THE
BAMBOO
PEOPLE

Congratulations

Puyallup Valley JACL Chapter

THE BAMBOO PEOPLE:

The Law and Japanese-Americans

Frank F. Chuman

Publisher's
Inc.

Del Mar, California

Library of Congress Catalog Card No. 76-4117
International Standard Book No. 0-89163-013-9

2　3　4　5　6　7　8　9

Printed in the United States of America

PREFACE

The Bamboo People is a legal history of the residents of the United States of Japanese descent, beginning with the first Japanese immigrants in 1869 and extending to the present time. It is part of the Japanese American Research Project of the University of California at Los Angeles, funded by the Japanese American Citizens League, the Carnegie Foundation, and the United States National Institute of Mental Health.

The author, Frank F. Chuman, was chosen for this task by Dr. Robert A. Wilson, associate professor at UCLA and director of the Research Project. Mr. Chuman, a practicing lawyer in Los Angeles, enjoys high credentials and is a past National President of the Japanese American Citizens League. His work, representing some six years of painstaking research, has an elegant simplicity of style that makes for both easy reading and clear understanding.

This is a history that needed to be written. It is a book done from the perspective of a Japanese-American, with his own observations, interpretations, and commentary upon the tragedy of racial discrimination and the dignity of those who endured it. Of course, I may vigorously disagree with certain details of Mr. Chuman's work,* but this in no way affects the legitimacy of his effort. *The Bamboo People* does not need my approval nor does my differing recollection of some of the events affect the validity of Mr. Chuman's overall statement. It is an important book for Japanese-Americans and others interested in a free society.

The Bamboo People is much more than an historical treatise. Robert Burns would say that it is illustrative of "man's inhumanity to man." As Mr. Chuman's work clearly confirms, truth is, indeed, stranger than fiction. As early as the mid-nineteenth century we find that California—now our most liberal state in public policy—exhibited racist tendencies in its reaction to the first Oriental immigration. Strong anti-Oriental

---

*Note: Most of my disagreement focuses upon the generalized depiction of those responsible for carrying out the policy of evacuation during World War II. For example, I found that General DeWitt preferred curfew to evacuation; that both military and civilian authorities welcomed and relied on the assistance of the JACL; that assurances made to the JACL were sincerely made and kept as far as humanly possible and were certainly not "mockery"; that the horse stalls of Santa Anita were completely remodeled into temporary housing and had no offensive odors when I inspected them; that property protection measures were quite adequate and administrative details were handled by civilian departmental administrations; and that while the evacuees suffered great hardships, many efforts were made to alleviate them. I knew of no federal officer charged with any responsibility for the evacuees who acted with callousness or indifference. The claims program for the indemnification of losses suffered in the evacuation was so designed as to resolve all doubts in favor of the claimant.

feeling continued in the days of Leland Stanford who, when Governor of California, spoke out against the admission of any Orientals to the United States. Today the great university that bears his name, as one of the progressive institutions in American education, would certainly decry such a stand. However, Stanford's protests came only a decade after Commodore Perry sailed into Tokyo Bay and ended a 230-year world isolation policy by the Japanese. It is also well to remember, as Mr. Chuman points out, that all during this period, the immigration policy of the United States was to grant admission to people of the free white race only. Seven years after the adoption of the Fourteenth Amendment, this policy was amended so as to admit blacks—but not Orientals.

Still another subsequent event is reminiscent of present-day confusion. In 1906 the San Francisco School Board segregated the public schools in order to preclude the entrance of Orientals into the system. This brought a national confrontation with the Japanese Government, which resulted in the "Gentlemen's Agreement" of 1908. But that agreement controlled the immigration policy regarding Japanese entrants to the United States only until the Oriental Exclusion Act of 1924. The act remained in effect until 1952 when, finally, the entire policy was about-faced to one of a modern policy of immigration without regard to race.

In view of this bleak history, it is well to remind ourselves that President Theodore Roosevelt, to whom we paid homage in my childhood with a ditty, "Here's to Teddy, rough and ready, population is his cry," had strong advice for the American people in 1906. He warned, "The attitude of hostility . . . toward the Japanese in this country . . . is most discreditable to us as a people and it may be fraught with the gravest consequences for the Nation." Later events proved this prophecy to be correct.

All of this and more is chronicled in The Bamboo People. I have read every word of this disquieting story of a race of people who came to our shores over a hundred years ago, who raised their families here, who endeavored to become part and parcel of our community, who fought side by side with us in war and peace, and yet were relegated to second-class citizenship and deprived of their liberty. Only recently have they been allowed full enjoyment of their constitutional rights. The story teaches a lesson in freedom to every person who prizes his liberty.

The Bamboo People is also a stimulating work. The drama of the oppressed keeps the reader's heart pitter-pattering, and their emotional entreaty starts the blood boiling. Its tragic lesson is an experience never to be forgotten. Perhaps I am oversensitive, having served during the early months of the Second World War as Civilian Coordinator of the Western Defense Command under General DeWitt. Exposed to the problems of security on the West Coast, both to our country as well as to the people of Japanese descent living there, I served during the hectic days during which the ultimate governmental policy was formulated. Contrary to Mr. Chuman's conclusions, I found the final decision for removal of the Japanese to be based upon the physical dangers then facing 110,000 people of Japanese descent then living in California, Oregon, and Washington. I did not expect any sabotage from Japanese residents; there had been none in Hawaii where the opportunity was greater; the O.N.I. and F.B.I. had a tight oversight of all nationality groups, especially the Japanese. The Department of Justice was poised for individual action that would have controlled any recalcitrant Japanese, as it had those of German and Italian origin who had defied authority. There was little strategic justification for the evacuation; these people of Japanese descent, many of them American citizens, did not pose a substantial military threat.

As Civilian Coordinator, however, I received hundreds of threatening messages against the Japanese community every day. This led to the curfew orders promulgated by General DeWitt and later held unconstitutional by U.S. District Court Judge Fee of Oregon. The Congress then authorized exclusion, and the agitation was such that the Western Defense Command decided upon a policy of evacuation. Looking back on it today, this was, of course, a mistake. Although the Supreme Court held the action constitutional, one must remember that even the Court's judgment can be no better than the information on which it is based. In my view, the military necessity for the action taken was lacking. "Security is like liberty in that many crimes are committed in its name." (*United States* vs. *Shaughnessy*, 338 U.S. 537, 551 [1950], J. Jackson dissenting.)

It is true that necessity had its own rules, but they are justified only as the sole remaining means available to preserve the paramount interests of the American people. Certainly other means were present here as was clearly disclosed in subsequent courses of action offered by the military establishment, such as enlistment. As a result, our fellow citizens of Japanese descent experienced great and unselfish sacrifice. They have borne it well. We are proud of the nobility that they have shown in their distress and hail their courage as being in the best tradition of our American citizenship. As Mr. Justice Brandeis said, we trust that the "inexorable law that nothing is settled until it is settled right" will prevail. We hope that our miscarriage will be a lesson to those who follow in the pathway to freedom.

Tom C. Clark

Associate Justice of the United
States Supreme Court (Ret.)

INTRODUCTION

In 1962 the Japanese American Citizens League (JACL) selected the University of California at Los Angeles (UCLA) to be a base for a comprehensive research project on the history of the Japanese and Japanese-Americans in the United States. The JACL felt that this great educational institution would be the most appropriate site for such a project because it is located in Southern California, an area that has had the largest mainland population of persons of Japanese ancestry in this country, both before and after World War II. This region had also produced many of the anti-Japanese statutes, court decisions, and anti-Japanese activities that seriously affected persons of Japanese ancestry.

In accepting the responsibility for this project, UCLA agreed to provide a repository in its newly constructed research library to house the anticipated mass of books, magazines, newspapers, diaries, personal letters, photographs, miscellaneous documents, and other memorabilia that the project was sure to generate. UCLA also agreed to keep in its research library repository the oral history interviews, tapes, and other informational data to be utilized in this research. Upon completion of the project, access to this material would be provided to other scholars who might desire to conduct further research on the subject of the Japanese in the United States.

UCLA designated that this program was to be known as the Japanese-American Research Project (JARP). A special JACL Japanese History Committee was appointed to coordinate the project.

The initial funding for the research project was given to UCLA by the JACL. Subsequently, the Carnegie Foundation and the United States National Institute of Mental Health furnished grants to UCLA in order that the university could continue on the project to its end.

The Japanese-American Research Project was originally programmed to document the entire general history of Japanese in the United States. However, it became apparent soon after the project was launched that the subject was of a considerably larger magnitude than anticipated. Therefore, the project was modified to key in on four main areas as they began to emerge from the research data. It was decided then that four separate basic accounts would be necessary: a "definitive" history, a three-generation sociological history, an agricultural history, a legal history.

In writing this legal history of the Japanese in the United States, I have attempted to do so in nonlegal language. I have therefore avoided using many technical terms contained in various state and federal court decisions in order to make this book more readable. Procedural issues discussed in these decisions have sometimes been eliminated, since the bases upon which the courts reached the stage of judgment are not relevant to their discussion.

As far as I know, every substantial aspect of the legal history of the Japanese in the mainland United States is included herein. Because of the vastly different circumstances that prevailed in Hawaii, after careful consideration I have decided that this is a separate story and should not be included in this account. Resource information and citations of court decisions are noted at the back of the book and in the index.

A note on Japanese names is in order. In Japan the family name comes first then the given name, as in Jones Mary. When the Japanese immigrants arrived here and took up life in the New World, many of them chose to follow American practice and put their given names first. Their American-born children and grandchildren, most of whom had American given names, invariably did so.

To keep things as lucid as possible, in this work the names of Japanese, in Japan or in America as representatives of the Japanese government, are given in Japanese style, with the family name first, since this is the way in which these individuals were always known. Japanese in America and American citizens of Japanese ancestry are referred to as they are known here, with the given name first. Thus the Japanese admiral who ordered the attack on Pearl Harbor is Yamamoto Isoroku, while the lovely young Sansei who typed the final manuscript with dedication and skill is Miss Susan Mori.

Many persons assisted in the writing of this book. I express my thanks and appreciation to them all. They include the eminent writer John Ball, Ralph Merritt, Dr. Clark Kerr, Dr. Franklin Murphy, Dr. Scott Miyakawa, Joe Grant Masaoka, Dr. David Saxon, and the various deans of the Departments of Humanities, Sociology, and History on the UCLA campus.

I acknowledge my debt to the members of the Executive Committee and particularly to Shigeo Wakamatsu, Chairman of the Japanese History Committee during the past thirteen years. The Committee provided the necessary funds for research, travel, the hiring of research assistants, and other expenses of this book. For its financial as well as moral support I am deeply grateful.

Many persons also assisted me in the course of my research. They include Chief Justice Earl Warren, Associate Justice Tom Clark, John J. McCloy, Phillip Sinnott, Pat Frayne, William Mason, Judge Robert W. Kenney, Togo Tanaka, Harry Honda (the editor of the *Pacific*

Citizen), and these eminent attorneys: A. L. Wirin, Edward J. Ennis, Saburo Kido, James Purcell, Wayne Collins, and Theodore Tamba.

My legal assistants, Lee Rosen and Patricia Barry, were most helpful in tracking down various court decisions that are cited in this book.

I reserve special thanks for my secretary, Mrs. Mary O'Dell. In the midst of pending legal matters that required constant attention in my office, she somehow managed to complete the first draft of the manuscript. Her conscientious efforts and her cheerfulness in spite of the pressures on her were invaluable.

To Paul M. DeFalla, my research assistant, I extend my deep thanks and gratitude. He provided the professional touch of a historian in organizing the mass of research material in an orderly fashion so as to make it possible for me to proceed efficiently in writing the manuscript.

To my parents, and to all the other Issei pioneers, whether living or deceased, I affectionately dedicate this work. It was their sacrifices, their determination, their contributions, and their nobility of spirit that have become the history of the Japanese in the United States. They actually lived such history. I have merely attempted to record it.

Frank F. Chuman

CONTENTS

1

Early Japanese Immigration to the United States (1869–1907)

THE FIRST KNOWN permanent immigrants from Japan to the continental United States entered San Francisco Harbor during the month of May 1869. They arrived aboard the Pacific Mail Steamship Company's side-wheeler *China*.

The pioneer immigrants had fled from the village of Aizu Wakamatsu. As followers of a certain Lord Matsudaira Katamori, they had been supporters of the dictatorial regime of the Tokugawa Shogun. In 1867, after bitter fighting, the forces in support of Emperor Mutsuhito, later known as Meiji, had restored him to his historic position as the titular supreme ruler of the nation. This had left the supporters of Lord Matsudaira in a dangerously exposed position. The trip to San Francisco saved some of them.

This handful of immigrants who came to California established a colony in Gold Hill, near the town of Coloma, in El Dorado County. They named their settlement after the village from which they had fled. They called it the Wakamatsu Tea and Silk Colony.

The settlers at Gold Hill brought with them 50,000 three-year-old mulberry trees for the purpose of silk farming. They also brought a large quantity of tea seeds, some grape seedlings, and many other varieties of plants and seeds native to Japan. With them also came a large assortment of bamboo roots. The bamboo was to be grown for food and for use in making artifacts.

After the Wakamatsu immigrants arrived, there was very little movement of people from Japan to the United States for two decades. During that period of time, the big Japanese migration was internal— from central and southern Japan to the northern island of Hokkaido. Between the time when the Wakamatsu settlers arrived in California and the year 1885, over 105,000 persons left their homes in lower Japan proper to settle in Hokkaido.[1] During that same period, only about 600 Japanese immigrants came to the United States.

Small as their numbers may have been, those Japanese were landing in California at precisely the time when a great conflict was building up on the Pacific Slope between the Chinese, who had been arriving there by the thousands since 1850, and the non-Oriental population.

CHINESE IMMIGRATION AND THE JAPANESE

The conflict had been in the making since 1848 when the gold rush had begun. That rush was on in 1850 when California was admitted to the Union as a free state. That same year the Taiping Rebellion broke out in China—it raged for fourteen years. During this period California continued to grow in population and develop as an American community. Orchards needed to be pruned and the fruit picked. Farms needed to be worked. Mines had to be operated. Highways and railroads needed to be built. Clothes had to be washed. Furniture and shoes had to be made. A source of "inexpensive" labor was of the essence. The answer? The Chinese from a war-torn China.

In 1869, the same year the Wakamatsu immigrants arrived, the great transcontinental railroad linking the eastern United States with the West Coast was finished. Now the whole of California began to be heavily populated with people from all over the United States—and a post–Civil War depression was beginning to creep with cat-feet upon the entire nation. Chinese labor became a glut on the California market. At least so said organized labor, which was by then beginning to flex its political muscle throughout the nation. By 1869 it was a foregone conclusion that the Chinese had to go. That was also the year when the new Japanese government at last decided to allow its subjects to go abroad.

Thirteen years later, in 1882, the conflict over Chinese immigration that had been building up on the West Coast since the end of the Civil War exploded into congressional action. The Chinese were abruptly excluded from immigrating into the United States. At precisely this time, Japanese began arriving in California in increasing numbers.

It had been an emissary of the United States, Commodore Matthew Perry of the U.S. Navy, with his fleet of "black ships," who had set into motion the whole process of exchanging goods and people between the United States and Japan. On July 8, 1853 Commodore Perry had unexpectedly steamed into Tokyo Bay and anchored off the town of Uraga. Under the implied but obvious threat of armed force, he requested of the Japanese a coaling station for his vessels. The Japanese were astounded and perplexed. They were also much impressed by the sight of Commodore Perry's four mighty ships that belched black smoke as big as thunderclouds from their stacks. After depositing his demands with the Tokugawa Shogun, Commodore Matthew Perry sailed away. But he promised the Japanese that he would be back the following year for an answer.

On March 31, 1854 he returned. This time he had seven smoke-belching ships. He effected a treaty between Japan and the United States known as the Treaty of Peace, Amity and Commerce.[2] The isolated, secluded Japanese were to be isolated no more.

On November 9, 1867, approximately thirteen years after Commodore Perry left Japan with his United States–Japan treaty in hand, the Tokugawa Shogun announced in Japan the "Imperial Restoration

Decree" by which Emperor Meiji was declared to be, henceforth, the acknowledged supreme secular and spiritual ruler of the Japanese nation. Among the acts of Emperor Meiji during the first years of his reign was his lifting of a ban prohibiting travel by his subjects to other countries of the world. The government would now issue passports. Thus, by a mere wave of the imperial pen, approximately 230 years of virtual isolation of the common Japanese national from the rest of the world was ended. Only eighteen months after Emperor Meiji was restored to his throne, the Wakamatsu immigrants began steaming through the Golden Gate into San Francisco Bay.

There is no record indicating that the Wakamatsu immigrants encountered any difficulties in being admitted to the country. Perhaps this was due to the fact that the purpose for their coming may have been known in advance. For some years past, Californians had been showing an increasing interest in silk farming. Here from Japan was a boatload of mulberry trees and experts in silk farming to go with them. In addition, the Wakamatsu immigrants did not wear "pig-tails" as did their fellow Asians, the Chinese. Also, there were only a few of them disembarking from the side-wheeler that had brought them. They had not arrived by the hundreds, as the Chinese had done.

IMMIGRATION STATUTES

Had the State of California wanted to prevent the Wakamatsu immigrants from entering the United States, it would have had to find an illegal way to prevent their landing on American soil. Article I, Section 8, Clause 3 of the United States Constitution provides that the *federal* government, through the Congress, shall have the sole power "to regulate commerce with foreign nations and among the several states and with the Indian tribes." In the commerce clause, the basic authority with regard to the immigration into the United States of persons from foreign countries was conferred upon the Congress. No other branch of government could infringe upon this congressional prerogative.

Also, under the constitutional provision, the United States of America as a sovereign nation, acting through its Congress, has the absolute power to encourage, to restrict, or to prohibit the entrance into the country of foreign nationals. This same power allows the United States to establish the standards and procedures by which aliens may be permitted entry into this country.

As a corollary to these powers, Congress also has the prerogative to establish the basis, the reasons, and the standards for the deportation of aliens. The United States Supreme Court has recognized and upheld the exclusive authority of the Congress in the matter of the immigration and deportation of aliens.[3] In addition, Article I, Section 8, Clause 3 of the Constitution establishes that the Congress is the sole authority in the nation with regard to the forming of "Uniform Rules of Naturalization."

Three years after the Constitution was ratified, the Congress, through the Act of March 26, 1790, decreed that "any alien, being a free white person who shall have resided within the limits and under the jurisdiction of the United States for a term of two years, may be admitted to become a citizen thereof."[4]

Five years later, on January 29, 1795, the Act of 1790 was amended to read that an alien asking to be admitted to citizenship "shall have declared his intention at least three years before his application that it was his bona fide intention to become a citizen of the United States and that he had resided within the United States five years at least within the state or territory where such court is held at the time of his application for admission to citizenship."[5]

The reference to "free white persons" was retained in the amended act and this restriction remained the law for over eighty years before it was changed. When it was revised in 1873, the change was to include American blacks and "persons of African nativity or descent." Thus, when the Wakamatsu immigrants arrived in America, they were fated to remain permanent aliens and could never become citizens, as they were neither white nor specifically black.

The United States has historically had a "color problem" of one type or another. One major difficulty has been the defining in a legal sense who is "white," an issue that plagued the courts of America for over 150 years. The naturalization statute of 1790 neatly set up that problem. It is compounded when it is approached from the opposite viewpoint: Who is not white? Is not a Japanese girl whose skin hue approximates the color of an Easter lily "white"? No, the courts have said at times. That's not what the founding fathers meant when Congress wrote the word "white" into the naturalization statute of 1790. Ever since then the courts and Congress have followed a tortuous and obscure path in establishing a national policy toward granting naturalization privileges to potential citizens other than "free white persons."

Second-guessing about what the founding fathers had meant by "free white person" depended on what political winds were blowing. In 1894 they blew ill for a Japanese named Saito. He was the first Japanese alien to run into the "white person" block at the level of the United States district court, when he attempted to become a naturalized citizen.

In re Saito, it is reported that Saito, a native of Japan, had applied for citizenship to the federal district court. There the issue revolved around the question of whether Saito, who had been deemed to be of the Mongolian race, was to be considered as being within the purview of the term "a free white person."[6]

The hue of Saito's complexion is not known, but it is known that the district court rejected his application—the court stated that it was perfectly clear from the earliest naturalization statutes that the Congress had intended to exclude from the privilege of American citizenship all races except the Caucasian race. Here, now, was a rejection based on race, not color.

The court then went on to justify its judgment in the *Saito* case by pointing out that its determination of the issue was consistent with the rejection by the Congress of certain attempts made in 1870 and 1873 to include Japanese and Chinese in the classes of persons eligible for naturalization. The court declared that the races of mankind are the white, the black, the yellow, and the brown. Since Saito belonged to the yellow, or Mongolian, race and not to the white race, it legally followed that he was ineligible for citizenship.[7]

Between 1869, when the Wakamatsu immigrants arrived in California, and 1882, when the Chinese were excluded, the actual number of immigrants arriving in the United States from Japan was relatively small. Therefore, no open hostility was directed at these newcomers during this period. However, it was inevitable that the resident Japanese would gradually become the indirect victims of the long-standing and numerous anti-Oriental statutes enacted by the California Legislature, even though these laws were specifically aimed at the ever-growing number of Chinese in that state.

CHINESE EXCLUSION

Not all of the Chinese who came to the United States remained. A great many of them went back to their homeland for one reason or another. But few in California took note of the statistics reflecting Chinese departures. All the statistics that most people were concerned with were those reflecting the number of Chinese arrivals. These statistics were impressive. Between the years 1820 and 1850, a span of time that roughly covers the Mexican period of California, only forty-six Chinese are on record as having come to the Golden State.[8] But between 1850, the year California was admitted to the

Union, and 1882, the year when the Chinese were excluded, over 280,000 Chinese were recorded as having entered the state.[9]

During the year 1852 alone, over 13,000 Chinese were recorded as having entered the country. The pressure in California against Chinese immigration began to mount early. In 1862, seven years before the Wakamatsu immigrants were to arrive, the newly elected governor of the state, Leland Stanford, in his inaugural address to the electorate, spoke forcefully of the undesirability of the Chinese.[10] But Chinese immigration was an international question, one not to be decided by a state. Thus, in July 1868 the United States and the Chinese Empire signed the so-called Burlingame Treaty.[11] This treaty guaranteed Chinese subjects "privileges, immunities and exemptions in respect to travel and residence in the United States as might be enjoyed by the Citizens or subjects of the most favored nations."

In 1875, in the case of *Chy Lung* vs. *Freeman*,[12] the Supreme Court of the United States held unconstitutional a California statute that assumed the right of the Golden State to exclude the Chinese from entering the United States via California. In this landmark case, the Court held that the Congress had exclusive jurisdiction in the establishing of standards of admissibility for aliens wishing to enter the United States. The Court concluded that no state could enact statutes affecting the entry of immigrants into its jurisdiction.

The Californians, now more numerous than ever since the transcontinental railroad had been finished (a railroad partly built by the Chinese), realized that their only hope for doing anything to stop Chinese immigration lay in Washington. Their political pressure in the Capital began to increase. As a result, the United States government saw to it that the Chinese Empire entered into an agreement, the terms of which permitted the United States to modify, restrict, or prohibit Chinese immigration to America through the instrumentality of American law. That was the Treaty of 1880.[13] Now the trap was set. It was sprung two years later. On May 6, 1882[14] the first congressional Chinese Exclusion Act went into effect.

This act provided for the suspension of immigration of Chinese laborers for a period of ten years. But the act did not stop there. It also specifically, by name, barred the Chinese from the privileges of naturalization. Henceforth, there was to be no question as to whether a foreign-born Chinese person was eligible for naturalization.

It was "undesirable" to be of Asian descent in the United States. And it was particularly bad in California because, notwithstanding the intent, purpose, and scope of the Civil Rights Act of 1866[15] and the Fourteenth Amendment to the United States Constitution (1868), the new California Constitution of May 7, 1879 lumped into one class all persons to be denied the right of suffrage—all "natives of China, idiots, and insane persons."[16]

This constitution went into effect before the congressional Act of 1882 specifically barring the Chinese from the privileges of citizenship through naturalization. Article XIX of this same constitution (the so-called Workingmen's Party Constitution) proclaimed that "the presence of foreigners ineligible to become citizens of the United States is declared to be dangerous to the well-being of the state."

This constitutional dictum automatically made the Wakamatsu immigrants at Gold Hill, who had arrived in California ten years before with their mulberry trees, "dangerous to the well-being of the state." Not being "white," they were clearly foreigners ineligible to become citizens of the country. But by 1879 the colony had disbanded because of lack of funds, and its members had drifted away. At this time, however, the Japanese were not as yet considered "dangerous to the well-being of the state." That blow, as reported, came in 1882.

THE SEARCH FOR JAPANESE LABOR

Although the first Chinese Exclusion Act did not go into effect until that year, it had been apparent to many persons that some such congressional action would be forthcoming. Thus, even before the exclusion statute was enacted, "labor agents" traveled extensively throughout Japan in an effort to encourage Japanese laborers to emigrate to the United States.

No attention was paid by these agents on either side of the Pacific, or their clients, to the fact that the California Legislature was always busy introducing anti-Oriental bills into the legislative hopper. On January 31, 1880 Assembly Bill No. 808 was introduced into the California Legislature for the purpose of amending Section 1880 of the state's Code of Civil Procedure so as to exclude as witnesses in a civil suit "all aliens ineligible for citizenship."

On January 18, 1885 California Senate Bill No. 2 was introduced. The purpose of this bill was to prohibit the issuance of licenses to drive a vehicle to all aliens who had not declared their intentions of becoming citizens of the United States. The Chinese were by far the most numerous aliens in California who were not permitted to make application for naturalization. Now these aliens could not drive a wagon, a vegetable cart, or a for-hire hack on the public streets.

Prior to 1884 the success of the labor agents in Japan was minimal, for a number of reasons. First, Japan was not interested in sending laborers or financially distressed farmers abroad out of pride in its national image. And certainly it did not want to risk exporting politically troublesome persons such as ex-Samurai to foreign countries.

However, the emperor was very interested in having some of his qualified subjects travel in search of a Western education. But these students were to return to Japan with their acquired knowledge of the Western world to help hasten Japan's own modernization.[17] Aside from the Wakamatsu tea and silk farmer immigrants, the first bona fide Japanese emigrants to the United States were persons seeking knowledge of the world outside their own country—a unique international experiment.

In 1884 the Japanese government adopted a policy of allowing its laboring classes to emigrate to foreign countries to work. In this year a convention was signed between the Japanese government and the Hawaiian sugar plantation owners permitting the plantation owners to import Japanese laborers under contract. At that time the Hawaiian Islands were still being governed under a constitutional monarchy, but they were also a protectorate of the United States under the Hawaiian monarch, King Kalakaua.

Although the first recorded immigrants from Japan to Hawaii, known as Gannen Mono, arrived in 1884, on January 20, 1885, 944 Japanese labor contract emigrants departed from Yokohama, aboard the City of Tokyo and sailed for the sugar plantations of Hawaii. Hawaii welcomed the news. But that was not the case within the continental United States, particularly within the state of California.

Shortly before, the Californians had been the most influential instigators of the Chinese Exclusion Act. Now these same Californians saw that another set of Asians, this time from Japan, were making themselves available for "cheap" contract labor. They commenced vigorous anti-Japanese agitation in Washington.

This political pressure on Washington was successful. On February 26, 1885, hardly a month after the Japanese immigrants had sailed from Yokohama for Hawaii, the United States Congress enacted a statute to "prohibit the importation and migration of foreigners and aliens under contract or agreement to perform labor in the United States, its territories, and the District of Columbia."[18]

This statute, of course, was born out of the fear that the Japanese contract laborers, now going to Hawaii, would use the islands as a hopping-off place from which to come to the mainland United States.

As matters turned out, this fear was well founded, for many of these Japanese did ultimately come to the United States.

The Japanese who left Hawaii chose to leave their jobs to look for better ones primarily because the Hawaiian plantation owners had not abided by the provisions of the contracts made by them. Although the plantation owners and the Japanese government had negotiated detailed agreements with reference to the immigrants' passage, food, wages, living quarters, and compulsory savings from the laborers' wages, complaints in other areas quickly developed. There was too much regimentation. The laborers complained that their personal rights were being violated. Various indignities were heaped on them. The language barrier was also a factor of misunderstanding and confusion.

Meanwhile, the number of immigrants from Japan coming directly to the mainland United States slowly began to increase, adding to those who were coming via Hawaii. Between the years 1884, when Japan legalized the emigration of laborers, and 1890, 2,270 Japanese immigrants entered the United States. During the next decade (1891–1900), 27,440 arrived.

Of this total number, the year 1898 accounted for 2,844 Japanese immigrant entries, and the year 1899, for 12,626. The majority of these immigrants from Japan settled on the Pacific Coast of the United States, with most of them choosing California as a place of residence.

This sizable influx of people to the Pacific states did not go unnoticed, particularly in California. As a result of the impassioned cry of "The Chinese Must Go!" the Chinese had finally been excluded. Now the slogan was "The Japs Must Go!"

JAPANESE IMMIGRATION AND THE COURTS

This cry was first heard in California in 1887, from the mouth of a certain Doctor O'Donnell from San Francisco. O'Donnell has come down to us in history as a man of doubtful character and an even more doubtful political reputation.[19] Mrs. Mary Coolidge, referring to O'Donnell in her *Chinese Immigration*, categorically states that the doctor had been "arrested several times for abortion" and that his "subsequent political record [sic] was notoriously disreputable." But to be a good anti-Orientalist, one did not have to be a reputable person in those days. Anybody would do.

While such "patriots" as O'Donnell were going about exhorting the populace to get rid of the resident Japanese aliens living in California, the immigration officials at the port of entry of San Francisco were exercising their discretion to prevent Japanese aliens from becoming residents by refusing them entry into the country.

In those days, the California immigration commissioner was an official appointed by the governor and served at his pleasure, although the commissioner worked under the authority of the United States secretary of the treasury.[20] Every now and then, a Japanese alien who was refused permission to land by the immigration commissioner would somehow find the ways and means to take his plight to court— sometimes all the way to the United States Supreme Court. That is how it has come to be a matter of record as to how the immigration machinery worked at ports of entry.

Such was the case involving Ekiu Nishimura, a twenty-five-year-old Japanese woman. Mrs. Nishimura arrived at San Francisco from Yokohama on May 7, 1891 on the S.S. *Belgic*. Commissioner of Immigration William H. Thornley refused to allow her to land because, in his judgment, she came within the purview of the Congressional Act of August 3, 1882.[21]

This act, besides imposing a head tax of fifty cents on all immigrants landing at a port of entry, excluded from entry persons deemed to be idiots, lunatics, convicts, or "persons likely to become a public charge."

Mrs. Nishimura pleaded that she had been married for two years to a man who had been a resident of the United States for the past year. She also contended that her husband, who had been unable to meet her at the port, had instructed her to proceed to a San Francisco hotel and wait for him there. She also produced $21 in United States currency, which, in 1891, was the average amount of American money brought by immigrants from foreign countries.[22] This sum, therefore, should have been enough to dismiss the charge that she was a person "likely to become a public charge." But Commissioner Thornley was not persuaded and refused her entry into the United States.

Since the S.S. *Belgic* was not scheduled to sail for several days, and feeling that a ship's hold was not a proper place to detain Mrs. Nishimura until the vessel departed, Commissioner Thornley allowed her to get off the boat and placed her in the custody of a Chinese Methodist mission nearby.

While at the mission, on May 13, four days after she had arrived at the port of San Francisco, Mrs. Nishimura filed a writ of habeas corpus against the commissioner of immigration, alleging that she was being illegally detained and restrained of her liberty. The following day, May 14, a new addition to the immigration bureaucracy was added in the person of John L. Hatch. He had been appointed as *inspector* of immigration.

Inspector Hatch interviewed Mrs. Nishimura and determined that Commissioner Thornley had made an error when he had ruled that she was not admissible under the Act of August 3, 1882. The inspector decided that Mrs. Nishimura was inadmissible under the Act of March 3, 1891[23] as "a person without visible means of support, without relatives or friends in the United States, and a person unable to care for herself, and liable to become a public charge."

Her only recourse now was an appeal to the United States Supreme Court. The question naturally arises as to how Mrs. Nishimura, and those who followed her, were able to secure the necessary legal assistance to carry their pleas to the higher courts of the United States. Almost from the beginning, they were assisted by a number of Christian missionary organizations who even at that time were dedicated to the concept of seeing justice done. Later on, the presidents of Stanford University and Claremont College and other distinguished Americans gave their aid and support in helping the Japanese to seek justice and to pursue their cases in the courts of appeal when it was necessary to do so.

Before the Supreme Court (*Ekiu Nishimura* vs. *U.S.*[24]) Mrs. Nishimura contended that giving an administrative official exclusive authority to determine her right to land in the United States deprived her of her liberty without due process of law and that the arbitrary findings of fact by such an administrative official could be reviewed by a court of law.

Supreme Court Justice Horace Gray brushed these contentions aside. He held that the Congress could entrust the final determination of facts to executive officers, that such executive officers were the exclusive judges of the existence of facts according to their own opinion of what the facts are and that no tribunal could reexamine such facts unless expressly authorized by statute. The Court decision concluded that because the inspector found that the petitioner was likely to become a public charge, she was within one of the classes of aliens excluded from admission by the first section of the Act of March 3, 1891.

In dealing with Mrs. Nishimura, the immigration inspector took no testimony under oath, nor did he keep a record of the unsworn testimony he did take. He allowed no witnesses to be heard, including Mrs. Nishimura herself. He filed no written findings of fact; he had thus decided solely upon his own inspection and examination the question of the right of Mrs. Nishimura to enter the United States.

The *Nishimura* case is noteworthy for at least two reasons. It was the first case involving a person of Japanese ancestry to be decided by the United States Supreme Court. In addition, the case very possibly induced the governments of Japan and the United States to look at their mutual treaties with an eye toward the protection of the rights of persons in either country. In 1894, two years after the *Nishimura* decision, a new treaty was entered into between the two nations.[25] The treaty included the right of persons "to have full liberty to enter, travel, or reside in any part of the territories of the other contracting party, and shall enjoy full and perfect protection for their persons and property."

Presumably, this international agreement would henceforth cause all courts in the United States to view more closely the arbitrary practices of immigration inspectors. However, the United States Supreme Court itself, in the *Nishimura* case, had offered no such suggestion to the lower courts. It had stated that, insofar as immigration officials were concerned, "so long as the officer was acting within the powers expressly conferred by Congress" that officers were to be the sole and exclusive judges of the existence of the facts upon which they made a final determination, and further, that such determination, standing on its own, satisfied the requirements of due process of law. Here the Supreme Court had not offered even a minimum degree of procedural protection under the due process clause of the Fourteenth Amendment.

While such officials as Inspector Hatch were excluding Japanese immigrants from the United States, the Japanese government was engaged in a herculean task to modernize her nation. To accomplish this Japan required raw materials with which to meet the needs of its expanding industrial complex. A few miles to the west lay the untapped resources of mainland China and Southeast Asia. Requests by Japan for access to these natural resources were either rejected or ignored by the Manchu government.

The answer, to Japan, lay at hand. By the 1890s she had built up a sizeable standing army, trained and led by officers educated in Europe. She had also built up an excellent navy under the guidance of England, herself a great naval power. She decided on an aggressive military campaign.

The Sino-Japanese War broke out in July 1894, but not before Japan had signed another major treaty with the United States in March of the same year. This was the Treaty of Commerce and Navigation proclaimed March 21, 1895.[26] The treaty was a tentative one and was not to go into effect until July 17, 1899. Obviously, neither the United

States nor Japan knew how long the coming war with China would last nor what its ultimate result would be.

The Sino-Japanese War lasted only a few months. China proved powerless to resist Japan's speed of action and superior weapons. After China capitulated, Japan took over control of Korea and Formosa. She also occupied large areas of the Chinese mainland in order to "protect the interests of Japan."[27]

But getting ready for the war had given the Japanese populace an uneasy glimpse of what national conscription could do to the individual and his family. Emigration from Japan, partly to seek a new life, but now also to escape conscription, increased noticeably. In 1890, four years before the Sino-Japanese War, only a little over 2,000 Japanese emigrated to the United States. However, by 1900, six years after the war, over 24,000 Japanese persons left Japan for the United States. Of this number, over 18,000 went to live in the Pacific states, over 10,000 of which took up residence in California.

ORGANIZED LABOR FIGHTS IMMIGRATION

If this heavy outflow of Japanese from their homeland did not arouse the concern of Emperor Meiji, it did heighten the activities of Dennis Kearney, the creator of the Workingmen's Party, whose cry of "The Chinese Must Go!" had been so effective a few years before. Now, during the month of May 1892, Kearney could be heard haranguing a crowd in that hotbed of anti-Orientalism, San Francisco. Kearney was enlightening his listeners about the newly discovered Japanese "menace."[28] In July he could be heard on the same theme in Sacramento. This time, his words were recorded by a shorthand reporter as Kearney berated "the foreign Shylocks who are rushing another breed of Asiatic slaves to fill up the gap made vacant by the Chinese who are shut out by our law—now Japs are being brought here in countless numbers to demoralize and discourage our domestic labor market and to be educated at our expense. We are paying out money to allow fully developed men who know no morals but vice to sit beside our daughters and debauch and demoralize them." Kearney closed this impassioned oration with "The Japs Must Go!"

Several more anti-Japanese immigration mass meetings were held in San Francisco, attended by such men as the mayor of San Francisco, James Phelan, and Professor Edward Alsward Ross of Stanford University. Present on the speakers' platform were several labor leaders and politicians. All of the speakers urged the enactment of a congressional statute, or such other measures as might be necessary, to achieve a total exclusion of all classes of Japanese immigrants other than members of the Japanese diplomatic staff. "Such a law," it was concluded, "has become a necessity, not only on the grounds set forth in the policy of the Chinese Exclusion Law, but because additional reasons resting on the fact that the assumed virtue of the Japanese, i.e., their partial adoption of American customs, makes them more dangerous as competitors."

In spite of the opposition, the dangerous "competitors" continued to arrive, with the immigration officials at ports of entry trying to keep out some whom they felt could be excluded. On July 11, 1901 Kaoru Yamataya, a Japanese woman, landed at Seattle, Washington (*Yamataya* vs. *Fisher*[29]). Three days after Miss Yamataya had entered the United States, an immigration inspector determined that she had entered the country in violation of the law. In the inspector's judgment, she was a "pauper" and therefore "likely to become a public charge." The secretary of the treasury then issued a warrant addressed to the inspector, commanding him to deport alien Yamataya at the expense of the vessel that had transported her to Seattle.[30]

Miss Yamataya filed a petition for a writ of habeas corpus. The writ was dismissed, and she was ordered remanded to the custody of the secretary of the treasury. She then appealed to the United States Supreme Court. Justice John Marshall Harlan affirmed the lower court's decision, dismissed the writ of habeas corpus, and ordered her returned to Japan.

In so doing, Justice Harlan affirmed that the Act of March 3, 1891 clearly provided that persons likely to become a public charge could be excluded from admission into the United States. He took note of the Treaty of 1895, which had become effective in July 1899, and held that the Act of March 3, 1891 was not in contravention of that treaty because it contained a provision that in matters involving "public security" local laws would apply, and the matter of whether a person was determined to be a "pauper" or a "person likely to become a public charge" was a matter of public security.

It may be noted that the Supreme Court retreated slightly from its harsh ruling in the *Nishimura* case.[31] In the *Yamataya* case, the Court held that an executive officer may not arbitrarily cause an alien who has entered the country, even though in an allegedly illegal manner, to be taken into custody and deported without first giving that person the opportunity to be heard on questions involving his possible rights to be or to remain in the United States. The Court affirmed that the principle of "due process of law" under the Fourteenth Amendment of the Constitution was to be recognized and applied by all courts. It concluded that aliens who had not acquired domicile in the United States should be deemed to have received due process of law if the alien had received a full hearing, in which case the decision of the executive official would not be subject to judicial review.

The full hearing in the *Yamataya* case had consisted of the young Japanese woman having received a notice of a hearing. But she did not know the English language well enough to understand the notice. The Court said that this fact was unfortunate but irrelevant. At least, by dictum, through the *Yamataya* case the Supreme Court established that there was a difference in procedural requirements of due process of law in cases where an alien had actually entered the country and was then in fact residing here. In such cases the secretary of the treasury or any of his executive officers could not cause such aliens to be taken into custody and deport them without first giving them an opportunity to be heard on the question of what rights they might have to be in or to remain in this country. [32]

Although Miss Yamataya had been ordered deported to Japan by the highest court in the land, the Court's decision did not please everybody. The decision had set some limits as to the procedures that the immigration officials were required to follow at such deportation hearings. Now, the immigration officials, at least, could not arbitrarily detain alien Japanese residing within the United States and, without according them a full hearing, summarily order them out of the country. It now became evident to organized labor in California that other methods would have to be used to prevent Japanese from entering the United States.

Author Roger Daniels writes:

On the second Sunday in May, 1905, delegates from sixty-seven local and near-by labor organizations met to form what became the Asiatic Exclusion League. From the day of the League's formation on May 14, 1905, until after the end of World War II, there was in California, an organized anti-Japanese movement that would eventually draw support from all segments of the state's population. In the beginning, the organized movement was an extension of the San Francisco labor unions. The most prominent labor leaders attending the initial meeting of the League were Patrick Henry McCarthy, head of the Building Trades Council of San Francisco, and Andrew Furuseth and Walter MacArthur, both of the Sailor's Union. A satellite of McCarthy, Olaf Tveitmoe, was named its president. All four of these men were immigrants from Europe. [33]

The anti-Japanese thunderclouds began to form in San Francisco in 1905. The so-called "Gentlemen's Agreement," which would begin the process of shutting the door to Japanese immigration to the United States, was now only three short years away.

2

The School Crisis of 1906 and the "Gentlemen's Agreement" of 1907/1908

N O SOONER WAS the war over between loser Imperial Russia and winner Imperial Japan when threats of war between the United States and Japan began to be muttered on both sides of the Pacific in 1906. The "crisis" between the United States and Japan did not arise over the question of who was to be in control of some part of our terrestrial globe; it arose over the fact that some children of Japanese ancestry were then attending the public schools in San Francisco. These children were innocent pawns in what was to develop into a full-scale international diplomatic chess game. The real issue was immigration from Japan to the United States.

In 1900 the Japanese government had discontinued the issuance of passports to its laborers who wanted to come directly to this country. This was the first "Gentlemen's Agreement" entered into between Japan and the United States over the issue of immigration. But the Japanese government continued to allow its nationals to go to Hawaii.

Now the Californians complained that many Japanese immigrants in Hawaii were leaving the islands to enter the United States, via Canada or Mexico, to settle not only in California, but also in other states along the Pacific Coast. The San Francisco-based Asiatic Exclusion League prevailed upon members of the legislatures of such states as Idaho, Montana, and Nevada to adopt resolutions and memorials similar to those the League had persuaded the California Legislature to forward to the Congress. In light of the actions taken by these various state legislatures, the Japanese government began to limit emigration into Hawaii.

In the month of April 1905, during the height of the agitation by the Asiatic Exclusion League, Japan temporarily suspended all emigration to Hawaii. By then, however, the tide of public feeling in the United States against Japanese immigration was so strong that the voluntary measures of the Japanese government to restrict emigration of its nationals to the United States had little effect on the thinking of the state legislatures. Their anti-Japanese resolutions and memorials to the Congress continued in a stream to Washington.

SCHOOL SEGREGATION IN SAN FRANCISCO

On April 1, 1905 the San Francisco Board of Education submitted to the board of supervisors a plan to segregate Japanese public-school children. In San Francisco, Chinese children were already going to a separate Chinese school.

One month later, on May 6, 1905, the San Francisco Board of Education again indicated its determination to "effect the establishment of separate schools for Chinese and Japanese pupils, not only for relieving the congestion presently prevailing in our schools, but also for the higher evil [sic] that our children should not be placed in any position where their youthful impression may be affected by association with pupils of the Mongolian race."[1] In addition to its findings of "congestion," the board of education had also found that the Japanese children in the San Francisco schools were "vicious, immoral, of an age and majority too advanced for safe association with the younger American children."[2] One of the Japanese children was Kazuye Togasaki, a girl who was then eight years old and in the third grade at the Hearst Grammar School. Subsequently, she became a physician and, prior to the evacuation in 1942, she delivered almost half of all the Japanese children born in San Francisco during one year. In the early 1970s she was chosen as one of San Francisco's "Women of the Year."

On October 11, 1906, the board of education formally approved a resolution to segregate the grammar-school children of Japanese ancestry into a separate institution.[3] The following Monday, Japanese children were refused admittance into the regular schools.

The resolution affected ninety-three children of Japanese ancestry, sixty-eight of whom were born in Japan and twenty-five of whom were born in the United States and were therefore American citizens. These students attended twenty-three different public schools scattered throughout San Francisco. Their grades ranged from the first to the eighth. As Dr. Togasaki reported in an interview with the author in 1974:

> When I showed up at my school, my teacher, Miss Hasse, took me into the classroom and told the rest of the children, "Children, say good-bye to Kazuye because she won't be able to come to this school anymore." She was obviously unhappy. So the children said good-bye to me and I went home with a "transfer" in my hand. My father was furious.

To the Japanese press and the public, anti-Japanese agitation in the United States had heretofore been based solely on a fear of competition and a loss of work if Japanese laborers were permitted into the United States. Now, when the news of the school segregation in San Francisco reached Japan, it was discovered by the Japanese public in general that the discrimination against the Japanese in the United States was really based upon an alleged racial inferiority of the Japanese people.

Japan was a proud nation with a national history reaching into antiquity. Its people had developed a high degree of skill in multiple areas of human activity, including the arts. They were steeped in religious and philosophical teachings that had been conceived before the Christian era of the Western world. Also, they had recently proved to the czar of Russia that on the field of battle they were to be reckoned with. And now for the Japanese as a race to be held in contempt as barbarians and to be abused and discriminated against by the people of any Western nation was not only totally unwarranted, but unwise.

The segregation of grammar-school children of Japanese ancestry in America was symptomatic; and it occurred at a time of increasing tension between the two countries not only in the domestic field, but also in the international arena. Both countries were now world military powers.

From 1900 to 1910 immigrant Japanese began to flow into several different states, although the largest Japanese population was still in California. Settlers from Japan were going to Washington and Oregon and were slowly venturing into Utah, Idaho, Colorado, and Montana.[4]

The newest immigrants were no longer engaged only in farm labor and in the mines: they began to settle in communities to work in domestic service, railroad construction, tenant farming, flower growing, and sugar beet production. They also found employment in salmon canneries, in lumber mills, and in small shops and stores such as bathhouses, barbershops, boardinghouses, laundries, and restaurants. They opened stores for the sale of merchandise, art, and craft goods. This dispersion of efforts to earn a living made the Japanese immigrants more vulnerable to attack and discrimination.

A factor that added impetus and strength to anti-Japanese agitation was the increasing support given to it by the American press. Heretofore, anti-Japanese sentiment had been relatively unorganized—it was mostly the work of diverse elements of the community and an occasional politician. Now there were well-organized anti-Japanese associations led by clever and effective people who were supported by the press.

In 1905 Olaf Tveitmoe, who was one of the more prominent labor leaders on the Pacific Coast, was president of the Asiatic Exclusion League. In addition, he was secretary of the Building Trades Council in San Francisco, a city that was now totally controlled by labor unions.

In the same year Tveitmoe also became president of the Japanese and Korean Exclusion League, an association that claimed a membership of 78,500 persons, three-fourths of whom lived in San Francisco. These two groups launched a vigorous and vicious anti-Japanese campaign in California and other western states. This campaign included aggressive buttonholing of congressmen, urging them to enact legislation that would restrict, or altogether prohibit, the immigration of Japanese into the United States. The influential *San Francisco Chronicle* and the *San Francisco Examiner* strongly supported the anti-Japanese platforms of these two organizations.[5]

The American press was again beginning to use the words "Yellow Peril" to instill fear of Japan as a military threat. A case can be made that there was some degree of justification for this apprehension. In 1895 Japan had emerged victorious in its war with China. Now, a scant ten years later, Japan had triumphed over Russia in the conflict known as the Russo-Japanese War of 1904–1905.

Russia and Japan had been competing with each other for years over the extension of their respective influences over Korea and Manchuria. In 1904 Japan attacked the Russian Pacific Fleet and crippled that force to such an extent that Russia was unable to prevent Japan from transporting elements of the Japanese army to Manchuria. Russia, a European nation then considered by the rest of the world as the greatest military power on earth, decided to punish the upstart Japanese nation. Japan's crippling of the czar's Pacific Fleet could not be left unchallenged. It was decided that Russia's mighty Baltic Fleet would crush the small island-nation of Japan, even though this meant sending the fleet halfway around the world.

In spite of being low on fuel and provisions, and with her sailors wearied by the long journey around Africa, into the Indian Ocean, and across the Sea of China, the mighty Baltic Fleet steamed proudly into the straits of Tsushima on its way to the main islands of Japan. Admiral Togo Heihachiro of Satsuma, however, lay waiting for the czar's ships at the mouth of the straits. In the historic engagement that followed, Admiral Togo completely destroyed the highly vaunted Russian Fleet.

In 1905 came the Treaty of Portsmouth. (Negotiated in the state of New Hampshire; President Theodore Roosevelt acting as mediator.) Russia surrendered to Japan her mines, railroads, and other properties in Manchuria. Russia also ceded to Japan one-half of the Kurile Islands, a chain that lay north of Hokkaido, and gave up exercising "influence" over Korea. She also transferred her leasehold of the Liaotung Peninsula in China to Japan. Japan, however, was very disappointed at President Roosevelt's failure to press Russia for monetary indemnification as well.[6]

Although Japan had been unable to have Russia pay for the war with money, it was generally acknowledged throughout the world that within a remarkably short time (less than forty years since the Meiji Restoration in 1867) Japan had emerged as a major military-imperialistic power, as an aggressive rival of the West, and as a possible threat to the Western nations in the Pacific, including the United States.[7] This country—the government and the press, as well as the public—began to look upon Japan's foreign policy with suspicion.[8]

Similarly, Great Britain, France, and the Netherlands, which owned vast colonies in the Far East, became increasingly apprehensive and began openly to express fears that Japan would eventually overrun the world.[9]

The Japanese people, however, did not consider themselves a threat to the world, and certainly not to the United States. They considered the United States to be a great and friendly nation, a nation that had not only awakened Japan from its long period of slumber during the Tokugawa Shogun regime, but had also been a source of great assistance in Japan's attainment of its existing condition as a modern, progressive nation.

A striking example of the good will that the citizens of Japan held toward America was demonstrated just after the earthquake of April 18, 1906 had devastated the city of San Francisco. At this time, bands of young hoodlums were roaming the streets, assaulting Japanese businessmen and shopkeepers. Restaurants owned and operated by Japanese were being boycotted and their customers threatened and harassed. A Japanese professor of seismology, investigating the results of the earthquake and fire, was assaulted and insulted in the streets. An architect, also sent from Japan to study the structural damage caused by the earthquake, was severely beaten. Meantime, the San Francisco Board of Education was considering segregating Japanese children in the schools.

But in spite of the personal indignities being heaped upon their fellow countrymen in San Francisco, the people of Japan, touched by the appalling conditions under which the citizens of San Francisco were then living, started a fund-raising drive throughout Japan for the city's relief. Over $246,000 was raised and sent to San Francisco through the Red Cross. This amount exceeded the total of all the monies received from all other countries of the world sent for the relief of the stricken community.

The School Crisis Begins

It is not surprising, then, that when the San Francisco Board of Education, on October 11, 1906 (while part of the city was still in rubble), passed a resolution to segregate Japanese schoolchildren of grammar school age, the Japanese press and the Japanese government reacted to the move with surprise and indignation. The offending board of education's resolution read as follows:

Resolved: That in accordance with Article X, Section 1662, of the School Law of California, principals are hereby directed to send all Chinese, Japanese, and Korean children to the Oriental public school, situated on the south side of Clay Street, between Powell and Mason Streets, on and after Monday, October 15, 1906.

The minutes of the proceedings of the board read:

The Board of Education has constructed a building on the site of that which had been the Chinese School, and instead of limiting it to the admission of Chinese, extended its operation to include, as per the resolution, Japanese and Korean children.[10]

On October 21, 1906, five days after the regular schools in San Francisco had been closed to Japanese children, the United States ambassador to Japan, Luke Wright, hurriedly sent a telegram from Tokyo to the United States Department of State: "All newspapers here publishing dispatches from the United States giving accounts of agitation in San Francisco for exclusion of Japanese, including alleged hostile utterances of member of Congress Kahn in public speeches; also action of school authorities in segregating Japanese children in public schools."

The Federal Government Intervenes

Wright's telegram caught Washington by surprise. Secretary of State Elihu Root replied to Wright that the trouble was so local that the department had not known of its existence until the newspapers were checked. The message apparently caught President Theodore Roosevelt off guard too. Roosevelt was understandably concerned; he immediately ordered Secretary of Commerce and Labor Victor H. Metcalf, a Californian, to go to San Francisco to investigate the situation. Metcalf arrived in San Francisco on October 31. The exemplary conduct of the ninety-three Japanese pupils was highly praised by their teachers, who considered them well behaved, studious, and remarkably bright. In his report to President Roosevelt, Metcalf noted that there had been seventy-six schools in San Francisco before the earthquake of April 18. Twenty-eight primary or grammar schools and two high schools had been destroyed by fire, and one high school was destroyed by earthquakes, leaving forty-five schools operative. The

Oriental school, to which the Japanese schoolchildren were ordered segregated, was in the burned out section of the city. Metcalf noted from maps that it would be "absolutely impossible" for some of the Japanese children residing in the remote sections of the city to attend the Oriental school.[11]

Despite these facts, Metcalf's efforts to have the school board's resolution rescinded were unsuccessful. In fact, after discussing the matter with the president of the board of education, Metcalf reported to President Roosevelt that it was hopeless to look for modification or repeal of the resolution. However, Metcalf added, the board of education was willing to submit the question of the legality of the resolution to the Supreme Court of California on an agreed statement of facts.[12]

Metcalf conferred with the justices of the supreme court. He was told that if the Treaty of Commerce and Navigation of 1895 with Japan contained a favored-nation clause that the court would unanimously hold that the resolution was in violation of the 1895 treaty.[13] However, Metcalf was told by Robert Devlin, the United States district attorney at San Francisco, that the Treaty of 1895 did not contain a "most favored nation" clause concerning education, although the treaty did provide a most favored nation clause concerning an alien's right to residence and travel (Article I) and a clause regarding matters of commerce and trade (Article II). Devlin's opinion was transmitted to S. Uyeno, Japanese consul in San Francisco, who had previously lodged a formal written protest with Washington in reference to the school resolution.

Secretary of State Root, struggling to resolve the school issue, declared that he disagreed with the opinion of Devlin and with the opinion of Attorney General William H. Moody, who had concurred with Devlin. Secretary Root felt that Article I of the Treaty of 1895 regarding rights to residence and travel was sufficient to guarantee the Japanese equal treatment in the matter of education. He wrote, "The whole purpose and end of the Treaty of [1895], was to do away with and prevent just such exclusions as are now provided by the San Francisco School Board. The resolution is completely subversive of the purpose and spirit of the treaty, and is, in my judgment, a violation of its terms."[14]

A careful reading of the treaty reflects no direct reference to the right of education on the part of Japanese aliens. Root's opinion undoubtedly reflected the intended spirit of the Treaty of 1895, but technically he was on somewhat shaky legal ground. Even assuming that the treaty did guarantee equal treatment in matters pertaining to education, separate school facilities might still have been legal under the Fourteenth Amendment since "equal" did not need to be "identical" under the "separate but equal" doctrine enunciated in a series of cases decided by the United States Supreme Court. These cases primarily involved Negroes in the areas of public transportation, public facilities, and public education. [15]

Although Metcalf left to Devlin the details of a federal suit against the resolution, both Devlin and Metcalf, and even Solicitor James B. Scott, the highest legal officer of the department, had little confidence in the suit's basic legal strength. They felt, however, that such a lawsuit would apply some psychological leverage against the board of education and might induce it to modify its stance. And although President Roosevelt instructed Root to proceed with the suit, he also had little confidence that it would solve the immediate problem with regard to the Japanese.

Meanwhile, in Tokyo Foreign Minister Hayashi Tadasu was becoming increasingly impatient. He sought information from Minister Aoki Shuzo in Washington as to what the United States government was doing to end this discriminatory action in San Francisco. Foreign Minister Hayashi began to see that the basis for the resolution was indeed racial in nature, and his feelings reflected the growing resentment of Japan over the conduct of American public officials in San Francisco. Ambassador Aoki replied that President Roosevelt was proceeding carefully on this matter, as grave constitutional issues were being raised by this "crisis." Aoki urged patience upon his foreign minister.

Secretary Metcalf departed for Washington on November 13, after two weeks of futile negotiations with the city officials in San Francisco.

It is not difficult to understand why the intercession of the federal government in the "school crisis" met with so much resistance. In the city and county elections of 1905, the Union Labor party had won a smashing victory; every Union Labor candidate, including the entire board of supervisors, was elected. Mayor Eugene H. Schmitz had also been reelected by a large majority. By this outcome labor controlled the entire government of San Francisco, and it was the labor unions who most strongly opposed the influx of Japanese into California. [16] Even the veiled threats of President Roosevelt to send in the army to quell the harassment of Japanese business interests and to suppress mob violence had little or no effect on the city officials. [17]

Roosevelt realized then that the school crisis could only be resolved by restricting the increasing influx of Japanese laborers. This was the adamant position of the city officials of San Francisco. Although Roosevelt deplored the manifestations of these anti-Japanese sentiments, he agreed that the Japanese immigration should be checked. However, he took a slightly different approach to a possible solution of the issue. He truly felt that the Japanese could not be readily assimilated, not because they were racially inferior, but because they were racially different.

President Roosevelt's Solution

Roosevelt was also concerned about a larger and more serious aspect caused by the San Francisco furor; he saw the complications of the Japanese immigration issue in terms of national defense. He had previously urged upon the Congress an increase in appropriations to build up the United States Navy so as to make it the dominant naval power of the world. Now he had a timely issue with which to press more vigorously upon the Congress the need to increase the U.S. Fleet to meet the threat of a possible war with Japan. He therefore capitalized on the immigration controversy to expand the U.S. naval construction program.[18]

In order to mollify the Japanese government, Roosevelt conceived of a plan to check the Japanese influx of immigration through an informal agreement. On December 4, 1906 in his message to the Congress, Roosevelt outlined various proposals that he hoped would bring about an amicable solution to the impasse involving the school crisis as well as the Japanese immigration problem. He stated:

Not only must we treat all nations fairly, but we must treat with justice and goodwill all immigrants who come here under the law. Whether they are Catholic or Protestant, Jew or gentile, whether they come from England or Germany, Russia, Japan or Italy, matters nothing. All we have a right to question is the man's conduct. If he is honest and upright in his dealings with his neighbors and with the state, then he is entitled to respect and good treatment. Especially do we need to remember our duty to the stranger within our gates. It is the sure sign of a low civilization, a low morality, to abuse or discriminate against or in any way humiliate such a stranger who has come here lawfully and who is conducting himself properly.

I am prompted to say this by the attitude of hostility here and there assumed toward the Japanese in this country. . . . it is most discreditable to use as a people, and it may be *fraught with the gravest consequences* [italics added] to the nation. . . .

A most unworthy feeling has manifested itself toward the Japanese—the feeling that has been shown in shutting them out from the common schools in San Francisco. . . . to shut them out from the public school is a wicked absurdity. I ask fair treatment for the Japanese. I ask it as due to ourselves because we must act uprightly toward all men.

I recommend to the Congress that an act be passed specifically providing for the naturalization of Japanese who come here intending to become American citizens.

I . . . earnestly recommend that the criminal and civil statutes of the United States be so amended and added to as to enable the President, acting for the United States Government, which is responsible in our international relations, to enforce the rights of aliens under treaties. The mob of a single city may at any time perform acts of lawless violence against some class of foreigners which would plunge us into war.

The President's message to Congress aroused a tremendous amount of good feeling in Japan. The naturalization proposal was received with particular enthusiasm and, if carried out, would have accomplished more than any one act to heal Japan's wounded pride. The message was published in full in the Japanese press. Editorial praises were showered upon the President for his understanding message.

But Theodore Roosevelt's words fell on deaf ears in the United States, especially along the Pacific Coast. Indeed, his message aroused indignation and incited condemnation. The press throughout California was almost unanimous in opposing the President's views. The California congressional delegation strongly criticized Roosevelt's message; once more, anti-Japanese memorials and petitions poured into Washington.[19] General public response was loud and angry. Roosevelt was shocked at the bitter reaction. He realized then that the anti-Japanese feeling was more deep-seated than he had heretofore imagined and that genuine racial feelings were involved.

The antipathy to the Japanese on the Pacific Slope, due not only to labor competition but also complicated by deep racial feelings, more than ever spurred Roosevelt to attempt to shape a policy to stop the influx of Japanese laborers and to remove the complaints of the Caucasian residents. No message to Congress, no threat of federal troops against local authorities would be effective. Rather, the solution would have to be found through bargaining with the city officials and the Japanese government to solve the school crisis that was inextricably tied to the immigration issue.

The delicate and complicated negotiations with Japan lasted over two months, from late December 1906 to late February 1907.[20] The city and county officials in San Francisco played a direct and important role in this international matter. Early in February 1907 Roosevelt invited the entire San Francisco Board of Education to Washington,

D.C. to discuss various proposals to be submitted to Japan. Mayor Schmitz also accepted the invitation and appeared in Washington with the board, even though he was at that time under indictment by the San Francisco Grand Jury for graft, bribery, and extortion, along with sixteen of the eighteen recently elected members of the board of supervisors. [21]

For Japan, "face" was an important although unspoken factor during these negotiations. To exclude laborers in return for allowing some grammar-school children to attend the public schools in San Francisco was an unpalatable *quid pro quo*. In addition, the Japanese public felt that the right to education was included in the Treaty of 1895. It was only after Japan was advised of its tenuous legal grounds that it went on to consider other alternatives.

The United States held that the right of a state to control its own school system was one of its fundamental principles. Lawsuits filed by the federal government in the Ninth Federal Circuit Court of California and in the California Supreme Court against the San Francisco school authorities were also not considered persuasive. Threats of war because of a violation of national dignity were proclaimed by jingoistic presses on both sides of the Pacific. Hundreds of telegrams were received by Schmitz and the school board supporting a firm stand on restricting laborers from Japan, with the Japanese themselves contributing to the aggravations when 700 Japanese laborers from Hawaii arrived in January and 200 more in February. [22]

JAPANESE IMMIGRATION IS LIMITED

The Japanese government contended that they had already stopped the emigration of laborers going directly to the mainland United States; those emigrants who went to Hawaii had a notation on the face of their passports that their travel was limited to the Hawaiian Islands. If their subjects in fact landed in Hawaii, Japan's responsibility had been fulfilled. If such subjects subsequently left Hawaii to travel to the mainland, such emigrants went of their own accord and free will and were not under the control of the Japanese government if they did so since the Territory of Hawaii was now a part of the United States. Thus, the power to control the entry of aliens from Hawaii to the mainland was within the jurisdiction of the United States.

An impasse in the discussions loomed. Finally, a major shift in the position of the Japanese government cleared the way for the settlement of the issue. The Japanese government conceded that it would not object if the United States prohibited the immigration from Hawaii to the mainland, although it was still unwilling to prohibit the emigration of laborers to Hawaii.[23] It further agreed to abandon the two legal proceedings against the school authorities.

In turn, the school authorities agreed to rescind their order and permit qualified nonadult Japanese to enter the public schools. But the prospective pupil was required to demonstrate a satisfactory familiarity with English, to be sixteen years of age or under, and to be within the age limits set for a given grade. The restrictions would apply to all alien children alike.

In accordance with the agreement arrived at between the two governments, an amendment, authorized by Secretary of State Root, was added to the pending immigration bill to implement the understanding. The amendment did not mention the Japanese by name, but it was clearly designed to prevent Japanese laborers from entering the continental United States when they held passports for Canada, Mexico, or Hawaii. With the passage of this legislation, the San Francisco Board of Education publicly announced its intention of revoking the segregation order.

Immigration Act of 1907

The Immigration Act of February 20, 1907,[24] among other provisions, expanded the categories of aliens "who shall be excluded from admission into the United States" into some twenty different classes including "persons hereinafter called contract laborers" (Section 2). The fourth proviso of Section 1 contained the key clause agreed upon by the city authorities, President Roosevelt, and the Japanese government. It stated as follows:

Provided further, that whenever the President shall be satisfied that passports issued by any foreign government to its citizens to go to any country other than the United States or to any insular possession of the United States or to the Canal Zone are being used for the purpose of enabling the holder to come to the continental territory of the United States to the *detriment of labor conditions therein,* the President may refuse to permit such citizens of the country issuing such passports to enter the continental territory of the United States from such other country or from such insular possessions or from the Canal Zone.

The act invested the circuit and district courts of the United States "with full and concurrent jurisdiction of all causes, civil and criminal, arising under any of the provisions of this act" (Section 29). It further created a commission to make inquiry, examination by subcommittee, or otherwise into the general subject of immigration (Section 38).[25] Several previous immigration acts were repealed by this new act but not those pertaining to immigration or exclusion of Chinese persons (Section 43).

The act was to take effect July 1, 1907; Mayor Schmitz was still in Washington, D.C. when it was enacted on February 20, 1907. While in Washington, Schmitz issued a statement that read in part as follows:

We have every reason to believe that the administration now shares, and that it will share our way of looking at the problem, and that the result we desire—the cessation of the immigration of Japanese, skilled and unskilled, to this country, will be speedily achieved. . . .

In view of our numerous interviews with the President and our understanding thereof, we feel that the question of whether the right at issue was or was not given by treaty has been passed, and has been absolutely eliminated from the controversy, and the proposition involved is one of comity and public policy. Such being the case, we are fully in accord with the view of the administration to the effect that the attainment of the exclusion of all Japanese laborers, skilled and unskilled, should not be complicated with or endangered by the exercise of segregation right by the school board, authorized by Section 1662 of the Political Code of the State of California.[26]

Schmitz returned to San Francisco on March 6, 1907. On March 13, 1907, the board of education rescinded its segregation order of October 11, 1906. The new resolution read, "Resolved, and ordered, that the following resolution, adopted by the Board of Education on October 11, 1906, be and the same is hereby repealed, excepting insofar as it applies to Chinese and Korean children."[27]

The two suits instituted by the United States Department of Justice on behalf of the Japanese children were dismissed. The Japanese children were again permitted to attend the regular public schools.

In accordance with previous understandings arrived at between the President and the San Francisco officials on March 14, 1907, the day after the San Francisco Board of Education rescinded its resolution of October 11, 1906, President Roosevelt issued a proclamation pursuant to the fourth proviso of Section 1 of the Immigration Act of February 20, 1907. The proclamation was in the form of an executive order and read as follows:

EXECUTIVE ORDER

Whereas, by the act entitled "An Act to regulate the immigration of aliens into the United States," approved February 20, 1907, whenever the President is satisfied that passports issued by any foreign government to its citizens to go to any country other than the United States or to any insular possession of the United States or to the Canal Zone, are being used for the purpose of enabling the holders to come to the continental territory of the United States to the detriment of labor conditions therein, it is made the duty of the President to refuse to permit such citizens of the country issuing such passports to enter the continental territory of the United States from such country or from such insular possession or from the Canal Zone;

And whereas, upon sufficient evidence produced before me by the Department of Commerce and Labor, I am satisfied that passports issued by the Government of Japan to citizens of that country or Korea and who are laborers, skilled or unskilled, to go to Mexico, to Canada and to Hawaii, are being used for the purpose of enabling the holders thereof to come to the continental territory of the United States to the detriment of labor conditions therein;

I hereby order that such citizens of Japan and Korea, to wit: Japanese or Korean laborers, skilled or unskilled, who have received passports to go to Mexico, Canada or Hawaii and come therefrom, be refused permission to enter the continental territory of the United States.

It is further ordered that the Secretary of Commerce and Labor be, and he hereby is, directed to take, through the Bureau of Immigration and Naturalization, such measures and to make and enforce such rules and regulations as may be necessary to carry this order into effect.

THEODORE ROOSEVELT
The White House
March 14, 1907

The proclamation was the first important measure to control Japanese immigration. In the Immigration Act of February 20, 1907 (Section 39), the President was authorized to enter into such international agreements as might be proper to prevent the immigration of aliens who, under the laws of the United States, were or may have been excluded from entering the United States and to regulate any matters pertaining to such immigration. [28]

President Roosevelt, having succeeded in arresting Japanese laborers entering the United States indirectly by his proclamation of March 14, 1907, then turned his attention to the restricting and controlling of Japanese laborers coming directly from Japan to this country.

Secretary of State Root pointed out to the Japanese government the undeniable right of the United States, sanctioned by the Treaty of 1895, to exclude immigrant laborers by legislation. He predicted that the United States government would exercise the right if Japan refused to "cooperate." If a reciprocal labor exclusion treaty could not be agreed upon, Root suggested that Japan herself impose the desired total restrictions upon the departure of Japanese emigrants for the United States.

On February 24, 1907, within four days of the enactment of the Immigration Act of February 20, 1907, Foreign Minister Hayashi responded to Root's suggestion. Hayashi pointed out to Root that under orders then in force by the Japanese government, no passports were being granted to either skilled or unskilled Japanese laborers for the mainland United States other than "settled agriculturists, or farmers owning or having an interest or share in their produce or crops." He concluded that "the Imperial Government confidently believes that a strict adhesion on their part to the foregoing order, coupled with the continuation of the existing practice of inserting in all labor passports the destination of the laborers will be sufficient to make the new legislation of the United States more satisfactory and obviate the necessity of adopting additional measures."[29]

The "Gentlemen's Agreement"

In January 1908 an exchange of correspondence was commenced between United States Ambassador Thomas J. O'Brien and Foreign Minister Hayashi for further discussions. This period of correspondence lasted until March 1908. The correspondence ultimately formed the basis of a series of "understandings" now known as the famous "Gentlemen's Agreement" of 1908.[30]

The "Gentlemen's Agreement" continued in force from 1908 until 1924, the year during which Congress enacted the Immigration Quota Law of May 26, 1924, also known as the "Japanese Exclusion Act," an act by which all Japanese, being "aliens ineligible to citizenship," were excluded from permanent immigration into the United States. Once again the U.S. had affronted the personal and national pride of the Japanese who felt that they had dealt with the problem of immigration since 1908 in good faith and in full cooperation with the United States government through the "Gentlemen's Agreement."

The "Gentlemen's Agreement" had been carefully and painstakingly worked out between United States Ambassador O'Brien and Japanese Foreign Minister Hayashi. Many problems had been raised; many suggestions had been offered and rejected in the flowery but restrained language of the diplomat. Repeated assurances of mutual helpfulness, accord, and accommodations had been tendered by both sides.[31]

Of particular concern to the United States were the following points:

1. That closer control be exercised by the Japanese government over the issuance of its passports so as to ensure that none were given to laborers. Otherwise, the fraudulent practices of "unscrupulous persons" at the application level and at the issuance level would frustrate any system set up by the Japanese government.

2. That a record system be established by both governments that would reflect detailed data on the identity of each Japanese person entering the United States.

3. That the Japanese government develop a policy that would induce Japanese steamship companies to return to Japan at company expense any Japanese subjects who had violated the conditions of their passports.

4. That the Japanese government assume some control over its subjects who had violated the conditions of their passports.

5. That a system be set up to register all Japanese aliens in the United States.

6. That the Japanese government further clarify its term "settled agriculturists" as the Japanese government applied that term to immigrants from Japan.

To these points of concern, Japan replied as follows:

1. The Japanese government was prepared to enforce and regulate the emigration of Japanese to the United States, and responsible authorities were instructed "to exercise the most careful scrutiny" of applicants to determine their actual status before issuance of passports. If fraud was discovered in applying for passports, the applicant, his parents, wife, and family would be denied issuance of any further passports.

2. There was no existing law in Japan to compel steamship companies to return subjects to Japan for violations of law while in the United States, and there was no realistic hope that such a law would be enacted by the Diet.

3. It was not practical to note on the face of the passport any warnings against fraud or to attach a note to the passport to that effect, but the Japanese authorities would issue a warning in "clear and unmistakable terms" against fraud to each applicant at the time he applied for his passport.

4. Japan's consular offices in the United States would institute a system of registering all Japanese aliens in the United States.

5. The term settled agriculturists was defined to mean "a person who had invested capital in the enterprise, and whose share in its

proceeds, if it is carried on in partnership, will be in proportion to the amount of his investment."

6. There was a fundamental difference between the labor situation in the Hawaiian Islands as compared with that in the United States. Because of the exceptional labor requirements of industry in Hawaii (presumably sugar cane and pineapple) to which the Territory owed its existing high standard of wealth and prosperity, the Japanese government hoped that the matter of Japanese emigration into Hawaii would be considered by the United States to be outside the scope of the discussions.

On February 21, 1908 Ambassador O'Brien expressed his pleasure and satisfaction "that the Japanese Government had broadened and made more specific its plans for the restriction of emigration to the United States."

The "Gentlemen's Agreement," it should be noted, was not a treaty. It circumvented a treaty originally suggested by Secretary of State Root and was in reality an "executive agreement" that reflected a compromise of conflicting viewpoints between the two countries. In the words of President Roosevelt, it would provide "a maximum of efficiency" with "a minimum of friction."[32] The agreement was deemed by both countries to be necessary and desirable and was designed so that Japan would exercise control over the departure of Japanese emigrants, and the United States would control the admission of such would-be immigrants.

The text of the "Gentlemen's Agreement" has never been published, so the exact stipulations of the agreement are not known.[33] However, the United States commissioner-general of immigration, to whom instructions were undoubtedly given for carrying into effect this new agreement, made the following statement in his annual report for 1908:

. . . an understanding has been reached with Japan that the existing policy of discouraging the emigration of its subjects should be continued, and should, by cooperation of the two governments, be made as effective as possible. This understanding contemplates that the Japanese Government shall issue passports to the continental United States only to such of its subjects as are non-laborers or are laborers who, in coming to the continent, seek to resume a formerly acquired domicile, to join a parent, wife, or children residing there, or to assume active control of an already possessed interest in a farming enterprise in this country; so that the three classes of laborers entitled to receive passports have come to be designated as "relatives," "former residents," and "settled agriculturalists." With respect to Hawaii, the Japanese Government, of its own volition, stated that . . . the issuance would be limited to "former residents," and "parents, wives and children of residents." The said government has been also exercising a careful supervision over the subject of the emigration of the laboring classes to foreign contiguous territory. [34]

As soon as the "Gentlemen's Agreement" had taken effect, immigration of Japanese into the United States began to decline. The figures tell the story. In 1907, 12,888 Japanese immigrants entered the United States; in 1908 the number had fallen to 8,340; and in 1909 it had decreased to 1,596. Soon, departures from the United States were exceeding arrivals.

It was not until 1913 that this condition reversed once more. Relatively large numbers of Japanese women of the working class began coming into the United States as the wives of Japanese laborers. These women, known as "picture brides," were married by proxy in Japan to men in the United States many of whom they had never met. This was accomplished by entering the woman on the husband's *koseki*, or family register, in Japan, as his wife. By presenting the husband's family register to the Japanese government in applying for a passport and to the visa officer of the United States Consulate in Japan, a woman, as a wife, was able to obtain a passport to proceed to the United States. [35] Later, this practice was challenged, as will be discussed.

While the "Gentlemen's Agreement" affected the domestic policy of both countries, the problem of the immigration of the Japanese into the United States was also considered by President Roosevelt in terms of United States foreign policy. Roosevelt, while following a policy of keeping out Japanese immigrants, behaved with scrupulous courtesy both to the Japanese as a nation and to the Japanese who were residing in the United States. In justifying the continued build-up of the United States Navy, he advised Secretary of the Navy Philander Knox in 1910 that:

> Our vital interest is to keep the Japanese out of our country, and at the same time preserve the good will of Japan. The vital interest of the Japanese, on the other hand, is in Manchuria and Korea. It is peculiarly our interest not to take any steps as regards Manchuria which will give the Japanese cause to feel, with or without reason, that we are hostile to them, or a menace—in however slight degree—to their interests. [36]

With Japan building up its army and navy and accelerating its expansionist program into mainland China, Korea, Taiwan, Manchuria, and the other parts of the Far East, Roosevelt accurately discerned the conflict that was developing concerning America's Far Eastern policy.

He was acutely conscious of the fact that present and future relations with Japan could only be preserved and strengthened by mutual understanding and close cooperation between the two countries. With the Philippines a major factor in the United States' defense of its interests in the Pacific and with the existing policy of immigration that was provoking the good will of China, Roosevelt considered international relations with Japan to be extremely delicate. He felt that any further outbursts of racial prejudice, mob violence, or general anti-Japanese legislation in the western states could seriously shake his balanced situation. He had earlier written to his son Kermit about his concern regarding the continuing hostility toward the Japanese by persons in the Pacific Coast states. On October 27, 1906 he was most emphatic: "I am being horribly bothered about the Japanese business. The infernal fools in California, and especially in San Francisco, insult the Japanese recklessly and in the event of war it will be the Nation as a whole which will pay the consequences."[37]

In the words of Professor A. Whitney Griswold, "Much more depended on the success of the 'Gentlemen's Agreement' than the mere exclusion of Japanese laborers. In Roosevelt's view, at least, it was the cornerstone of the entire Far Eastern policy of the United States."[38]

3

Early Alien Land Laws
and the Impact of
the Treaty of Commerce and
Navigation of 1911

T HE USE, ENJOYMENT, and ownership of land is perhaps one of the
most cherished rights desired by man. Land provides a man the
opportunity to "sink his roots" in society, to become a person with
status in his community. Land provides a man the site to build his
home, to raise his family, to grow his crops, and even to attain wealth.
In short, with the ownership of land, a man can more nearly control
his destiny. Without land ownership, there is a feeling of instability
and impermanence. There is a lack of tangible material possession
that a man can pass on to his progeny.

THE ORIGINS OF LAND OWNERSHIP IN AMERICA

In America the right of a state to decide, through its laws, who
should or should not be granted the privilege of the enjoyment
and ownership of land originated in the concept of land tenure that
was in force in England at the time of the colonization of North
America.

According to the common law of England, sole and absolute ownership of English land reposed in the king of the realm. In 1607, when
the colonization of America began, the reigning monarch was James I.
His subjects held only conditional and defeasible title to "ownership"
of land based on a grant from the king. The right of the king's subject
to the use of land depended on the subject's willingness to assume
certain obligations and responsibilities in favor of the crown, including the performance of military service for the king. Land held
by such a subject could not be transferred in "fee simple" to another
person.

It was held that an alien had no bonds of allegiance to the crown,
nor was he obligated to serve the king in any way. Therefore, the alien
had no legal standing in the courts of old England except by direct
appeal to the crown. Although an alien was subject to imprisonment,
execution, or arbitrary expulsion from the country, he could hold no
title to land, nor could he succeed to title to property by inheritance
because title to land could never devolve to an alien.

In America the power of a state to restrict or prohibit the use, enjoyment, or ownership of land also extended to the natural resources in
that state.

In *Geer* vs. *Connecticut*[1] the United States Supreme Court held that
a state could prohibit any person not a citizen of a state from using or

exploiting the natural resources of that state because such person had "no communal interest in the property." This case involved the right, or lack thereof, of nonresidents of Connecticut to hunt wild birds in the state.

In *Mager* vs. *Grima*, [2] the Supreme Court also upheld the right of the State of Louisiana to tax the legacy left by a Lousiana decedent to a nonresident alien, a French national. In this case, Chief Justice Roger B. Taney declared that each state had the power to refuse an alien the right to take either real or personal property within the state that the alien had inherited from a citizen resident.

In 1876, in the case of *McCready* vs. *Virginia*, [3] the United States Supreme Court upheld a Virginia statute that prohibited anyone not a citizen of Virginia from taking or planting oysters in the rivers within the territorial limits of the state. Chief Justice Morrison R. Waite held that the State has the right to say that the tidewaters and beds of a state are to be used by the people of that state and only by them.

The case of *Hauenstein* vs. *Lynham* [4] involved the issue of whether a Swiss citizen could inherit the proceeds of a sale of the estate of a decedent who had left no wife or children and who had died in Virginia without leaving a will, leaving his property in that state. In this case, Associate Justice Noah H. Swayne of the United States Supreme Court said, "The law of nations recognizes the liberty of every government to give to foreigners only such rights touching on immovable property within its territory as it may see fit to concede. In our country, the authority is primarily in the states wherein the property is situated." In old England it used to be the crown that granted foreigners only such rights as it saw "fit to concede." In America it was to be the state legislatures.

ANTI-JAPANESE LEGISLATION

If President Theodore Roosevelt had had hopes that his "Gentlemen's Agreement" with Japan over the question of immigration would lessen or perhaps even end anti-Japanese agitation in California or other western states, he was to be soon disappointed. In 1909, when the ink on the written portions of the "Gentlemen's Agreement" had hardly had time to dry thoroughly, the anti-Japanese movement in America had spread into Nevada, Oregon, and Montana. The Asiatic Exclusion League was still vigorously at work, with California as the center of anti-Japanese activities.

In the 1909 legislative session, no less than seventeen anti-Japanese bills were introduced in the California Legislature. But these attacks were no longer limited to attempts to restrict or exclude Japanese laborers. Now several bills were introduced to oppose naturalization privileges that had been recommended by President Roosevelt in his message to Congress of December 4, 1906. Other bills were aimed at limiting the age that Oriental children might be admitted to the public schools, while others opposed treaties with Japan that would affect or impair state laws relative to education, marriage, the right to vote, eligibility to hold office, or the exercise of the police powers of the state.[5]

The Alien Land Bill of 1909

Probably the most important bill considered by the state legislature during the 1909 session was Assembly Bill 78, introduced by Assemblyman A. M. Drew of Fresno. On January 15, 1909 the Assembly Judiciary Committee reported favorably on this measure known as the alien land bill.[6] The bill provided that an alien acquiring title to land within the state must become a citizen within five years or dispose of his holdings. Japanese were not mentioned by name, but their ineligibility for citizenship made it clear that the measure was directed at them. It was obviously a frontal attack on the Japanese, intended to drive them out of California at the same time Japanese laborers were becoming sharecroppers, tenants, or lessees; in some cases they were purchasing land on which to grow their crops.

Attempts had been made in the California Legislature as far back as 1889 to prohibit aliens from owning real property in the state. In the 1889 bills,[7] the word "alien" was used to prohibit ownership of land by noncitizens within the state, but it was intended to bar only the Chinese and the Japanese. However, the state legislature quickly realized that the word "alien" would include persons in the state from European countries who were aliens eligible for citizenship but who merely had not yet become naturalized citizens. To prevent "desirable" European aliens from land ownership was not at all what the California Legislature had had in mind.

The alien land bill was an attempt to amend Section 671 of the Civil Code of California enacted in 1872, which clearly provided that "any person, whether a citizen or alien, may take, hold and dispose of property, real or personal, within this state." President Roosevelt intervened to urge the defeat of Assembly Bill 78. The tumultuous debate that followed involved political pressures, both for and against the bill, promises, compromises, threats, and displays of overwrought emotions. The alien land bill was not enacted.

On February 3, 1909 the *San Francisco Chronicle* described the closing moments of the debate before this measure was defeated:

> Johnson, grasping the inspiration of a fleeting moment, in the midst of a fight which he knew was lost, held high over his shaggy head, the baby of Assemblyman Rowan Irwin, saying:
>
> "I would rather every foot of California was in its native wilderness than to be cursed by the foot of these invaders, who are a curse to the country, a menace to our institutions, and destructive of every principle of Americanism. I want no alien, white, red, black or yellow, to own a foot of land in the State of California."
>
> After characterizing the Japanese whom he said he intensely and unalterably hated, as "a bandy-legged bugaboo, miserable craven Simian, degenerated rotten little devils," [Assemblyman Nathan C.] Coghlan, with arms high in the air, trembling with emotion from head to foot, walked to the center of the aisle . . . to argue more.[8]

In the following election year of 1910, the platforms of the Republican, Democratic, and Socialist parties all contained exclusion planks. The Democratic party added another item to urge "the adoption of the Sanford Bill preventing Asiatics who are not eligible to citizenship from owning land in California."

Japanese Contributions to the Community

Here and there, however, there were some communities that were beginning to look favorably upon the Japanese immigrants. These aliens had established themselves as important elements in the labor supply, and some had become successful farmers and businessmen. Certain agricultural industries were beginning to depend on them for much of their trade, and exclusion would have seriously injured their business interests.

The immigrants from Japan, in their farming operations, had often purchased seemingly worthless, useless lands. Through patience, diligence, knowledge of intensive farming techniques used in Japan, and with backbreaking toil, they drained off the muddy marshlands, hauled away the rocks and roots, and grew crops of vegetables, berries, melons, fruits, and flowers. They were thereby materially contributing to the economic wealth of the state.

In addition, the State Commission of Labor had completed an investigation of the Japanese in California and had issued a favorable report on them. The *San Francisco Chronicle* published a summary of the report on May 30, 1910. The report concluded, "The competency of both Chinese and Japanese to meet all the requirements in the industries of the orchard, the vineyard, and the field is unquestioned and unquestionable."[9]

Members of the California Senate condemned this report because it tended to remove from politics the Japanese "laborer problem," an issue that had been a convenient political gimmick at election time. The senate then passed the following resolution:

> Whereas, the State Labor Commissioner has in his report concerning Japanese laborers, expressed his opinion of the necessity for such laborers in this State, and thus, without authority misrepresented the wishes of the peoples of this commonwealth, therefore be it resolved, that the opinion of such Labor Commissioner is hereby disapproved by this Senate.[10]

As if to further discredit the labor commissioner's report, four more bills were introduced in the 1911 session of the California Legislature "to regulate the ownership or possession of lands by aliens."[11] Although introduced by different assemblymen and senators, each of these bills contained the same clause: "No alien who is not eligible to citizenship under the Constitution and laws of the United States of America, shall acquire title to or own land or real property in the State of California, except as hereinafter provided." The battle against the Japanese was continuing.

THE TREATY OF COMMERCE AND NAVIGATION OF 1911

In the same year, another matter of extreme importance related to the Japanese problem was being discussed in Washington, D.C. Talks were being held there by representatives of both the United States and Japan on the subject of a new treaty to replace the 1895 Treaty of Commerce and Navigation then in effect. President William Howard Taft was personally involved in the negotiations, and, realizing that any outbreaks of anti-Japanese agitation or violence in America at this time would impair progress in the treaty negotiations with Japan, he invited California Governor-elect Hiram Johnson to Washington, D.C. to discuss California's perennial "Japanese problem."

As it so happened, San Francisco was at that time being strongly considered as the host city for the forthcoming Panama Pacific International Exposition to be held in 1915. Of course, San Francisco officials as well as all political leaders and business interests throughout California were most anxious to have the city selected as the site of the Exposition. Thus, when Johnson arrived in Washington, President Taft was in a position to present a proposition that the governor could not refuse. The President stated flatly that if violence against the Japanese broke out again in California because of newspaper propaganda or mass meetings, the city of San Francisco would definitely not be the site of the Exposition. An important international treaty was at stake.

Johnson saw the point. He promised the President that California would be kept quiet, at least until the new treaty was ratified. He kept his word.[12]

The new Treaty of Commerce and Navigation was signed on February 21, 1911, with Secretary of State Philander C. Knox signing for the United States and Baron Yasuya Uchida, Japanese ambassador to the United States, signing for Japan. The treaty, which was to become effective July 17, 1911, was to remain in force for twelve years or until the expiration of a six months' advance notice from either signatory of intention to terminate the treaty (Article XVII).

When news of the upcoming treaty became known on the West Coast, there was some agitation against it. Pacific Coast senators and congressmen received letters and telegrams urging them to oppose it. On February 22, 1911, two days before the United States Senate ratified the treaty, the California Senate passed a resolution protesting the omission of an "exclusion" clause in the new agreement and called upon the President and Senate to withdraw and refuse their assent to it. However, both of the United States senators from California, Frank P. Flint and George C. Perkins, stated that they were satisfied with the provisions of the new treaty, maintaining that it fully and completely protected the interests of the people of the Pacific Coast. The senators pointed out that if the treaty proved unsatisfactory, it could be cancelled on a six months' notice. Governor Johnson wisely remained silent on the subject and refused to engage in open debate. The public furor ran its course and subsided. The United States Senate ratified the treaty on February 24, 1911. On April 5 President Taft, by a proclamation, set forth the provisions of the treaty.

What should be kept in mind in analyzing this document is the respective positions taken by Japan and the United States. Japan opposed any exclusion act that would prohibit Japanese immigrants from entering the United States. (The United States had had the power to enact such an exclusion statute under Article II, Paragraph 3, of the Treaty of 1895.) Now the United States desired some assurance that Japan would control emigration of its subjects to this country.

The Treaty of 1911 eliminated Article II, Paragraph 3 of the Treaty of 1895, which had stated, "The stipulations contained in this and the preceding article do not in any way affect the laws, ordinances and regulations with regard to trade, the immigration of laborers, police and public security which are in force or which may hereafter be enacted in either of the two countries."

In its place, Japan attached the following declaration to the Treaty of 1911: "The Imperial Japanese Government is fully prepared to maintain with equal effectiveness the limitation and control which they have for the past three years exercised in regulation of the emigration of laborers to the United States." Here the Japanese government was referring to the existing "Gentlemen's Agreement" of 1908.

The Presidential Proclamation of April 5, 1911, contained the following statement: "The advise and consent of the Senate of the United States to the ratification of the said Treaty was given with the understanding that the Treaty shall not be deemed to repeal or affect any of the provisions of the Act of Congress entitled 'An Act to regulate the immigration of aliens into the United States approved February 20, 1907.'" Thus, no specific "exclusion" clause as had been asked for by the anti-Japanese forces had been considered necessary in the new treaty.

In any case, by its statements and assurances, the Japanese government had expressed its intention (as it had since 1908) of continuing to enforce the "Gentlemen's Agreement" regarding the emigration of Japanese laborers to the U.S. Also, the "Gentlemen's Agreement" had come to be recognized by the United States government as an acceptable method of regulating and restricting Japanese immigration.

A comparison of the Treaty of 1895 with the Treaty of 1911 reveals that although it is true that the United States eliminated from the Treaty of 1895 its Article II, Paragraph 3, the section that specifically granted the U.S. the right to exclude Japanese immigrants, it is also true that the United States conceded very little else, if anything, to Japan as a nation. And when it came to the rights of Japanese immigrants, the new treaty actually narrowed the legal rights and privileges of the individual Japanese entering or residing in the United States. According to the Treaty of 1895, citizens or subjects of each country were to have "full liberty to enter, travel or reside in any part of the territories of the other" and enjoy "full and perfect protection for their persons and property" (Article I). The Treaty of 1911 omits the words "full" before "liberty," and "any part" before the word "territories," and the phrase "full and perfect protection for their persons and property."

Also, the following paragraph, contained in the Treaty of 1895, was completely eliminated from the Treaty of 1911:

> They shall have free access to the courts of justice in pursuit and defense of their rights; they shall be at liberty equally with native citizens and subjects to choose and employ lawyers, advocates and representatives to pursue and defend their rights before such courts, and in all other matters connected with the administration of justice, they shall enjoy all the rights and privileges enjoyed by native citizens or subjects.

Furthermore, the clause in the Treaty of 1895 that read "the right to succession to personal estate, by will or otherwise and the disposal of property" was eliminated in the Treaty of 1911. Also, the clause "full and perfect protection for their persons and property," contained in the former Treaty of 1895, was changed in the Treaty of 1911 to merely state that "citizens and subjects shall receive . . . the most constant protection and security for their persons and properties." "Constant" protection is not necessarily "full and perfect" protection.

The anti-Japanese segments of the California public had been kept quiet during the negotiations involving the proposed Treaty of 1911; Governor Johnson's part of the bargain he had made with President Taft had been upheld. The treaty had been negotiated, signed, ratified, and proclaimed, and San Francisco became the site of the coming Exposition. As soon as this had been decided, the anti-Japanese activity in California began once again. This was soon reflected in the halls of the California capitol.

THE ALIEN LAND LAW OF 1913

The 1913 session of the California Legislature was flooded by more than thirty anti-Japanese measures.[13] Most of them dealt with the holding of agricultural land by Japanese. Various proposals were submitted. Aliens not eligible for citizenship and corporations with majority stock ownership by such aliens were to be prohibited from owning land. Other proposals prohibited acquisition of land by aliens who had not declared their intentions of becoming citizens but would allow leasing of land by such aliens. Other bills limited the rights to ownership of land to those specifically prescribed by treaties with the countries of such aliens. Some of the bills limited the leasing of agricultural land to ineligible aliens to three years and town or city lots to five years.

Out of this chaotic mass of proposed legislation there gradually emerged a bill that made specific reference to existing treaties between the United States and the countries from which aliens had come and that further tied eligibility for ownership of land to eligibility for citizenship. Senator Francis J. Heney and California Attorney General Ulysses S. Webb jointly drafted a bill that was to be known later as the Heney-Webb Alien Land Law. The bill tied the right of ownership of land by aliens "only to the extent and in the manner provided by the respective treaties then existing."

On May 2, 1913 the Heney-Webb bill was further amended during debate to permit ineligible aliens the privilege of holding land under lease for periods not to exceed three years. As amended, the Heney-Webb bill passed the senate and the assembly within two days and was sent to the governor for his signature on May 3. The governor, however, did not sign the bill until May 19, 1913, in deference to a request by United States Secretary of State William Jennings Bryan to be allowed time to state the position of the federal government.

Secretary of State Bryan had expressed the hope that the formula involving the issue of eligibility for citizenship would not be used as a basis for the right to ownership of land. Bryan had received a note from Japan's Ambassador Count Chinda Sutemi to the effect that the Japanese government was deeply pained to find that, in spite of Japan's constant friendly attitude toward the United States, anti-Japanese agitation was still continuing and indeed was increasing in intensity in the United States. Ambassador Chinda expressed his "earnest hope" that the President would endeavor to check the pending hostile Heney-Webb bill.

Secretary Bryan, in replying to Ambassador Chinda, at first attempted to minimize the impact of the bill by expressing an opinion that it was without political significance and was, rather, the result of a particular economic situation existing in California. The Japanese government, however, pointed out to Secretary Bryan that the bill was unfair and discriminatory toward the Japanese since it prohibited the right of land ownership to Japanese simply because they were ineligible for citizenship while granting the right to other aliens, even including nontreaty aliens.

All efforts of the federal government to stop the Heney-Webb bill failed, due partly to the fact that a Democratic party President, Woodrow Wilson, was dealing with a Republican party governor in California. The Alien Land Law was signed by the Governor on May 19, 1913, to go into effect on August 10, 1913.[14]

The Alien Land Law was unquestionably a law based on racial discrimination directed against the Japanese. It disregarded the basic spirit of the existing Treaty of 1911 and was completely inconsistent with the sentiments of amity and good will constantly being exchanged between the two governments.

However, the contention of the Japanese government, that the Alien Land Law of 1913 was in violation of the letter of the Treaty of 1911 by depriving the Japanese of the right to land ownership, was not legally tenable. The Treaty of 1911 contained no provision regarding the right of aliens to own land or to lease agricultural land, although Article I did contain the provision for the "lease of land for residential and commercial purposes." However, the foundation for racial discrimination against the Japanese through the Alien Land Law, and through other laws that were to be passed in the future against the Japanese, was the federal law that did not permit naturalization of peoples who could not specifically be classified as either "white" or "black."

There was nothing ambiguous about the motives or the intentions of State Attorney General Webb as the joint sponsor of the Alien Land Law. In a speech, which Webb delivered before the Commonwealth Club of San Francisco on August 9, 1913, he stated:

It is unimportant and foreign to the question, whether a particular race is inferior. The simple and single question is, is the race desirable. . . . It [the law] seeks to limit their presence by curtailing their privileges which they may enjoy here; for they will not come in large numbers and long abide with us if they may not acquire land. And it seeks to limit the numbers who will come by limiting the opportunities for their activity here when they arrive.[15]

Turning now to the actual law, known officially as the California

Alien Land Law of 1913, Section 1 permitted all aliens "eligible to citizenship" to acquire, possess, enjoy, transmit, and inherit real property, or any interest therein, in the same manner and to the same extent as citizens of the United States.

In Sections 2 and 3 the right of all other aliens "to acquire, possess, enjoy and transfer real property or any interest therein, and all corporations in which a majority of the issued capital stock is owned by aliens, is limited to the extent and for the purposes prescribed by any treaty now existing between the Government of the United States and the nation or country of which such alien or majority of stockholders of the corporation is a citizen or subject. Both the alien and a corporation may lease lands for agricultural purposes for a term not exceeding three years."

Section 4 provided that if any heir or devisee of real property was within the classes prescribed by treaty, such real property should be sold and the proceedings distributed to such heirs or devisees by order of court. Section 5 provided for escheat to the state of property held by aliens or corporations in violation of the act. Upon final judgment, the title to such real property would pass to the state. Section 6 provided that in the case of a violation of the law involving leasehold or other interest in real property less than fee, the value of such leasehold or other interest in such real property should then be sold, and the proceeds distributed by a court in accordance with the interests of the respective parties.

Although many lawsuits arose under the California Alien Land Law of 1913, most of the cases were superior court cases that were not appealed and, therefore, are not published as official court reports.[16] The only reported court case that arose under the Alien Land Law of 1913 was *Suwa* vs. *Johnson*,[17] from Sutter County.

Johnson was the owner and lessor of agricultural land. On February 1, 1917 he executed and delivered to Murayama, a Japanese alien, a lease of his lands for three years, from February 1, 1917 to January 31, 1920. Also on February 1, 1917, Johnson executed and delivered to one Suwa, also a Japanese alien, a lease of the same land for three years, from February 1, 1920 to January 31, 1923. It was understood by all the parties that both leases were solely for the benefit of Murayama. After Murayama had finished his lease for the first three years, but before he entered into possession of the three-year lease held in the name of Suwa, Johnson refused to allow Murayama to enter the land.

Suwa instituted proceedings to enforce his lease with Johnson. Johnson countered that Suwa was an alien who could not lease land for Murayama since Murayama would then possess a leasehold interest of more than three years.

The appeals court held that Johnson could not void his lease with Suwa on the grounds of Suwa's alienage. The court in affirming the judgment of the earlier superior court decision in favor of Suwa, held that the issue of alienage to void the lease could only be raised by the attorney general on behalf of the State in the manner provided by the Alien Land Law of 1913. The interest of Suwa could not be attacked by the lessor collaterally. Under the 1913 statute, the alien grantee took a defeasible estate in the leased land, free from attack by anyone except the government in a direct proceeding if any illegality had occurred in obtaining the lease.

Presiding Justice William M. Finch declared, "Where an owner had conveyed his title to an alien, he becomes as much a stranger to that title, as if he had never owned the property conveyed. To permit such a stranger [that is, Johnson] to attack an owner's title on the ground of alienage would not promote 'the peace of society' or protect the individual from 'arbitrary aggression.'"

The effect of this early decision was to affirm contractual relations between private citizens regarding the ownership and use of agricultural lands. Only the state attorney general's office could take the land away from an alien in an escheat proceeding and then only upon evidence that a violation of the Alien Land Law had transpired. For private citizens who had initially entered into contracts with aliens involving land, later to rescind or attempt to cancel such contracts on the basis that the alien was ineligible for citizenship, was felt by the court to cause interminable turmoil and confusion of land ownership.

The Alien Land Law of 1913 was the first legislation to deprive the Japanese of any substantial property rights. It applied the standards of "eligibility to citizenship" as used by Congress to the entirely different and unrelated area of land ownership. It excluded Japanese from land ownership solely on the basis that they were ineligible for citizenship.

This perversion of the federal naturalization statutes, as in the Alien Land Law as well as in subsequent legislation, was to cripple the economic progress of the Japanese in the United States for many years to come. In fact, it is reflected to the present day in the relatively weak economic position of the Japanese-Americans when compared with other immigrant groups and their descendants who were not so encumbered during the early critical years of West Coast development. To a degree the law also handicapped the development of California's economy because Japanese farmers were particularly noted for their willingness and ability to develop marginal lands into profitable, crop-bearing acreage.

4

Some Illustrative Cases Concerning Japanese Nationals and United States Immigration Policy

TRANSLATION.

IMPERIAL JAPANESE GOVERNMENT
PASSPORT.

（譯文）

No 85308 Uye Chuman.

Age 23 years and 6 months.

The competent Authorities and all whom it may concern are requested to allow the above named person proceeding to

California U. S. A.

to pass freely and without hindrance, and to give said person such protection and assistance as may be required.

The 16th day of the 8th month of the 40th year of Meiji (1907)

Viscount Tok Hayashi

His Imperial Japanese Majesty's
Minister of State for Foreign Affair

Name and Official Seal

J. W. Nicholson

Signature of the Bearer:

DISINFECTED
YOKOHAMA.
JUL 12 1907

PASSED ASSISTANT SURGEON
U. S. P. H. & M. H. S.

氏名 諒

任憑旅行無阻如有緊要事即請沿途各官加意照料善爲保佑

TRADUCTION.

LE GOUVERNEMENT IMPÉRIAL DU JAPON
PASSEPORT.

No 85308

Les Autorités compétentes sont priées de laisser passer librement la personne ci-dessus mentionnée, allant

et de lui donner aide et protection en cas de besoin.

Le   jour du   mois de la   année de meiji (19)

Noms et cachet officiel
du Ministre des Affaires Étrangères
de Sa Majesté l'Empereur du Japon.

Signature du porteur:

Between 1908 and 1925 there were thirty-four state or federal cases involving Japanese aliens that are reported as legal decisions in court records. Eight of these cases involved the issue of exclusion (denying an alien the right to enter and reside in the United States); twenty cases involved deportation (proceeding put in motion to deport an alien after he was already in the country); and the remaining six cases involved petitions by aliens for United States citizenship.

It may be helpful to describe briefly the trends in American immigration policy from the earliest days of the Republic to the year 1924, insofar as Japanese nationals are concerned. A cutoff date of 1924 is used because this was the year when Congress specifically excluded all Japanese nationals from entering the United States for permanent residence. Prior to 1924 the question of whether a Japanese national could or could not enter the United States for permanent residency was handled on a catch-as-catch-can basis.

A BRIEF HISTORY OF AMERICAN IMMIGRATION LAWS

The first hundred years of America's history represent a period during which immigration into the United States was unrestricted and unimpeded. The new nation needed, and indeed welcomed, immigrants from all parts of the world in order to provide a constant stream of "new blood" for the young and dynamic country.

There was but one early attempt by America to restrict immigration. This was through the Alien Act of 1798.[1] This act was a part of the Alien and Sedition Laws that authorized the President to expel from the United States any alien he deemed dangerous. They were enacted because, at this time, the former British colonies were still not at formal peace with England. The Alien Act of 1798 turned out to be a very unpopular law and was allowed to expire at the end of its statutory two-year term.

This brings us to the year 1800, when immigrants were still needed and their passage to America had to be made less hazardous. In the years 1819, 1847, 1848, and 1855, laws were passed to improve the general conditions on the ships that brought immigrants to the United States.[2] As late as 1864 it was still felt that immigrants were needed, and Congress enacted legislation that specifically encouraged immigration.[3] In Japan, at about this same time, the move toward the Meiji Restoration was gaining headway—a change in government in Japan that would, soon after taking place, allow Japanese nationals to emigrate freely.

Congress, however, did not intend to encourage immigration by Asiatics. Even then the Californians were trying to devise a way to get rid of the Chinese in their midst. In 1871 a Los Angeles mob massacred nineteen Chinese workers whose only offense had been their national origin.[4]

By 1864 there were groups in America that were beginning to raise their collective voices against any more general immigration to the United States. This opposition to any immigration at all became stronger during times of economic depression.

Thus, in 1875, the Congress began to enact legislation that not only aimed at restricting general immigration but also imposed qualitative restrictions and standards, defining what types or classes of persons were to be deemed inadmissible as immigrants to the United States.[5]

This act of 1875 barred from immigration "convicts" and "prostitutes" of whatever nationality. Then, in 1882, the Congress suspended the general immigration of Chinese, as Chinese. This was the first U.S. statute declaring a person inadmissible because of his race as such.[6] In subsequent years other Asiatic groups were to be placed under such prohibition.

During the same year another exclusionary amendment to the immigration laws was enacted. This one barred from immigration "idiots," "lunatics," "convicts" (again), and "persons likely to become a public charge." It also imposed a head tax of fifty cents on each immigrant admitted.[7]

Six years later (1888), the first amendment to the immigration law providing for deportation proceedings was enacted.[8] This amendment empowered immigration authorities to deport, within one year of his or her entry, any alien who had entered the United States in violation of the "contract labor" laws of the United States.

Three years later, in 1891, the general immigration laws were tightened, codified, and their exclusionary features expanded. Now the law denied immigration to (1) persons suffering from "loathsome" or contagious diseases, (2) persons previously convicted of a criminal offense involving "moral turpitude," (3) paupers, and (4) polygamists.[9] The 1891 law also provided for the deportation (within one year of entry) of aliens who had entered the country illegally. It provided for general and medical inspections of the would-be immigrants, with these inspections to be performed exclusively by agents of the federal government.

More amendments to the immigration laws followed in 1903,[10] to be followed by still another amending and codification of the laws in

1907.[11] These latest amendments further extended the range of ex-cludable would-be immigrants to (1) the feeble-minded, (2) children not accompanied by their parents, (3) persons suffering from such physical or mental defects as were likely to impair their ability to earn a living, (4) persons afflicted by tuberculosis, (5) persons who admitted having committed a crime involving moral turpitude, and (6) women coming to the United States for the purposes of prostitution or other immoral purposes.

Ten years later (1917), the Congress effected still another overall revision of immigration laws in order to coordinate the amendments made to previously enacted statutes.[12] These laws, for the first time, included a literacy test. Also, for the first time in history, America prohibited from immigration to its shores all Asiatic ethnic groups save one. It thus established an "Asiatic Barred Zone."

The exception was the Japanese. Japan had not been included in the Asiatic Barred Zone because of the "Gentlemen's Agreement" of 1908–1909. But the Japanese were not to escape total racial hostility at the immigration level for very long. Seven years after the Asiatic Barred Zone had been established, what was to be known as the Japa-nese Exclusion Act of 1924[13] was enacted by Congress. This act barred all Japanese from admission to the United States for permanent resi-dence. The anti-Oriental immigation ring was now closed.

THE ISSUE OF EXCLUSION

As has been stated, between 1908 and 1925 there were eight re-ported federal litigations involving Japanese aliens over the question of whether these aliens were excludable from the United States.

The entry status of these people was of utmost importance. Were they new would-be immigrants or were they returning resident aliens? If the alien was a newly entering would-be immigrant, his admission or refusal to admission would be based solely on a cursory, arbitrary hear-ing before an immigration inspector. However, if he claimed to be a returning resident alien and admission was refused out of hand in spite of his claim, he was entitled to a full hearing before the immigration authorities and entitled to all constitutional safeguards of procedural due process. This had been the dictum of the Supreme Court in the earlier case of *Yamataya* vs. *Fisher*.[14]

Of the eight cases involving exclusion, all of which originally came to court on petitions for writ of habeas corpus, five were from Hawaii,[15] two from California,[16] and one from the state of Washington.[17] Two of these cases resulted in the Japanese aliens being denied admission into the United States; in the six others the Federal Circuit Court of Appeals granted admission to the persons involved.

The case of *U.S.* vs. *Nakashima* (1908) involved a Japanese alien who had entered Hawaii in May 1902 from Japan. He later left Hawaii to live in San Jose, California, where he resided for over four years. He departed for a short visit to Japan without relinquishing his domicile in California. Upon attempting to reenter the United States, he was inspected by the Immigration Service and found to be afflicted with trachoma, an eye disease that the immigration inspector deemed to be dangerous and contagious and that therefore made Nakashima excludable under the Act of 1891.[18] The federal appeals court ordered that Nakashima was entitled to enter the United States, ruling that the provision excluding aliens afflicted with trachoma under the Act of 1891 applied only to newly entering immigrants and did not affect the right of alien residents to reenter the United States.

Suekichi Tsuji, in *U.S.* vs. *Tsuji* (1912), was a Japanese alien who was admitted into the Territory of Hawaii on July 27, 1906, where he resided for four years. In 1910 he departed for Japan on a visit. His wife, Masa, had previously entered Hawaii on August 28, 1906, but she did not accompany him when he left for the visit to Japan. When Tsuji returned to Hawaii on June 17, 1911, he was refused admission by immigration inspectors and was ordered deported to Japan for admitting to a crime involving moral turpitude, namely, that of having previously imported a woman, his wife, into the United States for purposes of prostitution. Before Tsuji had left Hawaii for Japan he had in fact been found guilty of the crime of bringing a woman into the country for immoral purposes and had served a three-month jail sentence. The issue in this case was whether Tsuji, having acquired domicile in Hawaii and having resided there for several years, could lawfully be excluded even though he had committed a crime involving moral turpitude in the United States before his visit to Japan. The court held that Tsuji was entitled to reenter the United States as a lawful resident because the Act of 1911, in effect at the time of the exclusion hearing, applied only to immigrants and not to Tsuji who was an alien resident.

In *U.S.* vs. *Tsurukichi Nakao* (1914) the alien, a Japanese subject, entered Hawaii in November 1892, where he resided for sixteen years until November 1908. He returned to Japan in 1908 without intending to relinquish his residence in Hawaii. On May 23, 1913 he presented himself at Honolulu, Hawaii as a domiciled alien. The immigration inspector discovered that Nakao was afflicted with trachoma, which was deemed to be a dangerous and contagious disease, and thereby found that he was excludable this time under the Act of March 3, 1907. The Federal Circuit Court of Appeals had found in 1908, in the U.S. vs. *Nakashima* case, that Nakashima was not excludable as a returning resident alien under the Act of March 3, 1891. The same court found in this case that Nakao was also not excludable as a returning resident alien under the Act of February 20, 1907.

In the case of *Ex parte Keisuke Sata* (1914), Keisuke Sata had left Japan in 1913 and landed in Seattle, Washington. He was examined at the time of entry, found to be free of any disease, and was permitted to enter the United States. Later the same year he was suddenly served with a warrant of arrest by the Immigration Service, taken into custody, and ordered deported on the ground that he was illegally in the country because he was afflicted with syphilis, a dangerous and contagious disease—a disease for which he would have been excludable if it had been discovered that he was suffering from it at the time of his entry.

The basis for the warrant was a letter from the medical division of the Immigration Service at Angel Island in San Francisco stating that Sata was afflicted with that disease. Sata argued at his deportation hearing that he was not afflicted as charged and that he was not being given a fair opportunity to challenge the contents of the accusing letter, a document he had known nothing about until he was arrested.

The Federal District Court of California agreed with Sata's arguments, ordered his release from custody, and cancelled his deportation hearing. The court released him because, at the time of entry, he had no knowledge of the accusatory letter, and he had had no opportunity to challenge the truth of its contents. Therefore, the deportation proceedings against him were irregular, and the court could intervene to protect his rights to due process of law as a resident alien.

This same federal court later upheld the proceedings of a special immigration inquiry hearing when the hearing was held before three members of the Immigration Service, only two of whom were officers and the third an ordinary clerk. This arrangement was in contravention of Section 25 of the Immigration Act of February 20, 1907, which provided that a board of special inquiry should consist of three members selected from immigration "officials." That was in the case of *Ex parte Momo Tomimatsu* (1916).

Momo Tomimatsu, a Japanese woman with a proper passport, attempted to enter the United States at San Francisco to join her husband who was domiciled in the United States. She was refused admission because she was afflicted with trachoma. She challenged the regularity of the proceedings that found her excludable, contending that the three-member panel that constituted the board of special inquiry was not legally constituted. Federal District Judge Maurice T. Dooling rejected this contention and ruled Mrs. Tomimatsu excludable, declaring that Section 25 of the Immigration Act of February 20, 1907 did not use the word "officers," but instead used the term "officials." He held: "There is nothing in the Act that the words immigration 'officials' may not include clerks."

In *Tatsukichi Kuwabara* vs. *U.S.* (1919) a Japanese alien came to Hawaii on July 12, 1917. He stated that he was a teacher, intending to teach in a Buddhist mission. The immigration inspector denied his admission and detained him for deportation on the ground that he was excludable as a laborer under Section 3 of the Act of February 5, 1917.

The Federal District Court of the Territory of Hawaii upheld the ruling of the Immigration Service, whereupon Kuwabara appealed to the Federal Circuit Court of Appeals on the ground that the profession of teaching was not to be classified as labor. It was a recognized learned profession. The court of appeals agreed with Kuwabara, reversed the decision of the federal district court, and ordered him released from custody. Justice Erskine M. Ross of the court of appeals held, "An alien who seeks to enter this country for the purpose of teaching the Japanese language, history, geography and arithmetic . . . is not to perform labor in this country within the meaning of the Act of February 5, 1917; . . . [he] may be properly regarded as belonging to a 'recognized learned profession.'"

In *Ex parte Hosaye Sakaguchi* (1922) the subject alien was a Japanese woman who arrived at the port of Seattle on December 23, 1919, carrying a Japanese passport. She was the proxy wife of Kuinobuemon Sakaguchi, a resident alien of Seattle. Three years before coming to Seattle, Hosaye, not then the proxy wife of Sakaguchi, had left Japan to go to Victoria, British Columbia as the proxy wife of another Japanese alien and lived with this person about six months. She left him and returned to Japan. After she had become the proxy wife of Sakaguchi, and before she arrived in Seattle to join him, he discovered that she had been married before. Thus when Hosaye arrived in Seattle in 1919, Sakaguchi refused to accept her as his wife. In addition, the purported husband had no means to support his proxy wife as he was not employed. The immigration inspector ordered her excludable as likely to become a public charge and detained her for deportation. The Federal Circuit Court of Appeals ordered her discharged from custody and granted her entrance into the United States on the basis that Hosaye, being Sakaguchi's wife when she left Japan a second time, was still his wife even though Sakaguchi refused to receive her as such, and as his wife she was entitled to be admitted into the United States.

The court further reviewed the facts and found the immigration inspector in error in refusing Mrs. Sakaguchi entry on the ground that she was "likely to become a public charge." She was an able-bodied woman, twenty-five years old, with a fair education. She had no mental or physical disabilities, she had knowledge of the English language, and she had also graduated from sewing school in Japan and knew flower arrangement. The court felt she could obtain employment as a seamstress or flower arranger. Finally, her well-to-do brother-in-law and her sister, who also resided in Seattle, were willing to care for her. In the light of all the evidence, the court ruled that Mrs. Sakaguchi was not "likely to become a public charge" and admitted her for permanent residence.

In *Kaneda* vs. *U.S.*, Buntaro Kaneda, a citizen of Japan, twenty-two years of age, arrived in Honolulu on October 6, 1919 as a first-class passenger on the S.S. *Korea Maru*. He stated that he was coming to Hawaii to investigate the living conditions of the Japanese residents in Hawaii and to report the facts to certain newspapers in Japan. Kaneda later admitted that these statements were false.

He was refused admission by a board of special inquiry, on the ground that he had committed a crime involving moral turpitude, to wit: perjury. Kaneda stated on appeal that he had been deprived of his liberty without due process of law and, further, that his false statements were not material as to his right to be admitted.

The federal court of appeals upheld the decision of the immigration inspector in declaring that if the questions asked of a would-be immigrant appeared to be fair and reasonable so as to enable the immigration officials to perform their duty, the officials were not therefore in violation of state law or of due process of law.

CASES INVOLVING DEPORTATION

In the field of immigration law there is a major distinction between exclusion and deportation. In an exclusion proceeding, the alien presents himself at a port of entry or territorial boundary of the United States and applies for admission into the country. Even though the alien has obtained a visa from the American consul in a foreign country, the Immigration Service is authorized to determine for itself whether or not the alien is admissible into the United States.

In a deportation proceeding, the alien has already entered the United States, legally or otherwise. Deportation involves the physical expulsion of the alien through congressional statutes. Such procedures have been legally upheld. The United States Supreme Court recently declared, "That aliens remain vulnerable to expulsion after long residence is a practice that bristles with severities. But it is a weapon of defense and reprisal confirmed by international law as a power inherent in every sovereign state. Such is the traditional power of the nation over the alien and we leave the law on the subject as we find it."[19]

The basis for deporting aliens after they have been legally admitted into the United States has been widening over the past several years. General Joseph Swing, former commissioner of immigration and naturalization, testified before the Senate Appropriations Committee hearings in 1954 that there were now 700 different grounds for deportation.[20] The number of these grounds and the basis for them have been criticized as too large and excessively severe.[21]

Although the courts have repeatedly stated that a deportation proceeding is a civil matter and that an order of deportation does not involve criminal punishment,[22] expulsion of an alien may actually separate him from his home and family and deprive him "of all that makes life worth living."[23] Its practical effect in many cases is to "send the alien into exile."[24]

Between 1908 and 1925 there were twenty reported cases of deportation proceedings involving Japanese aliens. Two of these cases involved proceedings under the authority of the Presidential Proclamation of March 14, 1907, popularly known as the "Gentlemen's Agreement." Seven of these cases were held under the authority of the Act of February 20, 1907. Of these nine cases, two were for illegal entry,[25] one involved a laborer,[26] and six were for offenses involving prostitution.[27]

Proceedings Under the "Gentlemen's Agreement"

Ex parte Hamaguchi involved a Japanese alien who crossed the Canadian border on foot from Vancouver, British Columbia to Blaine, Washington. He had originally been issued a passport in Japan with a visa for the Hawaiian Islands. He later obtained a visa to proceed to Vancouver. On October 5, 1907 he crossed the border into the United States. In Portland, Oregon he was served with a warrant of arrest on the charge that he "entered without inspection." He was deported.

In *Akira Ono* vs. *U.S.*, Ono, a Japanese alien, arrived by boat as a seaman at Galveston, Texas in 1915. He deserted the ship there. Three years later, he was arrested for "entering without inspection" and ordered deported.

In both of these above cases, the courts upheld the order of deportation on the grounds that the individuals involved were unskilled laborers who were prohibited under the "Gentlemen's Agreement" from entering the United States, and their admission into the United States as unskilled laborers was held detrimental to the labor conditions in this country.

Proceedings Under the Act of February 20, 1907

However, in *Ex parte Kunijiro Toguchi*, a Japanese alien age twenty-five, whose purpose for coming to America was to work in his uncle's store as a salesman, was permitted to remain in the United States, even though he admitted that no salary had been agreed upon between him and his employer. Toguchi was to work for his uncle, who owned a silk and dry goods store in Detroit, Michigan. The Immigration Service sought to charge Toguchi with violation of the alien contract labor provision of the Immigration Act of February 20, 1907, which prohibited the admission of aliens who were to be employed as cheap, unskilled laborers.

The court stated that Toguchi's employment was not that of a laborer within the definition of the Act of 1907. Moreover, the fact that no salary was agreed upon was immaterial because, under the employment arrangements with his uncle, it was presumed that Toguchi would receive a reasonable compensation.

Of the six cases of prostitution, *Suzuki* vs. *Higgins* and *Matsumura* vs. *Higgins* involved Japanese aliens who had been convicted of and imprisoned for importing female alien prostitutes into the United States. *Ex parte Hidekuni Iwata* involved a Japanese alien who owned and operated a "house" in Fresno, California. The house contained twelve cribs, or rooms, inhabited by prostitutes, and Iwata received rent for their use. *Toku Sakai* vs. *U.S.*, *U.S.* vs. *Kimi Yamamoto*, and *Tama Miyake* vs. *U.S.* involved women from Japan who had engaged in prostitution after being admitted into the United States. All six were ordered deported under the Act of February 20, 1907, which provided that aliens, who by their conduct, behavior, or activity, such as having become prostitutes, procurers, or engaged in any other unlawful commercialized vice, were deportable at any time after entry.

Proceedings Under the Immigration Act of February 5, 1917

Deportation proceedings for the remaining eleven cases were commenced against Japanese aliens under applicable sections of the Immigration Act of February 5, 1917. One involved the charge of illiteracy,[28] two were for offenses involving prostitution,[29] three were on charges involving persons "likely to become a public charge,"[30] one cited a conspiracy to conceal entering illegal aliens,[31] one involved a laborer who was thereby presumed prohibited from entering the United States,[32] one was for illegal entry,[33] one was for a crime involving moral turpitude (assault with a deadly weapon),[34] and one was for attempting to enter without a valid passport.[35]

In *Mototaro Eguchi* vs. *U.S.*, the deportation proceedings involved the Immigration Service, which had invoked the literacy test under the Immigration Act of 1917. Eguchi was a Japanese alien who had gone to Honolulu, Hawaii in 1906. He had worked as a plantation laborer there for ten years. On December 16, 1916 he left the Territory of Hawaii for Japan for a visit of less than seven months. While Eguchi was in Japan, Congress enacted the Immigration Act of February 5, 1917, which contained a new provision that all aliens must either be able to read the English language or the language of the alien's country of origin. When Eguchi returned to Hawaii on July 12, 1917, he was ordered deported when he admitted he could read neither Japanese nor English. Eguchi claimed that he was a returning permanent resident alien. Nevertheless, notwithstanding his previous status in the United States, a status he had acquired before the passage of the new law, the court held that he was deportable because he did not conform to the new requirements of literacy.

In *Ex parte Gin Kato*, Kato, a subject of Japan, had resided in the United States since 1884. His wife resided in Japan. Investigation by the Immigration Service revealed the fact that he was employed by, or had connection with, a house of prostitution. Kato contended that under Section 19 of the Immigration Act of February 5, 1917, he could not be deported because he had resided in the United States for more than five years and, further, that his deportation was in violation of the treaty between Japan and the United States proclaimed March 21, 1895.

The Federal District Court of Washington rejected both of Kato's contentions. The five-year statute of limitations regarding deportability did not apply to Section 19 of the Act of February 5, 1917, which specifically provided that managers, employees, or anyone else connected with a house of prostitution were deportable at any time, irrespective of the time of their entry into the United States. Furthermore, the court held, Section 2 of the Treaty of 1895 did not affect laws, ordinances, and regulations of the United States or of the states pertaining to matters of public morals, security, or protection. [36]

In *Nishimura* vs. *Mansfield* a Japanese alien named Shigetake Asakura was deported from the United States in 1915 on the ground that he was connected with a house of prostitution. This same person attempted to reenter the United States under the name of Nishimura and thus used false and misleading statements as to his true identity. He was ordered deported under Section 19 of the Immigration Act of February 5, 1917 because he had in fact entered the country illegally and without inspection.

In the three cases involving deportation based on the alien being "likely to become a public charge," *Ex parte Tsunetaro Machida* involved a Japanese alien who had served a term in prison for over one year on the charge of smuggling aliens into the United States from Mexico. Machida argued that his conviction and sentence were not grounds for deportation under Section 3 of the Act of February 5, 1917 because this section applied only to persons who were "likely to become a public charge," to be supported at public expense by reason of poverty, insanity, or disease. The federal court upheld the order of deportation, stating that when Machida was convicted of the crime and sentenced to prison, he had become a public charge at that time.

In *Ex parte Yoshimasa Nomura* the board of special inquiry concluded that Nomura was "likely to become a public charge" and ordered him deported. Nomura claimed that he was born in Hawaii on September 6, 1904 and was therefore a United States citizen. He stated that he had moved to California in 1912 and later had gone to Japan where he had resided for ten years. He then said he left Japan in 1922 and went to Mexico, where he had resided for five months. Now he desired to enter the United States as a citizen of this country. At the immigration hearing, Nomura admitted that he had answered several questions falsely, and that he had lived in Mexico for two years instead of five months, and that he had arrived in Mexico in 1920 instead of 1922. The court stated that it could not rely on the credibility of Nomura's statements and upheld the order of deportation on the basis that Nomura's false declarations, contradictions, and discrepancies as to his birth, arrivals and departures, and residences at various places created a strong doubt as to his claim of American citizenship.

Rokuji Tambara vs. *Weedin* involved a Japanese alien who was deaf. Based upon his disability, he was found to be a person "likely to become a public charge" and was therefore excludable under Section 3 of the Act of February 5, 1917. The court ignored two offers to employ Tambara that had been introduced into evidence at the immigration hearing and affirmed the order of deportation, declaring that an ailment such as deafness would "militate in a substantial way against his ability to earn a living, because the handicap would bar Tambara from many occupations."

Masanori Tanaka vs. *Weedin* involved a seaman employed on a Japanese steamship. In 1919, while the ship was at anchor in Tacoma, Washington, he deserted the ship. In 1923 he was arrested while employed as a laborer in a lumber camp. He was found deportable under the "Gentlemen's Agreement" of 1907, which prohibited the entry of Japanese aliens into the United States if it was detrimental to labor conditions in this country.

The court, in *Weedin* vs. *Tayokichi Yamada,* upheld an order of deportation charging a crime involving moral turpitude. Yamada had pleaded guilty to assault with a deadly weapon and had been sentenced to the state penitentiary for a period of two years. The court stated that such crimes do not come within the scope of the five-year statute of limitations, which precluded deportation of aliens if such aliens were not deported within five years after entry in the United States.

In the case of *Takeyo Koyama* vs. *Burnett*, the alien Japanese wife of a United States citizen had first arrived in Honolulu, on May 18, 1918. After residing in Hawaii for four years, she left Honolulu in June of 1922, taking her American-born child with her. A year later, she returned to Honolulu, in possession of a Japanese passport that permitted her to enter Hawaii only. Here, the Japanese government was adhering to its "Gentlemen's Agreement." The Immigration Service refused to allow Mrs. Koyama to go to the mainland to join her husband, who was now residing in Los Angeles. The refusal was on the ground that Mrs. Koyama was not in possession of a Japanese passport to the mainland even though she had technically already acquired U.S. residency because she had lived in the Territory of Hawaii for four years. The court upheld the order of deportation and refused her permission to join her husband on the mainland.

Weedin vs. *Banzo Okada* is a particularly interesting case because it established the legal fiction of U.S. residency for persons while they were sailing on vessels owned by the United States.

Section 19 of the Immigration Act of February 5, 1917 provided that any time within five years after entry, any alien, who at the time of entry was deemed to belong to an "excludable" class, could be taken into custody and deported.

Banzo Okada had entered the United States illegally in 1917. He then resided continuously in the United States for approximately four years. In June 1921 Okada shipped out as a member of the crew of a vessel owned by the United States Shipping Board. The ship touched at several foreign ports and returned to the United States two months later. On August 24, 1921 Okada left the vessel and resumed his residence in the United States. Thirty-two months later, on April 24, 1924, he was served with a warrant of deportation on the grounds that in 1917 he had entered the United States illegally, and that, up to the time he had left the country on board a ship, he had not resided in the United States continuously in order to fulfill the prescribed five-year term of residency called for by Section 19 of the Immigration Act of 1917.

At issue here was whether Okada had terminated his residency in the United States in 1921 by going aboard a ship and sailing away to foreign ports before he had acquired a continuous five-year residency in the United States. Federal Circuit Court of Appeals Judge Frank H. Rudkin dismissed the deportation order and held that Okada was not deportable in that he had been in the United States for more than five years. Here the court held that the five-year period commenced to run from the date of the prohibited entry in 1917 and that residence in the United States was not broken while Okada was aboard a United States vessel as a member of the crew. The court said:

> . . . the petitioner [Okada], while on board the steamship as one of its crew, was within the jurisdiction of the United States and was at all times under her protection, and amenable to her laws. An American vessel is deemed to be part of the territory of the state within which its home port is situated, and as such, is part of the territory of the United States.

PETITIONS FOR NATURALIZATION

As mentioned in Chapter One, the first Congress that convened in 1790 fulfilled the mandate of the newly ratified Constitution and prescribed a uniform rule of naturalization. The Act of 1790[37] restricted eligibility for naturalization to aliens who were "free white persons." Subsequent amendments to the naturalization laws[38] added other criteria, including a certain period of residence in the United States and the possession of good moral character. Later amendments added a written and oral test and the requirement of a general knowledge of American history and American institutions. These and other standards presumably were to establish whether the applicant for naturalization understood and adopted our historic principles of government and was therefore worthy on his own individual merits to be fully acceptable as a member of American society. However, the main and most important criterion for eligibility for citizenship turned out to be whether the applicant was of a certain "color." Regardless of a person's individual worth, unless he was also a member of a specific color, to wit, a "free white person," he was ineligible for citizenship. In the early days of our nation, the reference to "free white persons" was an obvious attempt to exclude nonwhites, that is, Negroes who had been brought into the United States as slaves.

But what was to be the policy of Congress with reference to other nonwhite persons, including American Indians who had been residing in the United States before the earliest English immigrant settlers in Jamestown? Should these American Indians, born in North America before this nation was established, be admitted to citizenship after the United States of America was founded? Not so, said the Congress, because the native American Indians were not "free white persons." They were of the "red" color. In addition, American Indians were members of tribes with their own set of laws that regulated the daily conduct of their lives outside the purview of American law and its institutions. These Indian tribes were considered to be foreign nations and not to be included within the purview of congressional legislation for naturalization. [39]

Persons from Japan, Korea, and China were considered to be of the "yellow" race, and the Filipinos were considered "brown," being of Malaysian extraction and therefore distinct from those of other Oriental descents.

The criterion that one must be a "free white person" to be eligible for citizenship was modified by the Congress in 1870 after the Civil War, when "persons of African nativity or descent" were granted naturalization privileges. [40] Then some "brown" people were accorded privileges of naturalization in 1940, [41] and the people of China were granted naturalization in 1943 as a gesture of good will toward the Chinese government, an ally of the United States in World War II. [42] In 1946, the people of the Philippine Islands were granted naturalization privileges [43] in recognition of their support of the United States during World War II and to keep a pledge made to the Philippine government that it would be granted independence after the end of the war with Japan. [44] It was not until 1952 that persons of the "yellow" races from

Japan and Korea were granted naturalization privileges.[45] With the removal of the barriers to naturalization for the Japanese and Koreans, the color qualification was completely eliminated as a condition of eligibility for naturalization. It took Congress 162 years, from 1790 to 1952, to eliminate completely "color" as a criterion for eligibility to citizenship.

In the early case of In re Saito,[46] the federal district court declared that the races of mankind were classified as white, black, yellow, and brown. Apparently the color "red" for American Indians was overlooked by the judge in classifying races of people by color. Here, the court, for the first time, equated the word "white" with race, declaring that it was the intent of the Congress to exclude from the privilege of citizenship all races except the Caucasian. Saito therefore was not eligible to apply for naturalization because he was of the Mongolian race, a race that was not included within the term "free white person." Here according to the classification of the court, the Mongolian race was defined as the "yellow" race.

Between 1908 and 1925, six cases were reported in both the state and federal courts, including the United States Supreme Court, that involved issues of the eligibility of Japanese aliens for naturalization.

Four of these cases involved Japanese aliens who had rendered military service to the United States and had been honorably discharged from the armed forces. Two of these men were denied naturalization out of hand. The other two were at one time granted citizenship through naturalization and subsequently had their citizenship certificates cancelled. The fifth case involved a Japanese alien who applied for and was granted citizenship through naturalization: he also had his certificate of citizenship subsequently cancelled by another court.

The case of In re Buntaro Kumagai[47] involved a Japanese alien who had been honorably discharged as a soldier in the regular army of the United States. In 1862, in recognition of services performed by aliens who had enlisted for military service, Congress enacted a law that provided that "any alien" who had been honorably discharged was eligible to apply for naturalization. This provision of the Act of 1862 had been incorporated into the Act of 1901 as Section 2166.[48]

In 1908 Kumagai applied for naturalization in the Federal District Court of the State of Washington. District Judge Cornelius H. Hanford denied his application for naturalization on the ground that although the word "any alien" was mentioned in the Act of 1862, and also in Section 2166 of the Act of 1901,[49] the words "any alien" meant any alien who was a "free white person" as contained in Section 2169 of the Act of 1901. Judge Hanford ruled that the Congress intended by the Act of 1901 to maintain a line of demarkation between races and to extend the privileges of naturalization only to those of the race that was predominant in this country. He concluded therefore that "as this applicant is of a different race, the court is constrained to deny his application on the ground that the laws enacted by Congress do not extend to the people of his race the privilege of becoming naturalized citizens of this country."

Another attempt at naturalization was made in *Bessho* vs. *U. S.* [50] (1910). Namiyo Bessho was a Japanese alien who filed a petition for naturalization in the Federal District Court of Norfolk, Virginia. He had been honorably discharged after five years' service in the United States Navy. Bessho applied for naturalization on the basis of a law enacted by Congress in 1894[51] that granted citizenship to "any alien" over twenty-one years of age who had enlisted in the navy or Marine Corps and had served five consecutive years in either branch. Bessho contended that the Act of 1894, under which he had filed his petition for naturalization, was not governed by Section 2169 of the Act of June 29, 1906,[52] which limited the privilege of naturalization only to "free white persons and persons of African nativity or descent" because the Act of 1894 only contained the general words "any alien" without qualifying or restricting these words.

Justice Nathan Goff of the Federal Circuit Court of Appeals rejected this argument also. He stated that because Section 2169 had not been repealed, it must be applied in conjunction with the Act of 1894. He declared that the act clearly indicated that the Congress intended to exclude all persons of the Mongolian race from the privilege of the naturalization laws, and that was that.

In the case of *Hidemitsu Toyota* vs. *U. S.*,[53] Hidemitsu Toyota was born in Japan and entered the United States in 1913. For ten years, between 1913 and 1923, he had served in the United States Coast Guard, a service that was a part of the naval forces of the United States during World War I. On May 14, 1921 he filed a petition for naturalization in the District Court for the State of Massachusetts on the basis of the Act of 1918,[54] which accorded naturalization privileges to "all aliens" who had served in the armed forces of the United States and who had been honorably discharged. The district court granted his petition for naturalization and the government appealed. The Federal Circuit Court of Appeals for the First Circuit cancelled the certificate of citizenship. Toyota then appealed to the United States Supreme Court. Associate Justice Pierce Butler upheld the decision of the court of appeals to cancel the certificate of citizenship. He reaffirmed the position that the words "any alien" described in Section 2169 of the Act of June 29, 1906 was an expression by Congress used to describe the person for whose benefit that act was passed. He declared that the words "any alien" did not enlarge the classes of aliens eligible for naturalization, the eligibility of which was based on distinctions of color or race. He stated, "It has long been the national policy to maintain the distinction of color and race, . . . [and] radical changes are not lightly to be deemed to have intended."

The case of *Ichizo Sato* vs. *Hall*[55] in 1923 involved a Japanese alien, Ichizo Sato, who had served in the United States Army during World War I. He applied for naturalization in the Territory of Hawaii in 1919 on the basis of an act passed by Congress on May 9, 1918,[56] an act that had amended the naturalization laws to permit "any alien" serving in the military and naval services of the United States during World War I to file a petition for naturalization. On January 21, 1919, based upon this 1918 amendment, Sato was granted citizenship by the United States District Court for the Territory of Hawaii. Sato later went to California. Anxious to exercise his newly acquired rights of franchise as a citizen, he requested that he be registered as a voter of Sacramento County.

County Clerk Harry W. Hall refused to place Sato's name on the register of voters on the ground that members of the yellow race were not entitled to naturalization and that, therefore, an order of the United States District Court for the Territory of Hawaii was void on its face. Sato asserted that the order of a federal court admitting him to citizenship was a final judgment, entered by a court of competent jurisdiction, and, therefore, not subject to collateral attack. The Superior Court of Sacramento County upheld County Clerk Hall. Sato appealed to the California Supreme Court. The issue was whether Sato was entitled to the privileges of citizenship under the general naturalization laws of the United States.

The California Supreme Court held that the privilege of citizenship rested solely with the Congress. The federal courts had no power to alter or extend the provisions of the naturalization laws. Justice Frank H. Kerrigan, speaking for the court, held that under the Act of 1862[57] and the Act of 1894, the words granting naturalization privileges to "any alien" meant "any alien of the white or black races." Thus, with reference to the Act of 1918,[58] Congress could not have intended a new and special meaning in the Act of 1918 to expand the scope of eligibility of citizenship to those of races other than white or black.

He concluded that "under no condition could a Japanese born in Japan be eligible to naturalization."

In *Yamashita* vs. *Hinkle*[59] Takuji Yamashita had filed an application for naturalization in the Superior Court of the State of Washington prior to 1906. His petition was granted and an entry of judgment declaring Yamashita a United States citizen was issued to him by the court. Relying on his new status, Yamashita organized a corporation and attempted to file articles of incorporation with the secretary of state of the State of Washington. Only United States citizens could organize corporations in Washington at that time. Secretary of State Hinkle refused to receive and file the articles of incorporation on the ground that Yamashita, being of the Japanese race, was at the time of his naturalization not eligible for citizenship. Yamashita filed a writ of mandamus in the State Supreme Court of Washington to compel the secretary of state to accept his corporate documents. The supreme court refused to issue the writ, and Yamashita then appealed to the United States Supreme Court. Associate Justice George Sutherland upheld the ruling of the state supreme court and declared the judgment of naturalization entered in the superior court null and void. The fact that Yamashita had obtained his certificate of citizenship before the Act of June 29, 1906 was of no consequence because Section 2169 only permitted "free white persons" to become naturalized.

THE DOOR IS CLOSED TO JAPANESE NATURALIZATION

The case of *Ozawa* vs. *U.S.*[60] decided by the United States Supreme Court on November 13, 1922, was to remain the landmark case for the next thirty years so far as the ineligibility to citizenship of Japanese aliens was concerned, that is, until the amendment to the naturalization laws in 1952 accorded naturalization privileges to Japanese aliens. When Ozawa's application for citizenship was denied, he appealed to the United States Supreme Court. There Associate Justice Sutherland firmly closed the door on all further attempts by Japanese aliens to obtain naturalization privileges, except those granted Japanese aliens who had served in World War I. Special legislation had been enacted through the efforts of Master Sergeant Tokutaro Slocum, a Japanese alien who served with the famous Rainbow Division in France in World War I, and about whom more will be said.

Ozawa contended that because Orientals were not specifically excluded from naturalization by Congress under Section 2169 of the Act of June 29, 1906,[61] he should be considered to be within the province of being considered the same as a "free white person."

Justice Sutherland rejected this contention and pointed out that from the beginning of the naturalization acts from 1790 to 1906, Congress had accorded the privilege of naturalization only to "white" persons and to persons of "African nativity." He stated that although Japanese were not specifically excluded from naturalization, the omission of Japanese did not imply that they were included within the provisions of Section 2169. It had been the intention of the Congress to confer the privilege of citizenship only upon that class of persons whom the founding fathers knew as white and to deny it to all who could not be so classified. "It is not enough to say that the framers of the statute [Section 2169] did not have in mind the brown or the yellow races of Asia. It is necessary to go further and be able to say that had these particular races been suggested, the language of the Act would have been so phrased as to include them within its privileges." "Free white persons" were meant to indicate only a person of what is popularly known as the "Caucasian race." Here, Justice Sutherland continued, "the appellant is clearly of a race which is not Caucasian, and therefore belongs entirely outside the zone on the negative side."

As if in apology to soften the harsh racial tones of his decision, Justice Sutherland concluded, "Of course, there is not implied either in the legislation or in our interpretation of it, any suggestion of individual unworthiness or racial inferiority."

5

The "Yellow Peril" Propaganda and the Resultant Alien Land Laws

THE ORIGIN OF the term "Yellow Peril" is difficult to trace. According to author Roger Daniels, the term "seems to be a direct translation of Kaiser Wilhelm II's vaporings about a *'gelbe gefahr'* threatening Europe and all Christendom (he meant a Chinese invasion a la Genghis Khan). First heard in English around the turn of the century, it was in wide public use in the United States by 1905. Most of those who used it meant to warn of an imminent invasion by Japan. But even before Japan became a world power, some Americans, usually Californians, expressed fears about the Orient. They feared China."[1]

This fear of an invasion of the United States by Asians through the West Coast of America was passionately expressed in the *New York Tribune* of May 1, 1869 by United States economist and advocate of the single tax, Henry George:

> The sixty thousand or one hundred thousand Mongolians on our western coast are the thin edge of the wedge which has for its base the five hundred million of Eastern Asia . . . The Chinaman can live where stronger than he would starve. Give him fair play and this quality enables him to drive out the stronger races . . . (unless Chinese immigration is checked) the youngest home of the nations must in its early manhood follow the path and meet the doom of Babylon, Ninevah and Rome . . . Here plain to the eye of him who chooses to see are dragon's teeth (which will) spring up around men marshalled for civil war.[2]

"YELLOW PERIL" PROPAGANDA IS USED AGAINST THE JAPANESE

Twenty years after Henry George talked about Chinese dragon's teeth, it was Japan that began to disturb the balance of power in the Far East. In 1894 she fought and won her first modern naval battle against the Chinese. Ten years later she totally wrecked the balance of power in the Far East by defeating the armed forces of czarist Russia. Very soon thereafter propaganda against "colored" immigration into the United States took on an even shriller tone than it had before. The "Yellow Peril" was afoot.

Two eminent writers from the East Coast took up the hue and cry: Madison Grant and Lathrop Stoddard. In an introduction to fellow racist Lathrop Stoddard's *The Rising Tide of Color Against White Supremacy*, written in 1920, Madison Grant wrote:

> Colored migration is a universal peril, menacing every part of the white world . . . the whole white race is exposed, immediately or ultimately, to the possibility of social sterilization and final replacement or absorption by the teeming colored races . . . there is no immediate danger of the world being swamped by black blood. But there is a very immediate danger that the white

stocks may be swamped by Asiatic blood . . . unless the "white man" erects and maintains artificial barriers . . . [he will] finally perish . . . White civilization is today "coterminous" with the white race.[3]

Subsequently, these writers were duly acknowledged by their peers, Hitler's Nazis. According to Roger Daniels, "Both of these writers were later 'discovered' by the Nazis; between 1933 and 1937, Stoddard had six editions in the Third Reich, while Grant had four."[4]

The fear of the growing military power of Japan was easily transferred by agitators to another area: the presence in the United States of immigrants from Japan. Through exaggerated reports of the number of Japanese entering America and their control or use of agricultural lands or through outright expressions of hatred for them, the agitators made a case that the apparently peaceful Japanese immigrants were in truth the sinister vanguard of an invading horde, bent solely on the conquest of the country. Not since this same charge had been made against Chinese immigrants in the 1880s had it been leveled against any other immigrant ethnic or national group.

The same general social charges that had at one time proliferated against the Chinese, and some earlier immigrant groups from Eastern Europe and the Mediterranean area, were then aimed at the Japanese. It was said that the Japanese immigrants could not be assimilated because of their vile habits, low standard of living, extremely high birthrate, and so on. Also they were tricky, cunning, and absolutely unreliable.

The most prominent politician to seize upon the "Yellow Peril" theme before World War I was Democrat James D. Phelan, a United States senator from California. Senator Phelan's anti-Oriental activities dated from the 1880s. He was concerned about the military strength of Japan, particularly after the Russo-Japanese War of 1904–1905. The senator insisted that the Pacific Coast would be an easy prey in case of an attack by Japan and accused the Japanese immigrants in California of being an "enemy within our gates."

In 1907 an American naval hero named Richmond P. Hobson, while campaigning for a seat in Congress in his home state of Alabama, proclaimed the "Yellow Peril" menace. His theme attracted wide attention, particularly when it was spread through the Hearst chain of newspapers. Hobson advocated a large navy, stating that by landing an army of exactly 1,207,700 men Japan could conquer the Pacific Coast. He also predicted that Japan, by taking over China, would "soon be able to command the military resources of the whole yellow race."[5]

Hobson's predictions of a racial war gained a vigorous proponent in the United States in the person of one Homer Lea, an anti-Japanese racist whose claim to fame lay in his self-proclaimed close relationship as advisor to Dr. Sun Yat-sen, the great Chinese leader who organized the long-oppressed Chinese peasants, overthrew the Manchu dynasty, and established the Chinese Republic in 1912. Lea, a hunchback who somehow became a general in the Chinese army, wrote of the urgent need of the United States to build up a large army and navy, so as to repel a military attack against the United States by Japan. In his book *The Valor of Ignorance*, first published in 1909, Lea told of a coming war between Japan and the United States, with Japan seizing the Philippine Islands, landing forces on the Pacific Coast, and overrunning Washington, Oregon, and California.[6]

Then, during and after World War I, the German propaganda machine in America functioned remarkably well in spreading the idea that the real enemy of the United States was Japan. In May 1915 the German agent George Sylvester Viereck arranged the distribution in America of some 300,000 copies of a pamphlet on the subject of the "Yellow Peril." Another pamphlet, published in 1916 under the auspices of the German Newspaper Association, warned that the United States should arm and prepare for war, not against Germany, from which the United States had nothing to fear, but against Japan, which, Viereck insisted, "wants a foothold on the Pacific Coast."[7] An American newspaperman, Edward Lyell Fox, suspected of being a part of the German propaganda machine, proposed to Franz von Papen, then presumably a captain in the German army but actually an espionage agent, that Germany provide some agents provocateurs to foment anti-Japanese riots in California in order to involve Japan and the United States in war.

Another effective method of spreading the fear of the "Yellow Peril" was through motion pictures, an art that was just developing into a great medium of communication. In 1916 International Film Service Corporation, which was part of the Hearst empire, produced a movie titled *Patria*, which showed attempts by Japan to conquer the United States by enlisting the aid of Mexico.

The most influential and certainly the most persuasive sources of "Yellow Peril" propaganda were military officers of the various branches of the armed forces of the United States stationed in Washington, D.C. The army and navy, in their war plans, had concluded early that the most probable enemy against which the United States should prepare was Japan. This view was concurred in and vigorously upheld by

Franklin Delano Roosevelt, who was assistant secretary of the navy during the years 1913 to 1920. Josephus Daniels, secretary of the navy under President Woodrow Wilson during World War I, and Rear Admiral Bradley A. Fiske, Chief of Naval Operations, were also obsessed with the "Yellow Peril." The army's point of view had its strongest supporters in Major General J. P. Story and Lieutenant General Adrian R. Chaffee, former Chief of Staff.

The Japanese government, during the period 1913 to 1919, was carrying on a policy toward China and other parts of the world that lent credence to these attitudes.

Japan's "continued subjugation of Korea; the Twenty-One Demands upon China; the Shantung question; the friction between Japanese and American troops in Siberia; the insistent Japanese demands for racial equality, raised first at the Versailles Peace Conference and later at Geneva"[8] are cases in point. The agitation to exclude further immigration of the Japanese into the United States, and to drive the Japanese farmers from their lands by more restrictive legislation, was materially influenced by Japanese-American relations in the much broader area of international power politics.

The anti-Japanese alien land laws were based primarily on emotional appeals to the public and claims that the Japanese farmer was threatening to "overrun" the farmlands of California and other states. In the summer of 1909, there were approximately 40,000 Japanese farmhands in the seven western states of California, Washington, Colorado, Utah, Oregon, Idaho, and Montana.[9] Of this number, approximately 30,000 were engaged in farming activities in California, and most were tenant farmers.

When the California Alien Land Law of 1913 was enacted, the number of Japanese who actually owned agricultural lands was insignificant. In 1912, according to the county assessor's reports, Japanese owned only 12,726 acres of farms as compared with more than 11,000,000 acres of improved farmlands in the state of California at that time. Even as late as 1920, when the Alien Land Law was approved as an initiative measure, the Japanese owned only 74,767 acres and leased 383,287 more for a total of 458,054 acres, or only 0.0164 percent of the 27,981,444 acres of farmlands then reported in operation by the California Board of Control.[10]

THE ALIEN LAND LAW OF 1920

Before discussing the campaign that resulted in the passage of the California Alien Land Law of 1920, some mention should be made of similar statutes in other states where Japanese were engaged in farming. In 1917 Arizona enacted a law providing that "no person not eligible to become a citizen of the United States shall acquire title to any property within this state."[11] The State of Washington, which in 1889 had enacted an alien land law also aimed at the Japanese, added further restrictions, this time against land tenancy and land leasing. It did so in 1921 and again in 1923, in order to align its alien land laws with those of California.[12]

In 1923 Oregon and Idaho also enacted legislation patterned after the California Alien Land Law. Then came Nebraska, Texas, Kansas, Louisiana, Montana, New Mexico, Minnesota, and Missouri.[13] But of all the alien land laws passed by the various states, the one enacted by California in 1920 was perhaps the most significant because of its comprehensiveness.[14]

James D. Phelan, the anti-Japanese crusader of the late 1880s and early 1900s, was again the most prominent person in the agitation for more restrictive alien land laws than those that had been enacted in California in 1913.[15] His efforts were a pure and simple political ploy to get himself reelected to a second term as a United States senator.

On March 31, 1919, before a special session of the California Legislature, Phelan launched his reelection campaign. He insisted that the Japanese were a menace economically, socially, and militarily. His platform called for a more stringent alien land law, abrogation of the "Gentlemen's Agreement," passage of a Japanese exclusion law, a larger navy, and the strengthening of the coastal defenses on the Pacific Slope. Phelan's slogan was "Keep California White."

Phelan considered that a "Jap is a Jap," and insisted that "the native Japanese are as undesirable as the imported."[16] The following day, April 1, 1919, state Senator J. M. Inman, a Republican from Sacramento County, obviously in coordination with Phelan, introduced an alien land act designed to plug up certain loopholes in the 1913 Alien Land Law.

However, the California Legislature, then controlled by members of the Republican party, was opposed to supporting Democrat Phelan for the United States Senate seat. Although Senator Inman had introduced the amendments to the Alien Land Law of 1913, the other members of the Republican party in the state legislature refused to consider the amendments to the act for fear Democrat Phelan would capitalize on its passage and win reelection to the Senate while carrying the banner of the opposition party. Governor Hiram Johnson refused to call a special session of the legislature to consider amendments to the 1913 law. The only way left for the anti-Japanese forces to seek the desired amendments was to place the measure on the ballot of the forthcoming general election of 1920 in the form of an initiative. By strenuous efforts, primarily those of the Native Sons and Daughters of the Golden West and the American Legion, the necessary signatures were obtained.

Once the measure was on the ballot, the anti-Japanese elements in California again united behind their common purpose. In September 1919 a reorganization meeting of the anti-Japanese forces convened in the offices of State Controller John S. Chambers, a Republican. Those present cut across party lines. The campaign was on, with the catch words "Save California from the Japs."

With Senator Inman as president, an organization called the California Oriental Exclusion League was formed and linked with counter-part organizations throughout the state.[17] In the south, it was the Los Angeles Anti-Asiatic Association; in the Sacramento Valley, the Fourteen Counties Association; in the Imperial Valley, the Alien Regulation League; and in the San Joaquin Valley, the Americanization League. But in this seeming diversity of supporters, there was unity. In addition to the endorsement of a more restrictive alien land law, the league groups approved the following five-point program:

1. Cancellation of the "Gentlemen's Agreement."

2. Exclusion of "picture brides."

3. Rigorous exclusion of Japanese as immigrants.

4. Confirmation of the policy that Asiatics should be forever barred from American citizenship.

5. Amendment of the federal Constitution providing that no child born in the United States should be given the rights of an American citizen unless both parents were of a race eligible for citizenship.

The Exclusion League programs and activities were further supported by four well-established and powerful anti-Japanese groups already in existence in California. They were the Native Sons and Daughters of the Golden West, the American Legion, the California State Federation of Labor, and the California State Grange.

Every major political figure in the state also supported this movement. Throughout the summer months of 1920, an emotional anti-

Japanese propaganda campaign was conducted. The Japanese were attacked for every conceivable thing, including their unbearable competition in the form of cheap labor, "constituting a yellow horde flooding the nation." They were accused of having a high birthrate, of being spies instead of farmers, of being sex fiends and rapists, and of mongrelizing white women. This propaganda was carried, with large headlines, in almost every newspaper throughout the state, with magazines, periodicals, and movies joining in the campaign.

Under this emotional barrage, the voters in California approved the Alien Land Law at the general election of November 2, 1920 by a margin of three-to-one (668,483 to 222,086), to become effective December 9, 1920.[18] The campaign, while successful in carrying every county in the state, was disappointing to the Oriental Exclusion League, which had optimistically forecast a ten-to-one margin of success for the measure instead of a mere three-to-one.

An ironic touch was the fact that Senator Phelan, the political candidate most instrumental in instigating the anti-Japanese program and in the passage of the Alien Land Law of 1920, was defeated in his bid for reelection.

The Alien Land Law of 1920 consisted of fourteen sections designed to plug loopholes in the earlier Alien Land Law of 1913. In the Alien Land Law of 1913, only the attorney general could institute escheat proceedings for violation of its provisions (Section 5). In the 1920 law, the attorney general, or district attorney of the proper county, could institute such proceedings (Section 7). The 1913 law permitted the lease of land to aliens up to a three-year period (Section 2). The 1920 law prohibited *any* leases of land to aliens (Section 8). The 1920 law also provided criminal penalties for persons who failed to file accounting of lands held on behalf of ineligible aliens or minors (Section 5[c]) and for persons who conspired to transfer real property to ineligible aliens (Section 10).

The 1920 law further prohibited corporations in which Japanese aliens held a majority of the stock from leasing or purchasing land (Section 3) and prohibited Japanese parents who were noncitizens from serving as guardians of property for their minor children (Section 4).

However, the heart of the newly approved Alien Land Law of 1920 was Section 9(a). Section 9 provided the following:

Every transfer of real property . . . shall be void as to the state and the interest thereby conveyed or sought to be conveyed shall escheat to the state if the property interest involved is such a character that an alien mentioned in

Section 2 hereof [aliens ineligible for citizenship or not allowed by treaty], is inhibited from acquiring, possessing, enjoying or transferring it, and if the conveyance is made with intent to prevent, evade or avoid escheat as provided for herein.

A prima facie presumption that the conveyance is made with such intent shall arise upon proof of any of the following groups of facts:

(a) The taking of the property in the name of a person other than the person mentioned in Section 2 hereof if the consideration is paid or agreed or understood to be paid by an alien mentioned in Section 2 hereof.

The enumeration in this section of certain presumptions shall not be so construed as to preclude other presumptions or inferences that reasonably may be made as to the existence of intent to prevent, evade or avoid escheat as provided for herein.

Stripped of its legal verbiage, Section 9(a) meant that if a Japanese alien furnished the funds to purchase land, and the title of such land was taken in the name of another person, such an act was presumed to be done with the intent to avoid the Alien Land Law and was therefore void, and the land was subject to escheat to the state.

Section 9(a) was upheld as constitutional for the next twenty-eight years, until it was struck down in the landmark case of *Oyama* vs. *California* in 1948 as violating the equal protection clause of the Fourteenth Amendment to the federal Constitution.

THE ALIEN LAND LAW IS TESTED IN COURT

Following the passage of the Alien Land Law of 1920, eleven landmark cases were reported during the next five years that directly involved either that law or the State of Washington Alien Land Law. (Other reported decisions that are not landmark cases involving the Alien Land Laws of California and other states will be discussed in a later chapter covering the period of 1925 to 1941.)

Of the eleven cases, nine were in California and two in the state of Washington. Six of the eleven cases were ultimately decided by the Supreme Court of the United States—the two in Washington and four in California.

The earliest case was one that had far-reaching beneficial results for Japanese aliens who purchased farmlands for their American-born minor children. Known as *Estate of Tetsubumi Yano,* it was decided by the California Supreme Court in 1922.[20]

Hayao Yano, a Japanese ineligible for United States citizenship, purchased fourteen acres of land in Sutter County valued at $3,000.

His daughter, Tetsubumi Yano, age two, was a native-born citizen of the United States. On October 23, 1920 he transferred title to the land to his daughter and filed a petition with the Superior Court of Sutter County to become the guardian of the person and estate (that is, the land) of his minor daughter. The guardianship proceedings were commenced before the Alien Land Law of 1920 went into effect on December 20, 1920. Hayao Yano admitted that his act of conveying the title to the land to his daughter, with himself as guardian, was the result of the laws in California, which did not permit him to buy the land for himself. The superior court denied his petition for letters of guardianship, and Yano appealed.

The California Supreme Court, by a six-to-one vote, reversed the decision of the superior court and held that Section 4 of the Alien Land Law of 1920 was unconstitutional, denying to the minor child equal protection of the laws guaranteed to her by the Fourteenth Amendment of the federal Constitution and by Section 21 of Article I of the state constitution, which granted rights, privileges, and immunities to all citizens. The court stated that the minor daughter, as an American citizen, was entitled to acquire and hold property, both real and personal, and that her infancy did not incapacitate her from becoming seized of the title to real estate. Furthermore, "the right of a father to be the guardian of his own minor child does not in any way depend upon or arise out of his nationality or his eligibility for citizenship in this country. It has no relation thereto."

In re Y. Akado[21] involved the arrest of, and criminal charges against, a Japanese alien for alleged violation of Section 10 of the 1920 Alien Land Law, which prohibited the acquisition of agricultural lands by aliens ineligible for citizenship.

On September 19, 1921 two men known only as Y. Akado and Cockrill agreed between themselves that Akado was to furnish the money to buy land in Sonoma County from a Mr. Sousa. The title to the property was to be taken in the name of Cockrill, but the land was to be controlled by Akado. Before the transfer of land was actually made to Cockrill, Akado was taken into custody on a warrant of arrest for conspiracy to violate Section 10. He applied for a writ of habeas corpus to secure his release from custody.

The writ was denied in the Superior Court of Sonoma County. Akado appealed. Section 10 provided that if two or more persons conspire to effect a transfer of real property, such acts were punishable by imprisonment in the county jail or state penitentiary not exceeding two years, or by a fine not exceeding $5,000, or both. Chief Justice Lucien Shaw of the California Supreme Court upheld the order denying the writ of habeas corpus. He stated:

> . . . it is to the interest of the state that all persons owning land should be effectively deterred from attempting to evade or frustrate the provisions of the act forbidding the acquisition of such land by such alien, by means of colorable conveyances and unrecorded trusts. It is therefore reasonable and proper to provide that the attempt to make such transfer, or an agreement or conspiracy to do so, should be punishable as a crime.

The serious impact of the results of In re Y. Akado was successfully avoided, however, in the case of In re K. Okahara,[22] which came before the same California Supreme Court one year later.

K. Okahara, a Japanese alien ineligible for citizenship, was arrested by the sheriff of Placer County, together with Toni Vicencio, and accused of unlawfully effecting the transfer of an interest in land in violation of the same Section 10 of the Alien Land Law of 1920. Okahara applied for a writ of habeas corpus to be released from custody. Okahara was ordered discharged from custody, and the order was upheld by the California Supreme Court. On March 20, 1922 Okahara executed a written contract with Vicencio, the owner, to transfer to Okahara for a five-year term some twenty acres of agricultural land in Placer County. Under this contract, Vicencio was described as the employer and Okahara an employee-contractor. Okahara was to clear the land, plant an orchard, and grow various vegetables, using his own tools and equipment, and was to receive 50 percent of the net proceeds from the sale of the products of the land.

Justice Emmet Seawell of the California Supreme Court, with five other justices concurring, held that such a contract did not transfer or convey any interest in real property, nor did it create a tenancy of any kind on the part of the cultivator of land (Okahara). At best, said Justice Seawell, Okahara was only a tenant in common of the crop, and the legal possession of the land was in the owner. It lacked the essential elements of a lease and bore all the characteristics of a sharecropping agreement. The court recognized that every agreement of contract to perform farm labor must of necessity give the physical right to go upon the premises on which the labor is to be done. However, such an agreement did not transfer an interest in land. Moreover "the fact that the crops are to be converted into money by the employee and divided on a net basis with the contractor could not work a transfer of any interest in the soil to the latter."

Justice Seawell must have had second thoughts about his cropping contract decision in the Okahara case, for in two subsequent California Supreme Court cases, arising out of Los Angeles County a year later and decided the same day, he ruled differently. In Jones vs. Webb[23] he held that where the landlord hired an employee to grow berries, vegetables, and farm crops for a monthly salary and a bonus, such use of the word "bonus" was a "disguise" and that the real intent of the parties was to lease land to the ineligible alien, an agreement that was prohibited by the 1920 law. In the case of In re Nose[24] the Japanese alien was to work the farm at a fixed wage plus an incentive of 50 percent of the net profits of the crops, an arrangement that, while appearing to be a cropping agreement, was held to be forbidden by the Alien Land Law of 1920.

THE ALIEN LAND LAWS REACH THE SUPREME COURT

Of the six Alien Land Law cases that reached the United States Supreme Court, the following four are considered definitive decisions touching on the following fundamental areas:

1. Whether the land laws of the State of Washington and the State of California were constitutional.

2. Whether the state could impose classifications as to the right of certain aliens to own property within their respective states.

3. Whether the classification for citizenship purposes by the Congress could be utilized in granting or prohibiting aliens from owning land within state boundaries.

4. Whether the Treaty of 1911 between the United States and Japan included the right of Japanese aliens to own agricultural land within the respective states.

Two of these cases were decided on November 12, 1923: Terrace vs. Thompson[25] and Porterfield vs. Webb.[26] The other two cases were decided one week later on November 19, 1923: Webb vs. O'Brien[27] and Frick vs. Webb.[28] In each of these four cases, Associate Justice Pierce Butler wrote the opinion for the Supreme Court.

In Terrace vs. Thompson, Terrace was a citizen of the United States and a resident of the state of Washington. He owned some agricultural land in King County, Washington. Terrace desired to lease this land to Nakatsuka, who was born in Japan and who was a farmer by occupation. Terrace brought suit against L. L. Thompson, the state attorney general, to enjoin him from enforcing the Alien Land Law of Washington (C.50, Laws of 1921). The law in Washington provided that such leases to aliens "who had not declared their intention to become citizens of the United States" were illegal, resulting in forfeiture of the land to the state, with additional provisions subjecting the landowner to prosecution and criminal penalties for the act of leasing land to such ineligible aliens.

Terrace contended that the Alien Land Law of 1921:

1. Took property of the parties without due process of law.

2. Prohibited the alien from following a common occupation of the community.

3. Violated the equal protection clause of the Fourteenth Amendment because the classification of ineligible aliens bore no reasonable relation to a legitimate legislative end.

4. Was contrary to Article I of the existing treaty between the United States and Japan because the law in question prohibited Japanese subjects from carrying on a trade.

The attorney general insisted that the Alien Land Law of 1921 was valid since the state could restrict leasing of land to persons who owed no allegiance to the state or the nation, and that the state was justified in classifying certain aliens as being prohibited from leasing land based on the public welfare and under the police power of the state.

Speaking for a unanimous court, Justice Butler upheld the validity of the Alien Land Law of 1921. Answering each of the arguments raised by appellant Terrace, he held:

1. The quality and allegiance of those who owned, occupied, and used the farmlands within the state's border were matters of highest importance and affected the safety and power of the state itself.

2. The issue was not the opportunity of the ineligible alien to earn a living in the common occupation of the community but had to do with the privilege of owning and controlling agricultural land within the state.

3. The rule established by Congress as to who is eligible for citizenship furnished a reasonable basis for classification in the state law, withholding from such alien the privilege of land ownership.

4. The United States–Japan Treaty of 1911 contained no provision giving Japanese the right to own or lease land for agricultural purposes. The right "to carry on trade" or "to own or lease and occupy homes, manufactories, warehouses and shops" or "to lease land for residential and commercial purposes" could not be said to include the right to own or lease or to have any title to or interest in land for agricultural purposes.

Porterfield vs. *Webb* was a California case wherein Porterfield sought to enjoin Attorney General U. S. Webb from enforcing the Alien Land Law of 1920. Porterfield was a citizen of the United States and a resident of California. He owned eighty acres of land in Los Angeles County. He desired to lease the land to Mizuno, a farmer who was born in Japan. As in *Terrace* vs. *Thompson*, the attorney general threatened to enforce the Alien Land Law of 1920, to forfeit the leasehold interest, and to prosecute Porterfield criminally for violating the law.

Substantially the same arguments advanced by Terrace in the Washington case were reiterated by Porterfield. However, Porterfield pointed out that there were eligible aliens who failed to declare their intention of becoming citizens of the United States, and therefore the provision establishing eligible aliens who had not declared their intention to become United States citizens, and aliens who were not eligible to become citizens, was arbitrary and unreasonable, and therefore the California law was invalid.

Supreme Court Justice Butler upheld the constitutionality of the California Alien Land Law. He brushed aside Porterfield's contention that the law was arbitrary or unreasonable because of the failure of the California Legislature to extend the prohibited class so as to include eligible aliens who had failed to declare their intentions to become citizens of the United States. He also repeated his previous decision that the treaty between the United States and Japan did not confer upon Japanese subjects the privilege of acquiring or leasing land for agricultural purposes.

Attorney General Webb, in asserting the validity of the California Alien Land Law, foresaw that the atmosphere in California, under which the Alien Land Law was passed by initiative, might be subject to inquiry by the justices of the United States Supreme Court to the effect that the law might be declared invalid because it was based on race discrimination against the Japanese. Webb answered this antic- ipated inquiry in the appellee's brief as follows:

> There is a valid classification between the aliens eligible for citizenship and aliens ineligible for citizenship. The classification is not one of racial discrim- ination. It is a question of recognizing the obvious fact that the American farm with its historical associations of cultivation and environment, including the home life of its occupants, cannot exist in competition with a farm devel- oped by Orientals with their totally different standards and ideas of cultivation of the soil, of living and social conditions.

One week later in *Webb* vs. *O'Brien*, sharecropping agreements, previously decided in *In re K. Okahara* to not be prohibited and reversed in *Jones* vs. *Webb* and *In re Nose*, were held by the United States Supreme Court to be prohibited under the California Alien Land Law of 1920.

O'Brien, a citizen of the United States and a resident of California, owned ten acres of agricultural land in Santa Clara County. Inouye, a farmer and a subject of Japan, desired to enter into a cropping con- tract covering the planting, cultivating, and harvesting of crops grown on the land. O'Brien instituted a suit to enjoin the attorney general from enforcing the Alien Land Law. The superior court granted the interlocutory injunction, and the attorney general appealed. Attorney General Webb contended that the State was interesting in preventing a sharecropping agreement because the alien ineligible for citizenship actually enjoyed the possession and dominion of land. O'Brien, rely- ing on *In re K. Okahara,* insisted that a sharecropping agreement was a contract for the performance of labor. Such a contract was not a con- veyance of land. As between the owner of property and the person cultivating the land, the relationship was that of employer-employee.

Justice Butler held that sharecropping agreements were also pro- hibited by the 1920 law. He held:

> The Act as a whole evidences legislative intention that ineligible aliens shall not be permitted to have or enjoy any privileges in respect to the use or the benefit of land for agricultural purposes. . . . The practical result of such a contract is that the cropper has use, control and benefit of land for agricul- tural purposes substantially similar to that granted to a lessee.

Justice Butler, revealing that he had been strongly influenced by the "Yellow Peril" propaganda against the Japanese, concluded:

Conceivably, by the use of such contracts, the population living on and cultivating the farmlands might come to be made up largely of ineligible aliens. The allegiance of the farmers to the state directly affects its strength and safety. We think it within the power of the state to deny to ineligible aliens the privilege to use agricultural lands within its borders.

In *Frick* vs. *Webb*, the companion case to *Webb* vs. *O'Brien*, Justice Butler also held that ownership of shares of stock by ineligible aliens in a California corporation engaged in agriculture constituted an interest in agricultural lands, and such ownership of stock was prohibited by the Alien Land Law of 1920.

Frick vs. *Webb* involved twenty-eight shares of capital stock of the Merced Farm Company, which owned 2,200 acres of farmland in California. Frick desired to sell his twenty-eight shares of stock to Satow, a native of Japan. Section 3 of the Act of 1920 prohibited ownership of shares of stock of any corporation owning real property where a majority of the members of the corporation were aliens ineligible for citizenship, unless such stock ownership was prescribed by treaty.

Justice Butler held that the Alien Land Law of 1920 was intended to forbid direct as well as indirect ownership and control of agricultural lands by ineligible aliens. He stated:

The right "to carry on trade" given by the treaty does not give the privilege to acquire the stock above described. To read the treaty to permit ineligible aliens to acquire such stock would be inconsistent with the intentions and purposes of the parties [sic]. We hold that the provisions of Section 3 above referred to do not conflict with the 14th Amendment, or with the treaty.

AMENDMENTS TO THE 1920 LAW

In 1923 the California Legislature further amended the California Alien Land Law of 1920 in several fundamentally important respects.[29]

1. Any real property acquired in violation of the 1920 law was deemed to escheat as of the date of such acquiring, as compared to the prior provision that the land was to escheat after proceedings had been instituted and a judgment of escheat to the State had been obtained in court (Section 7.)

2. Cropping contracts were declared to constitute an interest in real property (Section 8).

3. Aliens ineligible for citizenship, unless granted by treaty, could not acquire, possess, enjoy, use, cultivate, occupy, and transfer real property.

In addition, by a separate bill on May 31, 1923,[30] Section 1751(a) of the Code of Civil Procedure was amended to prohibit aliens ineligible for citizenship from being appointed guardians of any estate that consisted in whole or in part of real property. This amendment was obviously aimed at *Estate of Tetsubumi Yano*, the California Supreme Court decision of May 1, 1922. The court, barely a year earlier, had declared invalid Section 4 of the 1920 law prohibiting alien parents ineligible for citizenship from being appointed guardians of the estate of their American-born minor children.

The 1923 amendment to the 1920 law to the effect that escheat to the State was to be deemed to have occurred as of the date of such acquiring, that is, retroactively, was intended to preclude divestitures by ineligible Japanese aliens of their property interests before escheat proceedings had actually been instituted. Any Japanese person acquiring title or interest in any real property after 1923 was assuming a risk that the land acquired might later be declared invalid and subject to forfeiture.

It soon became evident that the Alien Land Law of 1920, and amendments thereto in 1923, coupled with the 1923 decisions of the United States Supreme Court, had dealt a severe blow to the agricultural interests of the Japanese, insofar as ownership of farmlands or farmlands controlled by Japanese was concerned. In 1930, only 191,427 acres[31] were farmlands owned or controlled by Japanese.[32] The working of these lands required the painstaking care of crops, innovative techniques of cultivation, more efficient production methods, and always the long, hard hours of toil. Japanese sweat and determination produced vegetables, fruits, and flowers—activities that in turn produced millions of dollars of agricultural wealth for the community, the state, and the nation.

The areas that made California one of the most important agricultural states in the nation included Marysville and the Suisun district; the great and fertile areas of the Vaca Valley; the San Joaquin and lower Sacramento valleys, where the muddy river bottoms were dredged to grow potatoes and rice; the beet fields and fruit orchards of the Santa Clara Valley; and extensive acreage used for berries, melons, and vegetables through the Coachella and Imperial valleys. These lands were worked by the Japanese.

The sugar beet fields of Oregon, Washington, Idaho, Utah, Colorado, and Montana produced vast returns, due in part to the efforts of Japanese farmers. In Arizona, Texas, Louisiana, Arkansas, and

Florida, Japanese farmers had settled to wrestle with the land and, by sheer stubborn patience, had developed rice fields, truck farms, and camellia culture.

The alien land laws of this era stood as symbols of racial intolerance and prejudice toward the Orientals, particularly toward the Japanese. Almost thirty years would pass before, in 1952, they would be declared unconstitutional on the ground that they were based on racial prejudice.[33] But by then the Japanese in America had suffered an incalculable economic setback from which they still have not fully recovered.

6

The End of the "Gentlemen's Agreement" and the Japanese Exclusion Act of 1924

I N THE YEAR 1924 the unfortunate use of two words by Japan's ambassador in a letter to the United States' secretary of state caused Congress to enact a law that totally excluded all Japanese from immigrating into the United States, thereby putting a sudden end to the existing "Gentlemen's Agreement" of 1908 between Japan and America.

The Japanese ambassador was Masanao Hanihara, who, on April 10, 1924, wrote a long letter to Secretary of State Charles Evans Hughes urging the importance of the continuation of the "Gentlemen's Agreement." The letter had been solicited from the ambassador by Hughes less than two weeks before.

INTERNATIONAL DEVELOPMENTS

In order to review the enactment of the Japanese Exclusion Act in its proper historical perspective, a short review of certain international developments that had been rapidly leading the United States and Japan to some type of confrontation is in order.

After the Russo-Japanese War, the United States had helped Japan obtain concessions from the Russians. When Japan vigorously began to develop her Russian-ceded interests in Manchuria, the United States became both irritated by and opposed to the expanding Japanese influence in Manchuria and China proper.

Ill feelings and tensions grew between the two countries when Japan reorganized the Russian railway system in Manchuria. Under the efficient management of Japanese business enterprise, it became a profitable venture primarily because Japan now offered lower sea and rail rates for shipments of goods from Japan and other countries into Manchuria. Also, Japan's aggressive economic expansion into China competed directly with American business interests, further aggravating the feelings of the United States. Strongly influenced by the U.S., Great Britain also became alarmed at the aggressive policies of Japan and attempted several countermoves against Japanese expansion.

In 1909 the United States made a direct attempt to check Japan's expansionist activities in Manchuria by trying to set up a bank in Mukden to finance developments by American business interests in mining, timber, and agriculture and to provide funds for the construction of a railway from Tsitsihar to Aigun along the Amur River. Japan promptly lodged a strong protest, and the project was abandoned.

In 1915, while Germany was at war in Europe, Japan entered into negotiations with China, negotiations that led to the Sino-Japanese Treaty. Through this treaty, China assigned to Japan the right to dispose of German interests in Shantung. This agreement between the two countries caused a flurry of diplomatic notes to be exchanged between the United States and Japan in an attempt by the United States to clarify Japan's ultimate intentions toward China. These diplomatic exchanges, known as the Lansing-Ishii Notes, finally came to declare that it was the intention of both countries to "encourage free and peaceful development of their trade in the Pacific region; to maintain the status quo in the region, and to defend the principle of the Open Door in China; to respect each other's territorial possessions; and to support by pacific means the independence and integrity of China."[1] These were agreements that would bear careful watching by both countries. It was now 1917.

The following year at the Paris Peace Conference in 1918, convened to decide the fate of a defeated Germany, China demanded restitution from Japan for the German leasehold in Shantung that she had assigned to Japan in 1915. The great powers decided in favor of Japan, an action that raised a storm of criticism in the United States. Japan remained in Shantung, which is part of China proper, where she was competing with United States business interests.

Controversies continued. In 1920, when Japan was feverishly expanding her naval construction program, she and the United States became embroiled in a contest over which country would control the Island of Yap, a speck of land in the Pacific Ocean that both countries desired as a fueling stop for their respective naval craft. This dispute grew to such magnitude that even the League of Nations eventually became involved in an attempt to resolve the issue. It was decided, but in a manner not completely satisfactory to either side.

The Washington Conference

In November 1921, in the hopes of restraining the current naval armaments race, the United States convened a conference involving itself, Japan, and Great Britain. The Washington Conference on Limitation of Armaments was one of the first such gatherings of nations in modern military history for the purpose of attempting arms limitations.

Japan was secretly anxious to reduce her military expenditures. She realized that a continuation of the spending of enormous amounts for military purposes would eventually lead her into bankruptcy. Before the Japanese delegates had left for the Washington Conference, Japan's Finance Minister Nishino Gen had privately expressed his opinion that his country's economy could not afford a prolonged armaments race. The delegates were therefore instructed to adopt a realistic posture at the conference and to avoid a direct clash with the United States.[2]

After several months of discussions, a naval armaments limitations agreement was concluded. The construction of capital ships by the parties involved was to be limited to the following ratio: United States, five; Great Britain, five; Japan, three. This ratio was developed in order to maintain the disparity between the major and secondary powers and at the same time avoid wastefulness among the major powers by eliminating excessive build-up of capital ships. Japan, which wanted to consider herself a major power, now found herself at the tail end of a 5:5:3 ratio. The militarists and jingoists in Japan were beside themselves with rage and frustration.

And that was not all. The Washington Conference, which ended in 1922, produced other far-reaching international results, all of them favorable to Great Britain and the United States and unfavorable to Japan. For instance, the Naval Armaments Limitation Treaty of 1922 abrogated the Anglo-Japanese Alliance of 1902. The United States had for many years desired to sever the military relationship between Great Britain and Japan because it felt that the alliance constituted a deterrence to America's future plans for expansion of its interests in the Pacific and in China.

The Naval Armaments Limitation Treaty of 1922 also abrogated the Lansing-Ishii Notes of 1917—agreements through which the United States had recognized that Japan had a "specific interest" in China. The United States had long felt that the Lansing-Ishii Notes were hampering her economic interests in China, and she desired a freer hand there in extending her penetration of markets in competition with Japan. The Japanese delegates to the Washington Conference had been most "realistic" in their bargaining with Great Britain and the United States.

The United States adjourned the Washington Conference well satisfied; her national and international interests had been protected, and an unlimited naval armament race among the great powers had been forestalled. However, while the results of the Washington Conference were being hailed in the United States, public opinion in Japan held that the naval formula established at the conference had been just another indication of discrimination against Japan as a nation.

Actually, Japan's Foreign Minister Baron Shidehara had been attempting all along to steer a moderate course of economic expansion in China, while at the same time assuming a cooperative and conciliatory attitude toward the United States and Great Britain with reference to Japan's military build-up. He also had Japan's financial position in mind. Unfortunately, the reason for Shidehara's conciliatory attitude was either not known or was not understood by the Japanese public.

Japanese newspapers and magazines, as well as an increasing number of political leaders, proclaimed that Japan had been forced to submit to Anglo-American pressures and that "the Western Powers entered into a blood-chilling conspiracy to topple Japan in the name of the Washington Naval Conference." According to the views of Japan's extremist military clique, the conference had marked "Japan's defeat in a bloodless naval battle."[3]

From this point forward, the militarists argued that so long as the United States continued to consider the Japanese inferior, as reflected in her continued discrimination against the Japanese, there could no longer be any hope of reconciliation between the two countries. Their argument was heard, and the power of Japan's military clique began to become increasingly dominant in Japanese domestic and foreign policies.

Meanwhile, in the United States, while the diplomatic and military delegates from Japan, Great Britain, and the United States had been meeting in Washington, D.C., another entirely different group of leaders was marshalling its forces in California and other western states for the purpose of carrying an anti-Japanese fight into the halls of Congress.

The Asiatic Barred Zone

The avowed goal of this group was to convince Congress to prohibit outright further immigration of Japanese into the United States. It had been done with the Chinese in 1882, and it had been done with almost all other Asiatic peoples of the world through the Asiatic Barred Zone Act of 1917—an action that created a clearly delineated geographical zone that included all of India, Burma, Siam (now Thailand), the Malay states, the Asiatic parts of Russia, sections of Arabia and Afghanistan, most of the Polynesian islands, the East Indian islands, Indochina (now Cambodia, Laos, and Vietnam), Java, Sumatra, Ceylon, Borneo, New Guinea, and the Celebes.

But the Japanese islands, although within the geographical area covered by the Asiatic Barred Zone, had been specifically exempted from its prohibitions because the issue of immigration from Japan was still functioning within the purview of the "Gentlemen's Agreement." Now the Congress was being pressed to abrogate this agreement through the enactment of an immigration law that would specifically bar the Japanese.

LIMITS ARE PLACED ON IMMIGRATION

The Japanese aside, the time appeared ripe for asking Congress to limit further immigration. Already, through its immigration laws of 1921, the Congress had for the first time not only restricted the number of immigrants to be allowed into the country, but it had also dealt with the issue of the "quality" of such immigrants. This was done by developing and enacting a national origins quota system based on the U.S. Census figures of 1910.

The Quota Immigration Act of 1921

The Quota Immigration Act of 1921 limited the number of aliens of any one nationality desiring to enter the United States for permanent residence to 3 percent of the number of foreign-born persons of that nationality who were in the United States in 1910.

That was the catch. By this device, the 3-percent quota allowable (in absolute numbers) to some countries was much larger than that which fell due for others. In its practical effect, the Quota Immigration Act gave first preference to persons from Northern and Western Europe[4] because in 1910 the census figures favored them.

The fact that the 1910 census figures were used as a basis for a quota system was not a coincidence. That year, and the previous one, had seen the greatest number of immigrants to the United States from England, Scotland, Ireland, Wales, and the Scandinavian countries. And these persons clearly were of a "white" complexion. Their large numbers were reflected in the 1910 census, as contrasted to the much smaller number of darker complexioned immigrants from Southern Europe and the Mediterranean countries who had not migrated to the U.S. in large numbers until after the end of World War I.

The Quota Immigration Act of 1921, originally scheduled to expire in one year, was later extended for another two years. However, this did not satisfy the anti-Japanese elements. The act did not exclude Japanese from immigration. The "Gentlemen's Agreement" was still the firm obstacle to total exclusion.

Efforts to Eliminate Japanese Immigration

The campaign to enlist support in Congress to exclude the Japanese was spearheaded by Virgil Stuart McClatchy of California, the owner of a chain of newspapers that included the *Sacramento Bee* and the

Fresno Bee. McClatchy was also the executive director of the Japanese Exclusion League of California. Later on he became the secretary of the California Joint Immigration Committee.

McClatchy prepared a statement on the menace of Japanese immigration and colonization in the United States that consisted of 138 paragraphs, and he submitted it to the United States Department of State.[5] His statement made no significant impact on the officials there. The statement, however, which had been previously reviewed by Congressman Albert Johnson (R.-Wash.), chairman of the House Committee on Immigration, was also readied for introduction to the United States Senate.

The statement, introduced into the Senate on July 21, 1921, carried the written endorsements of Hiram Johnson and Samuel M. Shortridge, both United States senators from California, as well as the endorsement of the California congressional delegation and the executive committees of various organizations such as the American Legion, the Native Sons and Daughters of the Golden West, the State Federation of Labor, the California Farm Bureau, the Federation of Women's Clubs, Veterans of Foreign Wars, and many other "patriotic" civic and fraternal bodies. At this same time the executive branch of the federal government was preparing to convene the Washington Conference to take place in November.

McClatchy's statement declared that the "steadily growing menace" of Japanese immigration was no longer a state or sectional problem but was a national one; that the "Gentlemen's Agreement" was a "grave error" on the part of the federal government; that the immigration of Japanese was not only "undesirable but dangerous to American interests" because the Japanese were "an unassimilable race" and, even when born here, were unfit "for the responsible duties of American citizenship."

"The extraordinary birth rate of such aliens" would cause the "inundation of the white population in this country by the yellow race," and "the whites would be speedily driven out of communities." The Japanese came here "not only with no desire to be absorbed and assimilated into the American 'melting pot' but with the determined and openly announced intent of establishing the Yamato race permanently on this continent." The Japanese "possess superior advantages in economic competition, partly because of racial characteristics, thrift, industry, low standards of living, willingness to work long hours without expensive pleasures . . . extraordinary co-operation and solidarity."

The statement declared that "we have surrendered to a foreign power our inalienable right to pass upon the number and eligibility of those who enter" and that the "Gentlemen's Agreement" should be cancelled because, even assuming that Japan had lived up to its intent in good faith, "it has failed utterly to accomplish the purposes for which it was avowedly entered into."

McClatchy's statement, while admittedly having a strong impact on some members of Congress, was not convincing enough to persuade other congressmen who felt that immigration of Japanese into the United States should either still be controlled by the continuation of the "Gentlemen's Agreement" or by a token quota allowed Japan on the same basis as immigrants from other countries of the world.

The Japanese Exclusion League prevailed upon Senator Johnson to organize congressional sentiment to vote for the total exclusion of the Japanese. Johnson organized the Executive Committee of Western States, which, in reality, was a steering committee for anti-Japanese activities in Congress. This committee consisted of one senator and one representative from each of the eleven western states to work on an anti-Japanese campaign in cooperation with the California delegation.[6]

In spite of McClatchy's statement in the Senate and Johnson's strenuous activities in the Congress, the Sixty-seventh Congress (1921–1922) took no action on the pending bill to exclude the Japanese.

Then, in 1923, Tokyo sustained a devastating earthquake, which, together with a widespread fire, resulted in vast property damage and hundreds of deaths in Tokyo and the surrounding area. The American people contributed over $12 million to Japan for relief and rehabilitation. This generous act of good will deeply touched the Japanese people, inducing them to think that the Americans were, after all, a warm and compassionate people.[7] Because of this humanitarian gesture, the Japanese people, including the Japanese government, could not understand how a large number of congressmen in Washington could be so strongly anti-Japanese in their thinking and in their public utterances. Moreover, the Japanese had completely underestimated the persistent efforts of the anti-Japanese forces in America in their anti-Japanese campaign, a campaign that had really begun almost twenty years before in 1905, when Japanese grammar-school children had been ordered segregated in the San Francisco public schools. The efforts of the Japanese Exclusion League were to bear fruit in the Sixty-eighth Congress, which convened in December 1923.

On December 5, 1923, Congressman Albert Johnson resubmitted a bill that he had first submitted in the previous congressional session. The following day, Senator Henry Cabot Lodge (R.-Mass.) introduced a similar bill in the Senate.[8]

Section 12(c) of the proposed immigration bill was designed to prohibit the immigration of "aliens ineligible for citizenship" under United States naturalization statutes by virtue of their not being of the "white" race. Congress was to consider this standard of eligibility as it pertained to the Japanese.

On February 8, 1924 Secretary of State Hughes addressed a letter to Congressman Johnson that said in part that "the practical effect of Section 12(c) is to single out Japanese immigrants for exclusion." His letter continued:

The Japanese are a sensitive people, and unquestionably would regard such a legislative enactment as fixing a stigma upon them. I regret to be compelled to say that I believe such legislative action would largely undo the work of the Washington Conference on Limitation of Armament, which so greatly improved our relations with Japan. The manifestation of American interest and generosity in providing relief to the sufferers from the recent earthquake disaster in Japan would not avail to diminish the resentment which would follow the enactment of such a measure, as this enactment would be regarded as an insult not to be palliated by any act of charity. It is useless to argue whether or not such a feeling would be justified; it is quite sufficient to say that it would exist. It has already been manifested in the discussions with Japan with respect to the pending of this measure, and no amount of argument can avail to remove it.[9]

Secretary of State Hughes suggested that the "Gentlemen's Agreement" be continued. He also saw no reason why it was necessary to completely exclude the Japanese even from the standpoint of American interests. On February 19, 1924 Hughes reiterated his admonition to Senator LeBaron Colt, (R.-R.I.), chairman of the Senate Committee on Immigration. On March 14, when Congressman Johnson made a report to the House, he supported Hughes and suggested that the pending legislation be changed "to meet . . . Hughes' suggestions as to administrative features that the control of immigration into the United States from Japan be as contained in 'our commercial treaties.'" The effect of this clause "as contained in our 'commercial treaties'" would have been to exempt nations, including Japan, from the exclusionary provisions of the immigration bill and to place the control again into the hands of the respective governments of Japan and the United States under the existing "Gentlemen's Agreement."

Meanwhile, hearings on the proposed immigration bills were being held by both the House and Senate Committees on Immigration. Arguments for and against exclusion of Japanese were sometimes bitterly, certainly stubbornly, advocated. Well-known proponents of the exclusion provisions were headed by spokesmen primarily from California, including McClatchy, former United States Senator James Phelan, United States Senator Shortridge, and California Attorney General U.S. Webb, all of whom adhered to the anti-Japanese arguments contained in McClatchy's statements previously submitted to the Senate on July , 1921. Most of the opponents of the exclusion bills were representatives of religious organizations who argued that such exclusion laws were not necessary and moreover violated principles of fairness and justice.

The anti-Japanese arguments so vigorously supported by the California congressional delegation prevailed. On March 24, 1924 the House Committee on Immigration recommended that Congress support the provision that "persons ineligible to citizenship shall not be admitted as immigrants." The committee further rejected the suggestions advanced by Hughes to continue the "Gentlemen's Agreement" on the ground that "the congressional prerogative of regulating immigration from Japan has been surrendered to the Japanese Government."[10] In the Senate, Senator Colt proposed a different measure that would leave "the Japanese question to be settled by diplomacy."

During the debates that raged in both houses of Congress, reference was made several times to the "Gentlemen's Agreement," both to the actual contents of the agreement as well as its effectiveness in controlling Japanese immigration into the United States. Complaints were voiced from several of the congressmen that the "Gentlemen's Agreement" was a secret document that no one had ever seen.

While the terms of the agreement were generally known, Secretary of State Hughes felt uneasy about this complaint. On March 7, 1924 Hughes suggested verbally to Japanese Ambassador Hanihara "that the Ambassador could write a letter to the Secretary . . . [in which] the [Gentlemen's] Agreement could be summarized in a brief and definite fashion and could be presented authoritatively."[11]

The Hanihara Letter

Ambassador Hanihara wrote a letter on April 10, 1924, which Secretary of State Hughes duly transmitted to the United States Senate the following day

The letter precipitated a furor in the Congress, and it ultimately proved to be the single most important factor in causing both the House and Senate Committees on Immigration suddenly and solidly to support the pending bill to exclude the Japanese. Further, it caused President Calvin Coolidge, who up to the time of the disclosure of the contents of the Hanihara letter had been working toward some diplomatic solution to the exclusion problem, to sign the bill excluding the Japanese on May 26, 1924.

Ambassador Hanihara had attempted, in his unfortunately worded letter, to explain that the "Gentlemen's Agreement" was in no way intended to restrict the sovereign right of the United States to regulate immigration. Instead, the agreement had been entered into because discriminatory legislation on the part of the United States would offend the national pride of a friendly nation. The letter asserted that the Japanese government had most scrupulously and faithfully carried out the terms of the agreement as a self-imposed restriction and that Japan was fully prepared to continue to conform to the agreement in the future. Hanihara pointed out that in the years 1908 to 1923 the total number of Japanese admitted to the United States had been 120,317, while the number of Japanese who had departed from the United States was 111,626. During those fifteen years, the excess of those admitted over those departed was only 8,691, for an annual average of only 579. Ambassador Hanihara continued:

Relying upon the confidence you [Hughes] have been good enough to show me at all times, I have stated or rather repeated all this to you very candidly and in the most friendly spirit, for I realize, as I believe you do, the *grave consequences* [italics added] which the enactment of the measure retaining that particular provision [excluding from immigration persons ineligible for citizenship] would inevitably bring upon the otherwise happy and eventually advantageous relations between our two countries.[12]

When the Hanihara letter was transmitted from Secretary of State Hughes to the Senate and printed in the *Congressional Record* for April 11, it received no particular attention for several days.

Suddenly, on April 14, Senator Lodge took the floor of the Senate to speak about the Hanihara letter. He characterized the letter as "improper" in that it contained a "veiled threat" against the United States. He declared:

The letter of the Japanese Ambassador has created a situation which makes it impossible for me to support the pending amendment. [The Senate Committee on Immigration had proposed an amendment to exempt Japan from the quota provisions of the bill.][13] The amendment has now assumed the dignity of a precedent, and I shall never consent to establish any precedent, which will give any nation the right to think that they can stop by threats or complaints the action of the United States when it determines who shall come within its gates and become part of its citizens.[14]

Other Senators quickly followed Senator Lodge's lead. Senator David A. Reed (R.-Penn.), who had originally favored the continuation of the "Gentlemen's Agreement," now changed his mind, saying:

I think the situation has changed. I think it ceases to be a question of whether this is a desirable method of restricting Japanese immigration. The letter of the Japanese Ambassador puts the unpleasant burden upon us of deciding whether we will permit our legislation to be controlled by apprehension of "grave consequences" with other nations, if we do not follow a particular line of legislative conduct. I, for one, feel compelled, on account of that veiled threat, to vote in favor of the exclusion and against the Committee amendment.

Ambassador Hanihara was astounded by the interpretation the Senate was putting on his letter to Secretary of State Hughes. Hanihara vehemently denied having intended any threat. He said he had not even meant to be discourteous. But the damage done by his unfortunate choice of those two words was beyond any hope of repair. The Senate rejected the committee's amendment to the proposed immigration law, which would have recognized the "Gentlemen's Agreement," by a vote of 76 to 2. The new amendment providing for the exclusion of any alien "ineligible for citizenship" was passed by a vote of 71 to 4.

President Coolidge, in an attempt to cool the congressional furor over the alleged "veiled threat" contained in Ambassador Hanihara's letter, suggested that the pending bill containing the exclusion provision be postponed for consideration until May 1926, in order to provide the President an opportunity to enter into negotiations with the Japanese government regarding the imminent danger in which the "Gentlemen's Agreement" now stood. The Congress summarily rejected the suggestion.

THE JAPANESE EXCLUSION ACT OF 1924

On May 15, 1924 the House passed the exclusion bill by a vote of 308 to 62, and, on May 19, after a House-Senate conference to harmonize minor aspects of the bill, the measure was sent to President Coolidge. On May 26 he signed the bill into law, to become effective on July 1. Officially, the bill was known as the Quota Immigration Law. Unofficially, it was known as the Japanese Exclusion Act.[15] The President declared, "In signing this bill, which in its main features I approve, I regret the impossibility of severing from it the exclusion provision which, in the light of existing law affects especially the Japanese."[16]

The law did, in effect, concern "especially the Japanese" as President Coolidge had put it. And it was affecting the Japanese without even naming them. Clause 13(c) of the law excluded them from immigration for permanent residence by merely stating that the quota was not to apply to "aliens ineligible for citizenship." The Japanese national could still come in as a tourist, student, government official, merchant, minister, or professor. But no more permanent Japanese residents, with their alleged high birthrate, were allowed.

Even if the law had granted Japan a quota on the same basis as the European nations, few Japanese would have been eligible. The new legislation restricted immigration to a quota based on the U.S. Census of 1890; only 2 percent of the number of foreign-born individuals of any given nationality then residing in the continental United States were eligible. Had the Japanese nation been granted such a quota, it would have amounted to only one hundred persons.

The Exclusion Act represented the culmination of almost twenty years of persistent and organized anti-Japanese activities in the United States. The Quota Immigration Law of 1924 was considered by Japan to be a direct blow to its national pride, to its international prestige, and to its status as a world power.

When the United States government advised the Japanese government that the law was an act of Congress over which the executive branch of the American government had no control, the Japanese government refused to accept this explanation. On May 31 Japan presented President Coolidge with a formal protest stating, "International discrimination in any form and on any subject, even if based on purely economic reasons, are opposed to the principles of justice and fairness upon which the friendly intercourse between nations must, in its final analysis, depend. . . . Still more unwelcome are discriminations based on race."

Race—that had been the issue. The real effect of the 1924 law was to brand the Japanese in particular, and all Orientals in general, as inferior, undesirable, and therefore not worthy to become permanent segments of American society. In Japan universal indignation came like a firestorm. Leading newspapers labeled the law as "inequitable and unjust," "a deliberate insult," and a "scar on the national honor of Japan." On the day that the exclusion law went into effect (July 1), the Japanese Parliament passed a resolution protesting the discriminatory law.

The Honorable Cyrus E. Woods, who had been American ambassador to Japan from August 1923 to June 1924, described the effect of the act as follows: "The Japanese Exclusion Act was, in my judgment, an international disaster of the first magnitude; a disaster to American diplomacy in the Far East, a disaster to American business, a disaster to religion and to the effective work of our American churches in Japan."[17]

The Japanese public was bewildered. Just the year before, after the terrible earthquake that had struck Tokyo, the American people had at once come to the help of Japan by contributing $12 million in relief aid. And now this? It was as though the Good Samaritan in the New Testament parable, after having delivered the wounded and bleeding traveler to the innkeeper with a gift for the traveler's keep, had suddenly drawn off, doubled up his fist, and planted a stunning blow on the face of the man he had just succored.

Unfortunately, the Act of 1924, in conjunction with the Immigration Act of February 5, 1917, was to govern American immigration policy for the next twenty-eight years, until the enactment of the Immigration and Nationality Act of December 24, 1952.[18]

7

New Attempts at Repression
(1924–1940)

AFTER THE PASSAGE of the Quota Immigration Law of 1924, the Japanese Exclusion League, led by V. S. McClatchy and former United States Senator James D. Phelan, lost its crusading fervor. It lay dormant for two years, and in 1926 it was formally dissolved.

Almost immediately there came into being another anti-Japanese racist organization known as the California Joint Immigration Committee. While many of the peripheral organizations that supported the old league did not join the new organization, the strongest supporters of the new group were the same ones that had previously been active in the Japanese Exclusion League, principally the Native Sons and Daughters of the Golden West, the American Legion, the American Federation of Labor, and the California State Grange. McClatchy continued his anti-Japanese activities for the California Joint Immigration Committee until his death in 1936.[1] Persons of Japanese ancestry continued to be buffeted about by forces either spearheaded or supported by the California Joint Immigration Committee.

The story of the Japanese in the United States between 1925 and 1941 is the story of the grim struggle of noncitizen and citizen alike to build their lives in the American community despite constant oppression and discrimination. It is the story of their tenacious clinging to their small homes and farms, their family shops and stores, while trying to plant their roots deeper into American soil, all the while fighting against relentless forces of discrimination aimed at discouraging them from establishing themselves as a rightful part of the community in which they had chosen to work and live.

DEMOGRAPHY OF THE JAPANESE IN AMERICA

It is interesting here to note exactly how large a "threat" the Japanese were to the American economy and to their local communities in terms of the number of Japanese, both noncitizen and citizen, their age distribution, their occupations, and their social structure.

In the year 1920, within the entire continental area of the United States, there were about 111,000 persons of Japanese ancestry. This population rose to nearly 139,000 by 1930, but during the next ten years, citizens and noncitizens had declined to approximately 127,000.[2] Of this total number in 1940, almost 90 percent lived in four western states: California, Oregon, Washington, and Arizona. Of these, almost 83 percent, or approximately 113,000 persons, resided in California, 11 percent in Washington, 3 percent in Oregon, and 3 percent in Arizona. In California the Japanese still constituted only 1.63 percent of the total population. In Washington they represented 0.008 percent and in Oregon and Arizona 0.003 percent.[3]

A study of the age distribution of persons of Japanese ancestry during the years between 1920 and 1940, shows a steadily rising number of United States citizens. In 1920 the median age of all Japanese males in the United States was 33.5 years, while the age for Japanese females was 23.3 years. In 1940, sixteen years after the prohibition of Japanese immigration into the United States, the median age for Japanese males had dropped to 23.6 years, and for females to 21.2 years. This reflected the births of new American citizens of Japanese ancestry as well as attrition within the older immigrant group.[4]

In 1940 almost all of the Japanese-born males residing in the United States had immigrated before 1924 and therefore were middle-aged; most of the noncitizen Japanese females, who were generally ten years younger, were in their thirties and forties.

After 1920 the increase in the Japanese population in this country was largely the result of children born here who were thus American citizens. In 1940, in the four cited Pacific states, more than one-half of the Japanese males were twenty-five years or younger; of the Japanese females, 59 percent were twenty-five or younger. In 1942, when anti-Japanese agitators were loudly proclaiming that persons of Japanese ancestry were a menace to the security of the United States, more than one-half of the entire population of persons of Japanese ancestry residing within the four Pacific Coast states were citizens of the United States of school or college age.[5]

DIVERSITY WITHIN THE JAPANESE COMMUNITY

Although anti-Japanese racists tended to consider all persons of Japanese ancestry alike, whether citizens or noncitizens, marked differences were rapidly developing between those persons of Japanese ancestry who had emigrated from Japan to the United States and those who were born and educated here. A third distinctive group included those born in the United States who went to Japan at an early age and later returned to their native country. Between 1920 and 1940 the differences among those three groups within the Japanese community became more and more distinguishable in language, customs, mode of dress, manners and social behavior, educational achievements, and vocational opportunities.

To dwell at length on the differences among these three groups is beyond the scope of this book. It should be noted, however, that some statutes, ordinances, and court decisions affected only those who were ineligible for citizenship, while other anti-Japanese attacks affected all three groups since such attacks were directed racially at all persons of Japanese heritage.

These three groups within the Japanese communities were known as Issei, Nisei, and Kibei. Translated literally, *Issei* (pronounced issay) means "first generation," or those persons, male and female, who were born in Japan and were the initial immigrants to the United States. *Nisei* (pronounced neesay) means "second generation," or the sons and daughters of first generation immigrants and, by virtue of their birth, American citizens. The term *Kibei* (pronounced keebay) refers to persons born in the United States, who at an early age were sent to Japan to live with relatives or to study and later returned.

The Issei

The Issei, who were born soon after the Meiji Restoration, had been strongly influenced by the culture of the previous Tokugawa regime as well as by the enlightened doctrines of the newly restored Emperor Meiji. The Issei were indoctrinated with the social and cultural customs of ancient Japan, customs transplanted almost entirely in their original form to the United States. In general, the lives of the Issei were characterized by deeply ingrained habits of personal discipline and devotion to their families. They seldom offered individual expressions of opinion in public and always displayed a continuing respect for wisdom, education, and the love of nature.

The Issei struggled to maintain a new life in the United States in spite of being subjected to unspeakable drudgery and almost unbearably strenuous physical labor in order to make a living. Most of the male Issei married later in life because of their need to be able to support a family before they "called" for a bride. Between 1910 and 1921 more than one-third of the Japanese marriages in America involved "picture brides," young women who exchanged their photographs with Issei in America through formal go-betweens.

Picture brides were usually from the same social class and prefecture as their prospective husbands. After the marriage had been registered on the husband's family record in Japan, these brides were issued passports to join their new husbands in the United States. In 1921, because of the furor raised by the United States government over this method of marriage and immigration, Japan voluntarily stopped the issuance of passports to picture brides, despite the fact that the program was working out quite well.

Although agriculture was the most important occupation of the

Issei, many were employed in other industries such as fishing, canning, mining, and railroad construction and maintenance. Others entered the service trades or opened small shops, boardinghouses, hotels, barbershops, and restaurants in areas where the early Issei and their Nisei children had congregated to form small communities.

A characteristic that every Issei carried within him was the deeply ingrained feeling that he was a member of a race separate and different from the other people in the United States. He had genuine pride in his ancient lineage and heritage. As Dr. Frank Miyamoto, professor of sociology and an associate dean at the University of Washington observed, "These early immigrants brought with them to the United States a proud heritage of a homogeneous culture."[6]

This unique individual and collective strength of the Issei generation was to sustain and comfort it during long years of suffering from merciless racist attacks. An intense pride of heritage gave the Issei comfort and the ability to endure property loss, the lack of material comforts, oppression, and frequent humiliation. Symbolic of the bamboo, these brave pioneers largely bent but did not break in the face of repeated onslaughts.

The Nisei

The members of the Nisei generation, while enjoying the legal advantages of United States citizenship, were strongly influenced in their early years by their Issei parents in respect to social values and cultural attitudes. Although the majority of the Nisei stood with their Issei parents in warding off the onslaughts of racial discrimination, the drudgery and oppression they saw being inflicted on them caused many of the Nisei to belittle their Japanese heritage in an attempt to establish their own personal and legal status. Difficulties arose in parent-child communications: usually parents could speak little English, while the Nisei often spoke Japanese in only crude and simple terms. The Issei parents, wiser than their Nisei children, quickly discerned that in a land of racial discrimination, the only future for their children lay in a Western education that could, in some small measure, provide the means for a better life.

Thus, the Issei parents literally sacrificed their working lives and limited their means in order to give their children educational opportunities. In most instances, the Nisei studied conscientiously, although they knew that their future in the United States was dim and uncertain. This conscientiousness manifested itself in many high scholastic achievements. But high achievements in high school, university, or college did not mean that the Nisei would succeed in society. The educated Nisei was to meet with disappointment, frustration, and bitter racial discrimination. He was called a "Jap" and was so deeply and so widely discriminated against that the educated Nisei was usually unable to find work except in the lowest type of employment in a non-Japanese company. With rare exceptions, he soon retreated into his own Japanese community to work at low paying jobs or to follow the trade and occupation of his Issei father.

During these years, the Nisei, with his outward Japanese physical features and his inward American cultural values, found himself a part of a hybrid generation. He was in the difficult position of being the offspring of parents of the Meiji era who were culturally tied to Japan, while growing up in the American community and embracing American values. The Nisei insisted that he was an American and asked that he be recognized as such, but, except in the schools, non-Japanese scorned him and refused to grant him acceptance.

On the other hand, if the same Nisei attempted to enter the Japanese-speaking community of his parents and the Kibei, he was considered to be too ill mannered and inadequately instructed in the Japanese language and culture to be acceptable. If the Nisei visited the land of his parents and ancestors, he was scorned as a foreigner and despised as the offspring of emigrants.

The Kibei

The Kibei group consisted of a small number of American-born Japanese who were sent at a relatively early age to live with relatives in Japan and to study there. A few of the Kibei were able to complete a university education abroad, usually in the private universities because the national universities were much more difficult to enter. The great majority of Kibei, however, received formal education only up to the junior high or high school level. Living in Japan during the Depression of the 1930s, many of them were swept up in the enthusiastic spirit of Japan's economic and military expansion policies in China and Manchuria.

Upon their return to the United States as adults, the Kibei found their vocational opportunities restricted because of their limited education in this country. They were most proficient in the Japanese language, which placed them close to the culture and social behavior of the Issei. Thus, between the Nisei and the Kibei, there arose a communication gap. Some Kibei spoke English proficiently, but most of them preferred to converse in Japanese due to their education overseas, and the Nisei spoke only rudimentary Japanese.

THE ECONOMY OF THE JAPANESE COMMUNITY

To complete a brief profile of the Japanese in the United States between 1920 and 1940, their economic activities need to be noted since the anti-Japanese attacks over these same years were not only racial in nature, but also economic in motivation.

The California Alien Land Law of 1920, and its subsequent amendments in 1923 and 1927 providing criminal penalties for those who conspired to violate the alien land laws, deterred the Japanese from owning, leasing, sharecropping, or enjoying farmlands. As noted, similar alien land laws were enacted in other western states. During this period there was a marked increase throughout California and other states of escheat actions brought against Japanese by local district attorneys or the state attorney generals. More than twenty-eight escheat lawsuits were filed in California alone against Japanese during this twenty-year period. The steady decline of Japanese-controlled farm acreage was also due to the submarginal lands that the Japanese farmer unsuccessfully attempted to cultivate. His lack of adequate capital, his loss of crops, and the low prices he was paid for his produce during the Depression were also factors in the decline in Japanese-owned farm acreage over the same twenty-year period.

The number of Japanese farmers decreased slightly over the twenty years, from 5,152 in 1920 to 5,135 in 1940. The total acreage owned, leased, or cultivated by Japanese farmers was reduced from 361,276 acres in 1920 to 220,094 acres in 1940, a decrease of almost 33 percent. But the gradually rising value of real estate in the midst of urban development, especially in California, caused these farmlands together with their buildings and improvements, to be valued in 1940 at over $65,780,000.[7]

Although the total acreage of farmlands was decreasing, farm operations were being markedly intensified. Forty-three percent of the Japanese on the Pacific Coast in 1940 were engaged in some type of farm operation, such as the production of vegetables, fruits, or greenhouse products. Many relatively small farms operated by Japanese were primarily devoted to the production of berries and vegetables. By 1940 the Japanese in the four western Pacific states, particularly California, aided in the production of 42 percent of the total commercial truck crop of these states, with a value estimated to be over $35 million per year. Although the Japanese farmers operated only 3.9 percent of all farmlands, and harvested on 25 percent of all crop land cultivated, they produced some 50 to 90 percent of such crops as celery, peppers, strawberries, cucumbers, artichokes, cauliflower, spinach, and tomatoes.[8]

In addition, some 26 percent of the gainfully employed Japanese worked in other related agricultural activities such as the wholesale or retail produce business. The small farmers soon became an integral part of the wholesale commission and brokerage houses that were organized to buy and sell farm products. By 1940 there were about 1,000 Japanese-owned or operated fruit and vegetable stores in Los Angeles County alone, employing around 5,000 workers, mostly Japanese, doing a business of over $25 million per year.[9]

REPRESSION AND HARASSMENT OF THE JAPANESE

After reviewing the demographic and economic distribution of the Japanese in the United States, it is appropriate to note the various methods of attack upon these people. The most obvious and effective ones were the restriction and prohibition of Japanese in their occupations and employment activities. The attack was carried on in several ways and on several fronts.

Employment Limited

For a period of ten years from 1923 to 1933, in virtually every session of the California Legislature bills were proposed, in either the Senate or the Assembly, prohibiting the employment of aliens in government and on public work projects sought by contractors, unless such aliens were "eligible for citizenship." These bills were obviously aimed at the Japanese who were not eligible for citizenship under the then existing federal naturalization laws.[10]

Large-Scale Deportations

The next method of attack upon Japanese aliens was a sweeping "dragnet" operation by immigration officers. They invaded homes, farms, boardinghouses, and business establishments to arrest aliens (usually without warrants) and to detain such aliens for deportation, often after only a cursory hearing. These proceedings resulted in many deportations or compulsory "voluntary departures." While there were many aliens from Japan who had illegally entered the United States either by way of Canada or Mexico, many more legal aliens were trapped in the dragnet and either summarily deported or granted "voluntary departure," with not only disastrous results to their employment and business activities but also agonizing separation from their wives and children.

Section 19(c) of the Immigration Act of 1917, in effect until 1948, provided for the suspension of deportation of aliens who, by reason of continuous residence in the United States for seven years, would sustain serious economic detriment to themselves or to their American-born spouses or children by such deportation. These persons were permitted to apply for suspension of deportation. But such aliens were required to be "eligible for citizenship." The Japanese alien, not being eligible for citizenship, was not, therefore, eligible for suspension of deportation during this period. He became eligible only in 1948 when ineligibility for citizenship was no longer an element for consideration.

The dragnet operation by the Immigration Service, especially in the Depression years of the 1930s, was not limited to the Japanese. Chinese, Mexicans, and persons of other nationalities were also swept up in mass arrests. Thousands of aliens, including aliens legally in the United States, were subjected to harassments, arrests, and deportation hearings based on officially sanctioned policies. The operating theory was that all aliens should be deported who were holding jobs that should be given to unemployed Americans. In 1931 William N. Doak, secretary of labor in President Herbert Hoover's administration, announced that "one way to provide work for unemployed Americans . . . [is] to oust any alien holding a job and deport him." Doak clarified his statement by adding, "There are 400,000 illegal aliens in the United States. Under the provisions of the Immigration laws, 100,000 of these aliens could be deported."[11]

One might ask: What did Doak intend to do about the remaining 300,000 illegal aliens?

The announced policy of United States Attorney General William Saxbe in 1974 for wholesale deportation of illegal aliens, mostly from Mexico, bears a melancholy resemblance to the statement of Secretary of Labor Doak in 1931.

As would be expected, the Japanese community expressed its hostility to the dragnet operations of the immigration officials in Los Angeles County. Several American owners of ranches employing Japanese aliens threatened to shoot any immigration inspector who "carried a gun." In many cases Japanese aliens obstinately refused to answer questions asked by immigration officers regarding their immigration status and instead retained attorneys to fight their alleged violation of status.[12]

In most instances where aliens were suspected of being illegally in the United States, the immigration officers arrested the aliens first, then telegraphed Washington, D.C. to request warrants of arrest. These warrants were then used to schedule formal deportation proceedings. In the' three-week period between February 21, 1931 and March 7, 1931, immigration officers checked and questioned several thousand suspected illegal aliens including Mexicans, Chinese, Japanese, and some others. Some 223 aliens were formally arrested. Of this number sixty-four agreed to depart voluntarily. They were taken to the Mexican border by truck and ordered out of the United States. One hundred thirty-eight warrants of arrest from Washington, D.C. were served on the rest of these aliens, including eighty on Mexican nationals, nineteen on Japanese, eight on Chinese, and eight on other nationalities; twenty-three aliens were later released. Among the nineteen Japanese aliens served with warrants of arrest, fourteen retained attorneys and strenuously fought charges that they were illegally residing in the United States.[13]

A clear pattern of Japanese aliens retaining attorneys to represent them developed during the 1920s and 1930s when the Japanese faced an ever increasing number of immigration or deportation proceedings. Although there were only twenty-eight cases reported during the sixteen years between 1908 and 1924, there were approximately sixty cases reported during the ten-year period between 1924 and 1934. The Japanese aliens concerned were subject primarily to immigration proceedings involving issues as to their right to enter, to reenter, or to remain in the United States. It may be reasonably assumed that many more aliens retained attorneys during exclusion or deportation hearings that were disposed of at the administrative level. Reported decisions only include appeals taken by the alien to the various federal district courts and federal courts of appeal.

The scope of these reported decisions indicates that Japanese aliens were vigorously contesting the issues during their immigration hearings. These decisions include those involving alien seamen;[14] prostitution;[15] the right to enter the United States;[16] the right to reenter the United States;[17] Communists;[18] aliens likely to become a public charge;[19] deportation involving the issue of residence in the United States for more or less than the five-year statute of limitations for deportation under the Immigration Act of 1917;[20] crimes involving moral turpitude;[21] issues involving fair hearings;[22] treaty traders;[23] aliens who remained in the United States after their legal period of stay had expired;[24] loss of United States citizenship by marriage to aliens;[25] and illegal entrants.[26]

A few of these reported decisions are of interest here due to the reasoning used by the various federal courts in deciding the fate of individuals. Although it is impossible to state the number of cases disposed of at the administrative level, or how fair the decisions rendered were, in those cases that reached the federal district courts and federal courts of appeal, and are therefore on record, the leniency and fairness in some of the judgments rendered are notable.

Alien Seamen. In one case, a Japanese alien had entered the United States illegally before 1919 and was employed as a fisherman on an American vessel. The ship sailed into Mexican waters in 1924, where it remained for several weeks. The alien did not leave the vessel until its return to Los Angeles. He was refused entry by the immigration inspector on the ground that the alien had left the United States by sailing into foreign waters. The court overruled the Immigration Service and held the alien seaman had never left the United States because the fishing boat was registered as a United States vessel. The vessel's return to Los Angeles did not constitute a new entry (*Ex parte T. Nagata*[27]).

Prostitution. Several Japanese aliens, all managing rooming houses in Seattle, Washington and in San Jose, El Centro, and San Francisco, California were deported for soliciting females to live in a room or for renting a room on the premises where such females were practicing prostitution.[28]

Right to Reenter the United States. Several cases involved Japanese aliens who claimed that they were entitled to reenter the United States having previously acquired residency status. Most of these cases dealt with the issue of whether the alien had resided in this country for more than five years before the Quota Immigration Law of 1924 was enacted. The proof of residency and continuous residence before 1924 was crucial in order to determine whether the alien was deportable. Under the Immigration Act of 1917, if an alien had resided continuously in the United States for five years or more before 1924, the alien was no longer deportable. After 1924, however, no matter how long the alien had resided in the United States after illegal entry, he was deportable. The courts held that the burden of proving continuous residency in the United States before or after 1924 was on the alien, and he had to be able to provide documents or other competent evidence (*Ex parte Keizo Kamiyama*[29]).

A particularly harsh court decision, denying a person's right to reenter the United States after twenty-one years of residence, involved a Japanese alien who first entered San Francisco illegally as a laborer in 1908. This alien married in the United States, had two American-born children, and lived with his family in San Francisco. The alien operated a restaurant in the city. In 1928 he returned to Japan. After a few months he attempted to reenter the United States but was denied admission. The court held that because of the five-year statute of limitations in the Immigration Act of 1917, the alien could not be ejected from the United States if he had remained in the country. But his long years of continuous illegal residence from 1907 to 1928 did not perfect his right to residence. His attempt to reenter the United States was considered a new entry. Since he was a laborer when he entered in 1907, he would have been barred from entry under the "Gentlemen's Agreement" anyway. The fact that he changed his occupation from laborer to that of a merchant did not change the situation so far as his right to reenter the United States was concerned (*Kaichiro Sugimoto* vs. *Nagle*[30]).

Crimes Involving Moral Turpitude. Various acts on the part of aliens were considered to be crimes involving moral turpitude and therefore deportable offenses.

In one case, the alien had earlier entered San Francisco from Hawaii as a sailor and had later deserted his ship. At the hearing, he showed a passport, and further testified that he was coming to the United States to buy breeding cattle for a dairy company in Japan, which was not true. False testimony at an immigration hearing was held to be a crime involving moral turpitude, and the alien was ordered deported (*Ex parte Keizo Shibata*[31]).

Pleading guilty to five counts of issuing bad checks and serving a state prison sentence were also considered proof of a crime involving moral turpitude, warranting deportation (*Nishimoto* vs. *Nagle*[32]).

An alien paid $200 to secure a reentry permit that stated he was another person who had entered the United States in 1906, when in fact he had entered the United States illegally in 1920. This act on the alien's part was also held to be a crime involving moral turpitude. He was convicted of the crime of conspiracy to violate immigration laws by impersonating another alien to obtain a reentry permit. This warranted deportation (*Shimi Miho* vs. *U. S.*[33]).

A conspiracy to pay another person to bring aliens illegally by boat into the United States was also considered a crime involving moral turpitude (*Yenkichi Ito* vs. *U. S.*[34]).

Fair Hearings. The court held that an immigration hearing in deportation proceedings was fair even though the alien was in custody, was interrogated in English, and had no counsel (*Ematsu Kishimoto* vs. *Carr*[35]).

However, where an alien was unable to speak English, frightened and in pain from a bullet wound in his arm inflicted upon him while he was trying to escape, and denied the right to cross-examine the immigration officer who arrested him because the officer did not appear for the immigration hearing, the court held that such circumstances violated fundamental principles of due process and were arbitrary and unfair. The alien was discharged from custody and deportation proceedings dismissed (*In re Sugano*[36]).

Treaty Traders. A treaty trader was a person engaged in international trade between the United States and the country of his nationality that had a treaty with the United States. The courts had considerable difficulty in determining what facts were necessary to be present for an alien to be admissible as a treaty trader, as provided for under the Treaty of Commerce and Navigation of 1911 between the United States and Japan. Since no standards or criteria had been set for the definition of treaty trader under the treaty, contradictory decisions were handed down, depending on how the court construed the words in the treaty "to engage in a commercial enterprise," in either applying a strictly narrow or a more liberal interpretation to that definition.

For example, a wife, a native of Japan, was denied entry into the United States by an immigration inspector on the ground that her husband, also a Japanese alien and an editor of a Japanese newspaper published and circulated only in San Francisco, was not engaged in foreign commerce. The court ordered the wife admitted on the ground that an alien admitted under the Treaty of Commerce and Navigation of 1911 was a treaty trader if such alien was engaged in a commercial enterprise, even though such an alien was not engaged in foreign commerce (*Shizuko Kumanomido* vs. *Nagle*[37]).

However, the wife of a Japanese alien who owned stock in a domestic corporation, a corporation that sold goods imported from Japan but was not a branch of a Japanese company, was denied entry to join her husband, although the husband had previously entered the United States as a treaty trader (*Ex parte Naoe Minamiji*[38]).

In the companion case of *Ex parte Haruye Suzuki*,[39] decided in the same court on the same day, the wife of a treaty trader was found admissible into the United States because her husband was a stockholder and vice president of The Mutual Trading Company, a California corporation organized by several local Japanese grocers to handle merchandise from Japan.

How the same federal court came to distinguish the two cases, so as to admit one wife to join her husband while denying another under the almost identical set of circumstances, is beyond comprehension.

Two years later in the same court, stock ownership in a company appeared to be of no significance in admitting a Japanese alien and his wife as treaty traders. The alien had entered the United States in 1926 as a treaty trader to carry on an import-export trade in San Pedro, California. He had previously owned a few shares of stock in the Japanese company in which he had been employed. However, before he went to Japan for a visit in 1930, he sold his shares in the company. The court ordered him readmitted as a treaty trader, stating that after several years in his particular occupation (more than four years), the act of selling his interest in the company for which he had been working did not cause him to lose his status as a treaty trader, as there was no evidence that he was going to engage in any other pursuit (*In re Katsujiro Akiyama*[40]).

In cases in which a treaty trader failed to maintain his status as such, he and his wife were subject to deportation. For example, an immigration inspector came upon the premises of a nursery and discovered a man and his wife both dressed in working clothes. The alien had been admitted into the United States as a foreign newspaper correspondent. They were both ordered deported because they had accepted other employment and thereby had forfeited their immigration status as treaty traders (*Kumaki Koga* vs. *Berkshire*[41]).

Escheat Actions

Another method of attacking the Japanese so as to prohibit and restrict their occupational activities was to institute escheat actions. State attorney generals and the district attorneys of the counties where farmlands were being used by the Japanese instituted many escheat actions against the Japanese farmers and their children. They even filed criminal actions against some non-Japanese on the ground that they had conspired with Japanese aliens in the sale of lands.

There was a marked increase in the number of alien land law escheat actions in the twenty-year period between 1920 and 1940. Up to 1920 there were eleven reported cases, nine in California and two in Washington. Between 1920 and 1940 there were twenty-eight reported cases, of which sixteen originated in California, eight in Washington, three in Arizona, and one in Oregon. The reported cases cited are only those alien land law escheat cases that were appealed to the appellate courts of their respective states, or to the United States Supreme Court. There were undoubtedly many more escheat cases that were originally instituted at the superior court level of these states, but they were not appealed.

The California Alien Land Law of 1920, passed by the voters as an initiative measure, became the model followed by other states. With minor variations, the main provisions of all of these state laws were similar in nature.

1. Only aliens who were eligible for citizenship or who filed a declaration of intention to become citizens were permitted to own, lease, enjoy, transmit, and inherit real property.

2. Aliens ineligible for citizenship were prohibited from owning, leasing, enjoying, transmitting, or inheriting land, except as allowed by treaty between the United States and the country of which the alien was a subject or citizen.

3. If payment for the land involved an alien ineligible for citizenship, and the title was taken in the name of another person, the transaction was presumed to be in violation of the Alien Land Law.

4. Any transaction between a non-Japanese owner of land and an alien ineligible for citizenship to purchase land was deemed a criminal conspiracy for which the non-Japanese could be prosecuted in a criminal action.

5. Stock corporations that owned land in which shares of stock were issued to or held by aliens ineligible for citizenship were prohibited.

By these provisions and other restrictions in the various states' alien land laws, the states sought to prevent the Japanese alien from engaging in agricultural occupations and, thus, to drive him out of the community in which he lived. But the Japanese fought back. Lawyers were retained by many aliens to analyze the land laws for some means to circumvent the harsh provisions or to discover a method by which the Japanese could continue their farming operations.

In many reported cases in which the state filed escheat actions to forfeit lands to the state purchased or leased for commercial, non-farming activities, the Treaty of Commerce and Navigation of 1911 was invoked. It was argued by the Japanese that such activities were not within the purview of the alien land laws. Some typical cases where this argument held up follow.

It was ordered that a pawnbroker in Seattle be issued a business license, notwithstanding a city ordinance that stated that a license could only be issued to citizens of the United States;[42] land purchased in Los Angeles for a health resort and sanitarium was considered to be trade within the treaty;[43] land leased to a corporation in Los Angeles to construct and operate a Japanese hospital was permitted as being a commercial activity within the definition of the treaty;[44] a city lot to construct a home, and not for use for agricultural purposes, was also permitted,[45] as was a lease of land for a garage business[46] and a pharmacy.[47]

During the 1920s and 1930s many Nisei were still minors. Where the Japanese aliens in escheat cases were able to persuade the courts that land had been purchased with the intent of making a gift of it to their minor children, the courts declared that there was no violation of the Alien Land Law and dismissed the escheat actions. The reasoning of the courts in actions involving minor children was concerned with whether the parent of the minor child was ineligible or eligible for citizenship, whether the parent could make a gift to his own child, and whether such gift would vest title and interest in the minor child. Thereafter, the parent had no legal interest in the property.

As early as 1925, two state courts anticipated the famous 1948 case of *Oyama* vs. *California*, decided by the United States Supreme Court, with reference to the validity of gifts of lands to minor children by aliens ineligible for citizenship.

Kosai and his wife, both Japanese aliens ineligible for citizenship, purchased land in King County, Washington. The title to the land was transferred to their minor child, Frank Kosai, a United States citizen. The Washington State Supreme Court held that a gift of land to the son did not violate the Washington Alien Land Law. It held that, in an escheat proceeding, the State must prove fraud in transferring title from the previous landowner to the minor child or ineligible aliens by clear and convincing evidence. Where there was evidence of an unrestricted, unqualified gift of land by alien parents to their minor child, the gift being beneficial to the minor, the acceptance of the land by the minor child was presumed, and the transfer of land was valid (*State* vs. *Kosai*[48]).

The Washington State Supreme Court reiterated the same position one year later in 1926 in another escheat action that alleged fraudulent intent in the conveyance of land to a minor child. The court maintained that all necessary facts constituting fraud must be clearly alleged and proven by the State. Thus, where farmlands purchased by Japanese aliens (husband and wife) were conveyed by warranty deed in the name of their minor child, a United States citizen, the court dismissed the escheat action (*State* vs. *Ishikawa*[49]).

The California courts extended the concept that the Japanese alien parent retained no further legal interest in land given to a minor child by declaring that persons other than parents, holding title to land as a trustee for the benefit of the minor child, also had no substantive interest in the land but merely held bare legal title to such property.

Kiyoko Nishi had purchased property for her minor child. The title to the property was taken in the name of Takeyama, a friend of Mrs. Nishi, who was an American citizen and who held title to the property as trustee for the benefit of the minor child. Payments to purchase the property were made by Mrs. Nishi. A creditor to whom Takeyama owed a personal debt of money attempted to levy on the property held by Takeyama as trustee. The court held that the property, standing in the name of the judgment debtor Takeyama and which he was holding as trustee, was not subject to a judgment to pay the personal debt of the trustee since such trust property belongs solely to the minor child and should therefore not be included as a part of the assets of the trustee.[50]

However, most of the escheat actions were unfavorable to the Japanese. For example, an employment contract in Los Angeles County between an employer, a United States citizen landowner, and a Japanese employee, who was ineligible for citizenship, was held to violate the California Alien Land Law of 1920. Under the contract, the employee was to receive a salary and a bonus. This bonus was a portion of the net profits. The court held that this contract was intended to disguise the real intent of the parties to effect or lease land to the employee,[51] an alien ineligible for citizenship. Also, in Los Angeles County, an employment contract that provided that the employee work for fixed wages and an incentive of 50 percent of the net profits from the sale of crops was declared illegal. The California Supreme Court held that this arrangement was a sharecropping agreement and thus a violation of the California Alien Land Law of 1920 as amended in 1923.[52]

Harsh consequences were suffered by a United States citizen landowner, one Cockrill, who agreed to take title to property in Sonoma County. The money for the purchase of the property was furnished by Ikeda, a Japanese subject ineligible for citizenship. The United States Supreme Court upheld a criminal indictment against Cockrill for conspiracy to violate the Alien Land Law of 1920, declaring that Section 9(c), which contained the provision that title to property taken in the name of another with funds furnished by an alien ineligible for citizenship raised a presumption to violate the Alien Land Law, did not violate the equal protection clause of the federal Constitution.[53]

Moreover, in a case that arose in Sutter County, California, where allegations in a criminal complaint to violate the Alien Land Laws of 1920, 1923, and 1927 were present, the California Supreme Court held that the burden is upon the defendant to show that he is not an alien ineligible for citizenship. Requiring such proof did not violate the Fourteenth Amendment to the Constitution; the Alien Land Law merely placed a burden "to overcome the presumption that he is not within the class of aliens ineligible for citizenship."[54]

An escheat proceeding by the State alleging a violation of the Alien Land Law of 1927 was held not to be a criminal or quasi-criminal proceeding but a civil proceeding to determine title to property. The alien was therefore not entitled to invoke the Fifth Amendment of the Constitution against self-incrimination in the escheat proceedings (*People* vs. *Nakamura*[55]).

Several escheat cases involved shares of stock in corporations organized to carry on farming operations. Shares of stock in King County, Washington, issued by White River Gardens, Inc., a corporation in which Japanese aliens exercised control, were escheated to the State. The court held that these stock arrangements were matters of pretense and a subterfuge to violate the Alien Land Law (*State* vs. *Hirabayashi*[56]).

In general, leases that were in effect between the landowners and the Japanese alien lessees before the alien land laws were enacted were held to be valid after these laws went into effect. The Washington Alien Land Law of 1921 did not expressly declare leases in effect on the date of the passage of the act to be invalid; therefore existing legal rights were held not to be impaired, and alien inhabitants of the state, as well as all other persons within its jurisdiction, were entitled to the protection of its laws in the absence of such specific legislative intent (*State* vs. *Natsuhara*[57]).

Options to purchase land in effect before the enactment of the Washington Alien Land Law were also held to be valid (*State* vs. *Kusumi*[58]).

Stricter Enforcement of Alien Land Laws

Besides escheat actions, various legislatures, especially the California Legislature, considered additional legislation to provide an even stricter enforcement of the alien land laws and also to restrict Japanese aliens even more in land use.

In 1925, to close the loophole in the Alien Land Law, A.B. 1270 was introduced in California to provide that every transfer of real property involving violations of the Alien Land Law was to be declared void as of the date of such transfer.[59] This provision was to affect title to *all* transactions involving land sold to Japanese aliens since the transactions would be considered retroactively. This law cast a cloud upon the title and interest of every transaction that had occurred even before the passage of the alien land laws. This bill was referred to the Committee on Judiciary where, fortunately, no further action was taken on it.

In 1937, another bill was introduced in the assembly (A.B. 1019) that provided that any contract or agreement in which an alien ineligible for citizenship was permitted to acquire, possess, use, cultivate, occupy, or transfer any interest in the land was void.[60] This bill also died in committee.

In the same year, Senate Bill 749 proposed to expand the scope of the Alien Land Law of 1920 so as to eliminate Japanese aliens from acquiring any interest in land by making it unlawful for such aliens "to acquire, possess, enjoy, use, cultivate, occupy or transfer real interest or any interest therein in the state and have in whole or in part the beneficial use thereof, or have possession, care or control of real property, agricultural lands or lands fit for agricultural purposes." This bill was referred to the Committee on Judiciary where no further action was taken.[61]

In 1939 additional procedural requirements relating to escheat actions were proposed by amending the Code of Civil Procedure. This was approved by the assembly but was not passed by the senate.[62]

On December 22, 1941, after Japan had attacked Pearl Harbor and the United States and Japan were at war, the California Assembly approved the creation of an interim assembly committee to conduct a probe of the various aspects of the Alien Land Law. This probe took the form of a house resolution, which read as follows:

House Resolution No. 39
Relative to the Alien Land Law

WHEREAS, an interim Assembly Committee on Governmental Efficiency and Economy was created by House Resolution No. 193 of the Regular Session of 1941; and

WHEREAS, this committee was vested with power to investigate the organization, functions and administration of the State Government and of each department, agency and subdivision thereof and the governments of the cities and counties of this State; and

WHEREAS, the administration, enforcement and application of the Alien Land Law (State. 1921, page LXXXIII) should be considered and studied by this committee; now, therefore, be it

RESOLVED BY THE ASSEMBLY OF THE STATE OF CALIFORNIA, that the Assembly Committee on Governmental Efficiency and Economy is hereby authorized and directed to investigate and study accurately and in detail the operation, effect, applicability, and enforcement of the Alien Land Law.[63]

Further Repression

In 1935 California Assemblyman William Moseley Jones proposed a bill that provided for the registration of aliens in the state who were ineligible for citizenship and over the age of twenty-one. Each alien ineligible for citizenship (that is, all Orientals) within six months after entering California, or after becoming twenty-one years of age in the state, was to file a written statement with the secretary of state, complete with name, address, birthplace, and the place of birth of mother and father. The registration book was to be a public record. Failure to so register would be a misdemeanor. For what purpose such a registration book was to be used or required was not explained. How this bill would be enforced—whether an alien was required to register each time he entered the state after residing in another state or county, how the law would be enforced as to aliens who had no knowledge of such a law, who would be empowered to enforce the law or to institute criminal proceedings, and where and in what form such a statement was to be obtained—was not mentioned. The bill was referred to the Committee on Elections without further action.[64]

Another bill, submitted in 1939, prohibited any farm organization, labor union, or chamber of commerce from electing, appointing, or retaining any alien ineligible for citizenship to represent it in any executive or administrative position. Violation of this law was also declared a misdemeanor. No action was taken on this bill.[65]

The California Legislature continued to pass resolution after resolution on other matters that pertained to "national defense" and the

"Oriental menace,"[66] repeatedly bombarding Congress with requests to restrict further immigration of aliens ineligible for citizenship,[67] although the Quota Immigration Law of 1924 had already accomplished this objective. The California Legislature also considered other measures to establish separate schools for children of Chinese, Japanese, or other Mongolian lineage[68] and to restrict the rights of aliens in various areas of business and the professions.[69]

In other states, such as Arizona, mobs assaulted the Japanese residing in the state. The Hearst press, commencing in the spring of 1935, began to write articles about "the inequitable Oriental competition sapping the economic life of America and retarding recovery."

About the same time, a mysterious Committee of One Thousand was formed in southern California and carried on calumnious attacks upon the Japanese. In its publication the *American Defender*, the committee accused the Japanese truck gardeners of spraying their vegetables with arsenic or using human excrement as fertilizer, thereby creating epidemics of "bacillary dysentery," and it charged that a Japanese army was then training in Peru. Typical of the utterances of the Committee of One Thousand is a passage in the *American Defender* on April 27, 1935. "Wherever the Japanese have settled, their nests pollute the communities like the running sores of leprosy. They exist like the yellowed, smoldering discarded butts in an over-full ash tray, vilifying the air with their loathsome smells, filling all who have misfortune to look upon them with a wholesome disgust and a desire to wash."[70]

As tensions between the United States and Japan mounted over the years, especially during the Depression, anti-Japanese feelings became more intense and accelerated. The racist attacks raged in local, state, and national presses; they were repeated on lecture platforms and in the legislative forums of the various states and in the Congress. The "Japanese problem" in the United States was discussed at international conferences, trade conventions, fraternal meetings, and the gatherings of community service organizations.

But in the midst of these attacks, various ostrich-like groups, both in the United States and Japan, were maintaining the fiction that the people of the two nations were devoted to each other, that both nations professed permanent and enduring affection and respect for each other, and that no point of real controversy existed to mar their traditional friendship. Streams of goodwill missions, friendship letters, and tributes to the Japanese in America served only to maintain the illusion that warm friendship and peace was in full bloom between the two nations and their people.

The grim realities of the situation during the period between 1924 and 1941 were evident in the Pacific Coast states, particularly in California.

California residents gradually found opposition to the Japanese an ever present issue, being applied to almost all their political, social, and economic problems . . . It colored every direct and indirect contact that they had with the Japanese.

Caught in the continuous cross-fire of this California-Japanese war were the resident Japanese. Always the victims of this weird transpacific struggle, they were the first casualties on the mainland after December 7, 1941, when the real war began.[71]

8

Japan and
the Road to War

ALTHOUGH THE FAMILY name Yamamoto in Japan is as common a surname as Smith is in the United States, the name Yamamoto Isoroku was eventually to become famous, not only in Japan, but throughout the world.

Yamamoto Isoroku was born in Nagaoka, Japan in 1884. His school teacher father, a former samurai, was fifty-six years old on the date of his son's birth; hence, Yamamato was named Isoroku, which means fifty-six. After completing his secondary school studies, Yamamoto Isoroku sought a military career in the Imperial Japanese Navy. His outstanding scholastic achievements, forceful personality, and his innovative naval training programs marked him for steady promotions, which led ultimately to the highest position in the Imperial Naval General Staff.

Standing five feet two inches high and erect in bearing, he was a calm, muscular athlete who excelled in swimming and Kendo (Japanese fencing). He was an entertaining storyteller, an enthusiastic bridge player, and an excellent poker player; he bid boldly at bridge in order to test the strength or weakness of his opponents' hands or to try new strategic moves.

He graduated first in his class from the strict Japanese Naval College at Etajima in 1904. One year later, Ensign Yamamoto lost two fingers of his left hand during the naval battle with the Russian Baltic Fleet off the Straits of Tsushima at the entrance to the Sea of Japan.

In 1919, at the age of thirty-five, he was assigned by the Naval General Staff to study petroleum engineering and aviation fuels at Harvard University. His two-year sojourn in the United States made a deep impression on him. Not only did it increase his admiration for the American people, but through it he also learned firsthand of the enormous natural resources of the United States. On his tours to the great industrial areas of Pennsylvania, Ohio, Michigan, and Illinois, he was overwhelmed by the sight of America's industrial strength. He noted the limited oil reserves in Japan as compared with the huge oil-producing areas of America's East Coast and the seemingly unlimited oil reserves of southwest Texas and California. He marveled at the energy, adaptability, and inventive genius of the high-speed modern mechanical processes in America. In later years, while in the highest echelons of Japan's High Command, he was to maintain vigorously, but unsuccessfully, that in any armed conflict with the United States, Japan could not possibly win.

In 1921 Yamamoto, now a commander, was ordered to Lake Kasumigaura, located a few miles northeast of Tokyo, as chief executive officer in a top secret project meant to develop Japan's naval air power. Although not previously a pilot, Yamamoto learned to fly and soon became Japan's leading naval expert in combat flight training and torpedo-bombing techniques.[1]

In 1925 he was transferred to the Japanese Embassy in Washington, D.C. as naval attaché with the rank of captain. From this post, he noted the increasing tension and ill-will between the United States and Japan, due primarily to Japan's policy in China and Manchuria. The United States was attempting to curb this aggression through repeated letters of protest to the Japanese government. These communications had little effect on an already powerful and growing military clique within the Japanese government.

Japan's foreign policy in China and Manchuria, its diplomatic relations with the United States, and American foreign policy had a severe impact on persons of Japanese ancestry in the United States. Of almost equal importance was the increasingly important role played by Yamamoto in the years following the passage of the Japanese Exclusion Act of 1924.

THE JAPANESE EXCLUSION ACT CAUSES CONTROVERSY

In Japan, the Exclusion Act continued to rankle the people and the press. To Japan, the shameful exclusion of its citizens and the refusal to consider them on an equal basis with Europeans as permanent immigrants into the United States continued to be a live issue before the public from 1924 until well into the 1930s. Each year from 1924 on, in the Annual Report to the Diet, the Japanese foreign minister expressed his regrets at his inability to resolve this vexing problem. Japanese publications constantly published articles on the injustices wrought by the Exclusion Act. Public and political leaders in Japan expressed vehement indignation over the racially discriminatory regulations.

To the Japanese nation and its people, the Japanese Exclusion Act of 1924 had become an issue of principle. Whether a few hundred Japanese were or were not admitted annually into the United States under its quota immigration formula became immaterial. The important question was whether Japan as a nation was entitled to respect and consideration, along with other nations, within the U.S. immigration policy. In other words, the Japanese government "asks of the United States government simply that proper consideration ordinarily given by one nation to the self respect of another, which after all, forms the basis of amicable international intercourse throughout the civilized world."[2]

For a period of almost ten years after the Washington Conference on Limitation of Armaments of 1921, Japan had attempted to pursue her economic and political interests without resorting to war under the moderate foreign policy of Foreign Minister Baron Shidehara Kijuro, who later became prime minister.

Japan's economic interests in China and Manchuria were born of the desperate need for natural resources and raw materials to supply her industrial economy and to provide convenient markets for her finished goods. But by 1931 Japan's efforts to expand deeper into China came into direct conflict with the rise of Chinese nationalist forces. In China, where there were enormous problems involving geographical distances, education and training of her vast manpower, and lack of industrial capabilities, General Chiang Kai-shek, successor to Dr. Sun Yat-sen, was valiantly struggling to unify China with one hand and attempting to repel the economic invaders from Japan with the other.[3]

In the 1920s there was little evidence in Japan of political and economic power clearly lodged in the Japanese people themselves or, in fact, of a truly representative Diet.[4] The political parties in Japan represented special interests. These parties could increase their power and influence in government only in relation to their support of Japan's industrial interests, particularly the *zaibatsu* (big business), which formed an industrial, commercial, and financial cartel. These industrial interests were in turn supported by the military as Japan extended her economic expansion further into China and Manchuria.

By the late 1920s, Baron Shidehara's foreign policies were more and more discredited by the industrial interests and military cliques. Inexorably, the military factions within the Japanese government grew increasingly impatient with Shidehara's moderation; the previously covert pressures of the business and military groups within the government now became open attempts to influence Japan's foreign policy. Business and military groups insisted that the nation's foreign and economic policies toward China and Manchuria become more "positive."

It was not until May 1930 that influential Americans and powerful organizations in the United States began to speak up against the inequities of the Japanese Exclusion Act. At the Seventeenth National Foreign Trade Convention in Los Angeles, J. J. Donovan, a leading industrialist from Bellingham, Washington, expressed his concern that anti-American attitudes in Japan were seriously affecting trade relations with that country. G. A. Witherow of the softwood lumber trade industry, also from the Northwest, deplored the Exclusion Act and called for "corrective measures" not only because of loss of trade with Japan but also "because of our long and genuine friendship dating back to Commodore Perry's time."

At the conclusion of the National Foreign Trade Convention, this gathering of businessmen passed a resolution that read in part, "This Convention favors strongly revision of the Immigration Act of 1924."[5]

Congressman Albert Johnson, who had sponsored the original amendment to the Quota Immigration Law of 1924, calling for the exclusion of the Japanese, was from the state of Washington. Whether men such as Donovan and Witherow had sufficient influence to persuade Congressman Johnson is not known. However, it is interesting to note that on the same day the resolution of the National Foreign Trade Convention was adopted, the following press release was issued from Washington, D.C. by Congressman Johnson:

> Chairman Johnson of the House Immigration Committee announced today that he expected to propose an amendment to the Immigration Act to give Japan its proportionate quota of immigrants. The proposed amendment would give an immigration quota to Japan of about one hundred and eighty a year, it is estimated by Labor Department officials.[6]

This press release reflected the gradual change of public and political attitudes in the United States toward Japanese immigration. Unfortunately, this change in attitude by Congress came six years too late. During the period from 1924 to 1930, other events were occurring, both in the United States and Japan, that were to cause further deterioration between these two countries. By now, mere public utterances of a change of heart and expressions of regret regarding former attitudes and injustice towards Japan and the Japanese could not stem the tide of conflict that loomed ahead.

THE GREAT DEPRESSION

The catastrophic event that directly affected the United States and Japan, and eventually reverberated throughout the entire world, was the collapse of the stock market in 1929. Millions of persons in the United States were thrown out of work, while unemployment figures rose to almost 25 percent. Business activities shuddered to a bankrupt stop. Fear and panic swept throughout the land. Life savings and deposits of millions were lost when thousands of banks failed. With declining sales and no money to borrow for industrial production, thousands of factories and mills closed.

In shops and stores inventories piled up and rotted, deteriorated, or decayed. The general population had no income to purchase goods;

there were no social security or unemployment benefits then. Long bread lines formed when people had no means to purchase food. In the cold winter months of 1929, shivering children huddled for warmth in unheated rooms for lack of coal or fuel. Able-bodied men, unable to find work, sold apples in the streets.

President Herbert Hoover, a mining engineer who had become a wealthy businessman and food administrator in war-torn Europe after World War I, struggled to bring order out of chaos. He commenced a public works employment program and declared a moratorium on home mortgage payments to prevent hundreds of thousands of homes from being foreclosed and families from being forced out without shelter. To bolster the hope and courage of the nation he promised "a car in every garage, a chicken in every pot." This rosy slogan did little to comfort the nation, for now the Great Depression had spread throughout the land.

In Japan, the world-wide depression brought the spinning wheels of industry to an abrupt halt. The slump in rice prices at home was aggravated by an overabundance of supply brought on by a bumper crop, and there was no market for it in other countries of the world. Japan's huge international market for silk and cotton, a market largely in the U.S. and upon which Japan largely depended for her economy, collapsed overnight.

Before the Great Depression, shipments of goods to the United States accounted for approximately 45 percent of Japan's total exports, of which more than 60 percent consisted of raw silk. Japan's other major exports to the U.S. were silk fabrics, tea, chinaware, and cotton goods. The Japanese economy had become so closely tied to the American market that even the slightest U.S. economic deviation directly affected Japan, particularly the Japanese silk cultivators and reelers, some of whom had speculated in the American stock market. In 1929, as now, it was widely recognized that "when America sneezes, Japan comes down with the flu." Thus, on October 29, when most of the 16,410,000 shares traded on the New York Stock Exchange plunged to new lows with billions of dollars lost, Japan was one of the first nations to feel the staggering impact of "Black Tuesday."[7]

To bolster its sagging export markets, Japan looked more eagerly across the Sea of Japan to the huge population of China and Manchuria and to that of areas in Southeast Asia. Between 1930 and 1932, after the initial shock of the Depression wore off, big business in Japan recovered its previous momentum, due largely to a government-sponsored export campaign.

THE BEGINNINGS OF FASCISM IN JAPAN

The Great Depression could be said to have triggered the beginning of Japanese fascism.[8] Under the impact of the Depression, Japan's military cliques gained control of the government and, through their strong-arm influence, over the political leaders of the country. They set out on a path leading to Japan's military–big business involvement on the Asian mainland. Japan's domestic policies and economic directions became clearly focused on imperialistic expansion with a zeal that ultimately became fanatic in intensity.

Japan's fascism followed the familiar pattern of government attacks on labor and peasant tenant unions and harsh restrictions on political parties that opposed the imperialistic policy. The military elements conspired with other extremist elements in the country to assassinate prominent politicians or business leaders who opposed the ruthless economic penetration into China and Manchuria. As the military cliques gained more influence and power they pushed through more expenditures from Japan's national budget for the construction of battleships, for a sharp increase in the conscription of men for military duty, and for military supplies and armaments.

England, with its far-flung empire extending across the world, became alarmed at the increasing power of Japan's army and navy, particularly around the countries and islands of Southeast Asia. This directly threatened England's lifelines to its territorial and overseas protectorates.

In 1930 England invited the United States and Japan to London to supplement the Washington Conference Pact of 1921, which had limited the holdings of capital ships by these three great powers. At the London Conference, the main topic was to be the limitations on the holdings of auxiliary warships. Yamamoto Isoroku was designated by Japan to be its chief delegate; he had been in Japan after his tour of duty as naval attaché to the Japanese Embassy in Washington, D.C.

The London Conference formally acknowledged Japan's right to maintain 6.9945 tons of cruisers and destroyers for every 10 United States and British tons. In addition, the United States delegates agreed to delay the construction of three heavy cruisers, for which appropriations had already been allocated, in order to give Japan 73 percent of naval parity with the United States until at least 1936. Best of all, from Yamamoto's point of view, no limitations were attached to the building of naval aircraft.[9]

However, Yamamoto returned to Japan frustrated and disillusioned because England and the United States had demanded and obtained an agreement that once again saw Japan compelled to accept a lesser ratio as compared with that of England and the United States. Japan had been insisting upon parity on all armanents with the other two great powers.

Yamamoto's announcement of a ratio less than parity again set off a public furor. Again the two Western powers had assigned a lesser role to Japan, based upon their concept that Japan was a racially inferior military power. The Japanese naval leadership refused to recognize the agreement, branding it as an encroachment upon its own authority. The Japanese nation erupted into confused debate. At the same time that the London Conference Agreement was being bitterly attacked, the battleship ratio of five for the United States, five for Great Britain, and three for Japan, agreed upon under the prior Washington Conference Pact of 1921, was also being openly denounced.

The Manchurian Incident

Professor Oka Yoshitake, a renowned historian at Tokyo University, described Japan's military aggression into Manchuria, beginning with the Manchurian incident of September 18, 1931, as "an undisguised counter attack by Japanese imperialism against the terms of the Washington agreements."[10]

The Manchurian incident referred to by Professor Oka, was a culmination of several years of secret planning by Japanese military extremists who held that Japan must "free" Manchuria from its Chinese warlord ruler, Marshal Chang Tso-lin. Manchuria was an answer to poverty in Japan, it was said. This vast undeveloped land, abundant in natural resources, would provide needed raw materials for Japan's industry and a market for her finished goods. Manchuria could be transformed into a civilized country for Japanese nationals, alleviate unemployment at home, and provide a new power base for Japan's expansionist programs, as well as become a buffer against the Soviet Union.[11]

On June 28, 1928 a staff officer of the crack Japanese Kwantung Army, without orders, commanded some troops from an engineer regiment to dynamite the special train in which Marshal Chang was traveling. Chang was fatally injured, thereby eliminating his power and influence in Manchuria. More Japanese troops were quietly sent into Manchuria over the next few years. In the summer of 1931, Japanese military fanatics, led by Lieutenant Colonel Ishihara Kanji and Colonel Itagaki Seishiro, took the next step to control Manchuria. At 10:00 P.M. on September 18, 1931, there was a detonation of dynamite on the tracks of the South Manchurian Railway near the barracks of the 7th Chinese Brigade, which was garrisoned in Mukden. The explosion had been planned by the Japanese.

Orders were issued to the Japanese troops massed nearby to fire on the Chinese barracks on the pretense that the Chinese troops had caused the explosion and that the Japanese were being sent in to "bring order." By morning, Mukden was in Japanese hands. Japan's recognition of Manchuria, renamed Manchukuo, was announced to the world a year later on September 15, 1932. Manchukuo became a puppet state of Japan.

Widespread Political Assassinations

Soon after the Manchurian incident there was a series of assassinations of Japanese political leaders who had opposed the aggressive imperialistic expansion into China. A rightist group of young army officers had earlier assassinated Prime Minister Hamaguchi Yuko in the Tokyo Station.[12] He had been shot in the stomach on November 14, 1930 but lingered on, suffering from debilitating surgeries for his wounds. He died on August 31, 1931. Baron Takuma Dan, the chief of the Mitsui cartel, was shot and killed on March 5, 1932 when he objected to the military expansion, stating that without ready cash, the big industrialists could not assist in the military campaign in China and Manchuria.[13] Prime Minister Inukai Tsuyoshi was assassinated on May 15, 1932 as he sat in the study of his official residence in Tokyo.[14]

In the early morning of February 26, 1936, the bloodiest rebellion of all took place. A fanatic squad of troops stationed in Tokyo tried to take over the government by eliminating some of the highest ranking political and moderate military leaders of the Japanese government. Finance Minister Takahashi Korekiyo was gunned down in his own home. The bedroom of Lord Privy Seal Admiral Viscount Saito Makoto was broken into and forty-seven bullets were poured into his body. Colonel Matsuo Denzo, the son-in-law of Prime Minister Okada Keisuke, was inadvertently shot and killed while the intended victim, Okada, managed to escape. General Watanabe Jotaro, inspector general of military education, was also cut down.[15] The rebels surrendered only when Emperor Hirohito himself appealed to them to put down their arms and leave the buildings.

THE PRELUDE TO WAR

Other events came tumbling over each other. In 1932 the United States Navy and the Imperial Japanese Navy both held war games and maneuvers in the Pacific Ocean.

One of the United States Navy games planned was a mock attack on Pearl Harbor. The Pacific Fleet at Hawaii thus staged a rehearsal for the events that were to transpire in 1941. The grand maneuvers included a test of the joint army and navy defense of Pearl Harbor. At dawn on a Sunday morning "enemy" carriers approaching Oahu from the northwest took the "defenders" completely by surprise. The attacking planes "sank" every U.S. battleship in the harbor and destroyed all the defending planes before they could get off the ground.[16] But the vulnerability of Pearl Harbor was apparently lost upon Secretary of State Henry L. Stimson and other high-ranking military and government personnel. These officials felt that the mere presence of the United States Fleet had a "steadying effect" on a Pacific enemy, that is, on the Japanese. They chose to think that Japan, a small island-nation in Asia, would never be audacious enough to dare an attack on Hawaii.

However, the results of the United States Navy war games in the Pacific were not ignored by Yamamoto Isoroku, now a rear admiral. The Japanese Imperial Navy held its grand naval maneuvers on October 26, 1932. Carrier-borne torpedo planes of "Fleet White" led by Admiral Yamamoto theoretically sank the battleships of "Fleet Blue," to prove again in most dramatic form the effectiveness of naval air power over the battleship.[17]

Japan Resigns From the League of Nations

The year 1932 also proved to be a year of challenges. The United States challenged Japan's growing aggressiveness in China. Japan challenged the United States, and other nations of the world, as to whether these nations could effectively deter Japan in her drive into China. On September 22, 1931 Secretary of State Stimson cabled the chief United States observer to the League of Nations in Switzerland:

It is apparent that the Japanese military have initiated a widely extended movement of aggression only after careful preparation. . . . The military chiefs and the Foreign Office of Japan are evidently sharply at variance as to intention and opinion. Consequently, it would be advisable . . . that nationalist feelings not be aroused against the Foreign Office in support of the Army.[18]

In the 1930s no power, including the United States, could have effectively opposed Japan's military aggressions. The United States Navy, half of it in mothballs, had never been weaker. Stimson had been told by the military chiefs that it would take at least five years to prepare for war with Japan. The West, weak and preoccupied with the Depression, could send no troops into the Orient to repel Japan. Not even the Soviet Union showed readiness to intervene because it was still struggling to get on its feet after the Communist revolution of 1918 that overthrew the czar.

But Stimson remained stubborn in opposing Japan's advances. On February 27, 1932 he carefully leaked a letter that he had written to United States Senator William E. Borah of Idaho, chairman of the Senate Foreign Relations Committee. The letter warned Japan that

any modification or abrogation of the structure of inter-locking treaties which were intended to safeguard the peace would release the United States from its obligation under any one of them. If Japan, with impunity, violated the Nine-Power Treaty guaranteeing the open door and territorial integrity of China, the United States could feel free to build capital ships beyond naval treaty limitations and to strengthen United States military establishments in the Philippines, Guam and Hawaii.[19]

This letter was to become known as the Stimson Doctrine. In effect it reiterated the open-door policy in China, enunciated by Secretary of State John Hays in 1899. Japan's answer to the Stimson Doctrine was to ignore it.

The League of Nations then sent an investigating team into China to ascertain what Japan was doing there. Lord Victor Lytton's committee returned in 1932 and sharply condemned Japan's imperialistic designs. The committee recommended that the League of Nations not recognize Manchukuo, either de jure or de facto, that Japan be asked to withdraw her troops from there, and that an international police force be established in Manchuria.

The Lytton report condemning Japan was approved by the League of Nations. Japan's answer was to give notice of withdrawal from the League, said withdrawal to be effective in two years. Japan felt it had nothing to fear from the withdrawal since the League of Nations was an ineffective organization without power to enforce its mandates. Freed from the moral restraints of being a member of the League, Japan quickly moved forward to consolidate its military gains throughout other parts of the Far East.

U.S.–Japan Relations Are Strained

In light of heightening tensions between Japan and the United States, it is interesting to note two proclamations that were announced pursuant to the provisions of the Quota Immigration Law of May 26, 1924. Authority had been conferred upon the President to adjust and revise the annual quotas each fiscal year for immigration of persons entering as permanent residents into the United States. In Proclamation No. 2048, dated June 16, 1933, and again in Proclamation No. 2283, dated April 28, 1938, President Franklin Roosevelt approved a revision of the numbers of the National Origin Immigration Quotas to grant 100 immigrants from Japan and a further quota of 100 from Yap and other Pacific islands under Japanese mandate for the respective succeeding fiscal years.[20]

What motivated the United States to recognize Japan by allowing the admission of 100 immigrants is not known. Perhaps the proclamations were a belated gesture of good will. Perhaps President Roosevelt felt that the proclamations could, in some way, slow down the pell-mell rush of Japan into the China mainland.

What is more revealing here is that Japan did not choose to send any emigrants to America following the announced revisions. By this time Japan's animosity toward the United States could not be overcome by these small gestures implying racial equality—not after several decades of bitter anti-Japanese immigration policies. In any event, there appears to be no record of any immigration from Japan into the United States following these proclamations.

Instead, there was an intensification of anti-American feelings in Japan, demonstrated by a series of provocative events meant deliberately to flout the United States. On December 12, 1937 Japanese naval aviators sank the United States gunboat *Panay* while she lay at anchor in the Yangtze River in China, although her American flag was clearly visible.

Earlier in the month, under the command of Colonel Hashimoto Kingoro, one of the extremist members of the army, a Japanese artillery regiment fired on the British gunboat *Ladybird* and later seized her. The Japanese were on the march everywhere in China. After the taking of Soochow, the road to Nanking and Shanghai was open. While Japanese military commanders were sternly issuing orders against any acts of misconduct by their soldiers, the orders were ignored and widespread looting, burning, and torturing of men, women, and children was prevalent "to teach the Chinese a lesson."[21]

President Roosevelt began to consider stronger measures. On October 5, 1937 he made a forceful speech in Chicago condemning all aggressors and equating the Japanese, by inference, with the Nazis and Fascists. "When an epidemic of physical disease starts to spread, the community approves and joins in a quarantine of the patients in order to protect the health of the community," Roosevelt declared. The following year, 1938, he sent Captain Royal Ingersoll, Chief of the

Navy's War Plans Division, to London with instructions to explore the implementation of a long-range naval blockade of Japan. The blockade would have stopped all Japanese traffic crossing a line roughly from Singapore through the Dutch East Indies, New Guinea, New Hebrides, and around to the east of Australia and New Zealand. While the British Admiralty approved the plan, Prime Minister Neville Chamberlain refused to join in such a blockade, and President Roosevelt was forced to abandon it. Then the United States broke off its commercial relations with Japan. On July 26, 1939 Secretary of State Cordell Hull dispatched a note to the Japanese ambassador saying that the United States was terminating the Treaty of Commerce and Navigation between the United States and Japan, signed in Washington on February 21, 1911. The notice stated that the treaty was to expire six months later, on January 26, 1940.[22]

The legal validity of this notice to abrogate the Treaty of 1911 merely by a note from the secretary of state to the Japanese ambassador is open to question. An international treaty, such as the Treaty of 1911, is considered to be the highest law of the land. Where the United States is a party to a treaty, even though such a treaty is terminable on notice, it can be terminated only by an act of Congress.

The notice to abrogate the Treaty of 1911 went almost unnoticed in the United States, which was readjusting its foreign policy to consider a more serious threat in Europe. On March 12, 1938 Hitler had seized Austria, and by September 1939 the German panzer troops had invaded Poland. Soon the Netherlands would fall, as would France. England was now struggling for its survival against the massive military power of Germany.

With the eyes of the United States turned more toward Europe than toward the Pacific, Japan was busy moving its military forces into other parts of Southeast Asia. In July 1940, after the fall of France, Tokyo extracted from the Vichy government an accord that recognized Japan's immediate military interests in Indochina. The accord also granted Japan the right to use the airfields and naval bases at Saigon and elsewhere. Admiral Jean Francois Darlan of France, lacking support from the Vichy, capitulated. Forty thousand Japanese troops quickly moved into southern Indochina and took control of the country.

Embargoes Are Declared on Goods to Japan

Japan's move into Indochina was countered by President Roosevelt. He immediately declared an embargo on various materials and supplies necessary for Japan's survival, including a long list of basic products such as chemicals, fibers, rubber, tin, tungsten, vanadium, and machine tools. On September 30, 1940 further embargoes were declared on aerial cameras, military searchlights, and fire control instruments.[23] Again, on December 20, 1940, a further embargo was declared to control the exportation of military equipment and munitions.[24] On July 26, 1941 President Roosevelt issued an order to freeze all Japanese assets in the United States and American territories. The British and the Dutch did the same with respect to their possessions. The freeze on funds by these three countries meant that the Japanese could not obtain any more currency with which to buy American, British, or Dutch supplies.[25]

Yamamoto Isoroku, now commander in chief of the combined Imperial Naval Fleet, had for years vociferously voiced his objections to the Japanese army's invasion of Manchuria. His opposition was lost in the clamor by the army to strengthen its foothold on the China mainland. Yamamoto had also opposed any military alliance with Germany or Italy because he knew that such an alliance would alienate Japan from the United States, Great Britain, and France. He favored the policy of carrying on trade between Japan and the other Asiatic countries. This moderate spirit, and particularly his opposition to any policy meant to antagonize the United States, subjected Yamamoto to bitter attacks by the right wing of the military and by other fanatical governmental officials. Yamamoto was considered to be too friendly to the United States. He was marked for assassination. As war clouds gathered, Yamamoto was assigned to sea duty so as to remove him from his enemies.

In July 1941 President Roosevelt played his strongest and most devastating trump card against Japan. He declared an embargo on petroleum products to Japan, including high-octane aviation fuel. Britain, China, and the Netherlands joined in imposing the same type of petroleum embargo, unofficially referred to as the "ABCD encirclement of Japan."

The oil embargo came as a bolt out of the blue to the Japanese military. The country's oil supplies were believed to be sufficient for a war with America lasting at most two years. Japan had two alternatives: to push further south until she took control of the Indonesian oil fields, or to negotiate with the ABCD powers for an easing of the embargo.[26]

JAPAN PREPARES FOR WAR

Ironically, and with eventual tragic results for him, Admiral Yamamoto was ordered by the Imperial High Command to prepare for war with the United States—the nation with which he had tried so hard to reach an amicable relationship. But as he was to state many times, before and during the war, while he opposed any antagonism toward the United States, once Japan had committed herself to a course of action, he as a good soldier had to obey without question, according to the code of *Bushido*.

While negotiations were proceeding in Washington, D.C. between Secretary of State Hull and Japan's Ambassador Admiral Nomura Kichisaburo and Special Envoy Kurusu Saburo, Yamamoto was preparing plans for the Japanese Naval Air Force to use in attacking Hawaii. Yamamoto's gamble was obvious: if his strategy was successful and if he was able to cripple or sink the United States Navy at Pearl Harbor, the United States would probably bargain for a negotiated settlement with Japan. His plans to bomb Pearl Harbor were meticulously prepared at Kanoya Air Base and later in a bay that closely resembled Pearl Harbor—Kagoshima Bay in Kyushu, the southernmost island of Japan.

While Admiral Yamamoto was intensely preparing for his sneak attack, Prime Minister Tojo Hideki, who also carried the portfolios of war minister and home minister—a combination that gave him virtual dictatorial powers in Japan—convened a historic liaison conference between the highest ranking military and cabinet officers of his nation. On November 1, 1941, for seventeen consecutive hours of debate, heated and often times anguished, they considered what they must do in the face of the recently proclaimed oil embargo. It was finally decided that Japan should continue to negotiate with the United States for concessions regarding the oil and other embargoes, which were slowly strangling Japan to death. The conference issued directives to Admiral Nomura and Special Envoy Kurusu that they were to continue negotiations with the United States in Washington, D.C. If a satisfactory agreement could not be reached by November 29, 1941, Japan would proceed with its plans to attack Pearl Harbor.

Having made this policy, the Imperial High Command, on November 26, 1941, ordered Admiral Yamamoto to weigh anchor from a place in the Kurile Islands in northern Japan, where he and his mighty armada were waiting, and ordered him to sail to Saiki Bay off the northeast corner of Kyushu to meet Admiral Nagumo Chuichi. Nagumo was to execute the plans for the attack on Pearl Harbor. Admiral Nagumo, aboard his flagship the aircraft carrier *Akagi*, was then to proceed to a point in the north Pacific about 2,300 miles northwest of Pearl

Harbor, where he was to arrive on Wednesday, December 3, 1941 to await further orders.

While Ambassador Nomura and Special Envoy Kurusu were waiting in the outer office of Secretary of State Hull to deliver the latest message from Tokyo—a message that was delayed in translation and therefore could not be delivered to Hull before noon on December 7—the order was flashed by Admiral Yamamoto to proceed with the plans to attack Pearl Harbor. The secret code for the attack was "Climb Mount Niitaka 1208."[27]

Navy Commander Fuchida of the Pearl Harbor Attack Squadron led his flyers off the aircraft carriers and roared toward Hawaii. By 3:05 A.M., December 8, Japan time (7:05 A.M. Hawaii time, 1:05 P.M. Washington, D.C. time, December 7), the attack squadron sighted the coast of the verdant island of Oahu, Hawaii.

The American Pacific Fleet, except for the aircraft carriers, which were at that time on the high seas between the Pacific Coast and the Hawaiian Islands, lay peacefully at anchor in Pearl Harbor on a quiet, sleepy Sunday morning. Breaking radio silence, Commander Fuchida signaled "to-to-to" ("attack, attack, attack"). The first torpedo bombs from his low-flying squadron were dropped at 7:49 A.M., December 7, 1941, Hawaii time (3:49 A.M., December 8, Tokyo time).

On December 8, 1941 the United States declared war on Japan. Whatever the other underlying causes of the war between the United States and Japan may have been, there is little question but that it was racial hostility that initially aggravated relations between the two powers.

9

Post–Pearl Harbor: "A Jap Is a Jap"

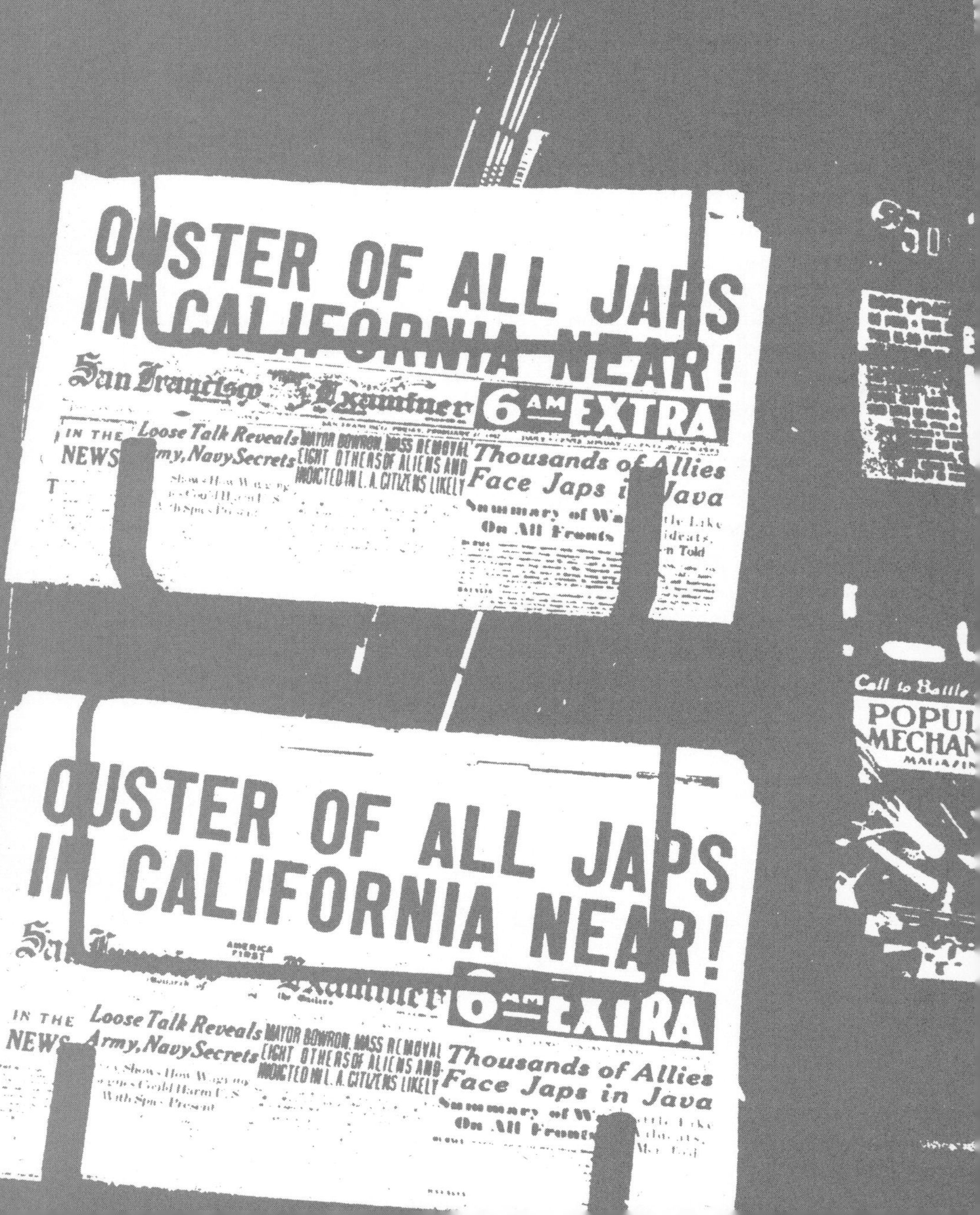

During World War II, ten concentration camps were constructed by the United States Army Corps of Engineers in seven western states. At the peak of their occupancy, these camps housed nearly 120,000 persons of Japanese ancestry, over 70,000 of whom were United States citizens. Almost all of the other inhabitants had lived in the United States from twenty to forty years but were not eligible to become citizens under the existing laws.[1]

The inhabitants in these ten camps were men, women, and children from all walks of life. They included the wealthy and the impoverished, the literate and the uneducated. These camps housed the feeble and the aged, the ill and the infirm, the blind and the lame, the injured as well as the healthy, and students from kindergarten through graduate school. Many of the evacuees were professional men and women: doctors, lawyers, architects, engineers, and university professors. There were also farmers, fishermen, flower growers, nurserymen, flower shop owners, restaurant managers, curio shopkeepers, and lessees of small rooming houses. Some were housemaids, houseboys, clerks, and salesmen.

Not one of these people had been accused, indicted, or convicted of any illegal or criminal act in any court or administrative proceeding. They had not been accorded any hearing, formal or informal, before being ordered into camp. No evidence had been presented against any of them by any law enforcement agency. No official of any city, county, state, or federal government had ever advised any of them, individually or collectively, of their civil or constitutional rights before or during the period of time that they were removed, transported to, and detained in these camps.

None of these persons had been provided with legal counsel; no opportunity was given them to subpoena witnesses, to produce documents in their defense, or to prove their innocence of any wrongdoing, in spite of the fact that all the courts of law were fully functioning during the entire period of the evacuation process from March 1942 to November 1942. No martial law had been declared during any part of the time that these persons were placed in these camps.

In most instances, whatever personal properties these persons possessed, such as tools, equipment, supplies, merchandise, food items, or farming utensils, had to be either abandoned, sold under distress conditions, or stored in sheds or garages, only to be later stolen. Crops and vegetables, ready for cutting or harvesting, had to be abandoned. Fishing vessels were beached, their nets, poles, hooks, and other equipment left hanging on the decks.

During the turmoil and confusion of the early days of the massive forced exodus, unprecedented in the United States, these people were allowed to take into the camps only what they could carry in suitcases. The "crime" charged against each of these nearly 120,000 persons was solely that they were of the same racial extraction as subjects of an enemy nation with which the United States was then at war.

The fact that the majority of the persons in these camps were United States citizens was considered irrelevant. Also, the fact that most of these same citizens had never been to Japan and could not speak, read, or write the Japanese language was also held immaterial. The fact that, in some instances, persons ordered into a camp were honorably discharged veterans of the United States armed forces was disregarded. The additional fact that sons, some daughters, fathers, husbands, and loved ones of those being ordered into these camps were then serving in the armed forces of the United States was ignored.

These ten concentration camps, euphemistically called "relocation centers," were located in seven states and housed the following number of persons.

Manzanar, California	10,000
Tule Lake, California	16,000
Poston, Arizona	20,000
Gila River, Arizona	15,000
Minidoka, Idaho	10,000
Heart Mountain, Wyoming	10,000
Granada, Colorado	8,000
Topaz, Utah	10,000
Rohrer, Arkansas	10,000
Jerome, Arkansas	10,000
TOTAL	119,000[2]

LIFE IN THE CAMPS

Most of these camps consisted of dreary tar-paper barracks, located in remote desert regions miles from any town or city. Their perimeters were guarded by barbed wire fences. Along them were wooden watchtowers manned day and night by military personnel of the United States Army. These guards, as part of military police companies, were fully equipped with sidearms, rifles, machine guns, jeeps, and trucks. From dusk to dawn, searchlights probed with their piercing beams of light along the barbed wire fences. Any persons attempting to escape from the confines of the camps were to be shot on sight. Cameras, knives, firearms, and even radios were considered contraband.[3] No one except authorized military personnel, or other officials of the United States government, could enter or leave the camps, and then only with the written permission of the camp director.

Since many excellent works have already been published about life within these concentration camps, no attempt will be made here to detail the psychological, sociological, or economic impact upon the inmates.[4]

Each family lived in one unit of a five-unit barrack, twenty feet wide by twenty feet long, which contained a crude wood- or coal-burning stove. Each inmate slept on a cotton mattress filled with straw and placed upon a single iron folding bed. The camps were bitterly cold in the wintertime and stifling in the summer months. Wind and dust swirled into the rooms from underneath the floor boards and penetrated everywhere. The fine powder could not be washed off even with frequent bathing because of the dust particles that constantly floated in the room.

Each "block," which contained some 300 residents, used a common latrine without partitions between the toilets. Washrooms with tubs for washing clothes contained no drying facilities; clothing was draped inside the rooms or outside the barracks to dry in the wind. Mess halls for each block had open bench tables, which allowed no privacy or opportunity for family communion.

Children roamed freely throughout the camp grounds seeking amusement, recreation, and diversion from boredom. Because of the acute shortage of qualified doctors, nurses, and technicians, necessary medical services were provided by the inmates themselves, many of whom had been rapidly trained to care for a heterogeneous community of people.

Yet, amidst the anguish of leaving their homes and communities, these splendid people, long innocent victims of racial bigotry, opportunistic politicians, and economic competitors, met their imprisonment with calmness and stoicism, with restraint, patience, and extraordinary fortitude.

Although the United States Army under Lieutenant General John L. DeWitt had removed the Japanese from the Pacific Coast states, the actual control of these ten camps was in the hands of a civilian agency. Executive Order No. 9102, signed by President Roosevelt on March 18, 1942, established the War Relocation Authority (WRA) under the Office of Emergency Management of the Executive Office of the President (7 Federal Register 2165). The WRA was authorized to "formulate and effectuate a program for the removal, from areas designated from time to time by the Secretary of War or appropriate military commander under the authority of Executive Order No. 9066 of February 19, 1942, of the persons or classes of persons designated under such Executive Order, and for their relocation, maintenance and supervision."

In March 1942 Dr. Milton Eisenhower, later to become the president of the University of Kansas, was appointed by President Roosevelt to be the first director. He was succeeded in June 1942 by Dillon Myer who was to serve throughout the war and to the end of the program. Myer had previously been acting administrator of the Agriculture Conservation Adjustment Administration in Washington, D.C. Amidst enormously difficult, and at times tumultuous, circumstances, Myer's humane and understanding administration did much to alleviate the bitterness and despair of the Japanese who had been herded into these camps.

Throughout their entire camp experience, these people faced their detention and their later return to their communities with dignity and inward strength, secure in the knowledge that they were not criminals serving their punishment but were the victims of hysteria, misunderstanding, and a long-standing racial hatred that had placed them in this inexorable situation.

The bold and unexpected attack on Pearl Harbor stunned the American people that early Sunday morning of December 7, 1941. An appreciable part of the great United States Pacific Fleet lay in devastated ruin in the harbor, either sunk, seriously damaged, capsized, or left burning. Thousands were dead. Planes on nearby Hickam Field lay like dead or crippled birds along the runway. Panic and fear swept the Hawaiian Islands with rumors that an invasion by Japanese army and naval forces was imminent.

Lieutenant General De Los Emmons was appointed military governor of Hawaii, and martial law was declared. Blackout precautions were taken. But no general evacuation of persons of Japanese ancestry was ordered by General Emmons throughout the entire war, in spite of the fact that approximately 38 percent of the entire population in Hawaii in 1942 was Japanese.

EVENTS LEADING TO THE EVACUATION

Immediately after Pearl Harbor, hundreds of Japanese aliens who were considered leaders within the Japanese community were apprehended by the FBI and detained at Sand Island, but most of them were soon released to rejoin their families. Americans of Japanese ancestry flocked to war industries to serve their country in the total effort. Thousands of other young men eagerly volunteered for active duty in the United States Army. The Hawaiian National Guard, composed principally of Americans of Japanese ancestry, was reactivated as a fighting unit. Later it was to perform heroically in combat in the bitter, muddy fighting in Italy and in France as the famed 100th Battalion of the 442nd Regimental Combat Team.

In spite of many wild rumors and false reports initially circulated, not one case of espionage, sabotage, or act of disloyalty was recorded on the part of either a Japanese alien or a United States citizen of Japanese ancestry in Hawaii. Instead, these persons joined hands with other residents of the islands to exert an all-out effort against their common enemy, Japan.

By August 1942, nine months after Pearl Harbor, Japan was master of all of Southeast Asia, including Hong Kong, French Indochina, Thailand, the Malay Peninsula, Sumatra, Java, Borneo, the Celebes, the Philippines, New Guinea, and the Solomon Islands. But despite these conquests, confidence in the loyalty of the Japanese-Americans on the Hawaiian Islands remained unimpaired throughout the entire war. Furthermore, the area of the Pacific surrounding the Hawaiian Islands was itself a combat area.[5]

On the mainland, however, the attitude toward persons of Japanese ancestry residing within the Western Defense Command area, under General DeWitt, was dramatically different.

During the first few weeks of December 1941, there existed a period of relative quiet, with no discernible agitation against the resident West Coast Japanese. There were rumors of poisoned vegetables, which the Los Angeles Times promptly reported as untrue. One small California newspaper proposed evacuation.[6]

However, on December 15, 1941 a careless statement to the press by Secretary of the Navy Frank Knox sent tremors of fear through the minds of western residents, the army, and other government officials. This statement was later to be exploited fully by politicians, various business interests, and genuine patriotic organizations.

Secretary Knox had made a hurried trip to the Hawaiian Islands to inspect the damage to the Pacific Fleet and to confer with military leaders and local officials. To reporters assembled in Washington, D.C. on his return he said, "The most effective fifth column work of the entire war was done in Hawaii, with the possible exception of

Norway." As it was to be proved later, there was not and never had been any "fifth column" activity by any part of the local population in Hawaii. The term fifth column did not properly describe what had happened in Hawaii. There was some espionage by paid consular agents, but that was a totally different matter.[7]

The fallacious statement by Secretary Knox was interpreted as accusing persons of Japanese ancestry in Hawaii of fifth column activity and predicting what might be expected from such persons on the West Coast. The racist press took up the clamor against the Japanese. Fears long implanted by years of propaganda against the "Yellow Peril" served to fuel the flames of prejudice. The Hearst publications and the *Los Angeles Times*, through editorials, columns, and news reports, aroused the public to the supposed danger in their midst.

Cries for Evacuation Are Heard

During January and early February of 1942, various organizations took up the hue and cry against the Japanese; their demands ranged from requests for surveillance by the army to complete evacuation, or internment, of all Japanese. These organizations included the California Department of the American Legion and many local posts, the Associated Farmers, the Grower-Shipper Vegetable Association, the Western Growers Protective Association, the California Farm Bureau, Americanism Educational League, Kilsoo Haan (a Korean who claimed support from certain nonexistent organizations), some labor unions, the Pacific League, and the California Joint Immigration Committee.[8]

Perhaps the most effective pressure upon government officials were the resolutions adopted by local posts and the state departments of the American Legion. The national convention of the American Legion on January 19, 1942 urged the evacuation and internment of all enemy aliens and nationals, which was interpreted to include all persons of Japanese descent, regardless of citizenship.

Radio commentators and journalists, such as John B. Hughes, Henry McLemore, and Walter Lippman, began a campaign of criticism against the War Department and the United States Department of Justice for their lack of action. They urged mass evacuation of all Japanese, citizens and aliens alike.[9]

On January 29, 1942 and again on February 5, Henry McLemore, a syndicated columnist for the *San Francisco Examiner*, a Hearst publication, demanded an immediate roundup of Japanese-Americans. He wrote:

> I am for the immediate removal of every Japanese on the West Coast in a point deep in the interior [*sic*].

Herd 'em up, pack 'em off and give 'em the inside room in the badlands. Let 'em be pinched, hurt, hungry, and dead up against it. . . . Let us have no patience with the enemy or with anyone whose veins carry his blood. . . . Personally, I hate the Japanese.[10]

Westbrook Pegler, long known for the venom in his pen, wrote, "The Japanese in California should be under guard to the last man and woman right now and to hell with habeas corpus."

The late Walter Lippman, a highly respected columnist and one of the most influential journalists in America, wrote a column on February 12, 1942 advocating the setting aside of the civil rights of Americans of Japanese ancestry. He said:

Since the outbreak of the Japanese war there has been no important sabotage on the Pacific Coast. From what we know about Hawaii and the fifth column in Europe, this is not, as some have liked to think, a sign that there is nothing to be feared. It is a sign that the blow is well organized and that it is held back until it can be struck with maximum effect.

Other organizations were also busy applying pressure on their local politicians to attack the Japanese. Congressman John Z. Anderson introduced H.J. Resolution 305 in the Seventy-seventh Congress (1942) that proposed an amendment to the Constitution to provide that persons born of parents ineligible for citizenship should not become citizens by virtue of their birth in the United States.

On January 30, 1942 the Los Angeles Chamber of Commerce, through its Washington representative Thomas B. Drake, presented a resolution to the West Coast congressional delegation, along with a draft resolution sponsored by Congressman John Costello of California that called for army control over aliens and dual citizens and for mass evacuation of aliens and their families. Two days earlier, on January 28, 1942, Congressman Martin Dies (Miss.), chairman of the Un-American Activities Committee, added his racist voice on the floor of the House of Representatives stating that "a fear of displeasing foreign powers, and a maudlin attitude towards fifth columnists was largely responsible for the unparalleled tragedy at Pearl Harbor."[11] The California Joint Immigration Committee met on February 1, 1942 and with the support of its member organizations urged the evacuation of all Japanese.

The earliest elected official to urge mass evacuation was Fletcher Bowron, a former superior court judge of Los Angeles County who had been a successful reform candidate for mayor of Los Angeles following the corrupt regime of Mayor Frank Shaw. Bowron had met with California State Attorney General Earl Warren, Tom Clark of the United

States Department of Justice, and General DeWitt regarding the "Japanese problem." On February 12, 1942, on Lincoln's birthday, Mayor Bowron made a radio address that included these words:[12]

If Lincoln were alive today, what would he do . . . to defend the nation against the Japanese horde . . . the people born on American soil who have secret loyalty to the Japanese Emperor?

There isn't a shadow of a doubt but that Lincoln, the mild mannered man whose memory we regard with almost saint-like reverence, would make short work of rounding up the Japanese and putting them where they could do no harm. The removal of all those of Japanese parentage must be effected before it is too late.[13]

The most authoritative words in favor of the mass evacuation of all Japanese came from Attorney General Warren. On February 21, 1942, he appeared before Congressman John H. Tolan's (Calif.) congressional committee, which had convened in California and later went to Portland and Seattle to study the Japanese evacuation.[14] Warren's words to the Tolan committee at the San Francisco session were remarkably similar to those to be written later by columnist Walter Lippman:

I am afraid many of our people in other parts of the country are of the opinion that because we have had no sabotage and no fifth column activities in this state since the beginning of the war, that means that none have been planned for us. But I take the view that this is the most ominous sign in our whole situation.

It convinces me more than perhaps any other factor that the sabotage that we are to get, the fifth column activities that we are to get, are timed just like Pearl Harbor was timed. . . . I believe the only reason we haven't had disaster in California is because it has been timed for a different date, and that when that time comes, if we don't do something about it, it is going to mean disaster both to California and our nation.

I want to say that the consensus of opinion [sic] among the law enforcement officers in this state is that there is more potential danger among the group of Japanese who were born in this country than from the alien Japanese who were born in Japan.

These ominous words of warning by the highest legal officer of California sent chills of terror throughout the entire state. Here was the state attorney general, presumably in close touch with Army Intelligence, Navy Intelligence, the FBI, and every law enforcement agency of the state, who unequivocally and emphatically recommended the incarceration of all the Japanese. He had given the same warning at the Conference of Sheriffs and District Attorneys of the State of California on February 2, 1942. He held that there was the strongest of suspicions that the Japanese as an entire race of people, men, women,

and children alike—especially United States citizens of Japanese ancestry—were poised to take disloyal action against the United States
at any moment, to move to commit acts of sabotage, espionage, and
disloyalty upon some mysterious signal to be issued to them by the
Japanese enemy.

Warren's suspicions were uttered by him as a statement of fact and
truth, in spite of repeated reports from the Army and Navy Intelligence
and the FBI, both in Hawaii and on the mainland of the United States,
that there had been no instance of any suspicious behavior by any
person of Japanese ancestry at any time. To this should be added the
fact that during the entire period of World War II, there was not one
instance of disloyalty by any person of Japanese ancestry, either in
Hawaii or on the mainland United States.

Nevertheless, it can be taken with reasonable certainty, that the
statement of Attorney General Warren on February 21, 1942 provided
the single most powerful voice for the ultimate decision of the United
States government to remove all persons of Japanese ancestry from the
Western Defense Command.

Later Warren was to become a powerful champion of human rights
and a staunch defender of individual civil rights as chief justice of the
Supreme Court of the United States.

Protest Against Evacuation Is Ignored

With the West Coast officials, led by Attorney General Warren,
almost solidly against the resident Japanese, the voices of a few fearless
non-Japanese private citizens who protested the mass evacuation were
lost in the clamor and ignored. One such voice in protest against the
proposed evacuation, though unpopular, was remarkably prophetic in
its declamation and should be recorded here. Louis Goldblatt, secretary
for the California State Industrial Union Council in San Francisco,
an affiliate of the Congress of Industrial Organizations, appeared before
the Tolan committee in California and stated:

We feel that a great deal of this problem has gotten out of hand . . . inas-
much as both the local and state authorities, instead of becoming bastions of
defense, of democracy and justice, joined the wolf pack when the cry came
out, "Let's get the yellow menace."

I think the only people who have shown a semblance of decency and honesty and forthrightness in this whole situation are the second generation
Japanese, who, on their own accord, have made a statement . . . that in their
opinion the thing they ought to do is get out of here. They are in accord with
evacuation . . . not in principle, but . . . because they realize that perhaps
the only thing they can do now to avoid vigilantism, mob rule and hysteria,

beatings and riots, is to evacuate. . . .

This entire episode of hysteria and mob chant against the native born Japanese will form a dark page of American history. It may well appear as one of the great victories won by the Axis Powers. [15]

J. Edgar Hoover, director of the FBI, was the only responsible high-ranking United States government official who went on record protesting the demand for the mass evacuation of the Japanese, which he stated was "based primarily upon public and political pressures rather than upon factual data."[16]

Further details of the pressures on the federal government calling for a mass evacuation of the Japanese are dealt with in other books specifically on the subject of the evacuation. Some of these sources are given in the footnotes of this chapter.

General DeWitt and the Western Defense Command

As noted, the attack on Pearl Harbor had produced a calm, competent judgment in Hawaii with reference to the loyalty of the Japanese-Americans by the military governor, General Emmons. The same attack produced panic and confusion at the Headquarters of the Western Defense Command and the Fourth Army at San Francisco's Presidio, a command that embraced the geographical area of the Pacific Coast states. General DeWitt was at the apex of this confusion. He was in fact the cause of much of it, and his uncertain judgment was eventually to become one of the contributing factors in the decision to evacuate Japanese-Americans from the Western Defense Command.

General DeWitt was sixty-two years of age in 1942, slight, wiry, and bespectacled. The son of an army general, he had been commissioned a lieutenant in the infantry when he was eighteen. He served in France during World War I as assistant chief of staff for supply. As a brigadier general, he later commanded troops in the Philippines. DeWitt was essentially an administrator with no combat experience during his entire army career except after the outbreak of World War II.[17] As a cautious, conservative officer in the twilight of his career, he was understandably determined there would be no Pearl Harbor on the West Coast. What is less well known was his longstanding prejudice toward Japanese-Americans. In fact, his racial prejudices extended to all other persons and soldiers of color in the United States Army. When he noted that some of the troops being sent to him as reinforcements after Pearl Harbor were Negroes, he protested to the army's chief of classification and assignment that, "You're filling too many colored troops upon the West Coast. There will be a great deal of public reaction out here due to the Jap situation. They feel they've got enough black-skinned people around them as it is, Filipinos and Japanese. . . . I'd rather have a white regiment."[18]

Fellow officers of General DeWitt noted his lack of leadership, his indecisiveness, his absence of combat experience, and his erratic, emotional thinking—thinking that was causing confusion at Fourth Army Headquarters. These officers included Major General Joseph W. Stilwell, later to become famous as "Vinegar Joe" of the Burma Campaign, who served under DeWitt as corps commander in charge of the defense of southern California, and Lieutenant General Leslie J. McNair, then deputy commander of the Army Ground Forces.[19]

The shortcomings of General DeWitt were to become increasingly more evident as public pressure mounted for the evacuation of Japanese-Americans from the West Coast.

PLANS FOR MASS EVACUATION BEGIN

In the first few days after Pearl Harbor, there was no concerted plan by either the United States Army or the United States Department of Justice for mass evacuation of aliens and citizens. As of December 9, 1941, General Brehon Somervell, of the army's G-4 (supply) ordered the construction of "facilities for the internment of alien enemies and other prisoners of war." But suddenly on the following day, December 10, the first proposal by the army for any kind of mass evacuation of Japanese-Americans was brought forward at a DeWitt staff conference in San Francisco. Plans for a mass roundup were drawn up locally and approved by General James Benedict, the commander of the San Francisco Bay area, but this plan was shelved. On December 10, General DeWitt recommended large-scale internment. He proposed "to collect all alien subjects fourteen years of age and over, of enemy nations and remove them to the interior of the United States and hold them under restraint after removal to prevent their surreptitious return."[20] This initial plan for evacuation called for removal of enemy aliens of all three Axis nations—Germany, Italy, and Japan—rather than only of persons of Japanese ancestry.[21]

In early 1942, when discussions were taking place to evacuate enemy aliens, there were, according to the 1940 census, the following approximate number of aliens of the Axis powers in California: 41,000 Japanese, 58,000 Italians, and 22,000 Germans. "Many of the German aliens were recent refugees from Nazi Germany. Most of the Germans, and a large proportion of the Japanese and Italians, lived in or near the principal cities and adjacent strategic areas."[22]

Immediately following Pearl Harbor, the FBI had apprehended German, Italian, and Japanese aliens who were suspected of "hostile intent or action against the national security." By December 13, within one week after the attack on Pearl Harbor, the Department of Justice had already interned a total of 831 alien residents of the Pacific Coast states, including 595 Japanese and 187 Germans.[23] After being apprehended, these aliens were placed in alien internment centers under the jurisdiction of the Department of Justice. These centers were located at Santa Fe, New Mexico; Missoula, Montana; Bismarck, North Dakota; Fort Sill, Oklahoma; and Crystal City, Texas. After administrative hearings conducted by officers of the Department of Justice, most of these Japanese aliens were later released to rejoin their families at the ten concentration camps where they were already incarcerated.

According to Edward Ennis, then assistant attorney general, United States Department of Justice, and chief of the Alien Internment Unit during World War II, "Whereas it was true that some Japanese aliens who had been interned had expressed sympathy towards Japan, there was no evidence that these same Japanese aliens had ever engaged in, or intended to engage in, espionage, sabotage, or [to] commit any other acts of disloyalty against the United States."

The Department of Justice, primarily through the FBI, Army Intelligence, and Navy Intelligence, had closely scrutinized the records of prospective enemy aliens long before Pearl Harbor. These agencies had compiled a list of those aliens against whom there were grounds for suspicion of disloyalty. It is reasonable to conclude, therefore, that with the immediate apprehension of these aliens, including Japanese, any major threat of disloyalty would have been effectively prevented.

That all such aliens suspected of disloyalty towards the United States had been interned quickly after the outbreak of World War II was a fact well known to General DeWitt. At this juncture of history, another person proved to be the key figure in the ultimate decision of the federal government to evacuate all Japanese-Americans.

Army Provost Marshal General Allen W. Gullion was the United States Army's highest ranking law enforcement officer. Gullion had previously served as Judge Advocate General, the highest legal officer within the army. As such, General Gullion had previously given his official opinion that within the United States, outside any zone of actual combat, where the civil courts were functioning the "military . . . does not have jurisdiction to participate in the arrest and tem-

porary holding of civilians who are citizens of the United States."
He suggested, however, that if federal troops were in actual control
(that is, under martial law), jurisdiction over citizen civilians might
be exercised.[24]

Thereupon (although martial law as such was never declared on the
Pacific Coast during the entire period of World War II), Chief of
Staff George C. Marshall, on December 11, 1941, promptly declared
the Pacific Coast states a "Theatre of Operations." While this declara-
tion was not made with the Japanese-Americans specifically in mind,
General Marshall created the necessary legal fiction that the Pacific
Coast was a war zone. He thus provided the army, and the courts, with
an excuse for placing civilian citizens under de facto military control.

On December 22, 1941 General Gullion, in an attempt to expand
his authority, formally requested the secretary of war to transfer the
responsibility for conduct of the enemy alien program from the Department of Justice to the War Department, a request that Secretary
of War Henry L. Stimson refused. Gullion then shifted his activities
to General DeWitt and recommended a mass roundup of all Japanese,
aliens and citizens alike. Gullion told DeWitt that he (Gullion) had
been visited by a representative of the Los Angeles Chamber of Commerce urging that all Japanese in the Los Angeles area be incarcerated.[25] General DeWitt surprisingly told Gullion:

> I'm very doubtful that it would be common sense procedure to try and
> intern . . . 117,000 Japanese in this theater. . . . I'd rather go along the
> way we are now . . . rather than attempt any such wholesale internment. . . .
> An American citizen, after all, is an American citizen. And while they all may
> not be loyal, I think we can weed the disloyal out of the loyal and lock them up
> if necessary.[26]

During the next month between December 26, 1941 and January
25, 1942, conferences were held constantly between General DeWitt,
James Rowe Jr., assistant attorney general, and Major Karl R. Bendetsen,
chief of the Aliens Division, Provost Marshal General's office, who
represented General Gullion. From these conferences, what appeared
to be a routine bureaucratic shuffle within the army command was
later to become a highly significant move. In all matters concerning
aliens, General DeWitt was to henceforth deal directly with the
Provost Marshal General's office.

As a result of this arrangement, the regular army command headquarters had little to do during January and February 1942 with reference to any plans and decisions for the Japanese evacuation. DeWitt
wanted fuller implementation of Presidential Proclamations 2525,

2526, and 2527, issued on December 7 and 8, 1941, which dealt with the control of Japanese (2525), German (2526), and Italian (2527) aliens.[27] He wanted the FBI to have blanket authority to "search, enter and arrest" all suspected individuals whether at their homes or places of business. United States Attorney General Francis Biddle complied, and on December 30, 1941 he informed the Provost Marshal General's office that he had authorized the issuance of search warrants for any home in which an enemy alien lived merely on the representation that there was reasonable cause to believe that there was contraband on the premises.

This move did not fully satisfy General DeWitt's abiding suspicions toward persons of Japanese ancestry. On January 20 and again on January 21, 1942, he voiced his apprehensions to Brigadier General Mark W. Clark of GHQ that an enemy raid on the West Coast would probably be accompanied by a "violent outburst of co-ordinated and controlled sabotage" among the Japanese population. As if to underscore this fear, an army intelligence bulletin referred to an "espionage now containing Japanese aliens, first and second generation Japanese, and other nations . . . thoroughly organized and working underground."[28]

On January 24, 1942 General DeWitt expressed an opinion that was later to become a principal argument for the ultimate evacuation of the entire Japanese population. These fears conveyed to General Gullion were later repeated by Walter Lippman and again by California Attorney General Warren. General DeWitt declared, "The fact that nothing has happened so far is more or less ominous, in that I feel that in view of the fact that we have had no sporadic attempts at sabotage, there is control being exercised and when we have it, it will be on a mass basis."[29]

DeWitt's statement was followed the next day by the public release of the Roberts Commission Report. A special commission chaired by Owen J. Roberts, associate justice of the Supreme Court of the United States, had been hastily convened in Hawaii to investigate the Japanese attack on Pearl Harbor. Although the conclusions it reached were proved false after the war was over, they were especially inflammatory toward all persons of Japanese ancestry at the time they were made. The report concluded that there had been widespread espionage in Pearl Harbor, both by Japanese consular agents and by Japanese residents of Oahu who "had no open relations with the Japanese foreign service."[30]

This conclusion had a devastating impact upon the general public in the Pacific Coast states. In spite of it, however, there was vigorous debate within the army, the navy, and the Department of Justice over the feasibility of the removing of all the citizens of Japanese ancestry. On February 1, 1942 Attorney General Biddle called a meeting in his office with representatives of the War Department and presented them with a proposed press release that included this statement: "The Department of War and the Department of Justice are in agreement that the present military situation does not at this time require the removal of American citizens of Japanese race."[31] This statement was objected to by Assistant Secretary of War John J. McCloy, General Gullion, and Major Bendetsen.

General DeWitt, who was still objecting to mass evacuation, was accused of "dragging his feet" in restricting the movements of Japanese-Americans. DeWitt was strongly supported in his position by General Clark of GHQ and Admiral Harold R. Stark, Chief of Naval Operations, who were both of the opinion that "from a military point of view," the Pacific Coast necessarily had a low priority as compared with Hawaii and the Far Pacific.

While it was DeWitt who was to testify later before the House Naval Affairs Committee in April 1943 that "a Jap is a Jap," the real power now pressing relentlessly forward for the mass evacuation was General Gullion. It was Gullion who warned Assistant Secretary of War McCloy of the "great danger" of Japanese sabotage on the West Coast. Because of the concentration of the Japanese population near strategic points, he recommended the exclusion of all Japanese from restricted zones. As DeWitt's administrative superior, it was Gullion who in effect overruled DeWitt, even though DeWitt's functional superior was in reality Secretary of War Stimson. As has been noted, Gullion had arranged for DeWitt to deal directly with the Provost Marshal General's office concerning the West Coast "alien problems," which were later to be expanded to include *all* citizens of Japanese ancestry.

As *Command Decisions,* the official publication of the Office of the Chief of Military History of the Department of the Army, was to comment:

It should be borne in mind that none of the enemy alien program recommendations submitted by General DeWitt through 16 February included American citizens of Japanese extraction. The concentration of the Japanese population near strategic points seemed, in itself, to be sinister in 1942. Actually, there was a greater proportionate concentration of German and Italian aliens near strategic points than there was of Japanese.

General DeWitt's Category A recommendations would have affected nine-tenths of the West Coast German alien population, and nearly three-fourths of the Italian aliens, but less than two-thirds of the Japanese aliens.

But Mr. Biddle questioned the necessity of forcibly excluding German and Italian aliens from all these areas . . . initially recommended by General DeWitt. In conclusion, he (Mr. Biddle) stated that, as he had been informally advised that all of Los Angeles County was going to be recommended as a Category A area, that the Department of Justice would have to step out of the picture because it did not have the physical means to carry out a mass evacuation of such scope. In conclusion, he stated that "the Department of Justice was not authorized under any circumstances to evacuate American citizens; if the Army for reasons of military necessity wanted that done in particular areas, the Army itself would have to do it."[32]

The ultimate decision, which was now rapidly deteriorating with reference to issues of constitutional rights and the responsibilities of either the army or civilian agencies, could now only be resolved by one person: President Franklin D. Roosevelt, Commander in Chief of the Armed Forces of the United States.

EXECUTIVE ORDER 9066

In the early afternoon of February 11, 1942, Secretary of War Stimson and Assistant Secretary of War McCloy went to the White House to learn whether or not the President would authorize the army to remove United States citizens as well as aliens of Japanese ancestry from restricted areas.

It is uncertain what was uppermost in President Roosevelt's mind when Stimson and McCloy attempted to discuss the "Japanese problem" that day. It may be assumed that the President was understandably preoccupied with monumental problems of domestic production of war materials, the total mobilization of manpower on the home front, and the far-flung military operations throughout the world. The evacuation of what he might have considered but a handful of citizens and aliens of Japanese ancestry could have appeared to President Roosevelt as a mere diversionary speck of dust compared to his other responsibilities.

On the other hand, Roosevelt may have heeded the clamoring of the West Coast congressional delegation and the other voices of the Far West. In the national election year of 1942, he would know that "cracking down" on the Japanese-Americans would be popular both on Capitol Hill and throughout the United States generally. In addition, he may have been convinced that Japanese, aliens and citizens alike, were dangerous to American security. He had vigorously pushed for mass internment of the Hawaiian Japanese–Americans, long after Military Governor General Emmons had rejected such a policy.

Apparently, without being particularly concerned that constitutional rights of United States citizens would be violated, that much-needed food production would be disrupted, that thousands of troops would be required by such an evacuation program, or that badly needed trucks and trains would be diverted from transportation of troops and supplies, President Roosevelt told Stimson and McCloy by telephone to go ahead and do anything they thought necessary under the circumstances. Immediately after the phone conference at the White House, McCloy informed Bendetsen, now a colonel:

> We have *carte blanche* to do what we want as far as the President is concerned. The President specifically authorized the evacuation of citizens. In doing so, he observed that there probably would be repercussions to such action, but said that what was to be done had to be dictated by the military necessity of the situation. Mr. Roosevelt's only qualification was "Be as reasonable as you can."

Mr. McCloy also told Colonel Bendetsen that he thought the President was prepared to sign an executive order giving the War Department the authority to carry out whatever action was decided upon.[33]

On February 17, 1942 there was another conference between Secretary of War Stimson and President Roosevelt regarding the decision to evacuate all Japanese from the West Coast.[34] On the afternoon of the same day, Stimson met with McCloy, General Clark, General Gullion, and Colonel Bendetsen. That evening at the home of Attorney General Biddle, with the same representatives present, General Gullion pulled from his pocket and read the draft of a proposed presidential executive order that would authorize the secretary of war to remove both citizens and aliens from areas that he might designate through his military commanders. Biddle accepted the draft without further argument since the President had already indicated to him that the removal order was a matter for military decision.[35]

On Thursday, February 19, 1942, President Roosevelt signed Executive Order 9066 that gave the army, through the secretary of war, the authority that General Gullion and Colonel Bendetsen had sought so long.[36] Using as justification a military necessity for "the successful prosecution of the war," the President empowered the military to designate "military areas" from which "any and all persons may be excluded" and to provide for such persons "transportation, food, shelter, and other accommodations as may be necessary . . . until other arrangements are made."

The words Japanese or Japanese-Americans never even appeared in Executive Order 9066, but the order was eventually used only against persons of Japanese ancestry. Although a mass removal of Germans and Italians was also authorized, no such evacuation took place. As Roger Daniels expressed it, "The myth of military necessity was used as a fig leaf for a particular variant of American racism."[37]

Five years later, historian Dr. Stetson Conn, then a civilian historian for the Department of the Army and later the army's chief of military history, was to analyze all contemporary evidence available to him during the evacuation period and was to find "little support for the argument that military necessity required a mass evacuation." He pointed rather to the machinations of General Gullion and of Colonel Bendetsen in bending the civilian heads of the War Department to their will, not General DeWitt as has been so popularly believed up to then. Conn concluded that "the only responsible commander who backed the War Department's plan as a measure required by military necessity was the President himself, as Commander in Chief."[38]

As the war on the continent of Europe had become more and more intense, due to the lightning-like speed and overwhelming might of the German Wehrmacht under Hitler, and with the Battle of Britain ominously looming ahead, on May 27, 1941 President Roosevelt declared the nation under an "unlimited national emergency." This required that the United States military, naval, air, and civilian defenses "be put on the basis of readiness to repel any and all acts or threats of aggression directed toward any part of the Western Hemisphere."[39] Later in the same year, on November 14, 1941, both United States citizens and aliens entering or leaving the United States were subject to certain rigorous restrictions.[40]

On December 7, 1941, following the attack on Pearl Harbor, President Roosevelt declared that a state of war existed between the United States and Japan and that "all natives, citizens, denizens or subjects of the Empire of Japan . . . are termed alien enemies" and that "alien enemies deemed dangerous to the public peace or safety of the United States by the Attorney General or the Secretary of War, as the case may be, are subject to summary apprehension."[41] By identical proclamations, alien Germans and Italians were also declared to be alien enemies.[42] Under these actions of December 7 and 8, 1941, vast powers were granted to the attorney general and to the secretary of war over alien enemies. The aliens could be barred from designated areas near military installations or any other localities connected with the national defense. Further restrictions could be imposed on places of abode, occupations, travel, and meetings.

Thus, on the face of it, Executive Order 9066 appeared to be a logical extension of authorization for protection of the United States during wartime against possible espionage and sabotage to national defense, materiel, premises, and utilities. It contained additional authorization that added United States citizens to the list of those persons who had been previously described as alien enemies.[43]

To add teeth to Executive Order No. 9066, Congress, on March 21, 1942, enacted Public Law 503, which provided as follows:

That whoever shall enter, remain in, leave, or commit any acts in any military area or military zone prescribed, under the authority of an Executive Order of the President, by the Secretary of War, or by any Military Commander designated by the Secretary of War, contrary to the restrictions applicable to any such area or zone or contrary to the order of the Secretary of War or any such Military Commander, shall, if it appears that he knew or should have known of the existence and extent of the restrictions or order and that his act was in violation thereof, be guilty of a misdemeanor and upon conviction shall be liable to a fine of not to exceed $5,000.00 or to imprisonment for not more than one year, or both, for each offense.[44]

ALL JAPANESE ARE INTERNED

Using Executive Order 9066 as leverage, General DeWitt now moved quickly to implement orders against United States citizens as well as aliens of Japanese ancestry. In his Public Proclamation No. 3 he established certain military areas and zones within the Western Defense Command that called for a curfew and ultimately the exclusion of all "alien Japanese, all alien Germans, all alien Italians, and all persons of Japanese ancestry."[45] A series of DeWitt "Civilian Exclusion Orders" followed from which "all persons of Japanese ancestry," both alien and nonalien, were ordered excluded at certain prescribed times from specific areas that he had established as military areas.

The mass evacuation itself took place over a period of eight months, from March 24, 1942 to November 3, 1942. Eventually, all the Pacific Coast states were emptied of all persons of Japanese ancestry.[46] General DeWitt's orders for mass evacuation of all persons of Japanese ancestry, but not of those of German and Italian ancestry, were based on "military necessity."

A memorandum from DeWitt to the secretary of war dated February 14, 1942, requesting authority to remove the Japanese, an authority that was duly delegated to him, is revealing on this point: "Racial affinities are not severed by migration. The Japanese race is an enemy race and while many second and third generation Japanese born on United States soil, possessed of United States citizenship, have become Americanized, the racial strains are undiluted." He concluded, "It therefore follows, that along the vital Pacific Coast, over 112,000 potential enemies of Japanese extraction are at large today."[47]

The 112,000 persons of a total Japanese population of 126,943 in all of the United States included men and women, citizens and aliens, the well and the sick, infants and the aged. It is doubtful that General DeWitt sincerely felt that some of these persons were "potential enemies," which he claimed were ready for "concerted action"; nor could he be really concerned with 7,000 children under the age of five years, or with 15,500 children under ten years of age. Nearly 50,000 of the 112,353 evacuees were women. Nearly 13,000 were males under fourteen years of age. Over 2,000 were over sixty-five years of age. Also, approximately 1,000 of the remaining males were hospitalized, institutionalized, or suffering from infirmities that reduced their possible military usefulness to zero. There were less than 46,000 Japanese males between the ages of fourteen and sixty-five, several thousand of whom were serving in the United States Army. Thus, the figure of 112,000 "potential enemies" was patently absurd.

But by the technique of "guilt based on racial ancestry," the blameless behavior of persons of Japanese ancestry was turned against them by General DeWitt: "The very fact that no sabotage has taken place to date is a disturbing and confirming indication that such action will be taken."

On July 19, 1943, after the Japanese had been entirely removed, General DeWitt submitted his final report, "Japanese Evacuation from the West Coast," a report that was transmitted to the secretary of war by the Chief of Staff. This final report accused the people of Japanese ancestry of being "populous, concentrated in residence, and . . . an unassimilated, tightly knit racial group. Their loyalties are unknown, and no means exist for distinguishing the loyal from the disloyal. Time does not permit any attempt to do so."[48]

Other charges contained in the final report were: (1) the distribution of the Japanese population was a threat to the national defense; (2) United States citizens of Japanese ancestry possessed dual citizenship by which such "dual" citizens were "tied" to Japan; (3) Japanese language schools were the creations and instruments of Imperial Japan for the dissemination of Japanese national ideas among the American-born; (4) religious views of resident Japanese were a danger to internal security; (5) the Kibei, discussed earlier, had strong ties to Japan; (6) the FBI had not completely removed all potentially dangerous or disloyal persons; (7) the threat of a Japanese invasion along the West

Coast was imminent; and (8) the evacuation was largely for the protection of the Japanese themselves.

It would not be until years later that each of these accusations was found to be exaggerated, hastily conceived, or entirely false and basically motivated by racial animosity. In time, all persons of Japanese ancestry residing in the United States were completely vindicated.

But in the heat and passions of war, the courts of law, from local tribunals to the Supreme Court of the United States, were persuaded by the words "military necessity" and believed that there was sufficient cause to find persons of Japanese ancestry in the United States "guilty" of the accusations against them, so as to justify their wholesale evacuation from the West Coast and their detention in concentration camps.[49]

10

The Founding of the JACL and the 442nd Regimental Combat Team

I N 1930 A NUMBER of organizations existed within the Japanese-American communities along the Pacific Coast to improve the legal status and welfare of both citizens and noncitizens. Clarence Arai, a prominent Seattle attorney, was one of many Nisei who proposed that these separate groups should combine into one national body to avoid obvious duplications of effort and to present a united front. He felt the new national organization should be made up entirely of United States citizens, a fact likely to impress vote-conscious politicians in Washington, D.C. As a name for the new national body, *Japanese American Citizens League* was proposed.

In 1930, over the Labor Day weekend, 181 delegates from all areas of the West Coast assembled in Seattle, Washington. A constitution was formally approved, the first national officers were elected, and the name Japanese American Citizens League was adopted.[1]

At this first convention of the JACL, resolutions were passed committing the organization to take immediate action in two important areas:

1. The repeal of Section 47 of the Immigration Act of 1917, known as the Cable Act, sponsored by Congressman John L. Cable of Ohio and passed by Congress on September 22, 1922.[2] The Cable Act provided that any American-born woman who married a person ineligible for citizenship would automatically lose her United States citizenship.

2. An amendment to the naturalization laws to allow Japanese veterans who had served in the United States armed forces during World War I to obtain naturalization. Oriental veterans of World War I had been denied the privilege of applying for United States citizenship because they were not of the "white race." Other aliens were allowed through special legislation passed by Congress to apply for United States citizenship upon being honorably discharged from military service during World War I.

THE JACL BECOMES INFLUENTIAL

The JACL decided to send representatives to Congress to urge the amendment of these two sections of the immigration and naturalization laws. In 1931, Miss Suma Sugi became the first Nisei to represent the JACL in Washington, D.C. Miss Sugi, now Mrs. Harry Yokotake of the Los Angeles City Board of Education, went to work for the repeal of the Cable Act.

The bill to repeal the act was not originated by the JACL; it was part of a larger legislative equal-rights package sponsored by the League of Women Voters. The Cable Act was considered to be discriminatory against women generally. Through the great efforts of Miss Sugi, as well as those of other dedicated women, the legislation was approved by both houses of Congress. President Roosevelt signed the bill repealing the Cable Act on June 25, 1936.[3]

In 1934 the JACL sent its second lobbyist, Tokutaro Slocum, to urge citizenship privileges for Orientals who had served honorably with the United States armed forces during World War I. Slocum, born in Japan with the name Nishimura, had been adopted when a youth by an American family named Slocum. Slocum had been a sergeant major with the 82nd (Rainbow) Division, made famous by the heroic deeds of Sergeant York. Slocum had been severely gassed during the bitter fighting against the German army at Meuse Argonne and again at St. Mihiel in France.

On December 10, 1918, while serving overseas, Slocum had filed a petition for naturalization. Federal District Judge John C. Lorne of Minot, North Dakota had granted Slocum his United States citizenship on June 28, 1921. The certificate of naturalization was later cancelled on January 10, 1923, after strenuous protests by the United States Immigration Service.

An outspoken, fire-breathing orator with sincere convictions, Slocum campaigned tirelessly in Congress to garner support for the bill. His wartime buddies, now in influential positions as officers of the American Legion, Veterans of Foreign Wars, Disabled American Veterans, and Spanish War Veterans, rallied to his cause. Physically exhausted from being gassed in France, living on meager funds, literally existing on water and crackers, he exhorted members of Congress to see the justice of his bill. Powerful groups opposed him, including the California Joint Immigration Committee led by V. S. McClatchy, its executive secretary, but they could not stop the persistent efforts of Slocum. H. R. 7170, sponsored by Congressman Clarence F. Lea of California, and S. 2508, sponsored by Senator Gerald Nye of North Dakota, passed the Congress. On June 24, 1935 President Roosevelt signed the Nye-Lea bill, which granted United States citizenship to approximately 500 Orientals, most of them of Japanese ancestry, who had served honorably with the United States armed forces during World War I.[4]

The repeal of the Cable Act in 1936 marked the first significant erosion of the inpregnable "white" requirements in the naturalization laws of the United States as these laws had been applied to Orientals since 1792. The passage of the Nye-Lea bill drove another wedge into the long-proclaimed position of the California Joint Immigration Committee to "Keep California for the Whites."

Over the ensuing years, the JACL increased its membership, and it had sixty-five chapters by 1942. The policy of the organization was to exert efforts to amend discriminatory laws through legislative activities, to test through lawsuits the constitutionality of various state and federal statutes, and to exercise the right of franchise so as to elect sympathetic public officials. Educational campaigns were launched to inform the American public of the efforts of the JACL to instill the principles of democracy and good citizenship in its members. Nisei were urged to cancel any dual citizenship status.

Dual citizenship was not held only by Nisei; it was a historic position of thousands of persons of European origin born here. While a person born in the United States acquired United States citizenship by birth, or by *jus soli* (right of the soil),[5] if the person's origins through his parents stemmed from Italy, Germany, Switzerland, or certain other countries in Europe, such a person was also claimed at birth as a citizen of that country through *jus sanguinis* (right of blood).

The claim of *jus sanguinis* over a person born abroad could only be made effective when such person was physically present in the country making the claim. Generally the claim applied only to compel military service or to allow employment in the country where citizenship in such country was a requirement.

From 1899 to 1925 Japan's Nationality Code had followed the European rule of *jus sanguinis*, holding that a child born anywhere was a Japanese citizen if his father was Japanese. In 1914 the Japanese on the West Coast themselves petitioned Japan to modify this dual citizenship law. Japan did exempt its law on March 16, 1914 and again in December 1925, to make it possible for a Japanese born in the United States or elsewhere to renounce his claim to Japanese citizenship.

After the Japanese Exclusion Act was passed by Congress in 1924, Japan revised her law to state that any person born abroad after December 1, 1925 was automatically released from the claim of Japanese citizenship; however, a child born in the United States or elsewhere could be registered with the Japanese consulate within fourteen days of birth in order to preserve the child's status as a dual citizen of Japan, if the parents so wished. Thousands of Nisei, whether born before or after December 1, 1925, renounced their Japanese citizenship due to the vigorous efforts of the JACL. Most of the Nisei who still retained

dual citizenship at the outbreak of World War II were simply either
ignorant of the requirements of the renunciation procedures or indif-
ferent to their status of still holding Japanese citizenship.

Other legislative campaigns undertaken by local chapters or by the
national JACL up to 1942 were efforts to defeat the Kramer bill,[6] which
provided that if the wife of a United States citizen was an alien "ineligible for citizenship," the children born abroad would be considered
aliens and not citizens of the United States. Other legislative efforts
of the organization were to combat discriminatory measures, particularly in California, such as laws that mitigated against employment of
citizens of Mongolian extraction.

The JACL was gaining considerable stature and recognition in the
Japanese and other communities when Pearl Harbor was attacked on
December 7, 1941. The JACL immediately wired President Roosevelt
as follows:

> In this solemn hour we pledge our fullest cooperation to you, Mr. President,
> and to our country. There cannot be any question. There must be no doubt.
> We in our hearts know we are Americans—loyal to America. We must prove
> that to all of you.

Within three short months after Pearl Harbor, the officers and members of the JACL were put to their severest test of leadership in guiding
persons of Japanese extraction through the turbulent period of the
evacuation.

THE JACL ASSUMES LEADERSHIP IN THE EVACUATION

The organization, whose membership was then composed of young
Nisei, had suddenly been compelled to assume the leadership of the
Japanese-American community. After the outbreak of World War II,
the older and more established Issei leaders had been arrested by the
FBI and placed in internment centers under the supervision of the
Alien Enemy Control Unit of the United States Department of Justice.
The awesome responsibility, and often bitterly controversial decisions
affecting the lives and futures of persons of Japanese ancestry that had
to be made, were now thrust into the hands of these young Japanese-
Americans.

By February 1942 the clamor to evacuate all the Japanese was becoming a political football in the state and national elections that year.
Soon afterwards, it was confirmed that United States citizens of Japanese ancestry were to be included in a mass evacuation of all Japanese.

In the same month Executive Order 9066 was signed by President Roosevelt. Mass hysteria and hatred toward the Japanese were spreading like a poisonous cloud over the heads of the Japanese-Americans. Racial prejudice, long-existent, became more blatant and vicious. Economic competitors in fishing, farming, flower growing, and commercial enterprises were eager to drive the Japanese out of the community. Law enforcement officials often feigned ignorance or expressed inability to cope with threats and assaults on the Japanese-Americans.

On Sunday, March 8, 1942, the JACL called an emergency meeting of the national council in San Francisco. Two hundred representatives from sixty-five chapters throughout the West Coast states attended to discuss the impact of Executive Order 9066. On the following day the delegates met with Colonel W. F. McGill, provost marshal, Western Defense Command; Tom C. Clark, assistant attorney general, United States Department of Justice, alien coordinator and chairman of the United States Government Committee on Evacuation, Western Defense Command; Richard M. Neustadt, regional director, Federal Social Security Agency; Herbert D. Armstrong, Federal Reserve Bank in San Francisco; W. B. Pollard of the Federal Reserve Bank in Washington, D.C.; Pearce Davis, assistant regional director of the Office of Defense, Health and Welfare; Wallace Howland, assistant to Assistant Attorney General Clark; and W. R. Thomas, San Francisco office of the Office of Price Administration.

At the meeting these government officials announced to the JACL delegates that the evacuation of all persons of Japanese ancestry, citizens and aliens alike, had already been decided upon. The Tolan congressional committee had also recommended the evacuation of all persons of Japanese ancestry.

Stunned by this shocking news, a special committee of eight representatives of the JACL met on March 10 with Assistant Attorney General Clark at the Whitcomb Hotel in San Francisco. Also present were Colonel McGill, Mr. Neustadt, and John J. McCloy, assistant secretary of war. At this meeting, solemn assurances were repeatedly given by these government officials that everything possible would be done to minimize personal hardships and property losses, that families would not be separated, that bank deposits would be fully protected, that the evacuees would not be forced into labor gangs, that the prevailing wage rates of the communities to which they would be evacuated would not be disrupted, that communities of Japanese-Americans would be established, and that agricultural operations would be continued and the proceeds from the sale of crops would be properly accounted for to the farmers evacuated.

The government officials were not present to seek approval or disapproval of the JACL to evacuate all persons of Japanese ancestry from the Pacific Coast states. This decision had already been made by the President of the United States and his representatives. Nothing said or done by the delegates could have changed the government decision that all the Japanese must leave the Western Defense Command.

The only issue to be decided at this special emergency session in San Francisco was whether the JACL as an organization, its officers and delegates as well as the other Japanese in communities throughout the West Coast, would evacuate in an orderly fashion or whether the government would be forced to take "drastic measures" at the point of a bayonet.

After the JACL leaders had met with the government officials, they returned to the national council meeting of the JACL and informed the delegates that the government officials had given solemn assurances that the mass evacuation would be effected with a minimum of personal hardships and property losses. The national council thereupon formally approved a motion to cooperate with the government in its policy of evacuating all the Japanese from the Pacific Coast states.

Before adjournment, JACL President Saburo Kido gave a "valedictory" speech before the tear-filled delegates whose sad responsibility it was to carry back to their chapter members the forced decision of the JACL to cooperate with the evacuation. President Kido said in part:

We are going into exile as our duty to our country, because the President and the military commanders of this area have deemed it necessary. We have pledged our full support to President Roosevelt and to the nation. This is a sacred promise which we shall keep as good patriotic citizens.

Ours is the call to quietly uproot ourselves from all that we know and hold dear, and to make our way into a wilderness of which we know not. Ours is not a spectacular front page type of duty to country, but rather a kind of behind the lines service which we have to win. "We also serve" must be our badge of courage in these trying days, for we also serve, each in his own way, this country of which we are so fond. What greater love, what greater testimony of one's loyalty could any one ask than this, leave your homes, your business, and your friends in order that your country may better fight a war?

Let us conquer whatever frontiers may await us with the same fortitude and patience as did our fathers and mothers who contributed more to the development of the West than most of us realize. Let us serve our country in the hardest way possible for us to serve, keeping in mind that we have the same objectives as 130 million other Americans, the ultimate and complete victory of democracy's forces.[7]

The words of the highest and most responsible officials of the federal government were still echoing in the ears of the JACL officials and delegates as they returned to their respective communities. The mass evacuation of the Japanese would be performed with a "minimum of personal hardships and property losses."[8]

HARDSHIPS ARE HEAPED UPON THE EVACUEES

What was considered to be the "minimum of personal hardships" was soon experienced by the Japanese, who were still in a state of shock from the experience of being uprooted from their homes, businesses, and farms. While tar-paper barracks were being constructed at the ten concentration camps, the evacuees were pushed, with unseeming haste on the part of the army, into race tracks, fairgrounds, or hastily constructed camps such as Santa Anita and Tanforan Race Tracks, Pomona County Fair Grounds, or Camp Walerga, near Sacramento. Tens of thousands of men, women, and children then went on to live for months on the cold, damp, concrete floors of horse stalls. The stalls, which formerly housed race horses, reeked of the overpowering odors of horse dung, urine, and sweat. The walls were still caked with the dirt and grime of the countless animals that had previously occupied these premises.

The assurance that there would be a "minimum of property losses" became an empty promise. Eventually, the losses reached monumental proportions, conservatively estimated at $400 million due to inaction, indifference, incompetence, and inadequate safeguards on the part of the responsible federal and army authorities. Dillon Myer, director of the War Relocation Authority, the agency to which the federal government transferred responsibility for the real and personal property of the Japanese in August 1942, wrote in his book *Uprooted Americans* that "evacuation incurred property problems had become snarled and material losses had already reached disturbing proportions."[9]

Myer noted several factors that contributed to the property problems inherited by the WRA:

1. The West Coast military authorities delayed in providing property protection, although an order from Assistant Secretary of War McCloy (on February 20, 1942, the day after evacuation was authorized)[10] had made such protection a definite responsibility of the Western Defense Command.

2. Property protection measures were inadequate to counteract initial losses or halt those that mounted throughout the period of exile.

3. Confusion was caused by the division of responsibility that existed in the initial stages among the Federal Reserve Bank of San Francisco, the Office of Alien Property Custodian, and the Farm Security Administration. Each agency had differing policies, and none of them was strong enough to prevent initial hardship to the evacuees.

4. Wartime hate, prejudice, and greed created indifference on the part of many West Coast law enforcement authorities toward investigating and prosecuting instances of destruction and pilferage of evacuees' property.

In his final report, Western Defense Commander General DeWitt explained the delay that occurred in carrying out this responsibility:

> . . . prior to March 10, the General Staff . . . had not engaged in any extensive planning or preparation for the [evacuation] program. The tactical duties imposed upon it were such that it was unable to do so and at the same time meet the responsibilities imposed on the Headquarters by the essentially military aspects of its missions.[11]

The statement of General DeWitt, while technically true before March 10, was not true after March 15, 1942. General DeWitt had, after that date, delegated authority to the Farm Security Administration "to institute and administer a program which will insure continuation of the proper use of agricultural lands voluntarily evacuated by enemy aliens and others designated by me, and which will insure fair and equitable arrangements between the evacuees and the operators of their property." Unfortunately, there was a further delay of several weeks before this delegation of authority actually became effective.

In addition, the United States Treasury Department had been given the authority by Executive Order 9102 "to assist persons removed . . . in the management of their property." The secretary of the treasury in turn delegated this authority to the Federal Reserve Bank of San Francisco, which was to be responsible for protection of urban evacuee properties.

However, both the Federal Reserve Bank of San Francisco and the Farm Security Administration, instead of taking direct responsibility to safeguard evacuee properties, "encouraged" evacuees to make their own arrangements for disposition of their property wherever possible. Both federal agencies stressed rapid liquidation of assets, stating that there were no facilities for storage of movable properties or arrangements for the disposition of automobiles during evacuation. At first the army prohibited evacuees from taking their automobiles even to the temporary assembly centers. If an evacuee did not dispose of his vehicle privately, he could sell it to the army or store it with the Federal Reserve Bank, at his risk and without insurance, in open spaces. Obviously, the cars would suffer rapid deterioration. By late fall of 1942, according to a Federal Reserve Bank report, all but 117 of the 2,000 cars thus stored had been "sold" to the bank. Then, the Federal Reserve Bank report stated, the army, "in consideration of the national interest during wartime, and in the interests of the evacuees themselves [!], decided to requisition these [117] vehicles."[12]

In April 1942, while the evacuation was moving relentlessly forward, the military authorities instructed the Federal Reserve Bank of San Francisco "to provide warehouse facilities in a manner which would not exhaust or burden facilities of that character already in existence," and to make every effort "to keep the number of warehouses at a minimum to limit guarding costs."

The bank accounts of evacuees fell victim to the manipulations of unscrupulous creditors. Such accounts were eagerly attached by them. Although the Federal Reserve Bank of San Francisco issued a special regulation on March 18, 1942 that any evacuee who felt he was in danger of being victimized could apply to the bank to have his account "frozen," the freezing order was used by the bank on only one occasion.[13]

The Farm Security Administration, charged with the responsibility of safeguarding evacuee farm crops and to account to the evacuees for any proceeds the agency received, did little or nothing with the result that farmers received almost no compensation for their produce.[14]

The physical properties of evacuees, which were stored in such places as vacant stores, churches, houses, garages, outbuildings, or barns, were frequently lost by fire, theft, or vandalism. Complaints by evacuees or the WRA were customarily ignored by local law enforcement agencies.

Mortgages on homes, buildings, lands, and farms as well as leases and other equitable interests in land were permanently lost. Dillon Myer stated in his report, "The loss of hundreds of property leases and the disappearance of a number of equities in land and buildings which had been built up over the major portion of a lifetime were among the most regrettable and least justifiable of all the many costs of the wartime evacuation."

Serious questions arise as to the good faith of the army and other federal government representatives relative to the assurances made by them to the JACL regarding a "minimum of personal hardships and losses" to be suffered by the evacuees. A charitable opinion of the entire evacuation program would hold that the disasters suffered by the Japanese were mostly due to administrative delays and confusion arising out of the fact that so many agencies were involved in implementing the evacuation orders. A more realistic view is that they were principally due to the callousness and indifference toward the basic human and property rights of the evacuees by the officers and local law enforcement agencies involved.

Regardless, the solemn assurances the federal officials made to the JACL proved to be mockery. These were the same assurances that the JACL officers and representatives had passed on to the Japanese community prior to the evacuation. As a direct result of the federal government's failure to live up to its commitments, an almost irretrievable loss of credibility was suffered by the JACL. Once in concentration camps, a good many of the evacuees blamed the organization for their plight.

Yet, in spite of being bitterly maligned by many fellow evacuees, the JACL members clung to their hopes that the inherent spirit of justice would manifest itself. Additional methods were considered by the JACL to seek recognition from the government of the irreproachable loyalty on the part of the Japanese-Americans.

NISEI ACCEPTED INTO THE ARMED FORCES

Over the Thanksgiving weekend of November 1942, two delegates from each of the ten concentration camps had been allowed to attend a special emergency national council meeting at the temporary headquarters of the organization in Salt Lake City, Utah. These delegates approved a resolution urging the federal government to accept Nisei into military service in order to establish their loyalty to the United States. Fearful citizens, various service organizations, the press, and military leaders such as General DeWitt and Colonel Bendetsen had loudly proclaimed that Nisei soldiers could not be trusted and that they would use radio transmitters, pistols, rifles, machine guns, and code signals to cause insidious uprisings among persons of Japanese ancestry against the United States.

In January 1943, to implement this resolution, three young Nisei members of the JACL obtained special approval to leave their camps to make a special trip to the White House. Their mission was to try to convince President Roosevelt that they belonged in the uniform of the United States Army. They were volunteering to fight for the United States against the common enemy. They wanted to discuss with Roosevelt their right as citizens to enter the army and to prove their loyalty to the United States.

They did not meet the President but did discuss their right to serve in the army with Secretary of War Henry L. Stimson and Assistant Secretary of War John J. McCloy, both of whom had previously recommended to President Roosevelt the signing of Executive Order 9066. The JACL delegates from the camps declared that the Nisei were ready to fight for the United States, but some of them did not want a racially segregated unit of Japanese-Americans. They felt instead that the Nisei soldiers should be dispersed throughout the army into whatever branch of service they might be assigned.

These three camp delegates felt differently, and they urged upon Stimson and McCloy that such dispersal would mean a complete loss of identity as citizens of Japanese ancestry. They argued that a segregated, all-Nisei outfit offered the best method to prove their loyalty to the public. The sincerity of the delegates and the uniqueness of a segregated Nisei unit apparently convinced Stimson and McCloy of the efficacy of the project. On January 28, 1943 Stimson announced plans to organize a Japanese-American combat team composed of Nisei volunteers from the mainland and from Hawaii. Stimson said, "It is the inherent right of every faithful citizen, regardless of ancestry, to bear arms in the Nation's battle."

On February 1, 1943 President Roosevelt wrote to Secretary Stimson as follows:

> The proposal of the War Department to organize a combat team consisting of loyal American citizens of Japanese descent has my full approval. The new combat team will add to the nearly 5,000 loyal Americans of Japanese ancestry who are already serving in the armed forces of our country.
>
> No loyal citizen of the United States should be denied the democratic right to exercise the responsibilities of his citizenship, regardless of ancestry. The principle on which this country was founded and which it has always been governed is that Americanism is not, and never was, a matter of race or ancestry. [15]

While General DeWitt still clung stubbornly to his fears, the three most powerful men in the United States government, Roosevelt, Stimson, and McCloy, completely reversed themselves and affirmed their faith in the loyalty of Japanese-Americans. The announcement by the War Department on February 1, 1943 regarding the establishment of such a segregated unit was declared by Dillon Myer to be "the most significant date of the last 10 months for persons of Japanese ancestry."[16] The War Department, after February 1, 1943, accepted only volunteers when it activated the 442nd Regimental Combat Team. But other Nisei found that, whether in the uniform of the United States Army or still waiting for the draft call in the camps, a cloud of suspicion of disloyalty continued to hover over them. It would not be until two years later, on January 21, 1944, that the Selective Service process of induction for Nisei would return to the same basis as it was for all other Americans.[17]

Dissension in the Camps Over Enlistment

It should be noted here that the decision of the JACL to urge the United States government to accept Nisei for enlistment in the armed forces was not entirely supported by other Nisei and Issei in the concentration camps. The Issei had seen their life earnings and properties swept away in the haste and confusion of the evacuation. Ineligible by law to become American citizens, the Issei were now all branded as "alien enemies." With no reliable news available to them, some of the Issei were susceptible to wild and exaggerated reports of the military successes of Japan. Having lost everything, some Issei even dreamed of being "rescued" by the Japanese government. Thus, any action by their Nisei progeny to join the United States Army did not meet with their approval.

Some Nisei in the camps opposed the JACL position regarding voluntary enlistment while they were still classified as 4-C (enemy aliens). They naturally resented this undeserved category. Other Nisei felt that the JACL should have urged the War Department to first reclassify all eligible Nisei still in camps as 1-A so as to be on an equal basis with other American citizens. A few, grievously disillusioned by the treatment of the United States government in stripping them of their human and constitutional rights as Americans, felt that the government should solve the resettlement problem before asking them to volunteer for military service. They were vociferous in this demand.

Angry, frustrated, confused, and disillusioned, many of the Japanese in the camps considered officers and members of the JACL as "traitors" to their people. Leaders of the JACL were made the scapegoats for the pitiful plight of the evacuees in general. Members of the JACL were physically attacked by dissident residents and sometimes threatened with death.

Saburo Kido, national president of the JACL, had presided over the momentous special emergency national council meeting at Salt Lake City in November 1942. Upon his return to Poston, a camp in Arizona to which he and his family had been evacuated, he was attacked by a group of angry residents for his endorsement of the enlistment program. Kido, a prominent attorney in the San Francisco Bay area, had been elected president in 1940 and was to serve for six years, an unprecedented three terms, covering the hectic days of the evacuation and the years to the end of World War II.

Kido's conviction that the American people and the American government would some day realize the terrible mistake they had made in accusing Japanese-Americans was to sustain him throughout the darkest days of the JACL. When this noble man was asked to sign a complaint for aggravated assault and battery against his assailants, he declined, stating from his hospital bed, "I understand their feelings and I forgive them all. The attackers do not know what they are doing. I am willing to sacrifice myself for my belief in American fair play, and for the right decisions made by the JACL."

Even while the Nisei G.I.s were preparing to fight in the trenches of Europe and in the foxholes of the Pacific, General DeWitt told the House Naval Affairs Subcommittee in San Francisco on April 13, 1943:

> There is developing a sentiment on the part of certain individuals to get the Japanese back to the Coast. I am opposing it with every means at my disposal. . . . A Jap's a Jap. They are a dangerous element, whether loyal or not. There is no way to determine their loyalty. . . . It makes no difference whether he is an American! Theoretically he is still a Japanese, and you can't change him. . . . You can't change him by giving him a piece of paper. [18]

It is ironic to note that while the War Department was accepting volunteers for the 442nd from the ten concentration camps, other eligible males of Japanese ancestry in these same camps, previously classified 1-A (eligible for immediate induction) were reclassified to 4-F (ineligible for induction) and still later reclassified to 4-C (enemy alien) by local draft boards. In addition, several months before Pearl Harbor, thousands of Nisei had been inducted into the United States Army. Most of these Nisei inductees had completed their basic training in various army camps. However, after Pearl Harbor hundreds of Nisei soldiers were summarily discharged from active military duty and sent to join their families in the concentration camps. Other Nisei soldiers were ordered to report to army camps in the interior of the United

States for assignment to noncombatant duties. These camps included Fort Riley, Kansas (cavalry), Fort Sheridan, Illinois (inductee processing), and Camp Grant, Illinois (quartermaster corps).

One Nisei soldier, an engineering major at UCLA, had been inducted into the army in November 1941 and had just completed his basic engineering training at Fort Leonard Wood, Missouri. After Pearl Harbor, when his outfit was ordered to Alaska to engage the enemy in the Kiska campaign, he was ordered to report to Fort Brady, Michigan, a military installation guarding the locks of the Sault Sainte Marie Canals. Although he was stationed with a military police unit at Fort Brady, he was issued no weapons, not even a sidearm. He complained bitterly to his parents and brother, who were at Manzanar, that if there was an attack by an enemy upon the locks, he could not defend the waterways except with his bare hands. He was later transferred to Camp Grant, Illinois for quartermaster duties. Yet, the War Department as early as June of 1942 sent G.I.s of the 100th Battalion from Hawaii to the mainland United States for combat training.

The 442nd Is Formed and Serves Heroically in Europe

Immediately after the Japanese attack on Pearl Harbor, the Hawaiian Territorial Guard was reactivated as the 100th Provisional Infantry Battalion. Six months later, on June 4, 1942, the army transport *Maui*, under convoy, steamed out of Hawaii carrying 1,432 men of the 100th Battalion for combat training on the mainland. As the vessel neared the Pacific Coast, navy blimps escorted the convoy into San Francisco Bay until the *Maui* docked at Oakland. The men went aboard three troop trains. Each train took a different route toward its destination, Camp McCoy, Wisconsin, a maneuvering area for the Wisconsin National Guard. On December 31, 1942 the 100th Battalion was ordered to Camp Shelby, Mississippi for further combat training. Within weeks, other soldiers, all volunteers, joined the 100th Battalion to become the cadre for the 442nd Regimental Combat Team, which had been activated on February 1, 1943.[19] Other units of the 442nd included the 522nd Field Artillery and the 232nd Engineers.

The 442nd was involved in long and arduous basic training for combat duty. It was bitterly cold at night in bivouac and bone-meltingly hot and humid during the day. The men not only had to contend with the Mississippi mud but also the snakes that slithered into their tents during warmer weather.

The 100th Battalion, now strengthened by an additional 2,686 newly enlisted men from Hawaii and 3,500 additional volunteers, formed the 442nd Regimental Combat Team. Except for high-ranking officers, the 442nd was totally composed of United States citizens of Japanese ancestry—men who were "alien enemies" according to Presidential Proclamation 2525 and Executive Order 9066. The 3,500 volunteers had all been recruited by the United States Army from the ten concentration camps in which they had previously been incarcerated.

During World War II, the 442nd Regimental Combat Team became famous as the most decorated unit of its size and length of service in American military history. The unit's motto was "Go for Broke," which in Hawaiian crapshooters' terms meant "shoot the works," or "all or nothing."

The final record of the 442nd at the end of World War II showed seven major campaigns in Europe, seven Presidential Unit Citations, 9,486 casualties, and 18,143 individual decorations, including:

Congressional Medal of Honor	1
Distinguished Service Crosses	52
Distinguished Service Medal	1
Silver Stars	560
Oak Leaf in lieu of second Silver Star	28
Legion of Merit Medals	22
Bronze Stars	4,000
Oak Leaf Clusters representing second Bronze Stars	1,200
Soldier's Medals	15
French Croix de Guerre	12
Palms representing second Croix de Guerre	2
Italian Crosses for Military Valor	2
Italian Medals for Military Valor	2[20]

No soldier assigned to the 442nd ever deserted the ranks, a record unmatched by any other American military outfit.

This distinguished unit took part in the invasion of Sicily, crossed into Italy, and forded the Rapido River while sustaining heavy casualties. The 442nd fought its way north past sharp and bitter resistance from the entrenched German army to assist in the capture of Rome. For outstanding accomplishment in combat in the vicinity of Serravezza, Carrara, and Fosdinovo, Italy, the 442nd was cited for special commendation by General Dwight D. Eisenhower, Chief of Staff.

On September 27, 1944 the battle-hardened but weary 442nd was ordered to Marseilles, France to fight near the area of Bastogne, where General Anthony McAuliffe had earlier said "nuts" to the German demand to surrender. Some 300 Texans of the 36th Division had been surrounded for a week in the Vosges Mountains and were in danger of total annihilation by a superior German force. On October 27, 1944, the 442nd threw itself into an all-out attack. It took the "Go for Broke" outfit only thirty-five minutes to smash the Nazi stronghold that had defied other Allied forces for five weeks.[21] It suffered 60 percent casualties—a greater number of dead and wounded than the 300 Texans it saved.

The 442nd, now famous throughout the European Theatre for extraordinary heroism and gallantry, was chosen to march up Constitution Avenue in Washington, D.C. on July 15, 1946, there to pass in review before President Harry S Truman and other notables.[22]

Nisei Also Serve Courageously in the Pacific

Other Nisei from both the Hawaiian Islands and continental United States served with courage and steadfastness in the Pacific Theatre alongside their fellow Americans. They served with gallantry as infantrymen in swampy, insect-infested jungles of the Pacific islands. They served with dedicated diligence in combat intelligence duties and as field interpreters and translators in interrogating Japanese prisoners of war. They crawled on their stomachs behind enemy lines into the midst of Japanese troops in order to confuse the enemy with misleading orders in the Japanese language. Their capture by the Japanese enemy would have meant indescribable death by torture. General Charles Willoughby, Chief of Staff for Intelligence to General Douglas MacArthur, stated after the war was over that these Nisei troops had shortened the Pacific Theatre war by at least two years and saved hundreds of thousands of American casualties.

Heroic, though unsung, deeds were performed by Nisei soldiers under General Joseph Stilwell in the China, Burma, and India Theatre of Operations. Stilwell said in tribute to them, "The Nisei bought an awful big hunk of America with their blood."

The special detachment in Burma under General Frank Merrill, known as Merrill's Marauders, included a number of courageous Nisei G.I.s. Nisei language specialists were assigned to navy and marine units throughout the Pacific area including Guam, Saipan, the Philippines, and Okinawa.

These were men who had previously been branded on the home front as being unworthy of trust and were suspected as "potential enemies." The proven valor of the Nisei G.I.s serving in World War II, now beginning to be widely noted in the United States, was perhaps the most important single factor in causing the American public to change its attitude from one of suspicion toward persons of Japanese ancestry to one of complete recognition and acceptance. Their loyalty, tested on the field of battle, could no longer be doubted.

11

Cases Concerning the Evacuation

NOTICE

Headquarters
~~rn~~ Defense Command
~~~~nd Fourth Army

~~~~be at San Francisco California
March 24 1942

Exclusion Order No. 1

Western Defense Command and Fourth Army
Wartime Civil Control Administration

INSTRUCTIONS TO ALL
JAPANESE
Living on Bainbridge Island

The following instructions must be observed

Go to the Civil Control Office at the Anderson Dock Store in Winslow
between 8:00 A.M. and 5:00 P.M. on March 25 1942
to receive further instructions.

As PREVIOUSLY STATED, martial law had been declared in Hawaii at the outbreak of the war but not on the mainland United States. All of the law courts, local, state, and federal, continued to function. The writ of habeas corpus had not been suspended. The guarantees of the Bill of Rights and other provisions of the Constitution protecting the civil liberties of all individuals were presumed; they had not been deemed as suspended by the existence of a state of war. [1]

Although the Western Defense Command had been declared by the War Department to be a military theatre of operations, public elections throughout the nation were not suspended, and none of the prerogatives of the courts or administrative agencies had been set aside. Especially pertinent was the continuance of the fundamental constitutional principle that persons not charged with offenses against the law of war could not be deprived of due process of law, nor could they be denied the benefits of a trial by jury in the absence of a valid declaration of martial law. [2]

The continued functioning of the courts during the evacuation program is illustrated in the case of *Regan* vs. *King*. [3] In June 1942, early in the evacuation period, John T. Regan, grand secretary of the Native Sons of the Golden West, filed a lawsuit against Cameron King, registrar of voters for the City and County of San Francisco in federal district court. Regan alleged that he was a citizen of the United States, a resident of the state of California, and a registered voter in San Francisco. He sued to compel King to strike from the register of voters names of "more than 2,600 Japanese of the full blood, born in the United States, residing in the State of California, of alien parents born in the Empire of Japan." Regan contended that his rights as an elector were impaired by King who permitted "ineligible persons of Japanese ancestry" to be electors of the state of California. King answered that such Japanese persons were entitled to be registered as voters because they were born in the United States and were therefore citizens.

The sole issue before Federal District Judge Adolphus F. St. Sure was whether a person of the Japanese race, born within the United States, was a citizen of the United States. Judge St. Sure noted the leading case of *U.S.* vs. *Wong Kim Ark*, [4] decided in 1898, which had clearly held that any person born in the United States, regardless of racial extraction, was a United States citizen under the provisions of Article 1 of the Fourteenth Amendment to the Constitution and that "all persons born or naturalized in the United States and subject to the jurisdiction thereof, are citizens of the United States and of the State wherein they reside."

Regan's attorney frankly stated in court that he was asking the judge to overrule the case of *U. S.* vs. *Wong Kim Ark* because he believed the decision was erroneous. Judge St. Sure pointed out that the *Wong Kim Ark* decision had been upheld by the Supreme Court of the United States in the later cases of *Morrison* vs. *California*[5] in 1934 and *Perkins* vs. *Elg*[6] in 1939.

In the *Morrison* case Justice Benjamin Cardozo of the Supreme Court stated, "A person of the Japanese race is a citizen of the United States if he was born within the United States." In the *Perkins* case Chief Justice Charles Evans Hughes held that "a child born here of alien parentage becomes a citizen of the United States."

Brushing aside the contentions of Regan's attorney, Judge St. Sure granted King's motion to dismiss the case, with these words, "It is unnecessary to discuss the arguments of counsel. In my opinion, the law is settled by the decisions of the Supreme Court just alluded to." His decision was affirmed on appeal.

In another case, a Japanese seaman, born in Japan and therefore classified as an "alien enemy," was held to have full legal rights to sue in federal district court during World War II in *Ex parte Kumezo Kawato*.[7] In this case Justice Hugo Black stated in part, "The President did not see fit to use his authority to exclude resident aliens from the courts. No existing statutes and proclamations bar the petitioner from the court. On the contrary, there exists clear authorization to resident enemy aliens to proceed in all the courts."

JAPANESE-AMERICANS ARE DENIED BASIC RIGHTS

But within one short year such rights of United States citizens as well as aliens were to be swept away in two cases involving Nisei who were convicted of the criminal charge of having violated a curfew order imposed by General DeWitt throughout the Western Defense Command. These two Nisei, Gordon Kiyoshi Hirabayashi, residing in Seattle, Washington, and Minoru Yasui, residing in Portland, Oregon, had been convicted in separate trials in the federal district courts of their respective residences.

Pursuant to Executive Order 9066, General DeWitt had issued Public Proclamation No. 1, dated March 2, 1942, in which he designated Military Area No. 1, which included, besides the southern part of Arizona, all the coastal regions of the three Pacific Coast states, including the cities of Seattle and Portland. Subsequently, Public Proclamation No. 3, dated March 24, 1942, declared that from March 27, 1942 on, "all alien Japanese, all alien Germans, all alien Italians, and all persons of Japanese ancestry, residing or being within the geographical limits of Military Area No. 1 . . . shall be within their place of residence between the hours of 8:00 p.m. and 6:00 a.m. which period is hereafter referred to as the hours of curfew."[8]

Public Law 503, enacted by Congress on March 21, 1942, had ratified Executive Order 9066. It provided that the violation of any order of any military commander was deemed to be a criminal offense punishable as a misdemeanor by fine or imprisonment or both.

Gordon Kiyoshi Hirabayashi, who is presently married to a Canadian citizen and is a professor of sociology at the University of Alberta in Edmonton, Canada, was born in Seattle in 1918. His parents had come from Japan to the United States and had never returned. Hirabayashi himself had never been to Japan nor had any connection or association with the Japanese in Japan. He attended the public schools in Seattle. At the time of his arrest, he was a senior at the University of Washington.

The evidence presented at a jury trial showed that Hirabayashi had failed to report to the Civil Control Station on May 11 or May 12, 1942, as directed, to register for evacuation from a military area. Hirabayashi admitted his failure to report, contending that it was his belief that he would be waiving his rights as an American citizen by so reporting. He was charged on a second count of being away from his place of residence after 8:00 P.M. on May 9, 1942. He also admitted the truth of this charge. The jury returned a verdict of guilty on both counts. He was sentenced to imprisonment for a term of three months on each count, the sentences to run concurrently.

Minoru Yasui, formerly a prominent practicing attorney in Denver, Colorado and now the director of the Denver Commission on Community Relations, was born in Oregon in 1916 of parents born in Japan. He entered the public schools in Oregon and also went to a Japanese language school for about three years. He later attended the University of Oregon from which he received both his A.B. and L.L.B. degrees. He was a member of the Bar of Oregon and a second lieutenant in the United States Army Infantry Reserve. He had been employed by the Japanese Consulate's Office in Chicago before the war, but he had resigned his position with the consulate as of December 8, 1941, the day after Pearl Harbor.

Yasui then took it upon himself to test the constitutionality of the curfew order then in effect. He discussed this intention with an agent of the FBI before voluntarily violating the order. After violating it, he requested that he be arrested so he could then attempt to obtain a writ of habeas corpus for his release and in this manner bring his case before the courts.

Subsequently, Judge Alger Fee of the federal district court ruled that the congressional act of March 21, 1942, then in effect as Public Law 503, was unconstitutional as it applied to American citizens. However, he held that in the case of Minoru Yasui, Public Law 503 was constitutional as defendant Yasui had renounced his citizenship "by reason of his course of conduct"—that is, by his having been an employee of the Japanese consul in Chicago. This in spite of the fact that Yasui had testified that at no time had he renounced his citizenship. Judge Fee sentenced defendant Yasui to one year's imprisonment—the maximum permitted by law for the violation.[9]

The Supreme Court later vacated the judgment and remanded the case for resentence and also ordered the court to strike its findings as to Yasui's alleged loss of United States citizenship.

Both of these cases, *Hirabayashi* vs. *U.S.*[10] and *Yasui* vs. *U.S.*,[11] were taken to the Court of Appeals for the Ninth Circuit and ultimately certified for review by the Supreme Court of the United States as companion cases since the cases involved the same constitutional issues. As discussed by Chief Justice Harlan Fiske Stone, who delivered the unanimous opinion of the Supreme Court, the issues before the Court were:

1. Whether the particular restrictions violated, namely that all persons of Japanese ancestry residing in such an area be within their place of residence between the hours of 8:00 P.M. and 6:00 A.M., were adopted by the military commander in the exercise of an unconstitutional delegation by Congress of its legislative power.

2. Whether the restrictions unconstitutionally discriminated between citizens of Japanese ancestry and those of other ancestries in violation of the Fifth Amendment.

With reference to the first issue, the Supreme Court denied that the curfew order of General DeWitt was an unconstitutional delegation by Congress of its legislative power. The logic of the Court was as follows:

1. Congress, by the act of March 21, 1942 (Public Law 503), provided criminal penalties for violation of orders of the military commander. Congress, by enacting Public Law 503, in effect ratified and confirmed the President's Executive Order 9066.

2. Congress, through Public Law 503, thus authorized the implementation of Executive Order 9066 on the part of the commanding officer in declaring the curfew order.

3. Since Congress and the President acted in cooperation with regard to any and all orders of the commanding officer, Congress and the executive both had constitutional authority to impose the curfew through the military authorities.

4. Since it was within the constitutional power of the Congress and the executive to prescribe the curfew order, said curfew order of General DeWitt was not an unlawful delegation of legislative power.

As to the second issue, the Supreme Court reasoned as follows:

1. The imposition of the curfew order was an emergency war measure. The war power of the national government is "the power to wage war successfully." This war power extends to every matter and activity so related to war as to substantially affect its conduct and progress.

2. The Constitution placed the responsibility for war-making upon the executive branch of the government, and the executive could delegate this responsibility to the military commander.

3. The military authorities determined that because of "attachments" of persons of Japanese ancestry to the Japanese enemy, including United States citizens of Japanese ancestry, these persons, as a group, having ethnic affiliation with an invading enemy, could be a greater source of danger than those of a different ancestry.

4. Distinctions between citizens because of their ancestry were by their very nature odious to a free people whose institutions were founded upon the doctrine of equality. Legislative classifications or discrimination based on race alone has often been held to be a denial of equal protection.

5. However, danger of espionage and sabotage in time of war and of threatened invasion calls upon the military authorities to scrutinize every relevant fact bearing on the loyalty of populations in the danger areas.

6. For the successful prosecution of the war, citizens of one ancestry may be placed in a different category from others.

7. The fact that attack on our shores was threatened by Japan rather than another enemy power set these citizens apart from others who had no particular associations with Japan.

8. The military commander, acting with the authorization of Congress and the executive, had constitutional power to appraise the danger in the light of facts of public notoriety. His appraisal of facts in the light of the authorized standard and the inferences that he drew from these facts involved the exercise of his informed judgment.

9. These facts, and the inferences that could be rationally drawn from them, supported the judgment of the military commander that danger of espionage and sabotage to our military resources was imminent and that the curfew order was an appropriate measure to meet it, based on "military necessity."

10. Since the findings of the military commander were adequately supported by basic facts in the light of knowledge then available, the curfew order was an appropriate means of minimizing the danger.

11. The Court therefore could not sit in review upon the wisdom of the military action or substitute the Court's judgment for the judgment of the military commander.

The purportedly rational and informed judgment of the military commander, solemnly noted as the truth by the Supreme Court and duly referred to in the decisions by Chief Justice Stone were the unknown behavior of persons of Japanese ancestry; possible espionage by persons of Japanese ancestry, particularly United States citizens; the protection from possible sabotage from Japanese who resided in or near three of the largest cities, Seattle, Portland, and Los Angeles, all three of which were within Military Area No. 1; the "solidarity" and "lack of assimilation," which precluded them from becoming an integral part of the majority population; the attendance of grammar-school children in the Japanese-language schools; the large number of dual citizens; and the difficulty in ascertaining and screening out by administrative hearings of suspected persons from the loyal, due to the compelling concern of national security.

Historically there was no threat of invasion of the Pacific Coast by the Japanese enemy during the entire period of the curfew and of the evacuation program—a fact well known to all responsible military authorities. It was, or should have been, known to General DeWitt. A substantial part of the Imperial Japanese Navy was sunk or crippled by the United States Navy in the battle of the Coral Sea in May 1942. The following month, at the battle of Midway, the rest of the Japanese

navy was destroyed or so damaged that there could have been no conceivable way for it to plan for, or to attempt, a major operation against
any part of the West Coast.

Thus, by the middle of 1942 it would have been physically impossible for Japan even to attempt an invasion of the United States. Still,
Japanese aliens and citizens alike were kept locked up in concentration
camps for another two years.

As Admiral Harold S. Stark, Chief of Naval Operations, and General Mark Clark of General Headquarters in Washington, D.C. had
emphatically stated several months before the evacuation, the Pacific
Coast states were not even considered to be a battle area and were of
low priority insofar as actual combat preparations were concerned to
repel a possible invasion threat by the Japanese enemy. Japan had
attained some quick victories at Guadalcanal, New Guinea, Guam,
and Wake Island early in December 1941, but by the middle of 1942
the tide of battle was rapidly changing in favor of the United States.

While it is true that everything was possible in wartime regarding
sabotage and espionage by any individual or group of persons conspiring
against the United States, the possibilities of such activities on the part
of the Japanese population were exaggerated to hysterical dimensions
by hostile, selfish interests and supported by the vacillating, irrational
judgments of General DeWitt.

"MILITARY NECESSITY" JUSTIFIED BY THE SUPREME COURT

Eighteen months after the *Hirabayashi* and *Yasui* cases, when commenting on the circumstances of the evacuation involved in *Korematsu
vs. U.S.*, a few of the justices of the Supreme Court were to have second
thoughts regarding the "facts" upon which General DeWitt had based
his judgment in issuing his curfew and exclusion orders. These justices
then declared General DeWitt's findings to have been "an accumula-
tion . . . of misinformation, half-truths, and insinuations that had for
years been directed against the Japanese Americans by people with
racial and economic prejudice—the same people who have been
among the foremost advocates of the evacuation."[12]

But by then permanent damage to the United States constitutional
process had already been done. In 1943 the justices of the Supreme
Court had concurred in converting a wartime folly into a principle of
law: the supremacy of the military judgment over civil judgment and
authority in time of war, even though a war might be being fought
thousands of miles away from the United States and might already be half
won. After 1943 the national policy of the United States government

would be grounded on the legal precedent that whether military intentions be good, wicked, or merely capricious, the actions of the military, if based on "findings" of "military necessity," would be upheld by the United States Supreme Court.

The decision of the Supreme Court in 1943 is appalling in light of the fact that most of its members on the bench before (and after) the *Hirabayashi* and *Yasui* cases had been vigorous champions of the human rights and civil liberties of Communists, common criminals, anarchists, and a host of other persons generally considered anathemas by the American people. For these persons, these same justices had been meticulously careful in defining procedural and substantive due process and had upheld the doctrine of separation of powers between the legislative and executive branches of government.

But the two decisions upheld the constitutionality of the curfew order enforced against a small group of persons just because they were of Japanese ancestry. They also sanctified into law and legal precedent justification of flagrant violations of constitutional rights of innocent individuals whose only crime was that they were racially identifiable. The decisions placed upon these persons the intolerable burden of being held guilty by association based on ethnic affiliation, although living under a constitutional form of government—a government whose basic precept as a democracy is recognized throughout the world.

By December 1944 the United States and the Allied forces were victorious on almost all fronts of World War II. They had inflicted heavy losses upon Japan and Germany; Italy had capitulated many months before. On December 18 the Supreme Court, by a vote of six to three, upheld the constitutionality of the mass evacuation of Japanese in the case of *Korematsu* vs. *U.S.* [13]

The majority opinion in the *Korematsu* case was written by Associate Justice Hugo Black, whose previous commitments in the field of civil rights and the protections of persons in criminal cases had won him high acclaim.

In his decision, Justice Black recited as fact that Korematsu, "an American citizen of Japanese descent, was convicted in a Federal District Court for remaining in San Leandro, California, a 'military area' contrary to Civilian Exclusion Order No. 34, of the Commanding General of the Western Command, United States Army, which order directed that after May 9, 1942, all persons of Japanese ancestry should be excluded from that area. No question is raised as to Petitioner's loyalty to the United States."

Fred Toyosaburo Korematsu was born in Oakland, California in 1919. He graduated from Oakland High School and became a nurseryman. He fell in love with a Caucasian girl and was anxious to remain near her. He was arrested for refusal to comply with the Civilian Exclusion Order No. 34. He was furnished bail awaiting trial but was not allowed his freedom. Instead, he was confined first at the Tanforan Racetrack, then in the county jail to await trial. He was convicted for violating the evacuation order, sentenced to five years probation, and then sent to a concentration camp.[14]

Justice Black and the five other justices, who upheld the evacuation order as being constitutional, refused to recognize the fact that the exclusion order and the order to report to an assembly center (to be later transported by the army to a concentration camp) were all part of one continuous process designed to remove the Japanese from their homes and to place them into one of these camps.

The majority of the Supreme Court also refused to concede that the only place to which Korematsu could have gone, by conforming to the exclusion order, was to a concentration camp. Justice Black evaded this fact in stating that "we cannot say either as a matter of fact or law, that his presence in that center [Tanforan Race Track] would have resulted in his detention in a relocation center." The only issue framed by the *Korematsu* case, said Justice Black, related to Korematsu remaining in the prohibited area in violation of the exclusion order. Black concluded that the order under which the petitioner (Korematsu) was convicted was valid.

For a short time after Executive Order 9066 went into effect on February 19, 1942, the Japanese were permitted to leave their homes "voluntarily" for places outside the Western Defense Command. However, because persons and officials in Utah, Idaho, Nevada, and New Mexico expressed their hostility to Japanese coming into these areas and threatened them with physical violence, the voluntary evacuation plan broke down.

Governors of all the western states opposed the voluntary resettlement of the Japanese in their states, except for Governor Ralph Carr of Colorado. The breakdown of the voluntary resettlement program, previously urged upon the Japanese by the federal government, caused General DeWitt hastily to establish the Wartime Civil Control Administration to place the Japanese temporarily in various assembly centers located at former race tracks, with Colonel Karl R. Bendetsen as director.[15]

On March 18, 1942 the War Relocation Authority was created by Executive Order 9102, and no further "voluntary" resettlement was permitted. After March 21, 1942 all Japanese persons were evacuated directly to one of the ten concentration camps, if the construction had been completed, or to an "assembly center" to await the completion of more camp facilities.

When Korematsu violated General DeWitt's Civilian Exclusion Order No. 34, he thereby created an extremely complicated legal and custodial situation between the federal courts and the army authorities. His violation of DeWitt's order caused Korematsu to be arrested and charged with violation of Public Law 503, a statute that was the "teeth" of the army's order.

After his arrest, Korematsu was allowed bail by the court. At this point, he should have been able to walk out of the courthouse a free man until the day of his trial. But the army seized him and kept him in custody. Being free on bail and at large would have been a violation of DeWitt's Order No. 34.

Korematsu was eventually convicted of having violated Public Law 503. At this point the court suspended his sentence and placed him on probation for five years. Again, Korematsu should have been free to walk out of the courthouse, but once again the army seized him and eventually sent him to a concentration camp. His being at large on probation would have still been in violation of General DeWitt's Order No. 34. After all, Korematsu was of Japanese descent.

The Supreme Court stated:

> To cast this case into outlines of racial prejudice, without reference to the real military dangers which were present, merely confuses the issue. Korematsu was not excluded from the Military Area because of hostility to him or his race. He was excluded because we are at war with the Japanese Empire, because the properly constituted military authorities feared an invasion of our West Coast and felt constrained to take proper security measures, because they decided that the military urgency of the situation demanded that all citizens of Japanese ancestry be segregated from the West Coast temporarily, and finally, because Congress, reposing its confidence at this time of war in our military leaders, as inevitably it must, determined that they should have the power to do just this.

Again the Court stated as it had stated in the *Hirabayashi* and *Yasui* cases, "Disloyal members of that [Japanese] population could not be readily isolated and separately dealt with which therefore required 'the temporary exclusion of the entire group' most of whom we have no doubt were loyal to this country."

Justice Black concluded as follows: "The judgment that exclusion of the whole group was for the same reason a military imperative answers the contention that the exclusion was in the nature of group punishment based on antagonism to those of Japanese origin. . . . We uphold the exclusion order as of the time it was made and when the petitioner violated it."

Three of the nine justices dissented in the *Korematsu* case: Justice Owen Roberts, Justice Frank Murphy, and Justice Robert H. Jackson. The one person on the Supreme Court who would have been expected to vote to uphold the validity of the evacuation of Korematsu was Justice Roberts.

Justice Roberts had been the chairman of the commission to investigate the attack on Pearl Harbor. The release of his report to the public in January 1942 had contained unproven allegations of fifth column activities by Japanese-Americans in Hawaii—allegations that had caused hysterical reactions on the West Coast against the Japanese. The Roberts report of January 25, 1942 concluded that there had been widespread espionage in Hawaii by persons of Japanese ancestry. The evacuation order had been, in part, based on the conclusions of Justice Roberts' report.

Therefore, it would seem to follow that Justice Roberts would have insisted that the evacuation order as it applied to Korematsu be upheld rather than to have had him released. Otherwise, such a person as Korematsu would have been at large to commit such acts as the Roberts report had alleged had been committed by the Japanese in Hawaii. Now, in contradiction of his own stated opinion in his report, Roberts voted with the minority of the Court to invalidate the exclusion order.

In his dissenting opinion, Justice Roberts flatly stated that "an assembly center was a euphemism for a prison," and that the exclusion order was "but a part of an over-all plan for forceable detention." Justice Roberts described the predicament of Korematsu as follows:

He was forbidden by Military Orders to leave the zone in which he lived; he was forbidden by Military Orders, after a date fixed [that is, May 9, 1942] to be found within that zone unless he were in an assembly center located in that zone.

The two conflicting orders, one which commanded him to stay, and the other which commanded him to go, were nothing but a cleverly devised trap to accomplish the real purpose of the military authority, which was to lock him up in a concentration camp. The only course by which the petitioner could avoid arrest and prosecution was to go to that camp according to instructions to be given him when he reported at a civil control center. We know that is a fact. Why should we set up a figmentary and artificial situation instead of addressing ourselves to the actualities of the case?

It is a case of convicting a citizen as a punishment for not submitting to imprisonment in a concentration camp, based on his ancestry, and solely because of his ancestry, without evidence or inquiry concerning his loyalty and good disposition towards the United States. . . . I need hardly labor the conclusion that constitutional rights have been violated. . . . I would reverse the judgment of conviction.

Justice Murphy stated:

I dissent, from this legalization of racism. Racial discrimination in any form and in any degree has no justifiable part whatever in our democratic way of life. It is unattractive in any setting but it is utterly revolting among a free people who have embraced the principles set forth in the Constitution of the United States. All residents of this nation are kin in some way by blood or culture to a foreign land. Yet they are primarily and necessarily a part of the new and distinct civilization of the United States. They must accordingly be treated at all times as the heirs of the American experiment and as entitled to all the rights and freedoms guaranteed by the Constitution.

The majority view of the *Korematsu* case remains to this day in the law books of the Supreme Court of the United States. Because of the *Korematsu* decision, the power of the military over the inhabitants of this nation is unlimited when exercised during a declared national emergency, even when no martial law has been declared. All the military has to do is to declare a "military necessity." The *Korematsu* case has affirmed that the Supreme Court will not review judgment on findings of the military. It was cited as the legal authority underpinning Title II of the Internal Security Act of 1950.[16]

DETENTION DECLARED UNCONSTITUTIONAL

Although the Supreme Court upheld the constitutionality of the evacuation order in the *Korematsu* case by a vote of six to three, the same Court, on the same day (December 18, 1944), unanimously declared the detention of persons of Japanese ancestry to be invalid in the case of *Ex parte Mitsuye Endo*,[17] which involved a Japanese-American girl born in the United States. The Supreme Court ordered her "unconditional release" by the War Relocation Authority.

To understand the impact of the *Endo* case, a brief review of the leave-clearance procedure, used to allow a detainee to leave a camp, is necessary. After all the Japanese had been removed from the West Coast and placed in concentration camps, the WRA attempted a selective sorting process of the evacuees who wished to leave these camps to be resettled in "nonstrategic" areas.

Reports of various investigative agencies of the federal government such as the FBI, Army Intelligence, Naval Intelligence, and the Provost Marshal General's office were utilized to conduct a record check of all applicants for leave clearance. Persons who appeared to have pro-Japanese sympathies were not allowed to leave but were instead transferred to the Tule Lake Camp near the Oregon-California border.[18]

All others considered "loyal" to the United States were cleared to leave the camps, but only if certain conditions had first been met to the satisfaction of the camp authorities. The applicants were required to have a definite job to which they could go, a home in which to live, and a friendly community to which they could be sent. Students whose high school, college, or professional education had been interrupted could also leave the camps if satisfactory conditions for their continuing education were also met. Other persons were permitted to leave the camps after clearance for temporary or seasonal work on farms, particularly in the sugar beet areas of eastern Oregon and Idaho. Details of the different types of leave clearances are described in *Uprooted Americans, Concentration Camps, USA,* and *America's Concentration Camps*.

These leave procedures were set up by the WRA on the basis of a commendable and understandable concern that such orderly leave procedures would be in the best interest of the Japanese who were in these camps and who wanted to go.

Mitsuye Endo was a United States citizen of Japanese ancestry. She was a California state employee at the time of the outbreak of World War II. Soon after the war, she was dismissed from state civil service under orders of the state personnel board. She had never attended a Japanese-language school and could neither read nor write Japanese. She was not a dual citizen. She had a brother serving in the United States Army. Her family did not even subscribe to a Japanese language newspaper. She had made application for leave clearance on February 19, 1943; it was granted to her on August 16, 1943, but she was not allowed to leave immediately. She had not made application for indefinite leave.

In her petition for a writ of habeas corpus, she alleged that she was a loyal and law-abiding citizen of the United States, that no charge had been made against her, that she was being unlawfully detained, and that she was confined in the relocation center under armed guard and held there against her will.

The Federal Government conceded that the United States Department of Justice and the WRA found her to be a loyal and law-abiding citizen. No claim was made that she was detained on any charge or that she was even suspected of disloyalty. The attorneys for the government further agreed that it was beyond the power of the WRA to detain citizens against whom no charges of disloyalty or subversiveness had been made. What the Government attorneys did insist upon, however, was that detention for an additional period after leave clearance had been granted was an essential step in the total evacuation program. Without such WRA control, there would be a disorderly migration of "unwanted" people to "unprepared communities," which would result in hardship and disorder. It was held necessary for the federal government to maintain control over the evacuated population for their "own peace and well-being" as well as for that of the nation. It was also argued that Executive Order 9102 authorized the WRA to make regulations to control situations created by the exercise of the powers conferred upon the WRA for protection against espionage and sabotage.

The Supreme Court of the United States, however, did not view the alleged humanitarian concern of the WRA in the same light. The Court declared that the act of March 21, 1942, which created the WRA, provided a program to remove the Japanese from their homes but not to detain them.

Justice William O. Douglas declared that "detention in Relocation Centers was no part of the original program of evacuation." He pointed out that the legislative history of the act establishing the WRA and the Executive Order 9066 authorizing the evacuation was silent on the power of the WRA to detain the evacuees. He delineated Executive Order 9066 and Executive Order 9102, and all the public proclamations including the 108 civilian exclusion orders issued by General DeWitt, as being war measures put into effect only to "remove from designated areas . . . persons whose removal is necessary in the interests of national security."

Justice Douglas went on to state that "the authority [of the WRA] to detain a citizen or to grant him a conditional release as protection against espionage or sabotage is exhausted at least when his loyalty is conceded." By this amazing line of reasoning, Douglas concluded that Mitsuye Endo was "entitled to an unconditional release by the War Relocation Authority."

Justice Murphy, who had dissented in the *Korematsu* case, concurred in the *Endo* case, stating:

> . . . detention in Relocation Centers of persons of Japanese ancestry regardless of loyalty is not only unauthorized by Congress or the Executive but is another example of the unconstitutional resort to racism inherent in the entire

evacuation program. Racial discrimination of this nature bears no reasonable relation to military necessity and is utterly foreign to the ideals and traditions of the American people."

Justice Roberts added:

. . . the court is squarely faced with a serious constitutional question, whether the relator's detention violated the guarantees of the Bill of Rights of the Federal Constitution and especially the guarantee of due process of law. There can be but one answer to that question. An admittedly loyal citizen has been deprived of her liberty for a period of years. Under the Constitution she should be free to come and go as she pleases. Instead, her liberty of motion and other innocent activities have been prohibited and conditioned. She should be discharged.

Within forty-eight hours after the *Endo* case had been decided, Major General H.C. Pratt, who had succeeded General DeWitt as the Western Defense Commander, revoked the West Coast mass exclusion orders effective as of January 2, 1945. With the exception of certain individuals, about whom more will be said later, the Japanese-Americans who had been locked up in concentration camps for periods of up to three years were "free" to go home again. But where was home now?

The evacuees' life savings were gone. Their properties had been either abandoned or disposed of under distress conditions. They had been stripped almost naked of their personal belongings. Their situation was close to desperate.

12

The Anti-Japanese Statutes Begin to Crack: Alien Land Laws and the Supreme Court Cases

Good legislation welcomes public notice; only improper and abusive legislation benefits by avoiding public notice.

Protect your pocketbook; protect your right to know about efforts to impose debt on you.

Vote "No" on Proposition 12.

JOHN B. LONG
General Manager California Newspaper Publishers Association

13	**REPEALING ALIEN LAND LAW.** Repeal of Initiative Act, Submitted by Legislature. Repeals inoperative law of 1920 which formerly denied aliens ineligible to citizenship the right to hold real estate in California.	**YES**
		NO

(For Full Text of Measure, See Page 41, Part II)

Analysis by the Legislative Counsel

This measure submits to the voters for approval or rejection an act of the Legislature which would repeal the initiative act adopted in 1920, commonly referred to as the Alien Land Law. Under Article IV, Section 1, of the California Constitution an initiative act adopted by the people cannot be repealed except by a vote of the people, unless otherwise provided in the initiative act, and no provision for repeal is contained in the 1920 initiative act.

The Alien Land Law prohibits the ownership of land or rights in land by aliens ineligible to citizenship under Federal naturalization laws, in the absence of a treaty to the contrary. It imposes similar restrictions upon companies, associations, and corporations, the majority of whose members or stockholders constitute such aliens, and provides for the escheat to the State of land held in violation of that law.

The Alien Land Law was declared invalid by the California Supreme Court in 1952 as a violation of the due process and equal protection clauses of the Fourteenth Amendment to the United States Constitution. (*Sei Fujii* v. *State*, 38 Cal. 2d 718). If the law retained any effect after this decision, it was rendered inoperative by a provision of the Federal Immigration and Nationality Act of 1952 making all races eligible for citizenship. (Sec. 311, Immigration and Nationality Act; 66 U.S. Statutes 239; 8 U.S. Code Annotated 1422.)

The measure would not affect pending court proceedings and provides that funds appropriated to pay claims against the State with respect to property escheated under the Alien Land Law continue to be available to pay judgments in such proceedings.

Argument in Favor of Repeal of Initiative Act

Vote "YES" on Proposition 13!

This Proposition will repeal an inoperative law

—It was declared UNCONSTITUTIONAL by the California Supreme Court in 1952

This Alien Property Initiative Act of 1920 was designed to bar aliens ineligible for citizenship by an Act of Congress passed in 1952. Thus, this 1920 Act is now meaningless and serves no useful purpose.

The Act of 1920 is today and was when enacted flagrantly inconsistent with American democratic principles. The last vestiges of this unfair law should be eliminated from our statute books.

To correct the unjust penalties of the law upon Japanese Americans, the Legislature passed a law in 1951 to make restitution for losses imposed by this now unconstitutional Alien Property Act. Again, in 1953, the Legislature enacted another remedial act to compensate a widow for the inequities caused by this Alien Property Act. The Legislature has done what it could do to relieve the injustices which have resulted.

Now, you can do your part in the final correction of historical inequities by your "YES" vote for this repeal.

This Proposition received the overwhelming vote of the California State Legislature and the signature of the Governor.

A "YES" vote on Proposition 13 is endorsed and supported by many prominent and respected individuals and organizations including: Governor Goodwin J. Knight; Attorney General Edmund G. Brown; the Los Angeles City Council; the Los Angeles County Board of Supervisors; Joseph Scott, attorney; Dore Schary, MGM Studios executive; the State Executive Committee of the Democratic Party; Carl Lindstrom, president, Los Angeles County Republican Assembly; Rollins MacFadyen, member executive committee, Los Angeles County Republican Central Committee; Louis R. Baker, chairman, ways and means committee, The American Legion, Department of California; Veterans of

To THE RETURNING farmers, "home" meant the prewar rural communities where they knew the soil and weather conditions and the familiar farms they had toiled on before the evacuation. They knew the kinds of crops to grow. They planned to borrow some starting capital from their neighborhood banks to purchase seeds and farm supplies. They hoped they could begin to associate themselves again with the various wholesale produce houses in the large cities, to which they would ship their crops.

But during the years of their incarceration, conditions had drastically changed in their old communities. Owners who had formerly rented the land to them were often hostile or would only do business at far above prewar rates. Often, the farming lands had disappeared. Factories, industrial plants, army barracks, or wartime housing developments had gobbled them up.

In some cases, where Japanese farmers were returning to lands they actually owned, they were confronted with threats of physical violence. Attempts were made to dynamite their homes, and they were plagued by vicious strangers who set fire to their homes and toolsheds. Some were subjected to the frightening experience of being shot at from ambush, both during the day and in the dark of night.

Secretary of the Interior Harold Ickes, to whose federal agency the War Relocation Authority had been transferred on February 29, 1944,[1] reported with indignation that by May 14, 1945 there had been twenty-four incidents of terrorism and violence, fifteen shootings, one attempted dynamiting, two arson cases, and five threatening visits made against Japanese farmers.[2]

LEGISLATIVE EFFORTS TO FURTHER RESTRICT LAND USE

The anti-Japanese forces, especially in California, had not been idle. Several years before the war, the California Legislature had passed a further restrictive amendment to the existing Alien Land Law in May 1927. It provided that if United States citizenship was at issue in connection with enforcement of the Alien Land Law, the cost of proving such United States citizenship must be borne by the individual involved.[3]

Another bill was submitted in the California Legislature in February 1935 that would have absolutely prohibited any alien "ineligible for citizenship" from engaging in agriculture under any circumstances.[4] It was aimed directly at the Japanese.

In 1937 a bill was introduced to prevent Japanese aliens from vesting titles to rural property in the names of their native-born children or from acting as "caretaking guardians" of land so acquired. This would have enabled the state to prosecute an individual accused of violating the law without having to resort to charges of conspiracy—charges that were difficult to prove in transactions involving the transfer of title to property to United States citizen children.[5]

Both the 1935 and the 1937 bills failed to pass. From then until the outbreak of World War II, however, no further serious attempts were made to restrict the use of land by Japanese farmers. When the war fever reached its height against persons of Japanese ancestry, nine separate anti-Japanese bills were introduced in the California Legislature in 1943.[6]

Before the evacuation of the Japanese in 1942, action by the California State Attorney General's office and local district attorneys' offices to institute escheat actions under the Alien Land Law was mostly sporadic and ineffective. Author Carey McWilliams has written:

Enforcement of the Alien Land Act of 1920 was vested in local law enforcement officials. When a "white person" in one of these counties wanted to lease land to a Japanese, he usually had no difficulty in doing so. Local district attorneys enforced the act when they wanted to enforce it, and they obligingly ignored evasions of the act when it suited their interests to do so. The act was easily by-passed; title to farm land was placed in the names of Hawaiian or American-born Japanese; verbal agreements were entered into, "gentlemen's agreements" that ran counter to the terms of written documents; Japanese were employed as "managers" instead of as "tenants." By these and other devices, and with the connivance of law enforcement officials, the act was blithely ignored. The amount of land escheated to the state under this statute is wholly negligible.[7]

The nine bills introduced in 1943 were designed to prohibit the ownership of property by alien Japanese and United States citizens of Japanese ancestry (AJR 3), to prohibit Japanese aliens from being guardians of property owned by their minor United States citizen children (SB 18, AB 23, AB 17, AB 374, AB 921, SB 140, and AB 31), and to provide for sale at public auction or private sale of escheated property (AB 493).

Two years later, eight more bills were introduced in the 1945 California Legislature that were designed further to prohibit ownership of property by alien Japanese or any person of Japanese ancestry.[8] Assembly Bill 2130 and Senate Bill 1293 provided that the burden of proving citizenship, eligibility for citizenship, or absence of Japanese ancestry was upon the defendant in an escheat action. Senate Bill 887 called for an appropriation of $100,000 to the attorney general to defray the expenses of enforcing the Alien Land Law. Assembly Bill 1682 and Senate Bill 139 provided for the proceeds from the sale of escheated property to be remitted one-half to the county where the land was situated and one-half to the California School Fund. Senate Bill 415 proposed that there be no statute of limitations to apply to any escheat actions then pending or commenced thereafter.[9]

ESCHEAT ACTIONS SEIZE PROPERTY

In 1945 the California Legislature enacted a measure to appropriate $200,000 to the state justice department to investigate and vigorously enforce the Alien Land Law of 1920 against the Japanese. By late 1946 more than sixty new escheat cases were filed against the Japanese charging them with violations of the Alien Land Law. These escheat actions were filed against both the Nisei and their parents in courts throughout California.

The thrust of these escheat actions was that property held in the name of a Nisei could be seized if it could be proved that it was purchased illegally by his Issei parents. More than twenty escheat actions had already been filed by the California Attorney General's office before 1945; the impetus given by the appropriation of $200,000 produced a total of eighty escheat cases that were in active stages of prosecution between 1944 and 1948.

Earl Warren, then attorney general of California, filed the twenty escheat actions against the Japanese in 1942. Warren explained that it was necessary for him to remove Japanese farmers from the vicinity of important military installations. In his successful campaign for governor of California that year, he called to the attention of the people his vigorous escheat actions against the Japanese.[10]

Robert Kenney succeeded Warren as attorney general in 1942 and was in office when the $200,000 was appropriated. In Kenney's words, he "inherited" these escheat proceedings. Contrary to his predecessor, Kenney was not enthusiastic about initiating actions against the absent Japanese, but he was constantly prodded by a number of persons who stood to profit from the forced sale of Japanese-owned land. By the end of 1945, Kenney's office did file at least forty cases in an attempt to prevent the return of evacuee farmers to the state's agriculture industry.

A review of escheat proceedings instituted by the California Attorney General's office under the Alien Land Law, taken from its own report,[11] showed the following interesting facts: From 1912 to 1946, the Attorney General's office had instituted seventy-six escheat proceedings against aliens "ineligible for naturalization." Of the seventy-six persons charged, seventy-three were Japanese, two were Chinese, and one was Indian (Hindu). No cases were filed against Koreans. The report on its face clearly shows that the Alien Land Law was enforced by the Attorney General's office almost exclusively against Japanese aliens. The intent of the law was clearly to drive the Japanese farmers out of agricultural activities.

One of the first pieces of farmland to be escheated to the State was that of a Mr. and Mrs. Fujita of Fresno County, who had purchased land in the name of their daughter Junko in 1917. Their land was confiscated by the State.

But in the same county, Takumi Sunada, a Nisei veteran of World War II won the right to hold his forty acres of vineyard when the State of California filed a disclaimer to the escheat action. Also in Fresno County, a case involving 320 acres of land owned by William Shiba was dismissed because of lack of evidence. In February 1947 Moto and George Asakawa of San Diego County won clear title to their property when the brothers instituted a suit against the State of California to have their property adjudged free of any escheat claims.

Another piece of farmland to be lost to the State was that of Yeizo Ikeda of Monterey County. Superior Court Judge H. G. Jorgenson ruled on August 28, 1946 that the Alien Land Law had been violated and escheated seventy-two acres to the State.

Meanwhile, several compromise settlements were made by various owners of property who had been accused of having violated the Alien Land Law. On September 16, 1946 Mrs. Fumiko Mitsuichi, a United States citizen, paid $75,000 to the State for seventy-one acres of truck garden land in West Los Angeles; she had originally paid $88,562.50 for the land in 1938. In January 1947 the State accepted settlements to quiet titles in five other pending escheat cases in Fresno County for the aggregate amount of $68,415.

The largest settlements in Fresno County were in two escheat suits in the Selma-Sanger area against Takei and Natsuye Iwamura and their children. The settlement to the State amounted to $29,625 for 100 acres of farmland. In the Reedley-Parlier area, the State compromised its suit against Tamigoro and Chisato Chiamori and their children upon payment by them of $24,502.50 to quiet title to sixty-two acres. Also in the Reedley area, Hanako Ishii Teraoka paid the sum of $10,400 to retain the rights to a forty-acre farm that she had received from her parents Keijiro and Mary Nakashima, and the sum of $3,887.50 was paid to the State to quiet title to land in the name of Fumiko Henel Akahori, daughter of Mitsuo and Umeji Akahori.

Bill Hosokawa, noted Nisei journalist and now associate editor of the *Denver Post*, noted in his book *Nisei: The Quiet Americans*, "Seven pieces of property were escheated and sold for a total of $57,864 and 12 cases were 'compromised' with the defendants settling the action by paying half of the appraised valuation of the land to the State. A total of $231,915 was paid to the State in these actions which amount to no more than blackmail."[12]

Another prominent Nisei journalist, Larry Tajiri, wrote early in 1946, "In 1940, 5,135 farms valued at approximately $66,000,000 were owned by American Japanese in California. With the wartime increases in the value of land and crops, this was a windfall awaiting those who could prove that the deeds were illegal. One of the biggest land grabs in history is on in California. And the Great Golden State, now one of the richest, proudest, and most populous in the nation, is in the uncomfortable position of being the grabber."[13]

However, among the eighty escheat cases either litigated through the years or ended by compromise, there was one in which the defendants refused to accept defeat in the state courts. Instead, they took their case to the United States Supreme Court. The case involved eight acres of farmland in San Diego County.

THE ALIEN LAND LAW IS SUCCESSFULLY CHALLENGED

Kajiro and Kohide Oyama were husband and wife, both born in Japan and therefore not eligible for United States citizenship. Their son Fred Yoshihiro Oyama was born in California in 1928. In 1934, when Fred was six years old, his parents purchased six acres of agricultural land for $4,000 with their own funds. Title to the property was taken in Fred's name and duly recorded. In 1935 the father petitioned to become the guardian of his son's person and estate, which was approved by the Superior Court of San Diego County. The California Supreme Court had already decided twelve years earlier in *Estate of Yano*[14] that parents, notwithstanding the fact that they were ineligible for citizenship, were nevertheless eligible to become legal guardians of the persons and estates of their minor children.

In 1937 two acres of land belonging to June Kushino, a minor, were sold to Fred Oyama for $1,500. The money for these two acres was also furnished by Fred's parents. The two acres were part of the estate of

June Kushino, which was being administered by her father, Ririchi Kushino, a Japanese alien. Title to the two acres was recorded in the name of Fred Y. Oyama, and the land so conveyed was added to his estate. The Superior Court of San Diego County approved the sale and made an order confirming the sale in the matter of the guardianship of June Kushino. After their respective purchases, both the first six acres and the subsequent two acres were cultivated by Mr. and Mrs. Oyama.

As guardian, Oyama made no annual accounting to the superior court as to receipts and expenditures related to his son's eight acres, nor did he file any report with the secretary of state of California regarding such receipts and expenditures, as required by Section 5 of the Alien Land Law of 1920. Notwithstanding, in 1936 and again in 1937, the father, as guardian, sought permission of the superior court to borrow $4,000, payable in six months, to finance the next season's crops. He placed the six acres into a mortgage as security for the loan. In both instances, the loans were approved by the court, and both loans were repaid on maturity.

In 1942 Fred and his family were forced to leave the Pacific Coast along with all other persons of Japanese ancestry. In 1944, when Fred was sixteen years of age and was still forbidden to return to his home, the State of California filed a petition to declare an escheat of the two parcels of property on the ground that the conveyances in 1934 and 1937 were obtained with the intent to violate and to evade the Alien Land Law. Both Fred and his father were named defendants in the escheat action. In 1946 the California Supreme Court, in the case of *People* vs. *Oyama*,[15] upheld the action of the state in escheating the two parcels.

Between the decision of the California Supreme Court in the *Oyama* case, which was handed down on October 31, 1946, and the final ruling by the United States Supreme Court on this same case on January 19, 1948,[16] two events of tremendous importance to the Japanese took place in California.

Proposition 15: The Voters Reject Further Discrimination

An amendment was introduced on May 18, 1945 and approved by the California Legislature, proposing a change in Section 17 of Article I of the Constitution of the State of California. The measure was considered necessary to ratify various amendments passed by the California Legislature to the Alien Land Law of 1920, which had been approved by a vote of the people as an initiative measure in the general elections of 1920. There was now a question in the California Legislature as to whether any subsequent amendments to the Alien Land Law passed by the legislature were valid since there was no provision in the 1920 initiative act empowering the California Legislature to enact amendments to the basic law. Measures approved by the people by initiative could only be amended by another measure put to the vote of the people.

Thus there appeared on the November 5, 1946 ballot, as Proposition 15, a measure entitled "Validation of Legislative Amendments to Alien Land Law." Senator Jack Tenney of Los Angeles County, long known for his anti-Japanese activities and the sponsor of numerous anti-Japanese bills in the California Legislature in 1943 and 1945, together with Senator Hugh M. Burns of Fresno County, who was later to become president pro tempore of the California Senate, stated in part:[17]

This amendment merely validates statutes pursuant to the Alien Land Laws heretofore enacted by the Legislature and now in full force and effect.

Its enactment by the people will close loopholes in legislative enactments based on constitutional grounds.

It is well known that Japanese aliens, in order to conceal true ownership of property, have indulged in all manner of subterfuges. These aliens have resorted to the use of "dummy" corporations, American-born Japanese children and other nefarious schemes and devices that, on the record, conceal the true identity of the owners of property.

Five days after the California Supreme Court handed down the *Oyama* decision, Proposition 15 came before the voters of California in the general election. The campaigns both for and against Proposition 15 were intense, sharp, and emotional. During weeks preceding the election, the Japanese American Citizens League had organized a legislative action group called the Anti-Discrimination Committee. A fund-raising drive was undertaken. Over $100,000 was raised among the Japanese-American communities in California and in other parts of the nation where Japanese-Americans resided.

Speakers were enlisted to discuss the inequities of the Alien Land Law, primarily as the law affected citizens of Japanese ancestry. Prominent leaders from the economic, political, social, and professional areas of the community were solicited for their support. Mike Masaoka, who had been the first mainland Nisei to volunteer for the famous 442nd Regimental Combat Team and who had only recently been honorably discharged from the United States Army, was assigned by the JACL to coordinate the state-wide campaign.

Press reports and brochures were released to newspapers throughout the state describing the contributions of Japanese aliens and citizens to the economic wealth of the state and nation. The loyalty of the alien parents and their citizen children was noted. The injustices of the measure were stressed.

On the night of the election, the returns showed that Proposition 15 had been defeated. The total vote was 797,067 in favor of the measure, 1,143,780 against. The Japanese American Citizens League hailed the results. Mike Masaoka, executive secretary of the JACL Anti-Discrimination Committee, was quoted in the November 9, 1946 issue of the *Pacific Citizen*:

> The election results prove that most Californians feel that Japanese Americans and their Issei parents have earned the right to justice and fair treatment. . . . They provide the first real public opinion poll of California citizens on an issue involving the state's residents of Japanese ancestry since 1920. . . . The lesson of the vote on Proposition 15 is that the war is over and the people of California will not approve discriminatory and prejudiced treatment of persons of Japanese ancestry.

A few days after Proposition 15 was rejected by the people of California, the attorneys for the Oyamas petitioned the California Supreme Court for a rehearing, listing among their arguments the defeat of Proposition 15 at the polls. The petition for rehearing was denied.

Oyama vs. California Reaches the Supreme Court

But the war was indeed over, and in its decision in *Oyama vs. California* the United States Supreme Court further proved that the hostilities were finished.

In approaching the Supreme Court, California Attorney General Kenney relied upon prior decisions of the California Supreme Court and the United States Supreme Court. These decisions included *Mott vs. Cline*,[18] which held that the State has the right to regulate the tenure and disposition of real property within its boundaries; *Webb vs. O'Brien*,[19] which had declared that the State could classify eligibility of ownership of land based on broad principles of national safety and public welfare; *In re Y. Akado*,[20] which held that the State had the power, in the absence of a treaty to the contrary, to forbid aliens to take or hold property within its limits.

The decisions of the Supreme Court of the United States included *Terrace* vs. *Thompson*[21] and *Porterfield* vs. *Webb*,[22] which upheld the power of the State to prohibit ineligible aliens from ownership of land in the absence of a treaty; *Morrison* vs. *California*[23] and *Cockrill* vs. *California*,[24] which had declared Section 9(a) of the Alien Land Law constitutional. Attorney General Kenney insisted that there was a rational basis for discrimination against aliens by racial classification. The distinction between eligible and ineligible aliens had been made by federal statutes, not by the State.

The Oyamas attacked the Alien Land Law of 1920 on several grounds:

1. That the law was unconstitutional because it was enacted for the purpose of, and administered in a manner to, discriminate against persons solely because of race.

2. That as to both alien father and citizen son, the law denied them due process of law as granted by Article I, Section 1 and Article I, Section 13 of the California Constitution, which guaranteed to all men the right to enjoy life, liberty, and property.

3. That as to both alien father and citizen son, the law deprived both of them of property without due process of law and denied them equal protection of the laws.

4. Citizen Fred Oyama further contended that the law violated a mandate of the California Constitution that "no citizen or class of citizens shall be granted privileges or immunities which, upon the same terms, shall not be granted to all citizens." (Article I, Section 21).

5. Fred Oyama also asserted that the law deprived him of privileges and immunities as a citizen, in violation of the Fourteenth Amendment to the United States Constitution.

Section 9(a) was the heart of the anti-Japanese Alien Land Law. It provided in part as follows:

A prima facie presumption that the conveyance is made with such intent [that is, to violate the Alien Land Law] shall arise upon proof of any of the following group of facts:

(a) The taking of the property in the name of a person other than the persons mentioned in Section 2 hereof [that is, United States citizens], if the consideration is paid or agreed or understood to be paid by an alien mentioned in Section 2 hereof [that is, aliens ineligible for citizenship].

The presumption in Section 9(a) operated as follows: If a citizen child has alien parents who are eligible for citizenship, and such eligible aliens furnish the money to purchase land and convey the land to their citizen child, there is a good and valid gift to the child. The gift by a parent to his own child is a normal, usual, and acceptable occurrence. The acceptance of the gift by the citizen child is presumed and protected by the courts because such gift is for the benefit of the child.

However, if the citizen child has alien parents ineligible for citizenship, the gift of land is illegal, invalid, and subject to escheat by the State. No matter when the transaction occurred, even many years before the escheat action, the citizen child had to produce affirmative proof as to the intent of his alien parents.

The citizen child of alien parents ineligible for citizenship faced a formidable burden of proof. The burden was greater on the citizen child whose alien parents were ineligible for citizenship based solely upon the fact that they were Japanese. As a result, the presumption operated unequally on different classes of citizens.

In an escheat action based on the Alien Land Law, the citizen child had not only to establish by the preponderance of evidence the intent of his father, but he also had to establish his intent by enough evidence to overcome both the State's evidence and the State's presumption. There was no way that the intent of the alien father ineligible for citizenship could be satisfactorily proven when the inquiry related to an issue as difficult to prove as "intent to prevent, evade, or avoid" escheat, particularly if the alien father ineligible for citizenship was deceased or not available to testify.

In such a case, the protection of the court could not be invoked to assist the citizen child born of ineligible aliens to presume the acceptance of a gift of land. Instead the court would take away the land of the citizen child on the ground that the gift was given with the "intent to prevent, evade, or avoid" escheat.

In upholding the Alien Land Law, Associate Justice Douglas L. Edmonds of the California Supreme Court stated that the law was enacted to define the right of which class of persons could own land within the state and, concurrently, that the State had the right to regulate the tenure and disposition of real property within its boundaries. The State also had the power, in the absence of a treaty to the contrary, to forbid aliens to take or hold property within its limits. The California Constitution also left to the legislature the power to regulate property rights with regard to all aliens ineligible for citizenship.

"Thus," declared Justice Edmonds, "the cases referred to by the Attorney General do not restrict the authority of the State, under its police power, to limit the right of aliens in regard to real property situated within its borders. It is sufficient if a rational basis is found for the classification."

He stated further, that in considering the Alien Land Law in connection with the "record" then before the court, there was no evidence that the statute was unconstitutionally applied or administered.

Justice Edmonds further declared that the State had established the right to ownership of land on the basis of eligibility for citizenship, a standard that had been determined by the United States Congress and that, therefore, when used by the State of California to determine which persons were to be allowed to own land in the state, did not amount to an unconstitutional delegation of legislative authority. "The clear and unmistakable purpose of the Alien Land Law at all times since it was enacted by the People as a initiative measure has been to place the ownership of real property in this state beyond the reach of an alien ineligible for citizenship."

Justice Edmonds concluded that "the evidence convincingly points to the conclusion that the minor son had no interest in the property, his name being only used as a subterfuge for the purpose of evading the Alien Land Law."

In upholding the constitutionality of the Alien Land Law, Justice Edmonds also overruled the contentions of the Oyamas that their rights, privileges, and immunities, under both the state and federal Constitutions, had been violated.

Section 9(a) Declared Unconstitutional

The *Oyama* case now moved to Washington, D.C., where it was accepted for review by the Supreme Court of the United States. On January 19, 1948, by a six to three decision, the Court reversed the decision of the California Supreme Court. The United States Supreme Court decision literally cut the heart out of the Alien Land Law, the presumption provision of Section 9(a), which was declared by the Supreme Court to violate the equal protection clause of Section 1 of the Fourteenth Amendment to the federal Constitution.

Three main constitutional issues were raised by the Oyamas for review as to the Alien Land Law of 1920:

1. Whether the law deprived Fred Oyama of the equal protection of the laws and of his privileges as an American citizen.

2. Whether the law denied Kajiro Oyama equal protection of the laws.

3. Whether the law contravened the due process clause by sanctioning a taking of property after expiration of the applicable limitations period.

Chief Justice Fred M. Vinson agreed with the Oyamas' first contention, that the Alien Land Law, as applied in this case, deprived Fred of the equal protection of California's laws and of his privileges as an American citizen. He held that the State of California had discriminated against Fred, a discrimination that was based solely on his parents' country of origin. He concluded that the compelling justification that would be needed to sustain discrimination of that nature was absent.

Since the Court agreed with Fred's first contention, he declared that it would not be necessary for the Supreme Court to review nor "reach their contentions; that the Alien Land Law denies ineligible aliens the equal protection of the laws, and that failure to apply any limitations period to escheat actions under that law takes property without due process of law."

Chief Justice Vinson, in discussing the case, came to grips with the statutory presumption of Section 9(a) of the Alien Land Law. The statutory presumption of Section 9(a) was "that any conveyance is with 'intent to prevent, evade, or avoid' escheat if an ineligible alien pays the consideration." Vinson pointed out that by federal statute, enacted before the Fourteenth Amendment, but vindicated by it, the states must accord to all citizens the right to take and hold real property.[25] California recognized both this right and the fact that infancy did not incapacitate a minor from holding realty. The State of California, in its brief, conceded this point.[26] It was also conceded by the State that under California law ineligible aliens might arrange gifts of agricultural land to their citizen children.[27] Likewise, when a minor citizen became the owner of agricultural land, by gift or otherwise, his parent could be appointed guardian of the estate, whether the parent was a citizen, an eligible alien, or an ineligible alien.[28] Once appointed, a guardian was entitled to have custody of the estate and to manage and husband it for the ward's benefit.[29]

Up to this point, Chief Justice Vinson noted that Fred was ostensibly on a par with minors of different lineage. He then went on:

At this point, however, the road forks. The California law pointed in one direction for minor citizens like Fred Oyama, whose parents cannot be naturalized, and in another for all other children—for minor citizens whose parents are either citizens or eligible aliens, and even for minors who are themselves aliens though eligible for naturalization.

For most minors, California had the customary rule that where a parent pays for a conveyance to a child, there is a presumption that a gift is intended. When a gift is thus presumed, and the deed is recorded in the child's name, the recording suffices for delivery. In the absence of evidence that the gift is disadvantageous, acceptance is also presumed. "The burden of proving that there was in fact no completed bona fide gift falls to him who would attack its validity" (that is, the State in this case).

Said Justice Vinson:

Fred Oyama, on the other hand, faced at the outset the necessity of overcoming a statutory presumption that conveyances financed by his father and recorded in Fred's name were not gifts at all.

. . . when it came to rebutting this statutory presumption, Fred Oyama ran into other obstacles, which, so far as we can ascertain, do not beset the path of most minor donees in California.

Thus the California courts said that the very fact that the transfer put the land beyond the father's power to deal with it directly—to deed it away, to borrow money on it, and to make free disposition of it in any other way—showed that the transfer was not complete, that it was merely colorable. The fact that the father attached no strings to the transfer was taken to indicate that he meant, in effect, to acquire the beneficial ownership himself. The California law purports to permit citizens' sons to take gifts of agricultural land from their fathers, regardless of the fathers' nationality. Yet, as indicated by this case, if the father is ineligible for citizenship, facts which would usually be considered indicia of the son's ownership are used to make that ownership suspect; if the father is not an ineligible alien, however, the same facts would be evidence that a completed gift was intended.

The Court noted that the cumulative effects of not only Section 9(a) but also the other statutory presumptions contained in the Alien Land Law clearly discriminated against Fred.

He was saddled with an onerous burden of proof which need not be borne by California children generally. . . . In short, Fred Oyama lost his gift, irretrievably and without compensation, solely because of the extraordinary obstacles which the State set before him.

The only basis for this discrimination against an American citizen, moreover, was the fact that his father was Japanese, and not American, Russian, Chinese, or English.

. . . only the most exceptional circumstances can excuse discrimination on that basis, in the face of the equal protection clause and a federal statute giving all citizens the right to own land. . . .

In the light most favorable to the State, this case presents a conflict between the State's right to formulate a policy of landholding within its bounds and the right of American citizens to own land anywhere in the United States. When these two rights clash, the rights of a citizen may not be subordinated merely because of his father's country of origin.

Justice Hugo Black with whom Justice William O. Douglas agreed in a concurring opinion, based their records for the reversal of the judgment of the California Supreme Court on sharper grounds. They bluntly stated that the Alien Land Law in actual effect singled out aliens of Japanese ancestry:

. . . the statute does not name the Japanese as such . . . and . . . its terms also apply to a comparatively small number of aliens from other countries. That the effect and purpose of the law is to discriminate against Japanese because they are Japanese is too plain to call for more than a statement of that well-known fact."

In addition, the California Supreme Court had said in the case of *Estate of Yano* that one purpose of the Alien Land Law was to "discourage the coming of Japanese into this State." Japanese had been permitted to come into the United States by previous immigration laws, even though they were not yet permitted to become citizens. Japanese who had emigrated to the United States could live in any one of the states. Once the Japanese had come into California, the State could not erect obstacles to prevent the immigration of people whom Congress had authorized to come into and remain in the country. To this extent, the Alien Land Law was in conflict with federal laws and treaties governing the immigration of aliens and their rights after arrival in this country.

"If there is any one purpose of the Fourteenth Amendment that is wholly outside the realm of doubt," stated Justices Black and Douglas, "it is that the Amendment was designed to bar States from denying to some groups, on account of their race or color, any rights, privileges, and opportunities accorded to other groups."

A

In 1853 Commodore Matthew Perry steamed into Tokyo Bay and set into motion the exchange of goods and people between Japan and the United States. The Treaty of Peace, Amity and Commerce formally acknowledged relations between the two countries and brought Japan out of isolation.

B

C

D

The first Japanese immigrants who came to the United States founded the Wakamatsu Tea and Silk Colony in 1869. Others followed, and their knowledge of intensive farming provided them with the ability to turn wasteland into rich, highly productive farmland. Fishing techniques were also brought from Japan, and the Japanese fishermen in the United States became extremely successful.

F

G

H

Top: On October 11, 1906 the San Francisco Board of Education approved a resolution to segregate the grammar-school children of Japanese ancestry into a separate institution. Ninety-three children were affected by this order, including Kazuye Togasaki (second row, third from the left), who later became a prominent physician in San Francisco.

Bottom: Discrimination continued to plague the Issei and their Nisei children throughout the first half of the twentieth century and became increasingly blatant as the United States moved toward war with Japan.

The bombing of Pearl Harbor was as shocking to people of Japanese ancestry as it was to the rest of the population in the United States. Although some German and Italian aliens were arrested when war was declared on the Axis powers, the Japanese alone were subjected to wholesale internment.

General John L. DeWitt

Right: Santa Anita Race Track, shown here, was among several locations used as temporary housing at the beginning of the evacuation. The evacuees were later transferred to the internment camps that were hastily built to house the 120,000 persons of Japanese ancestry.

Below: The 442nd Regimental Combat Team, the all-Nisei battalion, was the most-decorated unit ever to serve the United States armed forces. Several members of the unit are shown here making their way to the front in Italy in 1943

geant Tokutaro Slocum   O
Saburo Kido   P
Mike Masaoka

When the Japanese "moose" captured the heart of the American G.I., she also helped to open the door for immigration from Japan for the first time since 1924. The G.I. Fiancees Act of 1946 allowed thousands of war brides to enter the United States with their servicemen husbands.

Right: The Immigration and Nationality Act of 1952 made people of all races and nationalities eligible for American citizenship. Thousands of Issei, at last, were able to stand before federal judges and take the oath of allegiance.

Below: On February 19, 1976 several prominent members of Congress and the JACL looked on as President Gerald R. Ford formally rescinded Executive Order 9066.

R

S

Of interest in the concurring opinion is a reference made to the United Nations Charter.[30] The United States had pledged with other nations to "promise . . . universal respect for, and observance of, human rights and fundamental freedoms for all without distinction as to race, sex, language, or religion." Justice Black and Justice Douglas posed a rhetorical question to the State of California: "How can this nation be faithful to this international pledge if state laws which bar land ownership and occupancy by aliens on account of race are permitted to be enforced?"

They concluded that all previous decisions of the Supreme Court of the United States that had previously sustained state land laws that discriminated against people of Japanese origin residing in this country should be overruled.[31]

The concurring opinion of Justice Frank Murphy and Justice Wiley Rutledge was even sharper in its condemnation of the Alien Land Law. In declaring the Alien Land Law unconstitutional, they said, "The California statute in question . . . is nothing more than an outright racial discrimination. As such, it deserves constitutional condemnation. And since the very core of the statute is so defective, I consider it necessary to give voice to the fact even though I join in the opinion of the Court."

The State of California in its argument to the Supreme Court had disclaimed any implication that the Alien Land Law was racist in its origin, purpose, or effect. California had again contended that the statute was "entirely innocent" of the use of such factors. The law was grounded solely upon the reasonable distinctions created by Congress in its naturalization laws.

The concurring opinion examined the circumstances surrounding the original enactment of the law in 1913, its reenactment in 1920, and its subsequent applications against persons of Japanese ancestry. It noted the anti-Oriental "virus" that infected many persons in California. The repressive measures against the Chinese were later directed against the Japanese immigrants who were termed "Mongolian invaders." The intention of the 1913 law was to deal with the "Japanese menace" on a racial basis. Its purpose was to restrict Japanese farm competition. It was to discourage Japanese from entering California and to drive out those who were already there, on the basis that the Japanese were "inferior, undesirable and degenerate mongrels."

It was noted that there was nothing to indicate that the proponents of the law were at any time concerned with the use or ownership of farmlands by ineligible aliens other than those of Japanese origin. The concurring opinion of the Court stated:

> The Alien Land Law, in short, was designed to effect a purely racial discrimination, to prohibit a Japanese alien from owning or using agricultural land solely because he is a Japanese alien. It is rooted deeply in racial, economic, and social antagonisms. . . .
>
> Hence, the basic vice, the constitutional infirmity, of the Alien Land Law is that its discrimination rests upon an unreal racial foundation. It assumes that there is some racial characteristic, common to all Japanese aliens, that makes them unfit to own or use agricultural land in California. There is no such characteristic. None has even been suggested. The arguments in support of the statute make no attempt whatever to discover any true racial factor. They merely represent social and economic antagonisms which have been translated into false racial terms. As such, they cannot form the rationalization necessary to conform the statute to the requirements of the equal protection clause of the Fourteenth Amendment. Accordingly, I believe that the prior decisions of this Court giving sanction to this attempt to legalize racism should be overruled.[32]

Justices Murphy and Rutledge concluded:

> And so in origin, purpose, administration, and effect, the Alien Land Law does violence to the high ideals of the Constitution of the United States and the Charter of the United Nations. It is an unhappy facsimile, a disheartening reminder, of the racial policy pursued by those forces of evil whose destruction recently necessitated a devastating war. It is racism in one of its most malignant forms. Fortunately, the majority of the inhabitants of the United States, and the majority of those in California, reject racism and all of its implications. They recognize that under our Constitution, all persons are entitled to the equal protection of the laws without regard to their racial ancestry. Human liberty is in too great a peril today to warrant ignoring that principle in this case. For that reason I believe that the penalty of unconstitutionality should be imposed upon the Alien Land Law.

The defeat of Proposition 15 in November 1946 showed that the tide of anti-Japanese legislation could at least be stemmed. The victory by the Oyamas in the landmark case of 1948 demonstrated that this tide could be turned. The turning was slow but certain; the legal clock could now be turned back on the escheat cases that were already in litigation.

ALIEN LAND LAWS FACE FURTHER ATTACK

Of the approximately eighty escheat cases instituted by the Attorney General's office in California between the years 1942 and 1948, when the *Oyama* case was decided, eleven had already been disposed of in one of three ways. Two had resulted in land being escheated to the State. Three had been dismissed and the title holder was declared to have good and valid title to the land. Six were settled with the State on the basis of a compromise.[33] The compromise consisted of the American citizen, owner of the land then under escheat proceedings, paying one-half of the appraised value of the land under escheat. After receipt of the money the State dismissed the escheat action that resulted in the citizen owner being able to retain title to the land. The remaining sixty-nine cases were still in litigation.

In 1949 Assemblyman Augustus Hawkins introduced a bill to repeal the Alien Land Law of 1920 by submitting the proposed repeal to a vote of the people.[34] Hawkins' bill did not proceed beyond committee consideration, but another bill (A.B. 841) was later passed and placed on the November 6, 1956 ballot.

In 1951 the California Legislature passed S.B. 1490, sponsored by Senators Gerald J. O'Gara, Chris N. Jesperson, and George Miller Jr., for the purpose of appropriating funds by the legislature to reimburse those persons who had had their properties escheated by the State or who had paid money to effect a compromise with the State in order to retain their property. The California Legislature, in approving S.B. 1490, noted the fact that Section 9(a) of the Alien Land Law had been declared unconstitutional by the United States Supreme Court in the *Oyama* case.

It should also be noted that when the Supreme Court declared Section 9(a) unconstitutional, Attorney General Kenney had ordered a halt to all further proceedings of pending escheat actions. In 1951 he further ordered that all escheat actions be dismissed.

The memorable decision of the Supreme Court in *Oyama* vs. *California* had a dramatic effect on four more cases that also involved alien land laws. Three such cases were in California and one was in Oregon.

The next Alien Land Law case to be decided by the California Supreme Court was *Palermo* vs. *Stockton Theatres, Inc.*[35] on June 15, 1948. The issue centered on the possible infringement of a state statute upon the treaty powers of the federal government. The land involved was commercial property in the city of Stockton in San Joaquin County.

On January 3, 1930, the lessor, who was the owner of commercial land, executed a lease with a group of Japanese nationals for a term of ten years, commencing January 1, 1931. On December 22, 1934 the owner gave a written option to extend the terms of the lease for ten additional years. On January 16, 1935, the lessees, with the consent of the lessor, transferred their interest in the lease to Stockton Theatres, Inc., a California corporation, almost wholly owned by Japanese nationals. On July 26, 1939, almost two years before the start of World War II, the United States notified Japan that she desired to abrogate the Treaty of Commerce and Navigation between the two countries, to become effective on January 26, 1940.[36]

On February 14, 1940 the lessee (the corporation) served notice upon the lessor that it was exercising its option to renew the lease for an additional ten-year term, commencing January 1, 1941. On September 13, 1940 the parties entered into a written agreement to lease the premises for this stated additional term of ten years. On October 27, 1941 the original lessor died, and a new lessor became the owner of the premises. On October 19, 1944, during the war and while the Japanese lessees were in concentration camps, the lessor filed a demand upon the lessee to evacuate the premises. The lessor contended that the occupancy of the land by the lessee was illegal under the provisions of the California Alien Land Law.

The trial court gave judgment for the lessor. Judge M. G. Woodward held that the lease was void on the ground that the abrogation of the treaty between the United States and Japan nullified any leases in effect at the time of the abrogation since any leasehold interest under the Alien Land Law was subject to an existing treaty between the United States and Japan. In the absence of such treaty, a Japanese alien could not enter into a lease of commercial property in California.

The Federal District Court of Appeals reversed the decision of the trial court, and the California Supreme Court upheld the decision of the court of appeals. It affirmed unanimously that the abrogation of the treaty had no effect on the provisions of the Alien Land Law. The lease of September 13, 1940 was valid, including its contractual provisions for the option to renew the lease, irrespective of such abrogations.

The concurring opinion of Justice Jesse W. Carter and Justice Roger J. Traynor of the California Supreme Court contains some interesting language. They declared that the California Alien Land Law, upon which the facts of the case were based, was unconstitutional (as had been ruled in the *Oyama* case). They held that if the State could prohibit aliens ineligible for citizenship from owning or leasing real property, it would thereby effectively prevent such persons from conducting ordinary industrial or business enterprises. "The effect of such legis-lation is to impose upon the aliens ineligible for citizenship an eco-nomic status inferior to all others earning or living in the State. Such a discrimination cannot be sustained under the Fourteenth Amend-ment to the Constitution of the United States."

On March 29, 1949 the Oregon Supreme Court became the first highest tribunal of any state to declare an entire alien land law uncon-stitutional.[37] Judge James W. Crawford of the Circuit Court of Oregon of Multnomah County had held the Oregon Alien Land Law valid in the case of *Kenji Namba* vs. *McCourt*.[38]

Kenji Namba was born on May 25, 1925, in Multnomah County of parents of Japanese descent. He had served in the United States Army and had seen combat in Italy. His father, Etsuo Namba, was born in Japan and had been lawfully admitted into the United States. Florence Donald owned sixty-two acres of farmland, and in 1947 she attempted to lease the land to Kenji Namba and his father. The State of Oregon sought to invalidate the lease on the ground that the Treaty of Com-merce and Navigation entered into between the United States and Japan in 1911 had been terminated on July 26, 1939 (actually effective six months later). The abrogation of the treaty eliminated any right of a Japanese alien to own or lease agricultural land because the Oregon Alien Land Law permitted ownership or lease of agricultural lands only to the extent such a treaty between the United States and the nation of which such alien was subject permitted.

The Oregon Alien Land Law further contained the statutory pre-sumptions of intent to violate the law if the parties involved persons ineligible for citizenship, similar to those of the California Alien Land Law, after which it was patterned.[39]

Chief Justice George Rossman reversed the decision of the circuit court and declared that "Oregon Laws 1945, Chapter 436, infringes upon the equal protection clause of the Fourteenth Amendment. We hold that it is invalid."

In arriving at his clear-cut decision, Chief Justice Rossman noted that the state supreme court had not been required up to then to rule on the Oregon Alien Land Law since its enactment in 1923 nor on the 1945 ancillary measures. He stated that he was obliged to review, therefore, the decisions of the California Supreme Court, the State of Washington Supreme Court decisions, and particularly the recent decisions of the United States Supreme Court in *Oyama* vs. *California* and *Takahashi* vs. *Fish and Game Commission*.

He pointed out that according to the 1940 census, there were 1,617 Japanese aliens in Oregon.

Very likely death, the effects of evacuation, and other causes have reduced that number materially.

No one claims that any danger to our general welfare lurks in this small group of people who long ago lost the bloom of youth. The Exclusion Act makes it certain that their dwindling number will not be increased.

Our country cannot afford to create, by legislation or judicial construction, a ghetto for our ineligible aliens. And yet, if we deny to the alien who is lawfully here the normal means whereby he earns his livelihood, we thereby assign him to a lowered standard of living.

. . . our Alien Land Law must be deemed violative of the principles of law which protect from classification based upon color, race, and creed.

LANDMARK CASES CONFRONT RACIAL DISCRIMINATION

In two landmark cases, the Alien Land Laws of California were declared to violate the Fourteenth Amendment to the federal Constitution as being racially discriminatory against the Japanese. The first of these two cases, *Sei Fujii* vs. *State of California*,[40] was decided by the California Supreme Court on April 17, 1952. This case was followed three months later, on July 9, 1952, by the case of *Haruye Masaoka* vs. *State of California*.[41]

Sei Fujii, a Japanese alien who had come to the United States at an early age, had studied law at the University of Southern California. Later he became the owner-publisher of the *Kashu Mainichi*, a daily bilingual Japanese-English newspaper that was widely read in the Japanese community throughout southern California, especially in the farming areas of Los Angeles County. His knowledge of California laws and of the Constitution of the United States helped to make him a fearless fighter against injustices and inequities aimed at the Japanese. Various state and federal statutes and court decisions were constantly being pointed out by him through his newspaper as upholding racially discriminatory practices.

When the Supreme Court struck down Section 9(a) of the Alien Land Law in *Oyama* vs. *California*, Fujii felt that the time was ripe to make a frontal attack on the 1920 Alien Land Law in its entirety. In 1948, soon after the *Oyama* case had been decided, he bought a small amount of property in the eastern section of Los Angeles. A purchase similar to the Oyamas' was not what Fujii wanted; instead, he boldly took title in his own name as a Japanese alien. At the time of the purchase, there was no treaty between the United States and Japan that might have conferred upon him the right to own such land. The Cali-

fornia Supreme Court was therefore compelled to face the issue squarely: the possible right of a Japanese alien, ineligible for citizenship and
in the absence of a treaty, to purchase land in contravention of the
Alien Land Law.

The State of California promptly instituted an escheat action to
confiscate the property. Superior Court Judge Wilbur C. Curtis ruled
that the property did escheat to the State. Fujii appealed the judgment
of the superior court to the state supreme court. In a four to three decision, the state supreme court reversed the judgment of the superior
court. The supreme court declared that the provisions of the California
Alien Land Law barring aliens ineligible for citizenship from owning
land were in violation of the equal protection clauses of both the Constitution of the United States and the Constitution of California.

Chief Justice Phil S. Gibson, who wrote the majority opinion, stated
that the state law attempted to shift the blame of its racially discriminatory provisions against ownership of land by the Japanese to the
federal immigration laws. He pointed out that the standards of eligibility for naturalization imposed by Congress were not standards involving property rights:

> . . . there is no justification for a classification which operates to withhold
> property rights from some aliens, not because of anything they have done or
> any beliefs they hold, but solely because they are Japanese, and not French
> or Italian.
> The truth is that the right to earn a living in many occupations is insep-
> arably connected with the use and enjoyment of land. Farming, for example,
> is one of the most ancient and common ways of making a living. . . . Legis-
> lation which results in such discrimination imposes upon the ineligible alien
> an economic status inferior to that of all other persons living in the State and
> interferes with his right to earn a living.

He then declared that the constitutional theories upon which the
case of *Porterfield* vs. *Webb*[42] was based are "today without support and
must be abandoned." Justice Gibson concluded as follows:

> The California Alien Land Law is obviously designed and administered as
> an instrument effectuating racial discrimination, and the most searching
> examination discloses no circumstances justifying classification on that basis.
> There is nothing to indicate that those alien residents who are racially in-
> eligible for citizenship possess characteristics which are dangerous to the
> legitimate interests of the state, or that they, as a class, might use the land
> for purposes injurious to public morals, safety, or welfare. Accordingly, we
> hold that the Alien Land Law is invalid as in violation of the Fourteenth
> Amendment.

While the case of *Sei Fujii* vs. *State of California* was moving forward from the Superior Court of Los Angeles County to the California Supreme Court, another case, *Haruye Masaoka* vs. *State of California*, was also destined to be placed upon the law books of the California Supreme Court as a case in which the Alien Land Law was declared unconstitutional.

Haruye Masaoka, a petite, dignified, white-haired lady, was a widow whose husband had died many years before in Salt Lake City. She was an alien Japanese, ineligible for citizenship, who had no property or income other than a small pension. She had six sons, all born in the United States. During World War II, all six sons planned to enlist in the all-Nisei combat unit recruited from the concentration camps. The brothers persuaded the oldest among them, Joe Grant, not to volunteer because one of them had to care for their mother, an argument to which Joe Grant finally agreed. The other five enlisted and served with distinction in the 442nd Regimental Combat Team. Brother Mike was the first Nisei on the mainland United States to volunteer for this famed unit. The other brothers volunteered for the same unit immediately thereafter.

Ben Frank Masaoka was killed in action in October 1944 in the fierce battle to rescue the Lost Texas Battalion. Akira Ike Masaoka was severely wounded in the same action and is still totally disabled. Brothers Henry, Tadashi, and Mike were all wounded in action. Among them, the Masaoka brothers collected more than thirty medals for bravery in combat.[43]

After the war had ended, the five remaining brothers agreed among themselves to build a home for their aging mother where she could live out the rest of her life in relative comfort. Under Section 8 of the Alien Land Law, the sons could not make a gift of land to their mother. She would lose her home, her sons would lose their investment, and the property would escheat to the State.

To quiet title to the property and to determine whether or not the property had actually escheated to the State through the operation of the Alien Land Law (1 Deerings General Laws, Act 261), the mother, her sons, and their wives brought an action in the Superior Court of Los Angeles.

Judge Thurmond Clarke, later to be appointed to the Federal District Court of Southern California, quieted title in the mother and sons. On March 16, 1950 he held that the Alien Land Law was unconstitutional because it violated the Fourteenth Amendment to the Constitution. In his memorandum of opinion, Judge Clarke declared:[44]

I am satisfied that the Alien Land Law is directed against persons of Japanese ancestry solely because of their race. It is clear that the State Legislation which seeks to impair the constitutionally protected civil right to acquire, own and enjoy real property violates the due process and equal protection clause of the Fourteenth Amendment. Accordingly, I hold that the Alien Land Law of California under the facts in this case is unconstitutional because it violates the Fourteenth Amendment of the United States, both as to the alien mother and the citizen sons.

An appeal to the California Supreme Court by the State of California was dealt with by the court in summary fashion. The court merely stated, "Our decision in Sei Fujii vs. State of California . . . is controlling, and for the reasons there stated the judgment must be affirmed."[45]

Repeated blows by both the Supreme Court of the United States in Oyama vs. California and the state supreme courts in Kenji Namba vs. State of Oregon, Sei Fujii vs. State of California, and now Haruye Masaoka vs. State of California left the Alien Land Laws of these and other states of the western part of the United States torn and tattered symbols of an era of relentless racial animosity against the Japanese. The once grim barriers of economic and racial oppression had now been cracked open, and the rubble that remained was statutes of national and international embarrassment to the states that had originally enacted them.

PROPOSITION 13: THE ALIEN LAND LAW IS REPEALED

In order to sweep away the debris of the Alien Land Law from the statute books of California, the Japanese American Citizens League took the initiative and persuaded the California Legislature to repeal the Alien Land Law by putting the issue directly to a vote of the people. The repeal measure appeared on the November 4, 1956 general election ballot as Proposition 13.

The JACL again vigorously campaigned throughout the state. The 1956 effort was led by Joe Grant Masaoka, whose brother Mike, ten years before, had successfully directed the campaign to defeat Proposition 15.

Organizations and public bodies that in 1920 had so vehemently supported the enactment of the Alien Land Law were now prominently backing the repeal of this same notorious law. These organizations included the American Legion, the various county farm bureaus, the chambers of commerce, the city councils and county boards of supervisors, both major political parties, labor unions, and prominent newspapers such as the Los Angeles Times, the San Francisco Chronicle, and the Los Angeles Examiner.[46]

Proposition 13 to repeal the Alien Land Law was overwhelmingly approved by the voters of California on the night of November 6, 1956. Over 2.5 million voters approved the repeal by a two to one majority. The victory at the polls was noted by the *Pacific Citizen* on December 21, 1956:

> It was a tribute to the Issei whose love for the land kept them steadfast through years of discrimination. In only half a century the Issei had come full circle, accepted as equal citizens in the country they had adopted.
>
> America's Issei and Nisei, so recently removed from the harsh and discriminatory years of the war, today enjoy a freedom from statutory prejudice which persons of Japanese descent have not known since the first Alien Land Law was passed in 1913. On the agenda for tomorrow are the vestigial remnants of legislative prejudice in those remaining states where alien land laws—invalid and without meaning—still remain in the statutes, though the anti-Japanese activity which sponsored them has long since been forgotten.

The *Oyama, Palermo, Fujii,* and *Masaoka* decisions had the greatest beneficial impact upon persons of Japanese ancestry because they directly affected the largest number of individuals—those engaged in all kinds of agricultural activities, whether large or small. Other Japanese could now own not only farmlands but also all types of real property both for commercial and residential purposes. For the first time, the Japanese were given unrestricted opportunities to invest in land in order to establish their occupational and economic future on a firm basis. Until then, investments and purchases were made in fear and trepidation that their lands would at any time be forfeited to the State under escheat proceedings.

It may be fruitless to speculate on what might have been the economic and financial position of the Japanese had the Alien Land Laws not deterred and crippled the growth and development of their communities throughout the Pacific Coast states. Once unwanted lands of some sixty years before had been developed by them into rich agricultural complexes everywhere before the evacuation. During the population explosion after World War II, a phenomenon that affected the Pacific Coast more than any other part of the country, what had once been unwanted lands became desirable areas. People from all over the United States poured into the West, especially into California, to live in many new housing developments in the suburbs. Shopping centers sprang up in these suburbs, industrial and commercial complexes filling up much of the remaining space. Land prices rose at a rate never before experienced in American history. But until 1952, when the California Supreme Court at last struck down the Alien Land Law, the Japanese farmer could only bend his back to pick his crops as a tenant, instead of as an owner.

13
The Commercial Fishing Cases

FISHING IS AN age-old means of making a living. From the earliest days of human civilization to the present time, fishermen throughout the world have set sail in their boats, some to travel hundreds, sometimes thousands of miles in search of a catch. Fishermen use everything from crude poles, hooks, and nets to multi-million dollar, ocean-going refrigerated vessels equipped with the latest and most sophisticated electronic sonar devices. Millions of tons of fish are caught annually to help supply the never ceasing demand for food for millions of persons.

CONTRIBUTIONS OF EARLY JAPANESE FISHERMEN

It was natural that hundreds of Japanese who emigrated to the United States would engage in commercial fishing. Japan, their ancestral home, is an island empire surrounded by an ocean in which innumerable species of fish abound. These immigrant Japanese fishermen brought with them techniques and knowledge of fishing handed down from father to son. When they settled near harbors and along the ocean waters of America, they adapted their methods to their new fishing grounds. With better equipment and larger and faster vessels, these hardy people probed ever farther offshore in search of fish. By the time of the evacuation in 1942, the Japanese had been rapidly becoming a dominant force in the American West Coast fishing industry.

Home base to the hundreds of Japanese commercial fishermen in California were the great fishing harbors of Monterey, Terminal Island (Wilmington), San Pedro, and San Diego.

In 1892 six men were brought from Japan by an American fish cannery in Monterey to be employed as squid fishermen. In 1900 eight more fishermen were brought over from Japan by the same cannery to fish for salmon off San Francisco Bay. Other American canneries followed suit. By 1910 about 145 fishermen from Japan were employed by the various canneries in the Monterey area to fish for yellowtail, tuna, sea bass, smelt, rock cod, sardines, and barracuda.[1]

In 1896 Otsaburo Noda began diving for abalone near Monterey, at a place called Point Lobos. The work was arduous, slow, and exhausting because the abalone were attached to the rocks. Then he heard of someone in Japan who was developing a new method of abalone fishing. He contacted the Department of Agriculture and Commerce in Japan and asked for help. In October 1896 Kannosuke Otani came to visit Noda at the suggestion of the Japanese government. Otani was then experimenting with a specially devised suit to fish for abalone off the coast of Japan. His diving suit proved eminently useful, and soon fresh abalone became a popular seafood in California. Noda then tried exporting dried abalone to Japan. This venture also proved to be successful.

In the early 1900s the Monterey and San Francisco Bay areas were virgin grounds for commercial fishermen. Few of them had previously dared to challenge the swift, cold ocean currents, irregular wave patterns, and the damp, foggy weather of those sea areas. In 1930 Katsuyoshi Hamachi, a Japanese immigrant, noting that sardines were in great abundance in the Monterey–San Francisco areas, devised a strong, light net to catch sardines and increase his haul. It was a success and Hamachi prospered.

In 1902 more Japanese began to settle around the San Pedro Harbor area to fish for abalone and lobster. In 1910 other Japanese fishermen settled in Terminal Island near San Pedro. This colony eventually became the largest and most important Japanese fishing group. The population in the Terminal Island area included approximately 3,000 persons of Japanese ancestry; on February 28, 1942 they were all removed by naval authorities after being given only forty-eight hours' notice.[2] The navy then took possession of this area for shore facilities and an airstrip.

The harbor areas of San Diego, now a large base for the United States Navy, were settled by Japanese commercial fishermen beginning in 1899. This area became a busy harbor for fishermen who sailed into United States territorial waters or who roamed the seas farther south off Mexico and South America.

FISHERMEN ENCOUNTER ANTI-JAPANESE ATTACKS

Over the years, the immigrant fishermen from Japan were gradually replaced by their sons who were United States citizens. These Japanese-American fishermen encountered many anti-Japanese attacks from the California Legislature, various anti-Japanese organizations, and the press. They were constantly being assailed as being socially unassimilable, undesirable, and also potentially disloyal. Their economic competitors, who feared the increasing strength of the Japanese in the fishing industry, added their voices to those of others in expressions of racial hatred.

A particularly vicious, though unfounded, rumor was widely circulated for years by anti-Japanese elements: They claimed that the fishermen were former Japanese navy reservists and spies for the Japanese navy. The captains of the fishing vessels were said to be taking soundings of harbors, preparing hydrographical maps, and sending mysterious signals to the Japanese navy vessels. While these charges were strongly denied by the Japanese, and also by responsible Americans in the fishing industry, the denials had no discernible effect on the general population.

In 1942, the first year after Pearl Harbor, the president of the Coast Fishing Company stated:

As for the resident Japanese supplying the home government with information regarding harbors, coast lines, cities, etc., may I point out that at any local ship chandlery or other institution, including certain branches of our own government there may be had, by anyone, upon request or upon payment of a small fee, exact and up-to-date bathymetrical and topographical charts, maps, and pictures, giving marine and harbor soundings, land elevations and promontories, distances, locations and what not, all compiled by agencies of our government, and with the greatest exactitude. So, we are expected to believe that members of the local Japanese fishing fleet are busily engaged in mapping and plotting our harbors, coast lines, etc., and forwarding same to their home government, when common sense should tell us that every Japanese or other alien steamer entering our harbors probably has a personnel more capable of acquiring such information than are all members of the fleet combined.[3]

This significant piece of information fell on deaf ears.

The main attack by the anti-Japanese elements was an effort to prohibit the Japanese from obtaining commercial fishing licenses. Without such licenses the Japanese alien could not legally fish either in territorial waters off the coast of California or on the high seas and then bring his fish into California for sale. Commercial fishing licenses had been issued since 1909.[4] The earliest efforts to prohibit Japanese commercial fishermen from obtaining licenses commenced in 1919 and continued with varying intensity for the next twenty-six years, until 1945.

Eleven bills introduced in the California Legislature during these years were intended to limit commercial fishing licenses to "United States citizens."[5] Japanese nationals could not become citizens. Two bills attempted to limit issuances of licenses to United States citizens only or to "aliens eligible for citizenship."[6] Two other bills sought to limit licenses to United States citizens and to aliens who had "declared" their intentions of becoming United States citizens.[7] Japanese

nationals could not declare such intentions. Six bills did not mention
United States citizenship as a requirement but prohibited aliens in-
eligible for citizenship from being issued commercial fishing licenses.[8]
Four bills required at least one year continuous residence in the United
States or the state of California before making application for licens-
ing.[9] In only one bill were the words "alien Japanese" used.[10]

No matter what language was employed, these numerous bills over
the twenty-six years were all aimed at prohibiting the issuance of commercial fishing licenses to the Japanese as a distinct, specific racial
group. A survey taken of all commercial fishing licenses issued by the
Fish and Game Commission from 1930 to 1945 makes this fact clear.
This survey revealed that out of approximately 45,000 commercial
fishing licenses issued by the Fish and Game Commission of the State
of California during these fifteen years, only 2,400 had been applied
for by and issued to Japanese aliens.[11]

Of twenty-six bills introduced in the California Legislature between
1919 and 1945 to prohibit Japanese aliens from engaging in commercial
fishing, three were actually passed.

ALIENS DENIED FISHING LICENSES

In 1933 Section 990 of the Fish and Game Code was amended. The
amendment provided that persons who had not resided in the United
States or in the state of California for at least one year were prohibited
from bringing fish caught on the high seas into California for sale.[12]
An alien Japanese commercial fisherman tested this amendment in
the courts.

In 1935 T. Abe, who held a California commercial license, hired
a crew of Japanese aliens to fish from his vessel on the high seas off
the coast of California. None of his crew had resided in California or
within the United States for at least one year before coming into California with their catch. Thus, none of the crew members was eligible
to procure a commercial fishing license under the 1933 amendment to
Section 990. The Fish and Game Commission attempted to prevent
the fish from being unloaded in San Diego, charging that the crew had
violated Section 990.

Presiding Justice Charles R. Barnard of the California District Court
of Appeals in *T. Abe* vs. *Fish and Game Commission*[13] held that Section
990 was void and ineffective since the act discriminated between residents and nonresidents of the United States. He stated that this distinc-

tion was not a reasonable classification and constituted an "unequal exaction and a greater burden" upon nonresidents than upon residents in the same calling and under the same conditions. Section 990 was declared to be in violation of the equal protection clause of Section 1 of the Fourteenth Amendment to the Constitution. An appeal by the Fish and Game Commission for hearing before the California Supreme Court was denied on November 25, 1935.

In 1943, with the Japanese securely in their concentration camps, racists renewed their efforts to eliminate them from engaging in commercial fishing. The Japanese had no supporters; no politician dared to speak up for them in California. On the contrary, vituperative invectives against the Japanese invariably produced popular support for the politicians responsible.

The 1943 California Legislature quickly amended Section 990 of the Fish and Game Code.[14] This amendment provided:

A commercial fishing license may be issued to any person other than an alien Japanese. A commercial fishing license may be issued to a corporation only if said corporation is authorized to do business in this state, if none of the officers or directors thereof are alien Japanese, and if less than the majority of each class of stockholders thereof are alien Japanese.

There was no pretense that the 1943 amendment was enacted in the interest of "conservation"; both federal and state authorities were doing their utmost to encourage greater food production for wartime purposes. The amendment to Section 990 had but one intention: to discourage the return to California of alien Japanese commercial fishermen. The non-Japanese fishermen would thereby be free from the competition of these aliens.[15]

By 1945, two years later, Section 990 was amended again. On December 18, 1944 the Supreme Court of the United States had ordered the release of all loyal Japanese from the concentration camps in *Ex parte Endo*. General H. C. Pratt, commander of the Western Defense Command, had rescinded the Japanese Exclusion Order effective January 2, 1945. In response to that decision, a return to California on the part of many of the evacuated commercial fishermen was a reasonable certainty. As a consequence, another wave of proposals to prohibit Japanese aliens from returning to commercial fishing inundated the 1945 California Legislature.

The 1945 amendment to Section 990[16] was enacted because the members of the California Legislature foresaw that if the words "alien

Japanese" were retained in Section 990 of the 1943 amendment, it might be declared unconstitutional on the ground of discrimination since the amendment was directed against one specifically named racial group.

The 1945 amendment to Section 990 was not suggested by a legislative committee concerned with the conservation of fish in the high seas or in territorial waters of California; it was proposed by the Senate Fact-Finding Committee on Japanese Resettlement, a body that was studying the problems arising from the Japanese evacuees who were being released from the concentration camps and returning to their homes in California. In the senate committee's report, issued May 1, 1945, there appeared this frank explanation of the 1945 proposed amendment to Section 990:

> The committee gave little consideration to the problems of the use of fishing vessels on our coast owned and operated by Japanese, since this matter seems to have previously been covered by legislation. The committee, however, feels that there is danger of the present statute being declared unconstitutional, on the grounds of discrimination, since it is directed against alien Japanese. It is believed that this legal question can probably be eliminated by an amendment which has been proposed to the bill which would make it apply to any alien who is ineligible for citizenship. The committee has introduced Senate Bill 413 to make this change in the statute.

The 1945 amendment to Section 990 of the Fish and Game Code read as follows:

> A commercial fishing license may be issued to any person other than a person ineligible for citizenship. A corporation fishing license may be issued to a corporation only if said corporation is authorized to do business in this State, if none of the officers or directors thereof are persons ineligible for citizenship, and if less than the majority of each class of stockholders thereof are persons ineligible for citizenship.

RESTRICTIONS ON FISHING SUCCESSFULLY CHALLENGED

It was this 1945 amendment to Section 990 that prohibited Torao Takahashi from obtaining a commercial fishing license when he left the concentration camp at Manzanar, California in 1945 to resume his lifelong occupation. Takahashi was a Japanese alien who had been engaged in commercial fishing from 1915 to 1941. During this time he had been issued a commercial fishing license annually. In 1945, however, the Fish and Game Commission refused to issue a license to him because he was ineligible to become a United States citizen based upon his Japanese ancestry.

In 1947 he filed a suit against the Fish and Game Commission to compel it to issue him a license. Los Angeles County Superior Court Judge Henry M. Willis ordered the Fish and Game Commission to issue Takahashi a commercial fishing license, upholding the contention that Section 990 was unconstitutional because the statute discriminated against Takahashi solely because of his race.[17]

On appeal by the Fish and Game Commission, the California Supreme Court, in a four to three decision, reversed the decision of Judge Willis.[18] Justice Douglas L. Edmonds reasoned that the State of California, in its sovereign capacity as a trustee for all the people, held the fish and game as the property of the State. As a trustee, the State, in the interest of conservation (the basis urged by the Fish and Game Commission), could confer exclusive rights of fishing and hunting on its own citizens and expressly exclude aliens and nonresident citizens. Since the reduction of the number of persons eligible to fish bore a reasonable relation to the objects of conservation and was within the State's police power, the classification of who should have the right to fish or not to fish was bound to be reasonable. The prohibition of issuing fishing licenses to aliens ineligible for citizenship did not therefore deny such aliens their constitutional guarantees.

Takahashi then appealed to the Supreme Court of the United States.[19] On June 7, 1948, by a seven to two margin, the Supreme Court reversed the decision of the California Supreme Court and ordered the Fish and Game Commission to issue Takahashi a commercial fishing license.

Justice Hugo Black, speaking for the majority of the Court, brushed aside the argument that Section 990 was enacted by the California Legislature as a conservation measure. He held that a congressional standard for eligibility for citizenship could not be arbitrarily imposed by the State to deprive a permanent resident alien from making a living by fishing in the ocean. Such an arbitrary classification was invalid. He declared:

To whatever extent the fish in the three-mile belt off California may be "capable of ownership" by California, we think that "ownership" is inadequate to justify California in excluding any or all aliens who are lawful residents of the State from making a living by fishing in the ocean off its shores while permitting all others to do so.

It does not follow, as California seems to argue, that because the United States regulates immigration and naturalization in part on the basis of race and color classifications, a state can adopt one or more of the same classifications to prevent lawfully admitted aliens within its borders from earning a living in the same way that other state inhabitants earn their living. . . . State laws which impose discriminatory burdens upon the entrance or residence of aliens lawfully within the United States conflict with this constitutionally derived federal power to regulate immigration, and have accordingly been held invalid.

Justice Frank Murphy, who was joined by Justice Wiley Rutledge in the concurring opinion, reviewed the circumstances surrounding the 1945 amendment to Section 990. Justice Murphy declared that this section was the direct outgrowth of antagonism toward persons of Japanese ancestry, and they were therefore "not entitled to wear the cloak of constitutionality."

The statute in question is but one more manifestation of the anti-Japanese fever which has been evident in California in varying degrees since the turn of the century. That fever, of course, is traceable to the refusal or the inability of certain groups to adjust themselves economically and socially, relative to residents of Japanese ancestry. For some years prior to the Japanese attack on Pearl Harbor, these protagonists of intolerance had been leveling unfounded accusations and innuendoes against Japanese fishing crews operating off the coast of California. These fishermen numbered about a thousand and most of them had long resided in that State. It was claimed that they were engaged not only in fishing but in espionage and other illicit activities on behalf of the Japanese Government. As war with Japan approached and finally became a reality, these charges were repeated with increasing vigor. Yet full investigations by appropriate authorities failed to reveal any competent supporting evidence; not even one Japanese fisherman was arrested for alleged espionage. Such baseless accusations can only be viewed as an integral part of the long campaign to undermine the reputation of persons of Japanese background and to discourage their residence in California.

More specifically, these accusations were used to secure the passage of discriminatory fishing legislation.

We should not blink at the fact that Section 990, as now written, is a discriminatory piece of legislation having no relation whatever to any constitutionally cognizable interest of California. It was drawn against a background of racial and economic tension. It is directed in spirit and in effect solely against aliens of Japanese birth. It denies them commercial fishing rights not because they threaten the success of any conservation program, not because their fishing activities constitute a clear and present danger to the welfare of California or of the nation, but only because they are of Japanese stock, a stock which has had the misfortune to arouse antagonism among certain powerful interests. We need but unbutton the seemingly innocent words of Section 990 to discover beneath them the very negation of all the ideals of the equal protection clause. No more is necessary to warrant reversal of the judgment below.

14

The Japanese Evacuation Claims Act: The Federal Government Pays Ten Cents on the Dollar for Property Losses

ON DECEMBER 18, 1944 the Supreme Court of the United States had ruled in *Ex parte Mitsuye Endo* that the War Relocation Authority had no legal authority to detain a "concededly loyal" American citizen in these camps. As a result, the WRA had no legal authority to detain any person of Japanese ancestry against whom there was no evidence of disloyalty.

The WRA apparently anticipated the broad scope of the Supreme Court decision because on the same day the *Endo* decision was made known, it announced that all relocation centers would be closed before the end of 1945 and that the entire WRA program would be liquidated on June 30, 1946.[1] Both the War Department and the WRA had known ten days before that the Supreme Court would rule that the entire concentration camp program was unconstitutional.[2]

It was not mere coincidence, therefore, that on December 17, 1944, one day before the *Endo* decision, the War Department announced the revocation of the West Coast mass exclusion order of the Japanese, effective January 2, 1945.[3]

On December 18, 1944, when the WRA announced the closing of the camps, one of the ten camps had already been closed six months earlier. On June 30, 1944, the Jerome Relocation Center in Arkansas had been closed because many of the evacuees had resettled earlier in the states of Kentucky, Ohio, Illinois, Minnesota, and Wisconsin. The 5,000 remaining residents at Jerome had been transferred to other camps.[4]

Now, with the closing of all the camps having been announced, the relocation process of moving the evacuees out of the camps as quickly as possible became a program of urgency and compelling necessity. The field offices established by the WRA outside the camps and outside the Western Defense Command, such as in Chicago, Salt Lake City, Cleveland, Minneapolis, Des Moines, New York, Denver, Kansas City, and Boston, were ordered by the WRA to accelerate their activities in finding jobs and housing for the evacuees still remaining in the camps.[5] Additional field offices were now established by the WRA in Los Angeles, San Francisco, and Seattle to assist the evacuees who desired to return to the West Coast.[6]

THE EVACUEES LEAVE THE CAMPS

The WRA was inducing the evacuees to leave the camps by paying for their travel expenses to areas that had been selected by the evacuees or recommended by the various field offices. Speakers, mostly

Caucasian military officers who had commanded the Nisei either in the European or Pacific Theatres of Operations, and sometimes Nisei G.I.s themselves, were sent by the WRA to various communities, especially on the West Coast, to urge the residents to "accept" the Japanese back into their midst. One of them was Ben Kuroki, who had completed a total of fifty-eight missions including the devastating bombing raid on the oil fields of Ploesti in Rumania.

While thousands of evacuees did stream out of the camps, many thousands more adamantly refused to leave. The reluctance of the remaining evacuees is understandable. Of the approximately 44,000 persons who still remained in the concentration camps as of June 30, 1945, almost half were young people below the age of twenty. The rest were women or aging men whose sons had either volunteered or had been drafted into the United States Army after the selective service system was reinstated on January 20, 1944. More than 25,000 young Nisei men, mostly from the camps, were in uniform at the end of World War II. Several thousand more young people, both male and female, single and newly married, had left their parents to enter school in the East under the National Student Relocation Program or to seek employment and a new life in communities outside the Western Defense Command.

Thus, most of the evacuees who remained in the camps were minor children, women, aging men, or persons who were without funds to reestablish a new life elsewhere. The United States government, through the WRA, asked the evacuees to leave the camps and to go wherever: back to homes they no longer had, to jobs that had disappeared, to purchase or lease land with funds they did not have, or to go to strange communities to live because their former neighbors were still hostile to the Japanese.

In 1942, 110,000 Japanese had been ordered into these same ten concentration camps with unseemly haste and amid confusion. In 1945 and 1946 some of the same evacuees were now being ordered to leave the camps, helpless and penniless, because the government had not had the legal authority to detain them in the first place.

Again, the evacuees who refused to leave were herded about like cattle from camp to camp, together with other reluctant evacuees of camps that were being rapidly closed down. They were told to pack and be transported from closed camps to open camps by harassed officials who were striving to meet the deadlines imposed upon them by the WRA officials in Washington, D.C.

With grim faces, the WRA officials now told the reluctant Japanese that they could no longer stay in the camps, that they no longer belonged there, and that they should go "home." Some protesting evacuees were carried bodily into trains and busses, screaming and yelling to remain in their now familiar camp "homes."

On April 30, 1945 Dillon Myer, director of the WRA, appeared before the House Appropriations Subcommittee to ask for $25 million for fiscal year 1945–1946 to expedite the "relocation" of the residents who still were in the camps.[7]

Having received the requested appropriation, the WRA imposed further enforcement of the deadlines to close the camps. On July 13, 1945 the WRA announced a schedule of closing dates for all centers (except Tule Lake Center near Newell, California) to be between October 15 and December 15, 1945.[8] On August 1, 1945 Director Myer issued Administrative Notice 289, calling for the scheduled relocation of remaining residents during the last six weeks of operation of each WRA center.[9]

On December 1, 1945, three and a half months after the Japanese had surrendered on August 15, it was "triumphantly" announced by the WRA that the last relocation center, except Tule Lake, was closed, and all evacuees had left the camps.[10] The deadline previously announced by the WRA, to close the camps by June 30, 1946, was met on schedule. On June 30, 1946 the WRA relocation program was officially terminated.[11]

The total amount of the appropriations by the federal government to the WRA to evacuate, clothe, house, and feed the Japanese for three years and nine months in the ten concentration camps between March 21, 1942 and December 1, 1945, plus the administrative expenses to terminate the entire WRA program on June 30, 1946, was $160 million. An additional $56,482,638 was disbursed through the War Department for the Corps of Engineers to build the ten concentration camps. Still another $32,197,078 was charged by the War Department to the army for necessary army personnel, diverted during wartime, to supervise the evacuation of the Japanese under military orders of General DeWitt. Thus, the overall cost to the United States for the entire evacuation program totalled nearly a quarter of a billion dollars.[12] In addition, the Federal Reserve Bank in San Francisco in 1942 made an arbitrary and intentionally conservative estimate of anticipated property losses sustained by the Japanese to be some $400 million.

There is no way to estimate the actual economic losses to the evacuees. Included in these losses were the costs of professional equipment for doctors, dentists, and medical technicians. Also lost were the law books of attorneys, the merchandise and inventory of thousands of merchants, as well as the equipment, supplies, materials, counters, fixtures, and other improvements in countless shops and stores.

Also incalculable were losses of furniture, automobiles, equities in homes, lands, leasehold interests in buildings, and insurance policies. The costs of planting crops on the lands and the losses of farm supplies and equipment, fishing vessels and all of their nets, poles, and other equipment could not be accurately estimated. Not included in the economic losses were business items of good will and anticipatory profits. It is reasonably certain from available government sources that the total cost to the United States government plus the economic losses suffered by the evacuees totalled more than $700 million.

It was on the plight of the "returnees"—evacuees released from the camps and attempting to regain a toe hold on their disrupted lives—that the JACL now focused its concern. Saburo Kido was in his third term as national president of this organization. Soon after the end of World War II, Kido discussed with Mike Masaoka, the executive secretary of the JACL, the problems that confronted the Japanese as a consequence of the war and the evacuation. They both agreed that a national convention of the JACL was necessary to determine policies and programs to solve them.

THE JACL SEEKS COMPENSATION FOR EVACUEES

The first postwar national convention was held in Denver, Colorado in the spring of 1946, only a few months after the camps had been emptied of their inhabitants. Delegates gathered from all parts of the United States where they had resettled: from cities and towns in the Midwest and East as well as the Pacific Coast that had once been just names on the map to the Japanese. These places were now inhabited by hundreds, and in some instances even thousands, of Nisei and Issei. JACL members were living in such cities as Akron, Cincinnati, Detroit, Denver, Omaha, Chicago, Washington, D.C., Philadelphia, Twin Falls, New York, Baltimore, and dozens of other cities. The JACL now reached into communities throughout the entire United States. The breadth of its membership, as well as its growing strength and numbers, were to have tremendous clout in its legislative programs, not only in the halls of Congress, but also in the various state legislatures and local city councils.

Among the many topics discussed by the delegates and approved for action at the national convention was a mandate for the JACL to seek monetary compensation from the United States government for property losses suffered by the Japanese in the evacuation. When this objective was publicly announced by the JACL, many Nisei shook their heads in disbelief. Bill Hosokawa was to write,[13] quoting such Nisei, "The objectives seem over-ambitious; the Nisei had barely escaped being stripped of citizenship, their enemies had been close to success in their efforts to deport them. And when had anyone ever collected an indemnity from the government? Wasn't it wiser to let well enough alone?"

The answer for President Kido, Executive Secretary Masaoka, and the other JACL leaders was to assign Masaoka to Washington, D.C. to be their legislative representative to lobby for the program. Masaoka and his beautiful and gracious wife Etsu were undaunted by the obvious handicaps of their assignment. Masaoka, a champion debater and orator from the University of Utah, was a young and indomitable fighter for justice and fair play. Mrs. Masaoka's younger brother, Norman Mineta, was to become the mayor of San Jose, California and later the first Nisei congressman to be elected from the mainland United States.

Masaoka, on his limited budget, could not afford the extravagant, slickly organized legislative campaigns of wealthy corporate or other special interest lobbyists. What funds could not accomplish, his articulateness and burning sincerity in his concern with the plight of the Japanese could.

Long, weary walks from office to office to gain the ears of congressmen and senators was his method of getting legislators to listen to his pleas for justice, understanding, and fair play. At first the climate in Congress was hostile. Gradually, as he spoke, a few members began to listen. In time, more and more legislators began to support his cause. More frustrating days and months went by as he continued to trudge the marbled floors of Congress. Night and day, with his wife at his side, he studied the issues of the Japanese. He drafted letters and memorandums crammed with facts and figures regarding the injustices, past and present, directed toward the Japanese.

Committee hearings followed. His preparations for these hearings became legendary for the breadth and depth of his presentations. His prodigious efforts gradually began to bear fruit. Most important to his effectiveness were his reputation for complete integrity and the sincerity of his campaign to tell the truth about the Japanese. These were coupled with his selfless ability to seek advice upon which to plan his strategy to push his bills through Congress.

In 1946, Masaoka sought the assistance of the War Relocation Authority to draft a bill to submit to Congress to compensate evacuees for property losses. Prominent cabinet members such as Julius Krug, then secretary of the interior, were called to testify before the Congress in support of the measure. Other officials and leaders in communities throughout the United States were also called to add their support to the bill, which called for simple justice for the Japanese who had suffered so heavily during World War II.

THE EVACUATION CLAIMS ACT

Congress approved the bill (H.R.3999), and on July 2, 1948 President Harry S Truman signed the Japanese Evacuation Claims Act into law.[14] What is remarkable in the passage of this act is the fact that the Supreme Court of the United States had just four years before declared in the *Korematsu* case that the evacuation of the Japanese from the West Coast in 1942 was constitutional. Yet now both the Congress and the President recognized the "moral" responsibility toward the Japanese for the action taken against them during World War II and supported their plea to grant them some form of compensation for their property losses.

Under the Evacuation Claims Act, the evacuees were given until January 3, 1950, or eighteen months from its enactment, to file claims against the government. The Attorney General's office was given jurisdiction to determine "according to law" any claim by a person of Japanese ancestry against the United States arising on or after December 7, 1941, when such a claim would not be compensated for by insurance or otherwise, "for damages to or loss of real or personal property . . . that is a reasonable and natural consequence of the evacuation or exclusion from a military area in Arizona, Washington, Oregon, or California."

The act, however, contained several limitations. The attorney general could not consider claims "for damage or loss on account of death or personal injury, personal inconvenience, physical hardship, or mental suffering" (Sec. 2[4]). No claim could be filed "for loss of anticipated profits or loss of anticipated earnings" (Sec. 2[5]). In addition, the attorney general was to "adjudicate all claims filed . . . by award or order of dismissal . . . upon written findings of fact and reasons for the decision" (Sec. 4[a]). And the attorney general could not make an award exceeding $2,500 (Sec. 4[b]).

Before the deadline of January 3, 1950, a total of 23,689 claims were filed with the Attorney General's office, with the aggregate amount of property losses totalling $131,949,176.[15] These claims were broken down as follows:[16]

2,413 claims for sums less than $500

3,385 claims for sums between $501 and $1,000

8,409 claims for sums between $1,001 and $2,500

4,066 claims for sums between $2,501 and $5,000

4,630 claims for sums between $5,001 and $100,000

The above figures reflect that 60 percent of the claims were for less than $2,500, the statutory limit that could be paid directly to the claimants under the act from funds appropriated to the Attorney General's office. Forty percent of the claims were above $2,500, which would require special congressional appropriations to pay the claimants.

Claims Are Bogged Down by Restrictions

The Japanese Evacuation Claims Act was well intentioned and designed to provide some funds to the evacuees to reestablish their lives in their communities. The words contained in the preamble of the act, that the attorney general was to determine these claims "according to law," were construed by the Attorney General's office to mean an adjudication of these claims in a form of "judicial" proceeding. To prove a claim, the evacuee was now compelled to offer the sworn testimony of witnesses that the evacuee actually possessed the property that he claimed he owned at the time of the evacuation. The evidence in support of the claims was not admissible if based on hearsay or secondary evidence. The claims had to be supported by documentary or corroborative evidence, which in most cases was no longer available since such evidence had been destroyed, thrown away, or abandoned in the haste and confusion of the evacuation. Without such probative evidence, property losses could not be recognized. Thus, many claims were initially dismissed because of the "insufficiency of the evidence."

In addition, the requirement in the act that each award or order of dismissal was to be adjudicated by the Attorney General's office based upon "written findings of fact and reasons for the decision" meant lengthy reports to support the decision of claims involving, in many cases, only a few hundred dollars of losses.

Also, the statutory limitation of $2,500 meant that some 40 percent of the claimants would be forced to wait indefinitely for their awards.

Payments would have to be appropriated by Congress along with thousands of other similar items.

Because of these administrative and statutory limitations, the Attorney General's office in the entire year of 1950 processed only 211 claims and agreed to pay 137 of them. At that rate, it would have taken the government over 110 years to complete the processing. By the end of the program no one would have been alive to claim his award.

To further illustrate the aggravating features of the act, the 137 claimants had filed claims for property losses in the aggregate amount of $141,373, or an average of $1,030 each. The attorney general, after refusing to recognize many of the items in them because they were not supported by "evidence in accordance with the law," agreed to pay an aggregate amount of $62,500 for an average of $450 per claim, or only about 40 percent of the aggregate of the claimed losses. The remaining 74 of the 211 claims were dismissed because of the "insufficiency of the evidence," after an inordinately lengthy period of time was spent in "adjudicating" the dismissed claims and "filing findings of fact."

An appalling fact was that it was costing the government in salaries, office operating expenses, and investigating costs approximately $1,400 per case to decide that payments averaging $450 were equitable compensation for the evacuees.[17]

The JACL, concerned about the administrative operations of the act as well as the statutory limitations it contained, quickly returned to Congress to seek a more expeditious processing of the remaining claims. It proposed a procedure whereby compromise settlements could be made without the burdensome "findings of fact" and reasons for decision "according to law." Its efforts were given sympathetic attention by members of Congress.

An Amendment Speeds Up Settlement

On August 17, 1951, H.R. 3142, a bill that amended the Japanese Evacuation Claims Act of 1948, was signed into law by President Truman.[18] The 1951 amendment provided for appropriations of funds by the Congress for the payment of settlement awards "made by the Attorney General in compromise settlement of such claims upon the basis of affidavits and available government records satisfactory to him, in amounts which shall not in any case exceed either three-fourths of the amount, if any, of the claim attributable to compensable items thereof, or $2,500.00 whichever is less."

Under this amendment, further investigation of a majority of the claims was no longer necessary; the claimant could file an affidavit that he was possessed of certain properties at the time of his evacuation. The information in the affidavit would then be compared with forms and documents previously submitted by each evacuee to the WRA, the Federal Reserve Bank of San Francisco, the Farm Security Administration, or other federal agencies that had been charged with the responsibility of protecting the property of the evacuees at the time of their removal from the West Coast.

These government records were the basis for determining the monetary award to be arrived at by negotiations between the claimant and the Attorney General's office. The claimant would then have the option of compromising his award with the government at 75 percent of the actual award or, if the settlement agreed to was more than $2,500, he could accept the statutory maximum of $2,500.

The logjam of pending claims was loosened by this compromise procedure. Almost all of the remaining claims were quickly settled. In 1952, 15,354 claims amounting to $46,664,332 were compromised and settled for a total of $18,255,768. It cost only $43.27 in administrative overhead to settle an average claim of $773.65.

The final claim was paid in 1965, more than twenty-three years after the evacuation and seventeen years after the claims act was passed. The last claim was a compromise payment to Ed Koda, son of Keisaburo Koda, and to Mrs. Jean Koda, widow of Ed's brother William. The Kodas had owned nearly 4,000 acres of rice lands near South Dos Palos in the San Joaquin Valley. Their original claim was for $1,210,000. The Attorney General's office settled with them for $362,500.

In the end, a total of $38 million was paid by the federal government to the evacuees under the Evacuation Claims Act, which was less than ten cents for every dollar lost, based on the Federal Reserve Bank of San Francisco's 1942 estimate that property losses suffered by the Japanese totalled approximately $400 million.

Shortcomings of the Evacuation Claims Program

Although the evacuation claims program was conceived as a worthy measure, there were many serious shortcomings in the program that had become glaringly apparent when it came to a close in 1965.

1. The basis of valuation for property losses sustained by the evacuees was set at 1942 prices. Payments to the evacuees were made many years after the war ended, at a time when postwar inflationary prices had greatly reduced the purchasing power of the dollar.

2. This was further aggravated by the Attorney General's office, which refused to recognize a substantial number of the claims on the basis that ownership of many of the properties was not reflected in government records. Thus, such necessary items as furniture, stoves, household equipment, business supplies, and inventories, which the evacuees were forced to dispose of at distress prices or abandon, were not included.

3. A substantial number of claimants whose actual property losses were very substantial compromised and settled for $2,500. To request more than the statutory limit would have meant that the evacuees would have to wait for further appropriations from Congress. Sorely in need of immediate funds, these claimants decided to accept the $2,500.

4. Many of the claimants died while their claims were being processed. Additional expenses and delays ensued in efforts to file estate proceedings to distribute the awards to the heirs of the claimants.

5. The evacuees were never compensated for the money they might have earned during wartime through employment in shipyards or other defense industries, activities into which millions of their fellow Americans flocked to serve their country in the war effort. The loss of such wages, therefore, compounded their total losses.

The responsibility for safeguarding the property of the evacuees rested with the army, the Federal Reserve Bank of San Francisco, and the Farm Security Administration. As the WRA stated in its final report, "The Federal Government was slow to set up the machinery for safeguarding the property of the people who were to be evacuated."

Congressman Edgar A. Jonas of Illinois, a member of the congressional committee investigating the evacuation claims program in 1954 stated, "The evacuation orders, in many instances, gave the people affected desperately little time in which to settle their affairs. The governmental safeguards which were designed to prevent undue loss were somewhat tardily instituted, were not at once effectively publicized among the evacuees, and were never entirely successful."[19]

The inadequacy of the evacuation claims program was expressed by economist Kenneth Hansen in these words:

We haven't paid for these losses at all. In fact, the bill gets bigger every day. It's not a question of their temporary loss of rights, but has to be thought of in terms of their whole lives. They are still being denied the fruits of their earnings. The Nisei are paying the price today in the loss of opportunity and gains which they would have made had we not taken this outrageous action. Losses are still being compounded because of constantly increasing evaluation of often valuable lands they were forced to let go.[20]

And author Roger Daniels concurred:

For most American businessmen and the economy as a whole, World War II was a time of high profits, the prelude to affluence. Every identifiable socio-economic group in the United States, save one, profited from the war; for the Japanese Americans, it was a serious setback. Although most did not become impoverished, their economic progress was significantly retarded, not only during the war, but in the post-war period as well.[21]

The Questionnaire Program and the Nisei Draft Violators

SELECTIVE SERVICE SYSTEM—continued

23. List contributions you have made to any society, organization, or club:

Organization   *Place*   *Amount*   *Date*

----

24. List magazines and newspapers to which you have subscribed or have customarily read:

----

25. To the best of your knowledge, was your birth ever registered with any Japanese governmental agency for the purpose of establishing a claim to Japanese citizenship? _____

        (a) If so registered, have you applied for cancelation of such registration? _____

               (Yes or no)

        When?_____ Where? _____

26. Have you ever applied for repatriation to Japan? _____

27. Are you willing to serve in the armed forces of the United States on combat duty, wherever ordered? _____

28. Will you swear unqualified allegiance to the United States of America and faithfully defend the United States from any or all attack by foreign or domestic forces, and forswear any form of allegiance or obedience to the Japanese emperor, or any other foreign government, power, or organization? _____

_____   _____

      (Date)   (Signature)

NOTE.—Any person who knowingly and wilfully falsifies or conceals a material fact or makes a false or fraudulent statement or representation in any matter within the jurisdiction of any department or agency of the United States is liable to a fine of not more than $10,000 or 10 years' imprisonment, or both.

WRA-126, REV.   BUDGET NO. 13-R022-43
                                                  APPROVAL EXPIRES 7/31/43

WAR RELOCATION AUTHORITY

APPLICATION FOR LEAVE CLEARANCE

Relocation Center _____
Family No. _____
Center Address _____

1. _____   _____   _____

      (Surname)   (English given name)   (Japanese given name)

      (a) Alias _____

2. Names and ages of dependents you propose to take with you _____

3. Date of birth _____ Place of birth _____
    Citizenship _____

ARLY IN 1943, as the war against the Axis powers intensified, the
United States Army suddenly decided it needed additional fighting men. It was thought that some of these men could be drafted from
among the thousands of eligible males of Japanese ancestry who were
being detained in the camps. The War Department found itself ready
to change its policy of not allowing the enlistment of persons of Japanese ancestry.

In mid-January 1943 the War Relocation Authority officials were
summoned to a meeting in the office of Assistant Secretary of War
John J. McCloy. There, WRA Director Dillon Myer and his associates
were informed that the War Department had decided to recruit an
all-Nisei combat team of about 5,000 men to be drawn from both
the Hawaiian Islands and the concentration camps. The army then
directed the WRA to determine, by means of a questionnaire to be
answered as soon as possible by all Nisei males of military age in the
camps, the number and "loyalty" of such males. The WRA was eager
to accommodate the army in its request. It was certain it could supply
the army with ample evidence of the high number of eager volunteers
among the eligible Nisei males in the various camps. [1]

THE APPLICATION FOR LEAVE CLEARANCE

The WRA then made a mistake so appalling as to be almost beyond
belief. The army had requested that the WRA questionnaire be submitted only to eligible Nisei males of military age. But the WRA had
decided on its own to submit the questionnaire to all of the evacuees
who were seventeen years of age or over [2] —males and females, citizens
and noncitizens, the sick, the ailing, and the decrepit. The confusion
and anger caused among the evacuees was monumental because everyone concerned construed it to be an order to depart from the camps.
The questionnaire said so. [3]

Many of the Issei, particularly the elderly, as well as a considerable
number of Nisei, who felt it was their responsibility to care for their
parents, felt that they were in no position to leave camp at that time.
Wives with children had no desire to leave either. Where would they
go? Yet, here was the WRA asking them to sign forms titled "Application for Leave Clearance."

The WRA attempted to convince the inmates that the filling out
of the questionnaire did not mean that anyone would be forced to
leave, but the people who had experienced too many broken promises
from government officials did not believe these assurances. The evacuees suspected that the questionnaire was some sort of a ruse and that

the government would take unfavorable action against them based on their answers to the questions. As it later turned out, the evacuees were right. The "wrong" answers to the questionnaire were used against them as evidence to force them from the camps in which they were residing to a segregation center at Tule Lake near Newell, California and to brand them as "disloyal."[4] Thousands of evacuees refused to sign the questionnaire. Arguments about whether to even answer the questions split whole families asunder.

Question 27 read: "Are you willing to serve in the armed forces of the United States in combat duty, wherever ordered?"[5] (For the women, Army Nurse Corps or WAAC.) Presenting such a question to a sixty-year-old female was ridiculous. If the same question was posed to a Japanese male who was a national of Japan and he answered yes, it would have placed him in a terrible dilemma of being a traitor to the country of his citizenship while at the same time being declared an "enemy alien" by the country of his residence.

The psychological and emotional pressures, real or fancied, became almost unbearable to the Issei males as they struggled with the awful implications inherent in question 27. The next question was no better. Number 28 read: "Will you swear unqualified allegiance to the United States of America and faithfully defend the United States from any or all attack by foreign or domestic forces; and foreswear any form of allegiance or obedience to the Japanese Emperor, to any other government power or organization?"[6]

The Issei could not answer the first part yes because of the second part of the question. To "foreswear any form of allegiance or obedience to the Japanese Emperor" would leave them stateless, without legal or moral support from any country. The Issei were ineligible to become United States citizens by law. The Chinese, Filipino, and Hindu were now able to become citizens by amendments to the naturalization laws enacted by Congress during World War II, but not the Japanese. Thus, an Issei could not answer question 28 either yes or no without placing himself in a completely vulnerable position.

Resistance to the Questionnaire

The questionnaire caused further aggravation among a group of angry Nisei who bitterly resented the government and the army, which had subjected them to the evacuation in flagrant disregard of their constitutional rights as American citizens. These disgruntled Nisei resisted and opposed the efforts of the government to obtain responses to the questionnaire.

Joe Kurihara, a Nisei born in Hawaii, was typical of the embittered group. He was a veteran of the United States Army and had been wounded in action in World War I. Kurihara considered his imprisonment in the concentration camp as a personal insult and a direct question upon his own indisputable loyalty to the United States. He swore, after he was put behind barbed wire, "to become a 'Jap' a hundred per cent and never do another day's work to help this country fight this war."[7] He greatly influenced many other Nisei to oppose the government in its recruitment efforts to enlist Nisei volunteers, stating that the United States government had not been fair to American citizens of Japanese ancestry in its discriminatory policies and had impugned their loyalty.

Conflicts between the supporters of the JACL and some of the extremist Kibei had been simmering for a long time. Now these conflicts became more pronounced and violent after the questionnaire program was announced. As previously stated, the Kibei were American citizens of Japanese ancestry who had been sent to Japan at a relatively early age by their parents for either education or employment. Their knowledge of Japan and their ability to speak, read, and write Japanese caused them to be in closer contact with the Issei.

Some of the Kibei, whose sympathies were closer to Imperial Japan, saw the turmoil over the questionnaire as an opportunity to attack the Nisei and particularly the JACL leaders for the plight of the Japanese in the concentration camps. Even before the questionnaire was distributed by the WRA, the Kibei rebels accused some of the Nisei of collaborating with government officials, of being "informers" against the Kibei, and of urging the WRA to segregate the Kibei malcontents. Various leaders of the JACL were threatened with death or bodily injury. Ultimately, the most outspoken Kibei were removed from the various camps to Moab, Utah or to Leupp, Arizona where they remained until they were transferred to the segregation camp at Tule Lake.

After the questionnaire was sent out to all residents at the Heart Mountain center in Wyoming, a large group of other protesting Nisei formed a Citizens Congress at a meeting on February 11, 1943. One speaker expressed the point of view of many Nisei, not only in Wyoming, but also throughout all the concentration camps. His feelings are worth noting here:

The minds of many of us are still shrouded in doubt and confusion as to the true motives of our government when they invite our voluntary enlistment at the present time. It has not been explained why some American citizens, who patriotically volunteered, at the beginning of the war, were rejected by the Army. Furthermore, our government has permitted damaging propaganda to continue against us. Also, she has failed to reinstate us in the eyes of the American public. We are placed on the spot, and our course of action is in the balance scale of justice; for our government's honest interpretation of our stand will mean absolute vindication and admission of the wrong committed. On the other hand, if interpreted otherwise by misrepresentations and mis-understandings, it will amount to renewed condemnation of this group.

Although we have yellow skins, we too are Americans. We have an American upbringing, therefore we believe in fair play. Our firm conviction is that we would be useless Americans if we did not assert our constitutional rights now; for, unless our status as citizens is cleared and we are really fighting for the perpetuation of democracy, especially when our fathers, mothers, and families are in concentration camps, even though they are not charged with any crime.

We believe that our nation's good faith is to be found in whether it moves to restore full privileges at the earliest opportunity.[8]

And so, the turmoil and confusion raged on. Eventually, the WRA realized the error it had made in framing the questionnaire, and question 28 was rewritten to read, "Will you swear to abide by the laws of the United States and to take no action which would in any way interfere with the war efforts of the United States?"[9] This was a more proper question to ask the Issei, and most of them were able to answer affirmatively.

As the turmoil and confusion gradually subsided and long pent-up resentments were released, some of the questionnaires came in. But some evacuees, citizens and aliens alike, simply answered no to questions 27 and 28, out of resentment over their treatment at the hands of the government. Others refused to fill out the forms altogether.

In the end the questionnaire program, originally meant only to screen eligible male citizens for military service, turned out to be a trap for all the Japanese, just as the evacuees had feared. The WRA used the program to segregate the "loyal" from the ostensibly "disloyal," depending on how each individual had answered the questions in the "Application for Leave Clearance."[10] The WRA broke its word not to use the answers in the questionnaire for any other purpose than that which had been requested by the army. Those who had given flat yes answers to questions 27 and 28, even though they did not volunteer for the army out of choice or because they were otherwise not eligible, were subsequently permitted to leave the camps, provided that certain conditions of employment, residence, and "community acceptance" were present—conditions that, incidentally, were later to be declared unconstitutional by the United States Supreme Court in *Ex parte Mitsuye Endo*, a case discussed in a previous chapter.

Segregation of Evacuees

Those who answered questions 27 and 28 with an outright no or were equivocal in their answers were branded as being disloyal and were eventually segregated and sent to the Tule Lake center. Those who refused to fill out the questionnaire suffered the same fate.

A young Nisei mother who asked for repatriation to Japan explained:

I have American citizenship. It's no good, so what's the use. . . . I feel that we're not wanted in this country any longer. Before the evacuation I had thought that we were Americans, but our features are against us. . . . I found out about being an American. It's too late for me, but at least [in Japan] I can bring up my children so that they won't have to face the same kind of trouble I've experienced.

She and thousands of other persons, young and old, citizens and aliens, were considered "disloyal" and ordered to pack up and move into the segregation center at Tule Lake for the duration of the war. [11]

The total questionnaire program showed these final results. [12] Out of the nearly 78,000 inmates who were eligible to register, almost 75,000 eventually filled out the questionnaire. Approximately 6,700 of the registrants answered no to question 28, nearly 2,000 qualified their answers in one way or another and thus were set down in the government's books as "disloyal," and a few hundred simply left the question blank. The overwhelming majority—more than 65,000—answered yes to question 28. More than 1,200 Nisei volunteered for combat, and about two-thirds of them were eventually accepted for military service.

An analysis of the answers by camp clearly shows that internal local conditions modified the results. At five camps everyone registered; at four others a total of only thirty-six individuals—ten aliens and twenty-six citizens—refused to register; but at Tule Lake almost a third of the camp population of 3,216 people (1,360 citizens and 1,856 aliens) refused. Dorothy Swaine Thomas and Richard S. Nishimoto, who studied Tule Lake, concluded that administrative blunders were largely responsible for the high degree of nonregistration and disloyalty at Tule Lake; but to this, almost surely, must be added the factor of effective leadership among the "disloyal." Journalist Bill Hosokawa has stated that coercion by militant disloyals was also a consideration.

In all, some 11 percent of those eligible to register (about 7,500 evacuees) gave no or qualified answers to the loyalty question. At Tule Lake some 3,000 refused to register, many of them intimidated by gangs of ruffians against whom the WRA could not guarantee protection. [13]

Director Myer also explained that the no replies meant many things. Bill Hosokawa put it this way:

He felt most of them were the expressions of people who had failed to become integrated into their prewar communities, who were weary of fighting against discrimination, who were unhappy with the way they had been treated in the evacuation and angry with the government, who were discouraged about their future in the United States, even some who felt that they might have a more promising future if they went to Japan. But few were actively or even potentially disloyal to the United States; they were just fed up, and Myer could understand why they would be.[14]

Before the questionnaire program had been put into effect, the camp at Tule Lake had been just another camp with an ordinary mixed population of evacuees. The program turned it into a holding area for dissident "disloyals." This meant that now the "loyals" had to be transferred out of Tule Lake to other camps as the "disloyals" were transferred in.

DRAFT RESISTANCE BEGINS

As a result of the activities of the WRA in its efforts to accomplish this back-and-forth shuffling, the evacuees were once again subjected to confusion, hardships, inconveniences, and the disruption of their camp lives, such as they were. Thus, for many of the evacuees many things changed during the program. But one thing did not change and that was their 4-C classification as "enemy aliens" whether they had answered yes or no to questions 27 and 28. Then the local draft boards stepped into the picture and changed all that.

On January 24, 1944 the draft boards began to reclassify all 4-Cs of military age back to 1-A, regardless of which camp they might be interned in, including those at Tule Lake and those who were to be sent to Tule Lake after having been declared "disloyal" by the WRA.[15]

Here was a classic example of the bureaucratic right hand not paying any attention whatever to the judgment of the bureaucratic left hand. If the WRA considered certain eligible Japanese male citizens to be "disloyal" to the extent that it felt it necessary to segregate them in a special camp, why didn't the local draft boards also view these same persons as "disloyal" and simply leave them with their 4-C classification? Conversely, if the United States Selective Service authorities considered any eligible Japanese-American citizen of military age worthy of classification to a 1-A status for active service, why, at the same time, did the WRA insist that these same persons were so "disloyal" as to make it necessary to segregate them physically from the rest of the "loyal" community?

In the end thousands of Nisei had volunteered for active duty with the United States armed forces in order to show America their patriotism and for other excellent reasons. A former University of California student who volunteered for the all-Nisei combat team wrote to Monroe Deutsch, then president of the University of California,[16] "It was a hard decision . . . [but] I knew that this will be the only way that my family can resettle in Berkeley without prejudice and persecution." Other Nisei not only refused to volunteer during the questionnaire program but subsequently went on to refuse induction once they were reclassified to a 1-A status.

The United States Army had practiced racial discrimination against the Nisei long before Pearl Harbor. The navy, the Marine Corps, and the air force had a policy of not accepting Nisei, particularly those from the West Coast. Before World War II, no Nisei had ever been accepted into West Point or Annapolis. After Pearl Harbor many Nisei who were already in the uniform of the United States Army had been arbitrarily released from active service by transferring them to the Enlisted Reserve Corps "for the convenience of the Government," an obvious method used to discharge them from the army. Other Nisei in uniform, who were allowed to remain with their outfits, were assigned to permanent kitchen police (K.P.) duty or yard detail. When their non-Japanese buddies were shipped overseas, those Nisei were transferred to other units to continue their noncombat duties.

The principal reason for several hundred Nisei refusing induction was their strong conviction that they did not have an obligation to submit to military service under a government that had consistently and blatantly practiced discrimination against them based solely on their racial ancestry. The government had further violated their constitutional rights as American citizens by placing them in concentration camps where they were now branded as enemy aliens to boot.

This designation as an "enemy alien" was a shock to practically every Nisei who had been placed in a camp. They were American citizens. They had not been declared to be "enemy aliens" by the Presidential Proclamation of December 8, 1941 when the United States had declared war against Japan after the attack on Pearl Harbor. Subsequently, the Nisei committed no acts whatever of disloyalty or subversion against the United States. Even assuming some had, they would have had to have been accused in criminal proceedings as citizens, not as enemy aliens. Thus, when some Nisei began to receive their induction orders after being reclassified to 1-A, they refused to obey the orders.

Court Cases Involving Draft Violators

Several federal cases involving Nisei draft resisters produced utterly contradictory results.

Masaaki Kuwabara was a native-born American citizen of Japanese ancestry. He was a resident of San Pedro, California at the time of the evacuation. In the spring of 1942 he was evacuated from his home to the racetrack facilities of Santa Anita in Arcadia, California and was later transferred to a concentration camp in Jerome, Arkansas. He was ultimately transferred to the Tule Lake center after answering no to questions 27 and 28 of the questionnaire. He later admitted he was "disloyal," claiming that discrimination against him as an American citizen and his consequent detention at Tule Lake motivated him to form such a state of mind.

While at Tule Lake, the local draft board of Modoc County, California reclassified him from 4-C to 1-A (available for military service, Section 622.11 of the S.S.S. Regulations). The local board ordered him to report for a preinduction physical examination on May 3, 1944 (Section 629.2 of the S.S.S. Regulations). He refused to obey the order to report. The United States Grand Jury of Northern California charged Kuwabara with "failing to report for pre-induction physical examination in violation of Section 311 of the Selective Service and Training Act of 1940."[17]

In the case of *Masaaki Kuwabara et al.* vs. *United States,* [18] Kuwabara and twenty-five others similarly charged filed a motion to dismiss the proceedings. He stated, among other grounds, that he was being deprived of his liberty without due process of law. He also stated that his plea to the criminal charge was not voluntary because of his restraint and fear due to his confinement in the Tule Lake segregation center. (His fears were well grounded as will be discussed.)

Federal District Judge Louis E. Goodman granted the motion to dismiss but ordered Kuwabara returned to the Tule Lake center to be detained with the other evacuees since there was no other place to which Kuwabara could go.

Judge Goodman stated that just because the war power might allow the detention of Kuwabara at Tule Lake, the guarantees of the Bill of Rights and other constitutional provisions were not abrogated by the existence of the war. He observed that the issue raised by the motion in this case was without precedent. Nevertheless, the issue had to be resolved in the "light of the traditional and historical Anglo-American approach to the time honored doctrine of 'due process.' It must not give way to over-zealousness in an attempt to reach, via the criminal process, those whom we may regard as undesirable citizens." He concluded as follows: "It is shocking to the conscience that an American citizen be confined on the ground of disloyalty, and then, while so under duress and restraint, be compelled to serve in the armed forces, or be prosecuted for not yielding to such compulsion." Judge Goodman also released the other twenty-five Nisei similarly charged.

In Cheyenne, Wyoming, however, the federal court found Shigeru Fujii (and sixty-two others) guilty of the same charge as that which Kuwabara in California was found innocent and released. The defendants were charged with violating Section 311 of the Selective Training and Service Act, of "willfully refusing and failing to report for induction into the armed forces of the United States pursuant to an order of his local draft board."[19]

The circumstances under which Shigeru Fujii and the others were charged at Heart Mountain camp near Cody, Wyoming were markedly different from the conditions that existed at Tule Lake. Persons most opposed to the draft orders in Tule Lake were largely the Kibei and Nisei. At Heart Mountain, however, the draft opposers were led by Nisei, most of whom had never been to Japan nor wished to go to Japan to reside after the war. In the beginning, organized opposition to the draft was led by the Heart Mountain Congress of American Citizens, which was explicitly anti-WRA. This group also insisted that the JACL was not truly representative of the evacuee citizens. The leader of this group opposing the draft was Frank T. Inouye. He argued, "We must demand that our name be cleared; and have it read to the world that there had never been a justification for our evacuation, and that we are fighting, not to redeem ourselves or to clear our names, but for what we have always believed in."[20]

The influence of the Heart Mountain Congress of American Citizens was remarkably effective, as expressed by author Roger Daniels:

Initially the WRA had expected perhaps as many as 2,000 volunteers from Heart Mountain alone; as opposition to the whole program began to develop, its sights were lowered accordingly, and it was estimated that there would be 3,600 volunteers from all 10 camps; only some 1,200 had volunteered up to that time. But even on this diminished scale, the Heart Mountain participation was disproportionately small. . . . The number of volunteers from Heart Mountain was only thirty-eight young men, and half of them failed their physical examinations.[21]

Another person who emerged to lead the opposition to the draft was Kiyoshi Okamoto.[22] Born in Hawaii in the 1920s, he was educated in Los Angeles and became a construction engineer. He had never been to Japan and could not speak Japanese. He had been a principal supporter of the antiregistration (for the draft) and antivolunteer movement among the Nisei. His power and influence increased after the WRA arbitrarily used the questionnaire to effect the segregation program at Tule Lake. He began to speak up more openly after Frank Inouye was shipped away to Tule Lake. He pointed out the general injustices of the entire evacuation. He began to attack specific incidences by Caucasian staff members, acts of brutality, denial by the officials of free speech for evacuees, substandard living conditions within the camp, and the unsatisfactory working conditions of the evacuees.

In November 1943, instead of continuing his efforts through the Congress of American Citizens, Okamoto formed what he called a Fair Play Committee of One. He began to increase his agitation and boldly spoke to his fellow Nisei about doing something about their status. A large number of Nisei were attached to him, which resulted in the formation of a new group called the Fair Play Committee. The committee began to write articles about its cause in the *Rocky Shimpo*, a Japanese-American newspaper in Denver, Colorado and sought legal counsel to test in court the status of the Japanese in the camp. The committee solicited funds to finance its activities. It also began actively to counsel Nisei on resisting the draft. The committee's efforts were highly effective. In the first week of March 1944, twelve Nisei refused to board the bus to take their preinduction physical examinations. By the end of the same month, 54 of the 315 eligible male citizens refused to report for their physicals. The WRA, hoping to stop these resisters, took Okamoto into custody and quickly transferred him to Tule Lake as a "disloyal."[23]

Another leader of the Fair Play Committee then took Okamoto's place. He was twenty-seven-year-old Paul T. Nakadate[24] whose loyalty had been recognized by the WRA after a long interrogation. Nakadate simply felt that "democracy is sharing of equal responsibilities and sharing of equal rights." Nakadate strongly believed that the rights of the Nisei had been flagrantly and consistently violated by the United States government. Since he felt that his treatment had been unjust, he could no longer say whether he would serve in the United States Army, even though he had previously answered yes to questions 27 and 28 of the questionnaire. His answers failed to satisfy Heart Mountain Project Director Guy Robertson, and Nakadate was also transferred to Tule Lake.

After the leaders of the Fair Play Committee had been removed from Heart Mountain, Project Director Robertson decided to express his personal vindictiveness against the other draft resisters. At Robertson's insistence, a reluctant United States attorney, Carl L. Sackett, based in Cheyenne, Wyoming, caused the arrest of all the Nisei who had refused preinduction orders in late March and early April 1944.[25]

On May 10, 1944 a federal grand jury in Cheyenne, Wyoming indicted the draft resisters whose numbers had now grown to sixty-three. In his memorandum opinion Judge T. Blake Kennedy questioned their loyalty in these words, even though it had been stipulated by the government that these Nisei were loyal: "If they are truly loyal American citizens, they should embrace the opportunity to discharge the duties [of citizenship] by offering themselves in the cause of our National Defense."[26] An appeal to the Federal Circuit Court of Appeals in Denver, that the sixty-three Nisei had been deprived of their liberties without due process of law, was rejected in March 1945.[27] The Supreme Court of the United States refused to review the case.[28]

In both the *Kuwabara* and *Fujii* cases, the defendants stated that they would obey the induction orders if they were restored their rights as American citizens. In the case of *Shigeru Fujii et al.*, vs. *United States*, the three appeals justices[29] refused to meet the issue of whether the constitutional rights of the Nisei had been violated. Instead, the convictions were upheld on technical procedural grounds that bordered on the ludicrous rather than on substantial legal reasoning.

Justice Walter A. Huxman speaking for the Circuit Court of Appeals for the Tenth Circuit declared:

Two wrongs never make a right. One may not refuse to heed a lawful call of his government merely because in another way it may have injured him. Appellant was a citizen of the United States. He owed the same military service to his country that any other citizen did [in spite of the stipulation that the sixty-three Nisei had previously been classified by the same local board as 4-C]. Neither the fact that he was of Japanese ancestry nor the fact that his constitutional rights may have been invaded by sending him to a relocation center cancel this debt.

While the case of Shigeru Fujii and the other Nisei at Heart Mountain camp was being tried in the federal court of Cheyenne, Project Director Robertson was relentlessly pursuing the leaders of the Heart Mountain Fair Play Committee. At his insistence, the same federal grand jury that had indicted the sixty-three draft resisters handed down secret criminal indictments against the leaders—indictments that were made public only after Shigeru Fujii and the others had been convicted. The leaders, seven in number, were members of the Fair Play Committee's executive council. They were charged with "unlawful conspiracy to counsel, aid and abet violators of the draft."[30] The seven members included Robert Kiyoshi Okamoto, Isamu Sam Horino, Paul Takeo Nakadate, Tsutomu Wakaye, Frank Seishi Emi, Minoru Tamesa, and Gentaro Kubota. Charged with the same offense was James Matsumoto Omura, English editor of the *Rocky Shimpo.*

The criminal indictments charged the seven leaders and James Omura of entering into a conspiracy to counsel themselves and others to evade military service. Except for Gentaro Kubota, who was born in Japan, the defendants were American-born citizens of Japanese ancestry.

The seven members of the Fair Play Committee, who were now defendants in the case of *Kiyoshi Okamoto et al.* vs. *United States,* [31] contended that their convictions denied them their rights of freedom of speech, press, and assemblage guaranteed to them by the First Amendment of the Constitution. Defendant James Omura was acquitted in the federal district court; the seven leaders of the Fair Play Committee were found guilty.

On appeal, the same three justices of the Federal Circuit Court of Appeals who had upheld the convictions of the sixty-three Nisei a few months earlier on March 12, 1945 in *Shigeru Fujii et al.* vs. *United States,* reversed the convictions of the seven leaders in the case of *Kiyoshi Okamoto et al.* vs. *United States* on December 16, 1945.

Justice Sam G. Bratton of the court of appeals refused to recognize the principal contention of the seven leaders that the First Amendment of the Constitution had been infringed upon. He stated:

> While freedom of speech, freedom of the press and freedom of assembly as guaranteed by the First Amendment are fundamental rights, they are not in their nature absolute.
>
> These rights are not unbridled license to speak, publish or assemble without any responsibility whatever. Their exercise is subject to reasonable restriction required in order to protect the Government from destruction or serious injury.
>
> . . . the First Amendment in its full sweep does not protect one in speech, publication or assembly in furtherance of a conspiracy to promote evasion of an act reasonably designed to protect the Government against destruction by military force.

Having made this statement, Justice Bratton ordered the convictions of the Nisei reversed on the technical grounds that the trial judge in the federal district court had denied giving a certain jury instruction that had been requested by the defendants and had given the jury instructions that were erroneous.

In the trial before a jury in the federal district court, the defendants had submitted to the court a lengthy jury instruction, the substance of which was that in determining whether the defendants acted in good faith or bad faith, the jury might take into consideration several factors: (1) their sincerity or insincerity of belief as to their status and rights as American citizens of Japanese ancestry, who had been evacuated from their homes and detained in the relocation center; (2) the demand by the defendants that such status or rights be lawfully clarified by the court in determining the refusal of such persons to comply with the orders of the draft board; and (3) a determination of the sincerity and good faith of the defendants in such belief.

The judge in the federal district court trial refused to submit the above instruction to the jury as requested by the defendants. Instead, the judge instructed the jury as follows:

> They took the position that a test case should be filed, having for its purpose a test of the constitutionality of the Selective Training and Service Act as applied to them while detained in a relocation center. In this connection, you are instructed that a desire to have a test case for that purpose does not excuse failure to comply with the Selective Training and Service Act. . . . The Selective Training and Service Act provides that it is a violation of the law for anyone to counsel another to disobey the draft law or to assist or abet one to evade the draft law. And I charge you that it is a violation of the law, even though it is contended that the purpose was to create a case for the testing of the constitutionality of the law.

Justice Bratton held that this jury instruction by the trial judge was in error and that the jury instruction requested by the defendants should have been given to the jury. He held that the reversal in the case of *Kiyoshi Okamoto et al.* vs. *United States* was supported by a decision of the Supreme Court of the United States in *Keegan* vs. *United States*. [32]

The *Keegan* case involved American citizens of German blood who were members of the American Bund. Congress, by statute, had amended the Selective Training and Service Act, which provided that vacancies in the employment rolls of business or industry caused by induction of employees into the armed forces should not be filled by members of the Bund. Active agitation by the American Bund suggested that every eligible male of German blood (a United States citizen) ordered for induction into the armed forces of the United States should refuse military service until the act was revoked. In the *Keegan* case the Supreme Court of the United States had declared that the honesty and genuineness of those charged with counseling to oppose military service was material as to the guilt or innocence of those accused of violating the induction orders and that

to counsel merely refusal is not made criminal by the Act. . . . One with innocent motives, who honestly believes a law is unconstitutional, and therefore, not obligatory, may well counsel that the law shall not be obeyed; that its command shall be resisted until a court shall have held it valid, but this is not knowingly counselling, stealthily and by guile, to evade its command.

In citing the *Keegan* case, Justice Bratton wrote:

. . . it is clear that the trial court erred in giving the instruction to which inference had been made. In respect of the issue as to whether the appellants acted with honesty of purpose and innocence of motive in a good faith effort to bring about a test case to determine their exempt status under the Selective Service Act, the court should have instructed the jury in substantial harmony with the rule later enunciated in the *Keegan* case.

Of the other twenty-two Nisei who continued to resist the induction orders at Heart Mountain, between the summer of 1944 and the closing of the camp in November 1945, all were convicted for draft resistance, bringing the total of such convictions at Heart Mountain to eighty-five.[33]

It should be noted here that more than 700 men from Heart Mountain did board the bus for their draft physicals, and 385 of them were inducted. Of those, eleven were killed in action and fifty-two wounded.

The resistance to the draft at Heart Mountain concentration camp was not an isolated phenomenon. During World War II a total of 265 Nisei from the camps refused to obey the induction orders. They were charged with violation of the Selective Training and Service Act and were ultimately convicted. Eighty-one of the draft resisters were from Heart Mountain camp, 109 were from Gila River camp in Arizona, 33 were from Minidoka camp in Idaho, and 30 were from Amache camp in Colorado.[34]

Amnesty Is Granted to Draft Violators

By Executive Order 9814, dated December 23, 1946 (after the war was over), President Truman established the President's Amnesty

Board. The board was ordered to "examine and consider the cases of all persons convicted of violation of the Selective Training and Service Act of 1940 as amended. The board was to report to the attorney general its findings and its recommendations as to whether executive clemency should be granted or denied and, if executive clemency were granted, its recommendations with respect to the form that such clemency should take.

President Truman, after considering the report and recommendation of the board and of the attorney general, found that certain persons, including the 265 Nisei from the various concentration camps who had been convicted of violating the Selective Training and Service Act, "ought to have restored to them the political, civil and other rights of which they were deprived by reason of such conviction and which may not be restored to them unless they are pardoned."

On December 12, 1947, by Presidential Proclamation 2762, President Truman granted a full pardon to those persons convicted of violating the Selective Training and Service Act of 1940.[35] The names of all the 265 Nisei were included in the list attached to the proclamation.

As Roger Daniels has aptly expressed it:

This account of the "loyal" Japanese-American resistance . . . is highly significant. It calls into question the stereotype of the Japanese-American victim of oppression during World War II who met his fate with stoic resignation and responded only with superpatriotism.

Many Japanese-Americans, conforming to the JACL line, honestly felt that the only way they could ever find a place for themselves in America was by being better Americans than most. Whether or not this kind of passive submission is the proper way for free men to respond to injustice and racism is, of course, a matter of opinion. But it is important to note that not all loyal Japanese-Americans submitted; the resistance of the Heart Mountain *Fair Play Committee* and of other individuals and groups in the other camps, has been almost totally ignored and in some instances deliberately suppressed by chroniclers of the Japanese-Americans. . . . There are those, however, who will find more heroism in resistance than in patient resignation.[36]

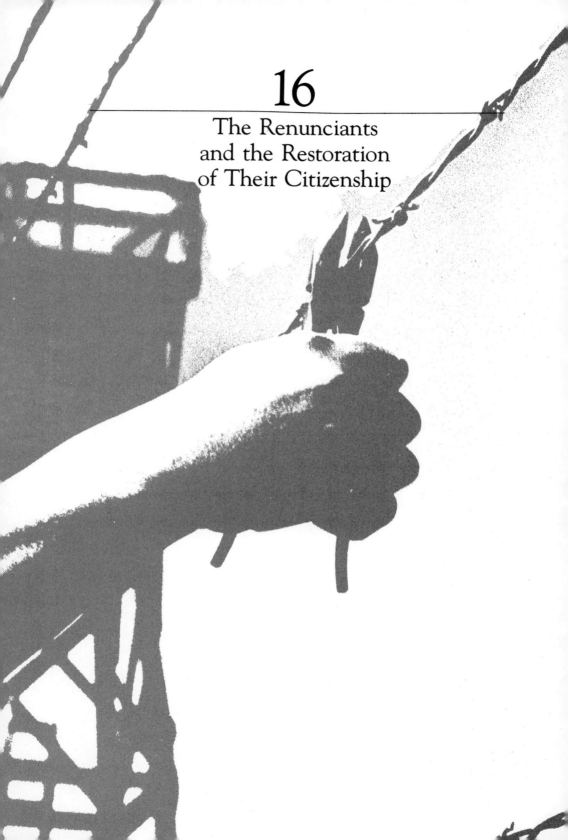

16

The Renunciants
and the Restoration
of Their Citizenship

IN FEBRUARY 1943, when the "Application for Leave Clearance" questionnaire was thrust upon all the evacuees by the WRA, the evacuees had been in camp for almost one year. These ten concentration camps were not normal communities. They were institutions behind barbed wire, normally as impregnable as the concrete walls of penal institutions. The evacuees were closely supervised and controlled by an all-Caucasian administration, backed by an armed company of military police that patrolled the outside perimeter of the camps in jeeps and trucks and kept a constant surveillance from watchtowers. In these institutions, the lives of the evacuees were regulated as to when, what, and how much they could eat and at what prescribed hours. Most evacuees, whether male or female, were issued identical clothing consisting of navy blue pea jackets, khaki pants, and heavy wool stockings.

The camps were ghettos of racially segregated and geographically isolated Japanese, miles from the feverish war efforts to which other persons in the United States were devoting their time and talents. Under conditions of enforced leisure, there was ample time and opportunity for gossip, for intrigue, and, more menacing, for self-seeking leaders of various factions to exercise their own embittered feelings upon bewildered, disillusioned, and helpless people. The enforced incarceration of these "inmates" provided a fertile breeding ground for the development of a type of "prison complex"[1] among the evacuees whose daily lives were filled with fears, rumors, and apprehensions.

The isolated atmosphere of the camps accentuated the psychological state of mind known as *anxiety neurosis*. The one overriding preoccupation of the evacuees was what they were to do to earn a living after the war. Belonging to a proud and self-reliant people whose culture traditionally did not call for dependence upon public charity, the evacuees now became fearful of having to look to the government for their daily needs if they were asked to leave the camps.

Parents became anxious about their children who, now without a normal family life, discipline, or guidance, were running freely throughout the camps. Under these primitive conditions, the school system furnished for the camp inmates was inadequate in spite of the many dedicated teachers who served in it. Learning about the virtues of American democracy while sitting in the barrack school buildings and looking at the barbed wire fences outside was sheer irony.

CALLS FOR RENUNCIATION BEGIN

The stress of life in the camps eroded what confidence in self and family the evacuees had had before their evacuation. The atmosphere of anxiety, fear, and exaggerated rumors was ideal for exploitation by embittered Issei, Nisei, and Kibei.

The argument that continued to rage in the camps went something like this: The Japanese, as a race of people, were unwanted in the United States and had been abandoned by the American people. Therefore, exhorted the leaders:

> Let's all return to Japan. Let us go to Japan where we can be with our own racially similar people. In Japan, we will not be hated or discriminated against as a race. We may have a difficult time adjusting to life in Japan in the beginning, but we will not be held in contempt by others. If we go to Japan, we don't need our United States citizenship. What good is citizenship in a country which refuses to treat us as equals? Why should we retain our citizenship which cannot protect us or give us fair and equal treatment? Demonstrate your contempt for the American constitutional principles and democratic ideals by renouncing your citizenship.[2]

To a large number of persons in the various camps, this argument made sense. It appealed to their disillusionment. It gave many people the hope of living again in a friendly environment in the land of their ancestors since the land of their choice had slammed the door in their faces and had trampled their will to regain a new life outside the camps.

Meanwhile, a demand that the "Japs" go "back to Japan" was echoed by politicians, pressure organizations, and the press. California State Senator Clarence C. Ward of Santa Barbara stumped the state urging that the evacuees be "interned" and eventually deported to Japan.[3] The race-baiting Martin Dies, chairman of the House of Representatives Special Committee to Investigate Un-American Activities, attacked the WRA for "molly-coddling the disloyal."

When the questionnaire program came to an end in June 1943, Tule Lake was designated by the WRA as a segregation camp. On August 16, 1943 Raymond R. Best relieved Harvey Coverly as project director at that site. A native of Michigan, Best was educated in Los Angeles, served with the Marine Corps in World War I, and later became involved in oil, banking, and general merchandising enterprises in Idaho. He was appointed to the Federal Land Bank at Spokane, Washington and worked for eight years as a soil conservationist with the Department of Agriculture. He had been with the WRA from its inception in 1942.[4]

The massive chess game to move people from one camp or another to the Tule Lake segregation center, and to compel persons at Tule

Lake to move from the center because they had answered the question-naire the "right" way, began in September 1943. These persons, now looked upon by the WRA as so many numbers instead of as human beings, were uprooted again. Twenty thousand individuals from nine camps throughout the United States were involved in this massive exchange. The segregation program took more than one month, with people being shuttled back and forth between camps to reach their ultimate destination. It required thirty-three troop trains to effect this move.[5] Over 6,000 "loyal" evacuees were ordered out of Tule Lake to make room for the "disloyal." Some of the evacuees were to say later that the traumatic experience of being ordered out of Tule Lake made some of the "loyal" give "disloyal" answers to the questionnaire to avoid being moved again.

Tule Lake segregation center had prepared well for the "disloyal" evacuees. The single-line barbed wire fence that formerly encircled the camp was now a double fence of barbed wire, eight feet high, and "manproof." The number of military police billeted outside the center had been increased to approximately 1,500 men. Besides the usual jeeps, trucks, and weapons carriers, a number of ominous-looking tanks were brought in to stand guard at the entrance of the center where everybody, including the public, could see them.[6]

Sociologists use the term *self-fulfilling prophecy* to describe the behavior of certain persons or groups of persons who perform in a violent or a vicious manner in a given social environment. If the pressures on such persons are too intense because of torments, insults, injuries, or injustices inflicted upon them in a period of violent, emotional disturbance, they may become what their tormentors accused them of being.

Having now been branded "disloyal" and "pro-Japanese" the trouble-makers, mostly young and active Kibei, began to agitate the WRA officials as soon as they arrived in Tule Lake. The self-government body, composed of old, conservative Tule Lake residents, was ousted. The "newly elected officers" for the evacuees called themselves the *Daihyo Sha Kai*, which in Japanese means Representative Body. Project Director Best said of this representative body,[7] "The strong men, troublemaker group was never representative of all the center residents . . . but it never ceased to terrify a majority of the peaceful citizens of Tule Lake."

The dissident extremists now began to impose pro-Japanese behavior upon other evacuees. The customary restraints in an open community were not present. To the residents who had chosen to go to Tule Lake, not because they were disloyal but because they wished to remain with their parents, and to those who gave lip service to disloyalty to avoid resettlement, living in Tule Lake for the rest of the war became a veritable nightmare.

Young toughs burst into the women's shower rooms, which had no keys or latches, shouting, "This is Japan, and men and women bathe together." The same groups broke up American-style dances held by the Nisei because the dances were not Japanese. Classes were formed to instruct girls in such niceties as sitting on the floor in proper Japanese style. The American flag, which had been hoisted by Nisei Boy Scouts in front of the administration building, was curtly ordered lowered by the young Kibei.[8]

A mysterious rash of accidents caused damage to camp equipment. Strikes were ordered in various service projects manned by the evacuees, without the consent of the workers. WRA officials were constantly harangued and criticized. Persons who spoke sympathetically of the WRA or against the dissidents were brutally beaten. Those working on the service projects, such as maintenance, garbage collection, kitchen service, and recreation, and earning $14, $16, and $18 per month, were compelled to stop and lost this meager income. The camp was in constant turmoil. Human misery mounted. Conditions deteriorated, with food deliveries interrupted, milk not being supplied, and garbage left uncollected.

Because of the chaotic conditions and the inability of the WRA officials to control the situation, the army decided on November 5, 1943 to move in to put a lid on the trouble. Martial law was declared eight days later and lasted for two months until January 14, 1944.[9] Two hundred men, mostly Kibei, were arrested and held in stockades without formal charges or trial.

Army control over Tule Lake caused sensational headlines throughout the West Coast, accusing all 20,000 evacuees of being "disloyal." The California Legislature demanded an investigation of the situation and approved a resolution to deport all the inmates at Tule Lake to Japan.[10] Congress also demanded an investigation.[11] United States Representative Clair Engle, whose California district included the center, made a quick trip to Tule Lake, but army control was so tight he could not even enter the camp.[12] Floodlights had been turned on at the watchtowers. Tanks rumbled into the camp and stood ponderous, menacing guard, their guns pointed straight at the frail tar-paper barracks that housed the residents. The inability of the WRA to control the wild, restless rebels was condemned by leading newspapers and denounced by scores of midwestern congressmen.

The abiding tragedy of the Tule Lake riots was that the great majority of the residents were victims of fellow inmates whose bitterness and anger over their treatment by the United States government was manifested in such extreme ways. They did what their tormentors outside the camp had "expected" them to do. The self-fulfilling prophecy manifested itself in still another disastrous way for thousands of evacuees who were United States citizens.

In Congress a group of Californians, including Jack Z. Anderson, John Costello, Alfred Elliott, Clair Engle, Leland Ford, Bertram ("Bud") Gearhardt, Carl Hinshaw, Leroy Johnston, John Phillips, Norris Poulson, Harry Shephard, and Richard Welch, felt that they should satisfy the demands of the West Coast exclusionist groups by making tough speeches on the floor of the House.[13] Also in the lead of the attacks against the Japanese were the American Legion, the Americanism Educational League, the California Joint Immigration Committee, the Hearst Press, and the *Los Angeles Times.*[14]

Loud and insistent voices, both from the Kibei extremists inside Tule Lake and from anti-Japanese elements outside the camps, called for a way for those in the camps to renounce their United States citizenship.

CONGRESS MAKES FORMAL RENUNCIATIONS POSSIBLE

In response, Congress, with extraordinary speed, approved the passage of an amendment to the Nationality Law of 1940 to enable those in the concentration camps to renounce their citizenship by merely filing a written declaration. On July 1, 1944 President Roosevelt signed Public Law 405. Section 801(i) of the law provided as follows:

Making in the United States a formal written renunciation of nationality in such form as may be prescribed by or before such officer as may be designated by the Attorney General, whenever the United States shall be in a state of war, and the Attorney General shall approve such renunciation as not contrary to the interests of national defense.[15]

When this bill was being considered in Congress, Attorney General Francis Biddle testified that there were between 300 and 1,000 persons of Japanese ancestry at the Tule Lake segregation center who had expressed a desire to renounce their citizenship and had asked for expatriation.[16] The measure was designed to deal specifically with the extremist, dissident group of rabid pro-Japanese Kibei who were loudly demanding to go to Japan, but during the winter of 1944 and the spring of 1945 some 5,700 applications, mostly from Tule Lake, were received.[17]

The Attorney General's office and the WRA had totally miscalculated the discouragement and loss of morale among the evacuees. The majority of the applicants were evacuees who were only reacting to an overwhelming fear originating both in the camp situation in which they found themselves and in not knowing what they would have to face in a hostile society outside. They were in a trap when the pro-Japanese pressure groups proposed a way out: Renounce American citizenship and ask for immediate repatriation. The active pro-Japanese organizations known as the *Hoshi-Dan* (Patriotic Society) and the *Hokoku* (Loyal to the Homeland Association) were made up primarily of belligerent young Kibei. The methods of persuasion used by them were very effective.

They terrorized the other residents of Tule Lake by invading their barracks and threatening to beat up the citizen families unless they renounced. They threatened the younger men over seventeen years of age with torture. They sent veiled threats to other evacuees who opposed the renunciation program. The members of the pro-Japanese organizations shaved their heads and performed calisthenics in military style at regular intervals in public places.

The residents, living in crowded blocks, never knew when someone next to them might be beaten or killed. Young girls had to stay in at night or risk attack. Young men of the *Hokoku* made the morning air hideous with the noise of their bugling (purchased by mail order from Sears), their goose-stepping military drills, and their shouts of "Banzai."[18]

The threats and beatings of undecided citizen evacuees were climaxed by the murder of Takeo Hitomi who had openly opposed the renunciation program.[19] He had been tabbed by the extremists as "number one Inu" (dog). Hitomi was general manager of Co-operative Enterprises, a merchandising project at Tule Lake where the evacuees could purchase various goods and materials from merchants outside the camp. News of his stabbing death by unknown assassins spread like wildfire throughout the tension-packed community. Panic gripped the center. Undecided citizens flocked by the thousands to renounce their citizenship as a means of insuring their safety.

Detailed hearings on the applications for renunciation had been established by the Attorney General's office to ascertain the true intentions of the citizens, but the applicants were now too far demoralized to state anything but the wish to cancel their citizenship. They had already been thoroughly coached by members of extremist organizations as to what to say to the hearing officers who interviewed them.

RENUNCIANTS SEEK REPATRIATION

Only a limited number of these renunciants applied for expatriation after World War II ended with the surrender of Japan. Over 4,000 Nisei and Kibei renunciants never wanted to go to Japan at all.[20] But those who remained in the United States now found themselves in a legal status without precedent. Those renunciant Nisei or Kibei who were born after 1924 and whose parents had not formally registered their births with the Japanese consul were now stateless. Those born before 1924 and who had been dual citizens were now aliens ineligible for citizenship in the land of their birth.

As mentioned previously, before the *Endo* decision was handed down on December 18, 1944, the army had rescinded the orders that had excluded Japanese from the West Coast. Now the evacuees could go back to California, Oregon, Washington, or Arizona. In addition, the WRA announced the closing of all the camps within the next twelve months.

What were the renunciants to do? They could only seek to rescind their renunciations in the federal courts of the United States.

The case of *Yuichi Inouye, Miye Mae Murakami, Tsutako Sumi and Mutsu Shimizu* vs. *Clark*, tried in the federal district court sitting in Los Angeles, involved four former United States citizens all residing in California at the time of their evacuation in 1942.[21]

Yuichi Inouye was seventeen years of age when he signed the written declaration of renunciation. He was an only son who, with his parents, had been evacuated to the Manzanar center. He later accompanied his parents to the Santa Fe internment center in New Mexico because his father had applied for repatriation to Japan. Young Inouye was considered "loyal" by the WRA officials. Inouye stated that he renounced his citizenship in order to accompany his parents to Japan. He did not know what he would do if he were left alone in the United States.

Miye Mae Murakami married a Japanese alien in September 1939. She and her family were evacuated in 1942. In February 1944 the family was transferred to the Tule Lake segregation center. Mrs. Murakami stated that she renounced her citizenship because she feared she would be separated from her husband who desired to return to Japan. She also stated that assaults, stabbings, and the general atmosphere of tension and hysteria at Tule Lake made her fear for her own safety if she did not renounce.

Tsutako Sumi, who was married to a Japanese alien, was the mother of three children, all born in the United States. She and her family were evacuated in 1942 to Tule Lake. She stated that she lived in a block surrounded by rabid pro-Japanese elements, and she was in daily fear of her life. Her husband forced her to renounce her citizenship to stop the threats against them.

Mutsu Shimizu, the wife of a Japanese alien, was also the mother of three children. In 1942 she and her family were evacuated to Manzanar in California and later transferred to Tule Lake. She stated that she renounced her citizenship because of threats and stabbings in her neighborhood. She was further coerced into renouncing her citizenship by her husband, who was an active leader in the pro-Japanese group.

All four of these persons claimed in court that their renunciations were not free and voluntary but were the result of undue influence, duress, and coercion. Federal District Judge Charles Cavanah, on special assignment in Los Angeles from Idaho, held that the renunciations of their United States citizenship were invalid, null, and void and ordered that their citizenship be restored to them.

As to Yuichi Inouye, Judge Cavanah stated that "it appears clear that the youth yielded to parental compulsion and [this is] a clear case of 'parental influence' in order to hold the family intact." Judge Cavanah further took note of the fact that there was no age requirement prescribed in Section 801(i) of Public Law 405 at which a person, who is a national of the United States by birth, shall lose his citizenship.

The requirement of age which renunciation of citizenship can be made, should not be left to conjecture in the face of Congressional silence, and the rights of citizenship are not to be destroyed by ambiguity."

At the time . . . Yuichi Inouye signed his application and its approval by the government, he, being under the legal age, the same is void.

Judge Cavanah discussed the concept of parental pressure further. He stated:

Where acts of a child done under the domination of the parent and which dominated the mind of the minor by unfair persuasion, it is regarded as induced by unfair persuasion and influence of the minor and is voidable.

The results, flowing from that parental domination, and the acts of fear constitute undue influence, duress and coercion, require them to be declared null and void. They should be considered in the light of the circumstances under which they were performed. Feebleness on one side and overpowering strength on the other imply duress.

Judge Cavanah, in restoring United States citizenship to Miye Mae Murakami, Tsutako Sumi, and Mutsu Shimizu, stated that none of them was guilty of any kind of disloyalty to the United States. He found, instead, that because of the conditions at Tule Lake, these women lacked sufficient free exercise of their will to make their renunciations voluntary. He declared:

Freedom of will is essential in the exercise of an act which is urged to be binding, and the right of citizenship being an important civil one, can only be waived as the result of free and intelligent choice. The mere fact that some of the plaintiffs, having stated that they knew the results of their renunciation does not remove the primary force and effect of duress, coercion and undue influence that caused them to renounce.

The Government appealed the decision of Judge Cavanah to the Ninth Circuit Court of Appeals where it was upheld in blunt language, harsh in expression, and biting in its effect.[22] Chief Judge William Denman, in sustaining the judgment of Federal District Judge Cavanah, delivered a scathing denunciation of government policy and its treatment of the evacuees at Tule Lake. He denounced the

unnecessarily cruel and inhuman treatment of these citizens (a) in a manner of their deportation for imprisonment and (b) in their incarceration for over two and a half years under conditions in major respects as degrading as those of a penitentiary and in important respects worse than in any federal penitentiary, and (c) in applying to them the Nazi-like doctrine of inherited racial enmity, stated by the Commanding General ordering the deportations as the major reason for that action.

(A) The racial deportation. Its unnecessary hardships and cruelty as affecting the attitude of scores of thousands of loyal Americans towards their citizenship in a country so ordering them into imprisonment. . . .

The emotion of free citizens contemplating the pathetic testing of the carrying capacity of stumbling infants lifting their bundles is not pertinent here. What is pertinent is what our incarcerated fellow citizens felt about it in their several years behind barbed wire under the machine guns of the soldiers in their prison's turrets. For, so far as concerns the psychology of the renunciations of those renouncing and their surrounding companions, the beguiling word "evacuation" meant deportation, "evacuees" meant prisoners, "relocation center" meant prison, and their single rooms, some crowding in six persons, meant cells, as they in fact were. Their true character is recognized in this opinion. . . .

(B) The incarceration at the Tule Lake stockade. . . . The barbed wire stockade surrounding the 18,000 people there was like that of the prison camps of the Germans. There were the same turrets for the soldiers and the same machine guns for those who might attempt to climb the high wiring. . . .

(C) General DeWitt's doctrine of enemy racism inherited by blood strain. . . . The major reason for General DeWitt's deportation orders is his belief that these citizens, descended of an eastern Asiatic race, can never be determined to be loyal Americans. . . .

The identity of this doctrine with that of the Hitler generals towards those having blood strains of a western Asiatic race as justifying the gas chambers of Dachau must have been realized by the educated Tule Lake persons of Japanese blood strain. . . .

Fear of reprisal if one failed to renounce his citizenship was for some the final pressure causing such renunciations. Such violence continuing over a year is another of the worse than penitentiary conditions considered supra.

Others feared such violence as of the German mobs if they returned to their homes after they were free to do so. . . .

The above facts in evidence add to our conclusion that the ultimate fact found of renunciation because of mental fear, intimidation and coercion necessarily follows from the probative facts.

In June 1947, approximately three months before the *Inouye* case was heard in the federal district court in Los Angeles, the federal district court in San Francisco considered a case involving 2,300 out of 5,371 American citizens of Japanese ancestry who had signed declarations renouncing their United States citizenship while in the Tule Lake segregation center. The case was heard before Judge Louis Goodman. Tadayasu Abo[23] and the others had sworn out writs of habeas corpus against District Director Irving Wixon of the United States Immigration Service in San Francisco, alleging that they were being unlawfully detained in custody for deportation to Japan. Wixon admitted that these persons were in his custody, under orders of the attorney general to remove them from the United States as alien enemies, pursuant to authority granted by the Alien Enemy Act of 1798.[24]

These 2,300 persons further sought to cancel their renunciations under procedures established under Section 801(i) of Public Law 405. It was claimed by them that their renunciations had been made under duress and coercion, induced by actions of the federal government and by factors involving "disloyal" residents. They contended that their state of mind, brought about by the evacuation and detention in the concentration camps, rendered them impotent to act freely, voluntarily, competently, and intelligently with respect to their acts of renouncing their citizenship. All these persons were possessed of dual citizenship of the United States and Japan.

The Government contended that at the time of their alleged renunciation, the petitioners were also citizens of Japan only when their renunciations were signed by them and approved by the government. The Government further asserted that many of the applicants were and had been "disloyal" to the United States.

Judge Goodman refused to recognize the contention of the Government that the renunciants could be legally deported to Japan under the Alien Enemy Act. He stated:

. . . absent any express declaration of Congressional intent, there is no justification for holding that under the Alien Enemy Act, a native-born resident American citizen, who renounces his American citizenship pursuant to Section 801(i) may be deported, at least as long as he continues to reside here.

Judge Goodman had earlier in his decision rejected the theory that a native-born resident American could, at the same time, be an alien and a citizen of a foreign state. He called this dual citizenship status "judicially unsound."

An American citizen as such, owes his entire allegiance to the United States and the United States is entitled to claim from him an indivisible loyalty. . . . It is constitutionally impossible for a resident citizen of the United States to have at the same time any allegiance to any foreign government.

Therefore, Judge Goodman pointed out:

Possession of Japanese citizenship, in Japan, by a native-born resident American citizen of Japanese ancestry does not, upon renunciation of American citizenship in the United States, convert that person into an alien until he has voluntarily departed from this country.

All that the expatriation statute (including Section 801[i]) purports to effect is termination of American citizenship. It in no way fixes or determines any particular alien nationality for the expatriate. By its terms, the Alien Enemy Act applies to subjects of hostile countries who are found within the United States and are "not actually naturalized" [50 U.S.C.A., Section 21].

Judge Goodman found that the 2,300 persons, even though they might have renounced their United States citizenship, were obviously not within the scope of Section 21. The writs of habeas corpus were granted to these renunciants, and their deportation to Japan was halted.

The following year, in a mass party action, 4,315 renunciants including the same 2,300 appeared before the same judge to be heard as to the validity of the renunciation of their United States citizenship.[25] The renunciants reiterated that internal pressures had been exerted upon them by pro-Japanese factions and that there were threats of violence against recalcitrant evacuees and their families. Other facts such as parental pressures, fear of community hostility on release, mass hysteria, the traumatic evacuation experiences, their loss of homes, isolation from the outside community, the guarded, overpopulated camps, inadequate and uncomfortable accommodations, and dreary unhealthful surroundings were alleged to have produced a neurosis of fear, anxiety, resentment, uncertainty, hopelessness, and a despair of eventual rehabilitation.

Judge Goodman declared that all the renunciations were void. He stated:

I am satisfied that such factors, singly or in combination, cast the taint of incompetency upon any act of renunciation made under their influence by American citizens interned without Constitutional sanction, as were the plaintiffs. . . .

Certainly the loss of American citizenship, described as "the highest hope of civilized man" (*United States* vs. *Schneiderman,* 320 U.S. 118), calls for the exercise of the most inflexible caution upon the part of the Government officials having the power to effectively take away "the priceless benefits" (*United States* vs. *Schneiderman,* supra).

In view of the admissions contained in the affidavits filed by the . . .[Government] herein, and the conceded purpose of Section 801(i), I have no doubt that there was a complete lack of constitutional authority for administrative, executive or military officers to detain and imprison American citizens at Tule Lake who were not charged criminally or subject to martial law.

In cancelling the renunciation, Judge Goodman concluded:

It is shocking to the conscience that an American citizen be confined without authority and then, while so under duress and restraint, for his Government to accept from him a surrender of his constitutional heritage.

The Government of the United States under the stress and necessities of national defense, committed error in accepting the renunciations of the greater number of the plaintiffs herein. The highest standards of public morality and the inexorable requirements of good conscience rests upon the Government in its dealings with its citizens. It must be slow to afflict and quick to make retribution. The Government must be neither reluctant nor evasive in correcting wrongs inflicted upon a citizen. By so doing, it demonstrates to the people of the world the fairness and justice of our form of society and law.

The Government was not satisfied with the two sweeping decisions of Judge Goodman as to the invalidity of the deportation orders and the renunciation of citizenship. It appealed to the Federal Circuit Court of Appeals for the Ninth District, which consisted of Chief Judge Denman and Circuit Judges Albert Stephens and William Orr.

Chief Judge Denman, who had written the scathing decision against the Government two years earlier on August 26, 1949 in the case of *Acheson* vs. *Murakami,* also wrote the opinion in the case of *Tadayasu Abo* vs. *McGrath.* [26]

The Government argued, on appeal, that the circuit court of appeals had decided the case of *Murakami* vs. *Acheson* on evidence that she had been coerced into committing an involuntary act of renunciation of citizenship. It asked this same court, in the present case, to apply the same standards of individual circumstances to determine the validity of such renunciations.

Chief Judge Denman held that all renunciants who were under the age of twenty-one years at the time they signed their renunciations were minors and incompetent to renounce. Their renunciations were cancelled, and the minors were restored to their United States citizenship.

As to the adult renunciants, Chief Judge Denman again noted the oppressive conditions that prevailed at Tule Lake, coupled with the inaction and ability of government officials to suppress the atmosphere of fear that pervaded the segregation center during the renunciation program. However, he accepted the position of the Government to the effect that the declaration of each renunciant should be individually determined as to the validity of the renunciation.

He imposed the evidentiary rule that the oppressive conditions at Tule Lake were part of each renunciant's case in that the conditions resulted in involuntary renunciations. However, these oppressive conditions were to be considered as rebuttable presumptions. He therefore required the Government to obtain additional evidence on each individual renunciant whom the Government wished to designate as a voluntary renunciant.

To implement this requirement on the government, to establish whether the actions were voluntary or involuntary, Chief Judge Denman remanded the case to Federal District Judge Goodman. Judge Denman allowed the Government ninety days to file further evidence showing such voluntary renunciation against any renunciant it desired to designate. If, within this ninety-day period of time, any of the renunciants were not designated by the Government by further evidence, the judgment invalidating the renunciation was to become final. For those renunciants designated as voluntary, further hearings would be conducted on an individual basis. If "substantial evidence" was presented by the Government against such renunciants, the burden of evidence was to shift upon such individuals to prove their involuntary action.

A fact of interest to be noted here is that on January 17, 1951, when Judge Denman remanded the 4,315 renunciants to the federal district court in San Francisco, these 4,315 persons were not in the Tule Lake segregation center; it had been closed as of February 1, 1946. These "disloyal" renunciants had all been released by the Department of Justice to relocate wherever they desired while they were awaiting the decision of the circuit court of appeals. Thus, the processing of these renunciants took place outside the camp.

To complete the melancholy history of the Tule Lake segregation program, some statistics from *Uprooted Americans,* written by Dillon S. Myer, director of the WRA, are appropriate here.[27]

Of a total of 120,000 people of Japanese ancestry who at some stage were the responsibility of the War Relocation Authority between 1942 and 1946, a total of 4,724 repatriates and expatriates sailed for Japan on five different dates—4 persons on June 11, 1942; 314 on September 2, 1943; 423 on November 25, 1945; 3,551 on December 29, 1945; and 432 on February 23, 1946. Of the 4,724 total number, 1,659 were alien repatriates; 1,949 were American citizens, all but about 100 were under 20 years of age, mostly children under 15 years of age accompanying repatriate parents; and 1,116 renunciants. This group of 1,116 renunciants who actually went to Japan was only about 20 percent of more than 5,700, who had applied for renunciation of their American citizenship earlier.

These figures cover the period up to February 23, 1946. On May 21, 1959 United States Attorney General William Rogers was quoted in the *Washington Post* as saying that there were "5,766 Nisei who renounced their citizenship, and 5,409 have since asked that it be returned. Only 357 failed to apply for a return of their citizenship in the United States. So far 4,978 have recovered status as United States citizens."

A recap as of May 21, 1959 reveals that of the 5,766 Nisei who had renounced their citizenship, 4,978 had already been granted restoration. This left 788 to whom restoration had not been granted. As of that date, 357 were known not to have asked for restoration of citizenship, leaving 431 unaccounted for. It is interesting to note that of the 1,116 Nisei renunciants who actually departed the United States for Japan, 685 were granted restoration along with the more than 4,000 others who remained in the United States. When it is considered that almost 40 percent of those who went to Japan were American citizens eighteen years of age or under, the tragic consequences of the unfortunate questionnaire program become glaringly apparent.

17
The Strandees

THE GENERAL TERM *strandees,* as applied to American citizens of Japanese ancestry, refers to those persons who had gone to Japan and who for various reasons had not returned to the United States before the outbreak of World War II. They lived in various parts of Japan during the war and suffered the shortages of food, fuel, and clothing along with the other inhabitants of that wartime country.

Many of these American citizens were of tender age. Some of the parents of these strandees had returned to Japan from the United States intending to live the rest of their lives in or near their ancestral homes. Many of them were discouraged and disillusioned by the relentless discrimination and prejudice that had faced them while in the United States. In almost all these cases, the parents had not acquired the fortune that they had dreamed of finding when they had set out for America years before.

In a few instances in which the citizens were in their teens or older, they were placed on a boat destined for Japan, with arrangements for their parents' relatives or friends to meet them at the docks of Yokohama or Kobe, there to be taken to the ancestral home or placed in some facility to obtain a formal Japanese education.

Before World War II, relatives in Japan often could not adequately support such children. Arrangements were therefore made by the parents of these youngsters to send money to maintain them. There was a financial advantage to this plan. Although incomes were small for the parents in the United States before World War II, in most instances averaging less than $100 per month, the American dollar was worth much more in Japan. Thus parents who could hardly support a child on $10 a month in the United States could quite adequately do so in Japan.

With this financial assistance from his parents, the child in Japan could be educated and incidentally learn Japanese. The parents often felt it was desirable for the child to know Japanese whether he was to remain in Japan or eventually to return to the United States.

A few of the strandees who had completed their high school education in the United States were sent by their parents to study Japanese at one of the many private language institutes or universities where foreign students were enrolled and where courses in Japanese were taught.

In the early 1940s, as war clouds loomed over the horizon, the United States ambassador to Japan, Joseph W. Grew, warned all American citizens of the threat of war between the United States and Japan. He had urged all American citizens throughout Japan to make arrangements to book passage and to return to the United States as soon as possible. Many hundreds of Americans of Japanese ancestry and other citizens, including students, visitors, businessmen, government officials, and missionaries, heeded Ambassador Grew's advice.

When World War II ended with Japan's surrender on August 15, 1945, most of the American citizens of Japanese ancestry who had been stranded in Japan were able to return to the United States. Since many of the passports issued before the outbreak of the war had expired, the strandees applied for new United States passports to the American consul in Tokyo. This was during the days of the occupation of Japan by the Allied powers under the command of General Douglas MacArthur. Hundreds of American citizens of Japanese ancestry who held dual citizenship were denied new passports by the American consul on the ground that they had lost their American citizenship while stranded in Japan during wartime.

Section 401(a) through (j) of the Nationality Act of 1940[1] specified ten different ways in which a "person who is a national of the United States, whether by birth or naturalization, shall lose his nationality." Briefly, such a person could lose his nationality by doing any of the following:

(a) Obtaining naturalization in a foreign state . . .

(b) Taking an oath . . . of allegiance to a foreign state . . .

(c) Entering, or serving in the armed forces of a foreign state . . .

(d) Accepting, or performing the duties of, any office, post, or employment under the government of a foreign state . . . for which only nationals of such state are eligible . . .

(e) Voting in a political election in a foreign state . . .

(f) Making a formal renunciation of nationality before a diplomatic or consular officer of the United States in a foreign state . . .

(g) Deserting the military or naval service of the United States in time of war . . .

(h) Committing any act of treason against, or attempting by force to overthrow or bearing arms against the United States . . .

(i) Making the United States a formal written renunciation of nationality . . .

(j) Departing from or remaining outside of the jurisdiction of the United States in time of war . . . for the purpose of evading or avoiding training and service in the land or naval forces of the United States.

Judicial proceedings were instituted by several hundred American citizens of Japanese ancestry against the secretary of state of the United States in an effort to obtain an adjudication of their claimed American citizenship in the federal district courts. They wished to establish whether, under Section 401, they should be deemed to have lost their American citizenship.

The strandees right to leave Japan to adjudicate this issue in the United States was made possible under Section 501 of the same Nationality Act of 1940.[2] Chapter V, Section 501 provided that "whenever a diplomatic or consular officer of the United States has reason to believe that a person while in a foreign state has lost his American nationality," the consular officer certifies the facts upon which his belief is based to the secretary of state. The person may then institute an action against the head of the department or agency, in these cases, the secretary of state of the United States, in the district court of the United States. The American consular officer in the foreign country issues to such nationals a "certificate of identity," which states that his nationality status is pending before the court. The national is permitted to leave the foreign state and is then admitted into the United States to contest his denial of nationality. The national is subject to deportation if the court decides that he is not a national of the United States.

CASES INVOLVING NATURALIZATION IN A FOREIGN STATE

Strandee Meiji Fujisawa left Japan and was admitted into the United States to adjudicate the issue as to whether he had lost his citizenship under Section 401(a), "obtaining naturalization in a foreign state."[3] Fujisawa was born in Imperial County, California. He went to Japan in 1939 to study Japanese and to prepare himself for employment in the import-export business between the United States and Japan. Possessed of dual citizenship, he renounced his Japanese citizenship before he left the United States. In accordance with Japanese law, the names of all members of the family are kept in a family register (*Koseki*) at the municipal office of the birth place of the parents. Fujisawa's father caused the name of Meiji, the son, to be removed from the family register in Japan.

Fujisawa continued his education in Japan after the outbreak of war between the United States and Japan. He graduated from a Japanese university in 1943. Upon graduation, he sought employment. He could not be hired in Japan because his name did not appear in his family register. He then reapplied for his Japanese citizenship, whereupon his name once again appeared in the family records. During the war he was employed by the Japanese government as an interpreter in a prisoner of war camp. After the surrender of Japan, he was employed as an interpreter by the United States Army of Occupation.

At his trial in the federal district court in Los Angeles, Fujisawa testified that he had remained loyal to the United States at all times. He had no intention of renouncing his United States citizenship, nor had he voted in any elections in Japan. He presented an affidavit executed by Thomas L. Blakemore, now a prominent attorney in Japan, who had lived in Japan for many years before he had returned to the United States prior to the outbreak of World War II. After the surrender of Japan, Blakemore was assigned to Japan to serve as chief of the Civil Affairs and Civil Liberties Branch under the Supreme Commander of Allied Powers (SCAP) during the military occupation of Japan. Blakemore's affidavit stated that Nisei living in Japan during the war years were subject to great hostility. They could not obtain employment or food rations unless their names were on their family register.

The court examined the forms submitted by Fujisawa to the municipal officer to recover his Japanese citizenship and found no evidence of allegiance to Japan or any intention of renouncing his United States citizenship. The court said the issue was whether Fujisawa had acted freely in recovering his Japanese citizenship. It held that Fujisawa had not acted freely and voluntarily in applying for his Japanese citizenship because of the coercive nature of the circumstances that compelled him to do so in order to find employment and to obtain food rations in order to survive. The court further noted his exemplary conduct in risking his own personal safety and incurring the wrath of the Japanese military authorities in charge of the prisoner of war camp when they discovered that he had assisted American prisoners and had protected and comforted them. His American citizenship was restored.

CASES INVOLVING SERVICE IN FOREIGN ARMED FORCES

Four cases involved the issue of whether strandees lost their United States citizenship under Section 401(c) by "entering or serving in the armed forces of a foreign state," in this instance, by serving in the Japanese army during wartime.

William S. Ishikawa[4] was born in Honolulu, Hawaii on July 1, 1916. He went to Japan in 1939 at the expense of the Japanese Foreign Office. During the war he was stationed in Nanking, China with the South Manchurian Railway Company. Being possessed of dual citizenship, he was considered a subject of Japan. He was conscripted into the Japanese army on May 4, 1945 and was discharged from the military service one week after Japan's surrender in August 1945.

At his trial in Hawaii, it was stipulated before Federal District Court Judge J. Frank McLaughlin that, under the military conscription laws of Japan, all male subjects of Japan who attained the age of twenty years were compelled to register for conscription. If any subject attempted to evade or delay the conscription order, the subject was punishable by imprisonment. Ishikawa testified that he was compelled to enter the Japanese army because he could not escape into free China. He also testified to having witnessed tortuous treatment inflicted by the dreaded Japanese military police (*Kempeitai*) upon Japanese subjects who refused to obey the conscription orders.

Judge McLaughlin held that Ishikawa did not lose his American citizenship under these circumstances, as Ishikawa's induction into the Japanese army had been involuntary. Ishikawa's citizenship was restored.

[Section 401(c)] . . . has been authoritatively construed as effecting expatriation only if the national of the United States entering or serving in the armed forces of a foreign state without express authority under the laws of the United States acted voluntarily and without legal or factual compulsion.

Federal District Judge Charles Cavanah, in Los Angeles, came to the same conclusion as Judge McLaughlin in Hawaii, in two companion cases, one involving Noboru Kato[5] and the other, George Y. Ozasa.[6]

Noboru Kato was born in Stockton, California in 1919. In 1933, when he was fourteen years old, he went to Japan to study. In 1940, when he had attained the age of twenty-one, he left college, intending to return to the United States. He did not return to America because his uncle with whom he was living, a Japanese army officer, informed him that he would be punished if he attempted to do so. Kato had received a deferment from the Japanese army to allow him to continue his education. He received his conscription order soon thereafter, and, for fear of being punished if he resisted, he entered the Japanese army. From August 1945 to 1948 he was a prisoner of war in a Russian prison. After his repatriation to Japan, he was employed by the United States Army of Occupation to educate the Japanese people concerning the American democratic system of government.

Judge Cavanah held that Kato had not lost his United States citizenship when he was drafted into the Japanese army. His conscription "was not of his free and voluntary act but was the result of coercion."

George Y. Ozasa was born in Oregon in 1921. He went to Japan in 1932 to be educated, with the intention of returning to the United States afterwards. He had registered in Japan with the American consul every two years as an American citizen until the outbreak of war with Japan. He was then drafted into the Japanese army.

Ozasa testified at his trial that when he received his conscription notice, he complied because he was afraid of military imprisonment and punishment. When the war ended in August 1945, he was discharged from the Japanese army and was later employed by the United States Army at an air force base in Miho. Judge Cavanah held that Ozasa did not lose his American citizenship "where his Japanese Army service was coerced upon him and his obedience to the conscription order was not free and voluntary."

The Supreme Court of the United States then decided a landmark case that involved the issue of loss of citizenship. Mitsugi Nishikawa[7] was born in Artesia, California in April 1916. He graduated from the University of California with a degree in engineering. He resided in the United States until August 1939, at which time he went to Japan for further studies. His name was entered in the family register in Japan. In 1940, while in Japan, he submitted to a physical exam as required under the Military Service Law of Japan. On March 1, 1941, having attained the age of twenty years, he was inducted into the Japanese army. Under the Military Service Law, imprisonment was provided for evasion of conscription. He served as a mechanic at various air force bases in China, Indochina, the Philippines, and Manchuria. He was severely beaten by Japanese air force soldiers when he expressed the opinion that Japan had no chance of winning the war. He was discharged in September 1945.

The United States Government contended that Nishikawa had lost his United States citizenship under Section 401(c) of the Nationality Act of 1940 by "entering, or serving in, the armed forces of a foreign state." Chief Justice Earl Warren delivered the opinion of the Supreme Court, holding that Nishikawa did not lose his United States citizenship. He stated that "no conduct results in expatriation unless the conduct is engaged in voluntarily."

Chief Justice Warren held that there should be a strict standard of proof in all expatriation cases. Thus, where a citizen claimant proves his birth in the United States, or acquisition of American citizenship in some other way, the burden of proof then shifts to the Government when the citizen contends that his loss of citizenship was involuntary. In the *Nishikawa* case the plaintiff stated that he was conscripted in a totalitarian country to whose conscription laws, with their penal sanctions, he was subject. The Government had the burden of persuading the "trier of fact by clear, convincing, and unequivocal evidence that the act showing renunciation of citizenship was voluntarily performed."

Nishikawa was held not to have lost his United States citizenship because the Government had not sustained that burden of proof on the record. Chief Justice Warren conceded that the Government assumed an "onerous" burden of proof in cases in which the basic right of citizenship is contended by the Government to have been lost by the citizen. But whenever the issue of voluntary action is contested by the citizen, the Government must, in each case, prove voluntary conduct by this "onerous" burden of proof, to the effect that the evidence of such conduct is "clear, convincing, and unequivocal." Otherwise the Government is deemed not to have sustained its burden of proof.

Justices Hugo Black and William O. Douglas concurred in the opinion. They stated that Nishikawa's American citizenship was his "constitutional birth right." Congress, therefore, "cannot involuntarily expatriate any citizen." Justices Felix Frankfurter and Harold Burton stated that "where an individual engages in conduct by command of a penal statute of another country to whose laws he is subject, the gravest doubt is cast on the applicability of the normal assumption—that what a person does, he does of his own free will."

CASES INVOLVING VOTING IN A FOREIGN STATE

Many other strandees returned to the United States from Japan after the end of the war with certificates of identity, issued by the American consul in Japan, for trial in the various federal district courts. These strandees were alleged to have lost their United States citizenship in Japan after World War II when Japan was an occupied country. General Douglas MacArthur had been appointed by the President of the United States to be Supreme Commander of Allied Powers of occupied Japan, with supreme authority to establish a new government for Japan and to regulate the defeated people of that country.

When these particular strandees applied for passports to return to the United States, their applications were denied by the American consul under the provisions of Section 401(e) that they had lost their

United States citizenship "by voting in a political election in a foreign state."

Up until the surrender of Japan, General MacArthur noted that the totalitarian form of government dominated by the military elements had ruthlessly and brutally controlled every aspect of life, with little regard for the wishes, desires, or aspirations of the people of Japan. In restructuring the government of Japan after World War II, General MacArthur had promulgated a new constitution for Japan in which the right of franchise was accorded to all qualified nationals. The right of franchise also included women. He felt strongly that universal right of franchise would have far-reaching effects in providing a democratic form of government in Japan. He encouraged free and open elections for all government offices from local villages up to the national Parliament.

To implement this policy, and to emphasize whole-hearted and widespread participation of all the people in the voting process, General MacArthur extolled the virtue of the power of the franchise through extensive news releases, posters, and radio broadcasts. American soldiers in jeeps also went into the remotest villages carrying the message of the power of the vote.

The word went out through all of Japan. "We must do as the great General says. We must please him by having everyone vote as he directs us to do. Let us all co-operate with his policy and he will then realize what we people desire in New Japan is the power of our individual vote." All the people flocked to the polls on election days in 1946 and 1947 to elect national as well as local officials.

Also, forceful pressures were applied by the local Japanese officials upon all the residents during the elections. It was hinted that if all the residents in the villages did not vote, their food rations would be discontinued. The Japanese, including those who possessed American citizenship, obeyed the "command" of General MacArthur to vote.

Unfortunately, General MacArthur's headquarters, and the general himself, did not caution those who possessed American citizenship that such citizens should not vote because by doing so they would be divested of their United States citizenship. Not being aware of this danger, thousands of American citizens, most of whom were of Japanese descent, voted. In all cases, the federal district courts restored American citizenship to those strandees. The main reasoning in these decisions held that when the Supreme Commander of Allied Powers of occupied Japan "ordered" and "supervised" the elections and when the military government "urged" all the residents of Japan to vote, it was unjust to say that these residents were acting of a free mind and with an intelligent choice.[8]

In addition to the main reason underlying the courts' decisions, some of the judges held that Japan was not a "foreign state" as provided in Section 401(e). They declared that when Japan was completely under the authority and power of the Supreme Commander of Allied Powers, Japan was not a "foreign state" within the meaning of Section 401(e).[9]

On September 12, 1951, in two other cases involving voting by strandees, which were decided the same day, Federal District Judge Frank McLaughlin of Hawaii went even further in ruling that the strandees did not lose their United States citizenship by voting in a political election in a foreign state. He declared that Section 401(e) of the Nationality Act of 1940 was unconstitutional.[10] In these two companion cases, Judge McLaughlin reasoned that American citizens of Japanese ancestry acquired their United States citizenship at birth as provided in the federal Constitution.[11]

Congress had power to make provisions and conditions of what acts may constitute loss of citizenship of persons who obtained their American citizenship by naturalization, but it could not divest the citizenship of a United States citizen who acquired his status by birth since citizenship by birth was grounded in the Constitution.[12] The only way, therefore, for a United States citizen who acquired his citizenship by birth to divest himself of his citizenship was by his own voluntary naturalization in a foreign state. He could not be divested of his birthright by any act of Congress.

In 1952, in the case of *Teruo Naito* vs. *Acheson*,[13] which also involved the voting issue, Federal District Court Judge William Byrne stated that "proof to bring about a loss of citizenship must be clear and unequivocal," and he held that Teruo Naito did not lose his citizenship. Judge Byrne defined the elements of the proof that were necessary for the Government to prove its case against an American citizen who claimed his act of losing his citizenship was not free and voluntary but the result of duress and coercion. He applied the standard of proof necessary in loss of citizenship in the cases of *Baumgartner* vs. *U.S.*[14] and *Schneiderman* vs. *U.S.*,[15] which had declared that such proof involving loss of citizenship must be clear and unequivocal. He held that the Government in the *Naito* case had not sustained its burden of proof.

Six years later the Supreme Court of the United States, in *Nishikawa vs. Dulles*, [16] added an additional "onerous" burden upon the Government in United States citizenship cases by including the word "convincing." At the present time any person involved in matters that concern the loss of his citizenship must be attacked by "clear, convincing, and unequivocal" evidence. In most instances, this burden of proof is virtually impossible for the Government to produce.

While there are no statistics as to exactly how many strandees returned to the United States as a result of these decisions, it is safe to say that there were probably over a thousand such persons in Japan at the time the war ended. Many of them reentered the United States with certificates of identity and ultimately regained their citizenship. Several hundred others, by supplying facts related to duress, coercion, or inadvertence and mistake at the time of their questioned acts, were issued passports by the American consuls and departed from Japan for their homes in America.

A small number chose to remain in Japan after the war, with or without their American citizenship. These persons frequently had married, were raising families in Japan, or had obtained some suitable employment that they were reluctant to leave. They had adjusted to life in Japan and chose her as their adopted country.

STRANDEES CONVICTED AS TRAITORS

However, two persons of Japanese ancestry who held dual nationalities lost their American citizenships after being convicted of treason for their actions in Japan during World War II. Tomoya Kawakita and Iva Ikuko Toguri D'Aquino were tried for treason under Article III, Section 3 of the federal Constitution. The punishment upon conviction of treason can be drastic.

Whoever, owing allegiance to the United States, levies war against them or adheres to their enemies, giving them aid and comfort within the United States or elsewhere, is guilty of treason and shall suffer death, or shall be imprisoned not less than five years and fined not less than $10,000; and shall be incapable of holding any office under the United States. [17]

Tomoya Kawakita

Tomoya Kawakita, the son of a wealthy truck farmer and produce merchant, was born in 1921 in Calexico, California. His parents were born in Japan. In 1939, shortly before he turned eighteen, he went to

Japan with his father to visit his grandfather. As a United States citizen, he traveled on an American passport.[18] He remained in Japan after his father returned home, and in March 1941 he entered Meiji University. After completing his schooling in 1943, he placed his name in the family register.[19] In 1944 he obtained employment as an English interpreter with the Oeyama Nickel Industry Co., Ltd., where American prisoners of war were put to work in the mines and factory. He worked there throughout the war, until Japan's surrender.

In December 1945 he decided to return to the United States. He went to the American consul at Yokohama, stated that he was a United States citizen, and was issued a passport. He returned to California in 1946.

On a balmy September day in 1947, a giant department store in the eastern section of Los Angeles was bustling with customers. Sergeant William L. Bruce of Garden Grove, California brushed by a husky short man of Japanese ancestry. Something clicked in Bruce's mind. His memory flashed back to the days, only two short years before, when he was a prisoner of war at the Oeyama mine. Bruce recognized the man as the English interpreter who had mistreated his fellow soldiers. He followed him out of the store and jotted down the license number of his car. He then reported the man and the various acts committed by him to the FBI.

The FBI conducted a careful and intensive investigation of the accusations over the next several months. The information was submitted to the federal grand jury in Los Angeles, and an indictment was handed down, charging Kawakita with the crime of treason on fifteen counts relating to his treatment of the prisoners of war. The period of time covered by the indictment was between August 8, 1944 and August 15, 1945. The original number of fifteen counts was later reduced to thirteen. Kawakita, called "Meatball" by the prisoners of war, went on trial before a jury in a courtroom in Los Angeles presided over by Federal District Judge William C. Mathes.

Kawakita denied any mistreatment of the prisoners of war in the Oeyama mine. He also contended that he had expatriated himself of his American citizenship and offered as evidence the entry of his name in the family register, his change in registration at Meiji University from American to Japanese, his change of residence from California to Japan, his trip to China on a Japanese passport during wartime, and his avowed allegiance to the emperor of Japan. He insisted that he could not legally be compelled to stand trial as an American citizen for acts committed in Japan.

On September 2, 1948, some twelve weeks later, after eight days of deliberations, the jury found Kawakita guilty on eight counts of treason. It also found that he had not lost his American citizenship. The death sentence was imposed on Kawakita by Judge Mathes.[20]

The Supreme Court of the United States in *Tomoya Kawakita* vs. *U.S.*, by a four to three decision, rejected Kawakita's contentions and upheld both his conviction and death sentence.[21] Justice William O. Douglas, in delivering the opinion of the Court, noted that although Kawakita had entered his name in the family register in Japan in 1943, after the war had ended he had applied for and was issued an American passport in 1945 upon taking an oath of allegiance to the United States. The entry of his name in the family register, said Justice Douglas, was merely a recognition of the Japanese citizenship that Kawakita had acquired at birth. This did not constitute an act of expatriation in spite of his later acts that were consistent with Japanese citizenship.

Justice Douglas held that under the Constitution, the crime of treason contained no territorial limitations. An American citizen living outside the United States who had not effectively expatriated himself under American law could still be guilty of treason. "He cannot turn it into a fair weather citizenship, retaining it for possible contingent benefits but meanwhile playing the part of the traitor. An American citizen owes allegiance to the United States wherever he may reside." Sufficient evidence was also found to show that Kawakita manifested "a long, persistent and continuous course of conduct directed against the American prisoners and going beyond any conceivable duty of an interpreter."

After the death sentence was imposed, Kawakita was remanded into the custody of the United States Marshal and transported to Alcatraz, the federal prison on an island in San Francisco Bay.

On November 2, 1953, President Dwight D. Eisenhower commuted his death sentence to life imprisonment. After almost sixteen years at Alcatraz, President John F. Kennedy, in one of his last official acts, granted Kawakita a presidential pardon on condition that he be returned to Japan and never seek entry into the United States.

Iva Ikuko Toguri D'Aquino

Iva Ikuko Toguri D'Aquino was born in Los Angeles, California on July 4, 1916. She attended public schools in Calexico, San Diego,

Compton, and Los Angeles. She received her B.A. in zoology from UCLA in 1940 and continued her postgraduate studies at the same university until 1941.

In July 1941 she left the United States for Japan to visit her mother's only sister who was in failing health. Because of difficulties in establishing her United States citizenship to obtain a passport, the State Department issued her a certificate of identification, valid for six months. In November 1941, becoming alarmed at war talks in Japan, she tried to book passage on the Japanese steamship *Tatsuta Maru,* which was to sail for the United States on December 2. Her travel papers from the American consul and the Japanese authorities were never received.

Stranded in Japan after the outbreak of war, she applied for evacuation from Japan through the Swiss legation. Again she encountered difficulties in proving her United States citizenship. In spite of these difficulties and harassment by Japanese authorities, however, she adamantly refused to renounce her American citizenship. Because of her lack of Japanese citizenship, she encountered considerable difficulty in obtaining employment in wartime Japan. In November 1943 she was finally accepted for employment as an announcer by Radio Tokyo. The Imperial Japanese Army was exploiting the shortwave radio equipment of Radio Tokyo to beam a special program known as "Zero Hour" directly to the Allied soldiers serving in the Pacific.

The program was directed by a staff of three Allied prisoners of war, Major Charles Cousen, an Australian infantry battalion commander, Captain Wallace Ince, an American, and Lieutenant Norman Reyes, an officer in the Philippine army.

Miss Toguri was told by the staff that the program she was to announce would consist of music interspersed with news commentaries and propaganda. The program was intended to be used as an instrument of psychological warfare to cause the Allied troops to become homesick, tired, and disgusted with the war. She was ordered to read the scripts exactly as they were given to her.

She was one of eighteen English-speaking women announcers, all of whom broadcast over "Zero Hour" in perfect unaccented English. Only Miss Toguri was American; the other young women were citizens of Japan, Canada, England, Switzerland, and Germany.[22]

As the American G.I.s listened to the popular dance records, rumors, and news from the home front, they mockingly labeled the voice heard nightly as "Tokyo Rose." Sitting in steaming jungles, cut off from everything, often suffering from malaria, lying tensely in wait for soft footsteps of fanatical Japanese troops, the voice they heard began to take on shape, form, and personality. A belief spread throughout the Pacific that there was only one Tokyo Rose although none of the eighteen announcers, including Miss Toguri, ever identified herself by that name. At the end of the war in August 1945, correspondents from various news agencies rushed into Tokyo in the hope of finding Tokyo Rose.

The events that led to the discovery of Iva Toguri D'Aquino (she married Felipe D'Aquino, a Portuguese national, in April 1945) were so bizarre as to be incredible. It was said that a reporter for a well-known news agency had bribed former employees of Radio Tokyo to identify Mrs. D'Aquino as Tokyo Rose. Other witnesses, who were purported to have seen and heard Mrs. D'Aquino announce herself as Tokyo Rose, were offered trips to the United States to testify against her. In September 1945 the United States Army placed Mrs. D'Aquino under arrest, but after their investigation she was released since there was no evidence that she was the legendary voice. A month later, on October 17, 1945, she was arrested again on orders from Washington and held incommunicado for ten months in Sugamo prison in Tokyo. She was detained in the same prison where major Japanese war-crime prisoners were kept. Eight months later, on May 1, 1946, following more intensive investigations, the army again gave her a full and unconditional clearance.

While she was in Sugamo prison, the FBI also investigated the matter. On orders from the Department of Justice, she was ordered released from prison on October 25, 1946 by telegram, which stated "no prosecution contemplated."

Following her release, she again filed papers to obtain an American passport. Once more, she encountered difficulties. While still in Tokyo, she was arrested for the third time on August 26, 1948 on the authority of the Supreme Command for the Allied Powers, based on a complaint issued by the Department of Justice, which had previously cleared her. She was placed on board a United States Army transport and sent to San Francisco, arriving on September 25, 1948.

On October 8, 1948, in federal district court in San Francisco, she was arraigned and charged with treason on eight counts of overt acts for various broadcasts that she had made over Radio Tokyo between November 1, 1943 and August 13, 1945. She pleaded innocent to the charges and was brought to trial before a jury.

During the trial the federal prosecutor stated that the broadcasts allegedly made by her had been recorded by the United States government monitoring station in Hawaii (these recordings had previously cleared her), but the recordings had been destroyed as a matter of "routine." The reporter who had "discovered" Tokyo Rose, after allegedly bribing witnesses to identify her, was never called as a government witness. The defense proved that the witnesses who had been bribed had indeed testified falsely before the federal grand jury, which had returned the indictment against her.

The jury trial lasted fifty-six days and cost the government over $500,000. It was the longest and most expensive trial on record at that time. After four weary days of deliberations, the jury reported to Judge Michael J. Roche that they were unable to reach a verdict. The judge sternly admonished the jury to keep in mind the length and cost of the trial. The jury finally brought in a verdict that Mrs. D'Aquino was innocent of seven of the counts and guilty of one count.

Count VI, on which she was adjudged guilty, read as follows:

That on a day during October 1944, the exact date being to the Grand Jurors unknown, defendant in the offices of the Broadcasting Corporation of Japan did speak into a microphone concerning the loss of ships.

The broadcast that Mrs. D'Aquino was purported to have made occurred after the United States had lost many ships in a bitter naval battle in Leyte Gulf off the Philippines. She is alleged to have stated, "Now you fellows have lost all your ships. You really are orphans of the Pacific. Now, how do you think you will ever get home?"

On October 7, 1949 Judge Roche sentenced Mrs. D'Aquino to ten years in a federal prison and fined her $10,000. As in the case of Tomoya Kawakita, she automatically lost her United States citizenship, a status that she had for many years insisted she had but that she had never been able to prove to the satisfaction of the United States government authorities.

The United States Court of Appeals for the Ninth Circuit upheld the conviction.[23] Chief Judge Walter L. Pope held that her detention in Sugamo prison for almost one year did not constitute a denial of her constitutional right to a speedy trial. He ruled further that the missing recordings did not constitute a deliberate suppression of the evidence by the United States government to deny her due process of law. He further stated that although she contended that her broadcasts were made under duress and coercion by Japanese military authorities, and thus were not voluntary or with the intent to commit treason, there was sufficient evidence for the jury to decide the issue. Judge Pope declared:

We think that the citizen owing allegiance to the United States must manifest a determination to resist commands and orders until such time as he is faced with the alternative of immediate injury or death. Were any other rule to be applied, traitors in the enemy country would by that fact alone be shielded from any requirement of resistance. The person claiming the defense of coercion and duress must be a person whose resistance has brought him to the last ditch.

Her further appeals to the Supreme Court of the United States were denied,[24] and she spent six and a half years in the federal women's prison in Alderson, West Virginia.

Just prior to her release from prison, scheduled for January 28, 1956, she was served with a warrant for her arrest for deportation to Japan by the immigration officers of the district office of the Immigration Service in Chicago, headed by District Director R. H. Robinson. She was ordered to leave the United States for Japan by April 13, 1956 or face deportation proceedings. The Immigration Service predicated its warrant for deportation on the basis that she was no longer a national or a citizen of the United States by reason of her conviction for treason.[25]

The deportation hearings scheduled in the summer of 1956 raised several complex legal issues:

1. Was Iva D'Aquino a stateless alien, a stateless person, a dual national, a Japanese national, or a Portuguese national because of her marriage to a Portuguese national?

2. Could a person who acquired United States citizenship by birth under the federal Constitution be dispossessed of his citizenship by an act of Congress or must there be a constitutional amendment?

3. Could a person who possessed dual citizenship at birth be compelled to leave the United States after conviction of treason?

4. Was Mrs. D'Aquino deportable to another country even though under an act of Congress she was considered an "undesirable resident" of the United States?

The Immigration Service, after struggling with these issues, finally dismissed deportation proceedings against her in 1958.

Supporters of Iva Ikuko Toguri D'Aquino have attempted on three different occasions to obtain a presidential pardon for her: the first in 1954 from President Dwight D. Eisenhower, the second in 1968 during the administration of President Lyndon B. Johnson, and the third in 1968 during President Richard M. Nixon's term. None of these applications was granted.

The Japanese American Citizens League at its national convention in Portland, Oregon passed a resolution on July 24, 1974 to seek "all executive or other remedies available under the law." The group contended, "It is now apparent that much of the evidence and the conduct of her trial were highly questionable and prejudicial and that, in view of the motivations and climate of public hysteria at the time of the trial, the verdict is a blot on the integrity of American jurisprudence."[26]

18

The Japanese "Moose"
Captures
the American G.I.

ON AUGUST 15, 1945, at 11:30 P.M., Emperor Hirohito spoke to his defeated subjects by radio. His message of surrender was beamed throughout the entire nation of Japan and to the fighting forces situated throughout China, the Philippines, Southeast Asia, and some of the islands of the Pacific:

Should we continue to fight, it would not only result in an ultimate collapse and obliteration of the Japanese nation, but also it would lead to the total extinction of human civilization. . . .

It is according to the dictate of time and fate that we have resolved to pave the way for a grand peace for all the generations to come by enduring the un-endurable and suffering what is insufferable.[1]

On September 2, 1945 representatives of the Japanese government boarded the United States battleship *Missouri,* lying at anchor in Tokyo Bay, to sign the instrument of surrender. Japan, which had boasted up to then of never having been defeated in war or having been invaded

by enemy troops, became on this day a subjugated nation under the command of General Douglas MacArthur, Supreme Commander of the Allied Powers.

Commenting on this period, former ambassador to Japan Edwin Reischauer has written:

Japan entered upon one of the most significant phases, and certainly the most unusual, of its long history. Indeed, the period of six and a half years of American occupation and tutelage was to prove unique in the record of human experience. Never before had one advanced nation attempted to reform, from within, the supposed faults of another advanced nation. Never before had a military occupation of one world power by another proved so satisfactory to the victors and at the same time so tolerable to the vanquished. When the peace treaty finally went into effect on April 28, 1952, most Americans and Japanese shared a general satisfaction with the period of occupation which was coming to an end.[2]

THE ARMY OF OCCUPATION ENTERS JAPAN

On September 6, 1945, four days after the instrument of surrender had been signed by Japan, the United States Army of Occupation poured into Japan. The American soldiers were understandably wary of the reception they would receive from the defeated Japanese. The Japanese fighting forces during the war had shown their traditional courage, tenacity, skill, and determination to die rather than surrender. The Japanese fighting men had been deeply inculcated with the belief that there was shame in surrender, hence their utter contempt of death, their own or their foes. This was part of the ancient code of the Samurai, called *Bushido* (Way of the Warrior).

The American G.I.s were told that the Japanese women would fight to protect their honor with knives and bamboo spears and that their children would clutch mines to their chests and throw their small bodies beneath American tanks. They expected sullen hostility, hatred, and violence.

The Japanese people, exhausted, starving, shelterless, and spiritually shattered, feared ruthless subjugation under army occupation at the hands of the dreaded enemy soldiers. They feared murder and rape by "barbaric" American soldiers bent on plunder and further destruction.[3]

The details of the American occupation policies under Supreme Commander General MacArthur, relative to the demilitarization, democratization, and rehabilitation of the Japanese nation, are not within the purview of this book. What is pertinent, however, is the impact that the United States Army of Occupation had on the immigration laws of the United States.

In general, the American soldier as a representative of an invading army of occupation was extremely well behaved. The Japanese men had expected massacre; instead they were most often treated with kindness and gallantry. The American G.I. went into the cities, towns, and villages throughout the islands of conquered Japan with a warm and nonchalant informality, giving cigarettes to the men and candy bars to the children.

As a consequence, the women of Japan, particularly the young unmarried women, gradually began to change their attitude toward the Americans. Most of the young women had no immoral intent in mind; they were merely responding to the soldiers' kindness and courtesy. They had never known such treatment from Japanese males. The traditional role of women in Japan was to be content with an inferior position in life. No outward manifestation of love or affection had been permitted in public between male and female. In a land, which for centuries had placed the women in the home and in the kitchen, with marriages prearranged by parents, love between men and women in many instances was only incidental. The chivalry of the American G.I. was a new and exciting experience.

The women-hungry G.I.s quickly took advantage of the special situation and gladly responded to the friendly overtures of these petite, graceful, gentle Japanese women. Acquaintances between the American G.I.s and the black-haired, seemingly shy, but subtly aggressive women quickly blossomed into romance for thousands of couples. Soon, almost every American G.I. during his tour of duty had his own special "moose," a slang term derived from the Japanese word *musume* for girl. While most of the "mooses" were girls whom the G.I. had met in bars, cafes, night clubs, and military clubs throughout Japan, some girls who became "mooses" of the G.I.s were from good families and represented the finest of Japanese womankind.

Although most of these romances died when the G.I.s were rotated back to the United States for discharge from military duty, many of the officers and enlisted men were serious in their intentions toward their Japanese sweethearts. Upon being notified of their imminent return home, thousands of American G.I.s expressed a desire to marry their "mooses" and take them to the United States.[4]

In 1946, however, any American G.I. who wished to marry a Japanese girl and bring her to the United States ran into a legal obstacle. The Japanese Exclusion Act of 1924 did not permit the entry of persons of Japanese ancestry into the United States for permanent residence.

Under this act, only persons "eligible for citizenship" were allowed to enter the United States as immigrants. Japanese fiancées were "ineligible for citizenship."

However, other Orientals could enter the United States as immigrants. On December 17, 1943, as a gesture of good will and friendship toward China, our ally during World War II, the old Chinese Exclusion Act, which had been on the books since 1882, had been repealed. Under a 1943 amendment, the Chinese were made eligible for both immigration and naturalization. A special quota for Chinese persons had been established in addition to the existing quota of 100 for non-Orientals born in China and eligible for naturalization.[5] On July 2, 1946 persons belonging to races indigenous to India were granted the privilege of admission to the United States as immigrants and were also declared eligible for naturalization.[6]

THE G.I. FIANCEES ACT

Thus, the only Orientals in 1946 not eligible for naturalization were the Japanese and the Koreans. The anguished cries of dismay of both the "mooses" and their G.I. fiancés were heard by sympathetic and understanding ears. With the JACL actively supporting the bill, Congress enacted an exception to the restrictive Japanese Exclusion Act of 1924. On June 29, 1946 Congress approved Public Law 471, designed "to facilitate the admission into the United States of the alien fiancées or fiancés of members of the Armed Forces of the United States."[7] Under this bill, known as the G.I. Fiancees Act, an alien fiancée of an American G.I. who had served in the armed forces during World War II would be admitted into the United States as a nonimmigrant temporary visitor for a period of three months. To obtain this visitor's visa, satisfactory evidence had to be presented to the American consul in Japan of the good faith marriage intention. Within this three-month period, the parties were to conclude a valid marriage in the United States. The Japanese "moose," now a bride, would then be allowed to remain in the United States as a permanent resident alien.

The G.I. Fiancees Act of 1946, which was to expire December 31, 1948, was extended to April 1, 1949.[8] On August 19, 1950 the law was further liberalized; spouses and minor children of members of the American armed forces, regardless of race, were permitted to enter the United States for permanent residence as nonquota immigrants, but only if the marriage had occurred before March 19, 1952.[9] At last, upon their discharge or rotation back to the United States, American

G.I.s could bring their Japanese wives and children home with them. This act, which was sponsored by the JACL, was of particular benefit to aliens of Japanese and Korean ancestry.

Accurate statistics are not available since 1952, but it may be conservatively estimated that under the G.I. Fiancees Act of 1946, and its extensions, more than 40,000 Japanese women entered the United States. These war brides are now residing in all parts of America. Consequently, rice, soy sauce, sushi, tempura, and various types of candies and cakes have now become an integral part of the stock-in-trade in many supermarkets. The long counters displaying Japanese food are silent proof of the power of the Japanese "moose," who captured not only the heart of the American G.I. but also his stomach.

19
Suspension of
Deportation

FTER THE END of World War II, thousands of Issei who were attempting to rehabilitate themselves from the effects of the economically crushing experience of the evacuation were faced with a new situation—one perhaps even more frightening and more devastating than the evacuation to a concentration camp and subsequent life there. They were served with warrants of arrest by U.S. Immigration Service officers, taken into custody, and told either to depart voluntarily from the United States for Japan at their own expense, or, if they lacked the funds (which most of them did), they would be deported to Japan by the United States government. In most of these cases, the aliens involved were, at the time these "orders" were made, married to United States citizens and had citizen children.

It was ironic, tragic, and incongruous that in 1946 new immigrants from Japan, looking forward eagerly to joining their future husbands, were being met by smiling officers of the U.S. Immigration Service and admitted into the U.S. At the same time, however, because of a section of the Immigration Act of 1917, long-time residents, some of whom had been in America for over twenty years, were being summoned before grim-faced officers of the Immigration Service and ordered to leave the country.

Admittedly, several hundred cases involved Japanese aliens who had not been legally admitted into the United States. They had walked across the U.S.–Mexican or U.S.–Canadian borders, had been smuggled into the United States on small boats or in the trunks of cars, or had managed to enter as "wetbacks" by swimming across the Rio Grande, which divides Mexico from the state of Texas. These aliens had successfully eluded the clutches of the immigration officers for years, had settled down in the United States, and had obtained employment or started their own businesses. In most cases these aliens had married and raised families that included children born in America.

In a majority of cases, however, the Japanese aliens had entered the United States legally before the outbreak of World War II. Section 3 of the Immigration Act of 1917[1] had permitted persons from Japan to be admitted as ministers, teachers, students, visitors, and merchants. These persons were classified as nonimmigrants since Japanese could not enter the United States for permanent residence.[2] Section 3 further provided that "such persons . . . who fail to maintain in the United States a status or occupation placing them within the excepted classes shall be deemed to be in the United States contrary to law, and shall be subject to deportation as provided in Section 19 of this Act."

The Japanese who had entered legally as nonimmigrants had had their stay in the United States renewed from time to time by applying for, and having granted, approval by the Immigration Service for additional periods. The sudden outbreak of the war with Japan had made any further extensions of stay in the United States impossible since they were now classified as "alien enemies" by the Presidential Proclamation of December 8, 1941.

While in the concentration camps, each of these aliens, whether he had initially entered the United States legally or illegally, was interviewed by an officer of the United States Immigration Service. In most instances, the interviews were recorded and later made a part of the alien's file. During the more than three years that these aliens were in the camps, their legal periods of stay expired so that they were in the United States "contrary to law." In the case of treaty traders, their commercial activities between the United States and Japan had been abruptly terminated by the war. Students had not been able to continue their education in the colleges and universities to which they had previously been admitted since they could not leave the camps. Aliens who had entered the United States illegally were naturally without status.

Aliens then deemed by the Immigration Service to be in the United States "contrary to law" could not have been deported or required to depart voluntarily for Japan during World War II as obviously no transportation was available. However, once the war was over and the aliens had been released from the camps and travel between the United States and Japan became possible, the Immigration Service immediately pounced upon these helpless people and instituted proceedings to remove them from the country.

Particularly pathetic were cases in which an alien was ordered to leave when his spouse and children wanted to remain in the United States where they had been born. The family was now to be split up, with attendant hardships upon every member. The American citizen spouses and children did not want to go to Japan, which to them was a strange and foreign country.

The basis for a heart-rending decision as to whether the alien should return to Japan alone or take the members of his family out of their own country was Section 19(c) of the Immigration Act of 1917, which provided that:

(c) In the case of any alien . . . who is deportable under any law of the United States and who has proved good moral character for the preceding five years, the Attorney General may (1) permit such alien to depart the United States to any country of his choice at his own expense, in lieu of deportation, or (2) suspend deportation of such alien if not racially inadmissible or ineligible for naturalization in the United States, if he finds that such deportation would result in serious economic detriment to a citizen or legally resident alien who is the spouse, parent, or minor child of such deportable alien.

Again, up to 1946, the racially discriminatory clause "aliens ineligible for naturalization" prevented aliens from Japan from applying for suspension of deportation.[2] The only significant groups of aliens "ineligible for citizenship" in 1946 were persons born in Japan and Korea. All other persons from Asiatic countries, including Chinese, Filipinos, and Hindus, through various amendments passed by Congress during World War II, were eligible for naturalization.

The ugly, racially discriminatory statute that had squeezed the Japanese alien in almost every area of his activity in the United States now rose up to confront him again. In all parts of the United States where these Japanese people were now residing, when they were served with warrants of arrest they desperately sought legal advice to find ways by which the Immigration Service could be prevented from executing the orders.

Attorneys representing these aliens in 1946 and 1947 applied for suspension of deportation in the hope of merely delaying the inevitable date of departure. Appeals of orders of deportation were filed with the Board of Immigration Appeals to further delay their execution. Injunctions were filed in the federal district courts to halt the actions of immigration officers, pending further appeals of the deportation orders. Pleas for bills poured into offices of congressmen and senators in other attempts to delay their departure. The JACL, which had successfully sponsored the G.I. Fiancees Act, now launched a vigorous legislative campaign in the halls of Congress to prevent the involuntary departure of long-time resident Japanese aliens from the United States.

The JACL pointed out to the congressmen and senators that regardless of whether these Japanese aliens had initially entered the United States legally or illegally, each of them had conducted himself in a law-abiding manner. They had worked hard in the fields and the farms or in their small shops and stores. They had raised their sons and daughters to be worthy American citizens. They had paid their share of taxes. Their thrift and self-reliance had kept them off relief rolls before World War II. They had borne the strains of war and the consequences of the evacuation with patience and fortitude. These aliens, whether male or female, were middle-aged or elderly. Because of their destitution as a result of the evacuation, these unfortunate aliens would find it virtually impossible to subsist in Japan, a nation that had exhausted its resources during the war just ended.

The JACL also reminded the members of Congress that these aliens had produced sons who had served in the armed forces of the United States in the war against Japan and Germany, including many in the famed 442nd Regimental Combat Team. These sons, and daughters, had also served in other military assignments as soldier-interpreters and translators. Many of them were with the Army of Occupation in Japan.

The impassioned pleas of the JACL on behalf of these helpless deportable aliens were heeded. On July 1, 1948 Congress approved H.R. 3566.[3] This bill amended Section 19(c) of the Immigration Act of 1917 to read as follows:

(c) In the case of any alien . . . who is deportable under any law of the United States and who has proved good moral character for the preceding five years, the Attorney General may . . . (2) suspend deportation of such alien, if he is not ineligible for naturalization, or if ineligible, such ineligibility would result in serious economic detriment to a citizen or legally resident alien who is the spouse, or minor child of such deportable alien; or (b) that such alien has resided continuously in the United States for seven years or more and is residing in the United States upon the effective date of this Act.

Subsection (c)(2)(b) was specifically added to include persons who did not have a spouse, parent, or minor child, so that such single, divorced, or widowed persons could also be permitted to apply individually for suspension of deportation.

The amendment to Section 19(c) of the Immigration Act of 1917 was carefully drafted by the JACL to include those Japanese aliens who were residing in the United States at the outbreak of World War II, who remained in the United States throughout the war years, and who did not depart from the United States after the end of the war.

It is conservatively estimated that over a thousand of these aliens, temporarily placed in imminent peril of being compelled to leave the United States, were eventually approved for permanent residence. These "deportable" aliens were now once again able to breathe more easily and set about to rebuild their lives in the country of their choice.

20

The Immigration and Nationality Act of 1952

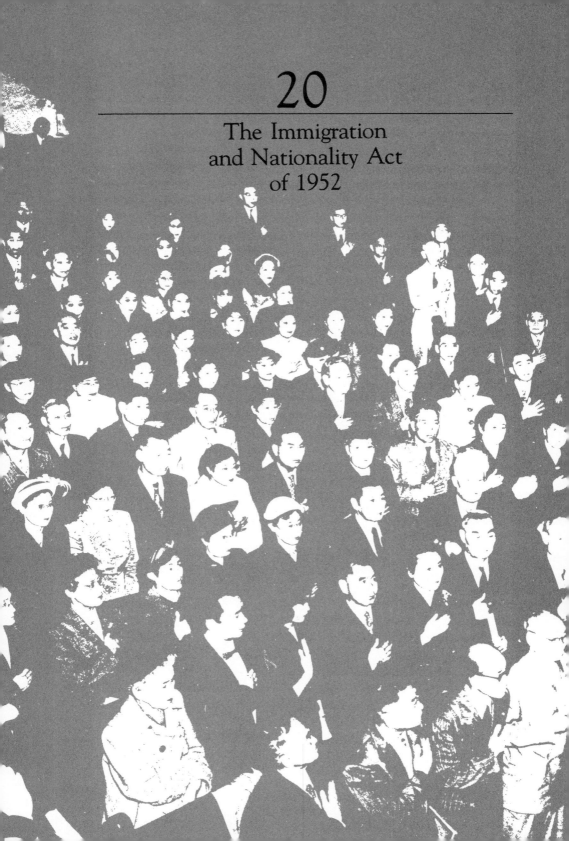

T HE ASIA-PACIFIC TRIANGLE is a term that appears throughout Section 202(a) of the Immigration and Nationality Act of 1952, popularly called the Walter-McCarran Act[1] after Congressman Francis E. Walter of Pennsylvania and Senator Pat McCarran of Nevada who sponsored the bills in their respective houses of Congress. This legislation brought within one comprehensive statute the multitude of laws that had previously governed the immigration and naturalization procedures of the United States. The new law perpetuated many of the immigration policies of the earlier statutes, but with some significant modifications. In brief, the new act

1. Made all races eligible for naturalization and eliminated race as a bar to immigration.

2. Eliminated discrimination between sexes with respect to immigration.

3. Introduced a system of selective immigration by giving a quota preference to skilled aliens whose services were urgently needed in the United States.

4. Placed a limit on the use of the governing country's quota by natives of colonies and dependent areas.

5. Provided an escape clause permitting the immigration of certain former voluntary members of proscribed organizations.

6. Broadened the grounds for the exclusion and deportation of aliens.

7. Curtailed procedures for the adjustment of status of nonimmigrant aliens into the United States to that of permanent resident aliens.

8. Afforded greater procedural safeguards to aliens subject to deportation.

The groundwork for this new act was laid in 1947 when the Senate authorized an investigation and study of the immigration and naturalization systems of the United States.[2] Every aspect of the immigration and naturalization policies of the United States government was reviewed between July and November 1948. Testimony was heard from representatives of government, from scores of voluntary, civic, social, and ethnic organizations in Washington, D.C., on the West Coast, the Mexican border, New Orleans, Miami, New York, along the Canadian border, and from Havana, Cuba.

The findings of the Senate Judiciary Committee, based on this staff study submitted to the Senate on April 20, 1950, were contained in a 925-page report, "The Immigration and Naturalization Systems of the United States."[3] Subsequently, during 1950 and 1951, Senator McCarran, chairman of the Senate Judiciary Committee, and Congressman Walter, chairman of the House Subcommittee on Immigration, introduced omnibus immigration and nationality legislation.

THE IMMIGRATION AND NATIONALITY ACT IS PASSED

After much debate in both the House and the Senate, a new immigration and nationality act was approved by the Eighty-second Congress and presented to the White House on June 11, 1952. Two weeks later, on June 25, President Truman vetoed the bill because he felt it was too restrictive.[4] The House quickly overrode the President's veto by a vote of 278 to 113 on June 26. On June 27 the Senate overrode the President's veto by a vote of 57 to 26, and the Immigration and Nationality Act of 1952 became law, with the Asia-Pacific Triangle as an integral part of the statute.

The Asia-Pacific Triangle, a specifically delineated section of the world, includes the continent of Asia and almost the entire span of the Pacific Ocean. All of the earth's surface between 60 degrees east and 165 degrees west longitude and from the North Pole south to 25 degrees south latitude is included (see map, page 313). Within this triangle there are twenty independent countries ranging from Afghanistan to Western Samoa. Sixteen subquota sections, from Australia's Christmas Island to Portugal's Timor, are also among the twenty-three immigration quota areas contained by this vast slice of the globe. It encompasses practically all of Asia proper, outside of some areas of the Soviet Union, and almost all of the Pacific islands north of Australia and New Zealand.

Well over half of the world's population live and work within this triangle.[5] Racial ancestry determined the quota area to which a person was chargeable for immigration purposes. Regardless of whether a person may have been born outside the Asia-Pacific Triangle, if his ancestry originated within that area he was chargeable to the quotas allotted to the countries within it.

Clearly the Immigration and Nationality Act of 1952 was specifically designed to restrict Asiatic immigration into the United States. For the first time since 1924, however, the Walter-McCarran Act did make possible the general immigration of persons from Japan to the

United States for permanent residence but Japan was allotted only 185 immigrants per year.

Also, a Caucasian born in England or Germany, for example, could enter the United States for permanent residence under the quota allotted to these Asiatic countries. However, if a person was born in England or Germany but his racial ancestry was in the Asia-Pacific Triangle, Japan, for example, that person of Japanese ancestry could not enter the United States under the English or German quota but was chargeable to the Japanese quota.

THE JACL SUPPORTS THE ACT OF 1952

In spite of its obviously racially discriminatory features, the Walter-McCarran Act was supported by the Japanese American Citizens League. After President Truman vetoed the bill in June 1952, the JACL was one of the organizations to exert persuasive pressure on members of Congress to override the veto. For this effort, the JACL was severely criticized for compromising its principles. The JACL worked strenuously to effect the passage of this particular act, despite its racially discriminatory features, because it made naturalization possible for the Issei.

Equality in immigration and naturalization privileges had been a basic objective of the JACL ever since it had been organized in 1930. One of the first actions of the fledgling organization had been to petition Congress to repeal the Japanese Exclusion Act of 1924[6] and to extend naturalization privileges to resident Japanese aliens. Persons from Japan had not been eligible for citizenship since 1790.[7]

In 1948 the JACL had enlisted the sympathetic support of Congressman Walter Judd of Minnesota, a former missionary in China. Congressman Judd sponsored a bill to extend naturalization privileges to resident aliens of Japanese ancestry. The "equality in naturalization" features of the Judd bill were incorporated in the Walter-McCarran Act of 1952. The JACL committed itself to the Walter-McCarran Act because it eliminated race as a disqualification to immigration and naturalization and in spite of the fact that it contained the features of the Asia-Pacific Triangle. That could be dealt with later.

The Walter-McCarran Act directly benefited the Japanese in Japan and the Japanese in the United States in the following ways:

1. By removing race as a qualification for naturalization. Some 500 discriminatory and restrictive laws and ordinances directed against

persons of Japanese ancestry throughout the United States became null, void, or "inoperative."

2. By making all resident aliens in the United States eligible for naturalization.

3. By removing the Japanese from the humiliating status of inferiority under which they had been held and which had contributed to the outbreak of the Pacific war.

4. By granting equality in immigration and citizenship to Japanese resident aliens, this act recognized the parents of the Japanese-American fighting men who had distinguished themselves in both the Pacific and European Theatres of World War II and the parents of all other Americans of Japanese ancestry.

5. By recognizing that persons of Japanese ancestry were loyal, law-abiding, and deserving of full acceptance as worthy members of the American community.[8]

The pernicious features of the Walter-McCarran Act were at no time either approved or condoned by the JACL, as some individuals and organizations once believed.[9] It was an instance of half a loaf being better than none. The racial features of the national origins quota system, compounded by the bigotry of the Asia-Pacific Triangle, were still deplored by the JACL.

The Japanese Exclusion Act of 1924 represented a high point of racial intolerance in United States immigration laws; the Immigration and Nationality Act of 1952, enacted twenty-eight years later, represented the first general relaxation of these ethnic restrictions.

Section 311 of the Walter-McCarran Act stated, "The right of a person to become a naturalized citizen of the United States shall not be denied or abridged because of race or sex or because such person is married." The barrier of race that had existed for 162 years collapsed on June 27, 1952.

THE ISSEI BECOME NATURALIZED

For the Issei, passage of the Walter-McCarran Act was the realization of something they had thought impossible. Now they enrolled by the thousands in citizenship courses sponsored by churches, JACL chapters, and other organizations. Bill Hosakawa has aptly expressed this period:

If they wondered why the rights of their citizen offspring had been abridged in the hysteria of the war, they were too polite to ask and too busy studying for their citizenship examinations to challenge the instructor. And in time, tiny

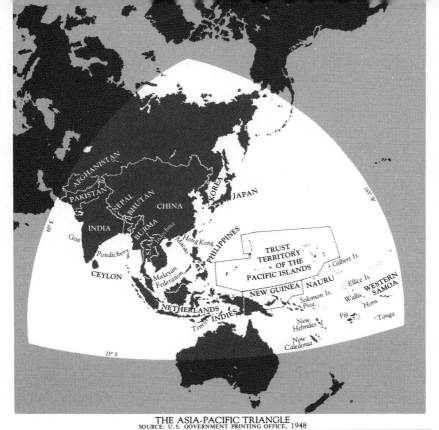

THE ASIA-PACIFIC TRIANGLE
SOURCE: U.S. GOVERNMENT PRINTING OFFICE, 1948

INDIA   Separate quota area in large type.   *Hong Kong*   Colony or other dependent area in small type.

old ladies bent by toil, gray-haired old men gnarled by a lifetime of labor, men and women in their sixties and seventies and eighties—usually accompanied by their proud Nisei children and even their Sansei grandchildren—stood before federal judges and took the oath of allegiance as America's newest citizens. It was a privilege and an honor that had been a long time coming.[10]

The gales of World War II had beaten mercilessly upon their heads, stripping them of their property as well as their civil rights. These aliens bore noble sons and daughters who were imprinted with the same marks of "shame" solely because of their ancestry. Yet, father and son, mother and daughter, all endured stoically and dauntlessly in the center of the storm.

These "bamboo plants" both young and old, bent to the ground to shelter themselves against the tumultuous force. Their resistance was reinforced by the strength of their own convictions as well as their own knowledge that they were without guilt.

In 1952 the American people, through their elected representatives in Congress, "accepted" these persons of Japanese ancestry through the passage of the Walter-McCarran Act.

21

Statutes and Court Decisions that Affected Persons of Japanese Ancestry

THE LONG YEARS before 1952 were marked by oppression, discrimination, racial animosity, and contempt toward persons of Japanese ancestry in the United States. The years from 1952 to the present may be described as the period in which the Japanese became known as "the most respected minority group in America." The rapidity of their acceptance as "worthy citizens" in almost every area of American life has been phenomenal. Wherever the Japanese now reside, work, play, or serve, they are often acclaimed for their neat and beautiful homes, their conscientiousness, and their good relationships with their fellows. They are also recognized as enthusiastic sportsmen as well as sincere and dedicated supporters of community projects through their churches and other organizations.

Yet, the Issei and the Nisei have not really changed from what they have been; their basic characteristics remain the same. Their cultural heritage has always been a finely balanced amalgamation of Japanese customs, ethics, and morality, blended with the newer heritage of American democracy.

Now Presidents of the United States, members of Congress, high-ranking military officers, government officials, state and local politicians, organizations once bitterly anti-Japanese, the press and other media of communication, and the American public all recognize the economic and social status of persons of Japanese ancestry with whole-hearted approval. Perhaps the reason for this change of attitude is that the American public now sees Japanese-Americans as Americans who happen to be of Japanese ancestry rather than as "Japs." The rapid recognition of the Japanese as "worthy citizens" may be based partly on a public desire to rectify as quickly as possible the wrong and unfair treatment imposed upon them by removing them from their homes and placing them in concentration camps during World War II.

The years following 1952 saw Issei, Nisei, and now Sansei residing throughout virtually every state of the Union, including the Deep South. As of the 1970 federal census, approximately 285,000 persons of Japanese ancestry were residing not only in the western United States but also within such states as Mississippi, New Hampshire, North Dakota, Vermont, Alabama, Arkansas, Delaware, Iowa, Kentucky, Louisiana, and Maine.

The pioneer immigrants from Japan were now reaching their seventies, eighties, and even nineties and were gradually disappearing from the American scene. Some of their sons and daughters were now in the prime of life, in their forties, fifties, and some in their sixties. The

Nisei, by and large, were settled in their homes, gradually accumulating seniority in employment, and busy raising their third-generation children, the Sansei. The Sansei were "as American as apple pie" in thought and behavior, completely integrated in their schools and communities, and many had attended the prestigious colleges and universities in the Midwest and East—something that was all but unattainable to most of the Nisei generation.

The Issei pioneers had not suffered hardships in the United States in vain. They now saw with pride their Nisei children able to step into professions for which they had been educated and into which, before World War II, they had not been able to enter because of racial discrimination and prejudice.

Throughout the United States the Nisei are now judges, lawyers, engineers, social workers, psychologists, teachers, accountants, journalists, scientists, chemists, architects, soil conservationists, highly skilled farmers, space physicists, doctors, nurses, and well-trained businessmen. Thousands of others work shoulder to shoulder with fellow Americans in civil service employment, shops, stores, factories, and businesses. Nisei serve on commissions, boards, and agencies. They have been elected to various offices as city councilmen, mayors, state legislators, county sheriffs and officers in other areas of law enforcement, and to the United States Congress. They have won recognition in the areas of painting, sculpture, dance, music, and theater. They are leaders in PTAs, veterans organizations, service clubs, and other church, community, and civic organizations. They are in the United States Foreign Service. They have attained high ranks in the armed forces. They have been accepted into the service academies of the army, the navy, and the air force.

While the Japanese were rapidly entering the mainstream of American life, a series of statutes and court decisions after 1952 helped them in their postwar adjustment. These legal steps may be divided into two parts: those that directly affected persons of Japanese ancestry and those that did not involve persons of Japanese ancestry as such but affected them as a racial minority, together with other ethnic minorities, in the attainment of equality for all.

BENEFITS FOR POSTAL SERVICE EMPLOYEES

There were several hundred Nisei employees in the postal service at the time of the outbreak of World War II. They had passed competitive written and oral examinations administered by the Federal Civil

Service Commission and had been assigned as postmen or clerical and supervisory workers. As classified federal civil service employees, they were eligible for promotions or entitled to increases in pay depending upon their years of service, rank, or seniority. When these federal employees were ordered into concentration camps, they lost their status. Many of the employees remained in the camps during the entire war. Others had relocated outside these camps. When they applied for their former jobs, they were refused. If they were rehired, they were placed in the status they had held at the date of their termination; the time spent in a camp was to be "dead time," during which increases in pay and promotions had passed them by.

On July 15, 1952 Congress approved Public Law 545,[1] which provided that each officer and each regular or substitute employee of Japanese ancestry in the postal service on the effective day of the act

(1) Who, at any time during the period beginning December 7, 1941, and ending September 3, 1945, solely by reason of any policy or program of the Federal Government with respect to persons of Japanese ancestry in the interests of the national security during such period, (A) was separated from his position in the postal field service or classified civil service, as the case may be, (B) lost opportunity for or was denied probational appointment from a civil service register of eligibles to any such position, or (C) was denied reinstatement to any such position; or

(2) Who, after having been separated from his position in the postal field service or classified civil service, as the case may be, at any time during such period, in order to enter the Armed Forces of the United States, either lost opportunity for or was denied probational appointment from a civil service register of eligibles to any such position or was denied reinstatement to any such position, solely by reason of any such policy or program of the Federal Government, shall have the grade, time in grade, and rate of compensation in the postal field service or the time in grade and rate of compensation in the classified civil service, as the case may be, which he would have attained automatically if such policy or program of the Federal Government had not been in effect.

MORE STRANDEES REGAIN UNITED STATES CITIZENSHIP

Several more cases involved strandees who, while residing in Japan during World War II, had either been drafted in the Japanese army, had voted in the Japanese elections, or had taught school in Japan.[2] They were all restored their United States citizenship in federal court proceedings after they had been issued certificates of identity by the American consul in Japan. They had been allowed to return to the United States to contest the loss of their citizenship. Thus, in *Acheson* vs. *Okimura*,[3] Associate Justice William O. Douglas of the Supreme Court of the United States held that where service in the Japanese army was evidenced by physical beatings by the Japanese military if a draftee refused to serve, there was adequate evidence that such military service was performed under compulsion, which nullified the loss of citizenship.

In four other cases involving strandees, the federal courts applied the standard of proof required in the case of *Nishikawa* vs. *Dulles*:[4] where United States citizens assert that their acts were not voluntary, the Government must bear the "onerous" burden of proving that such acts were voluntary by "clear, convincing, and unequivocal" evidence, individual by individual. Citizenship of all four of these strandees was ordered restored where the Government failed to meet its burden of proof.[5]

In 1952 there was still a veritable mountain of pending federal cases in the United States involving American citizens of Japanese ancestry who claimed that their act of voting in the Japanese elections had been inadvertent or had been committed because of the urgings of General Douglas MacArthur during the period of the occupation of Japan. The expenses of travel from Japan to the United States and the additional cost of litigation had placed a heavy burden upon the litigants and would place the same burdens upon other strandees who hoped to return to the United States if their applications for United States passports were denied by the American consul in Japan.

Congress was informed of the plight of these strandees. At the urging of the JACL a solution to the problem of United States citizens who had lost their citizenship by voting in the various political elections held in occupied Japan was found.[6]

Congress passed a bill known as Public Law 515 on July 20, 1954.[7] Under this law, any person who had lost United States citizenship solely by reason of having voted in any political election or plebiscite held in Japan between September 2, 1945 and April 27, 1952, inclusive, could within two years after the passage of the act, appear before any diplomatic or consular officer and take an oath of allegiance to the United States. A copy of the oath was sufficient evidence before any court or federal agency that such a person had not lost his United States citizenship.

Hundreds of Nisei did take an oath of allegiance to the United States, which restored their citizenship in the federal courts where their cases were pending. Others were able to show this document to the American consul for the issuance of a new passport.

THE RECLAMATION ACT OF 1902 IS AMENDED

On June 17, 1902 Congress had passed an act prohibiting the employment of "Mongolian" labor in the construction of reclamation projects.[8] The Reclamation Act of 1902 was aimed principally against the Japanese because the Chinese had been excluded since 1882.

In its post–World War II efforts to stimulate the development of industry, particularly in the Far West, Congress was confronted with a problem in employing both available laborers and highly skilled engineers of Japanese ("Mongolian") ancestry to work on these projects. The Reclamation Act was a barrier to the employment of these persons.

On May 10, 1956, over half a century after the original legislation, Congress passed Public Law 517,[9] which struck the word "Mongolian" from the Reclamation Act of 1902. The successful effort to eliminate this racially discriminatory word from the statutes of the United States was spearheaded by a distinguished member of Congress, Spark Matsunaga of Hawaii, a veteran of the famed 442nd Regimental Combat Team.

CONGRESS FURTHER AMENDS THE EVACUATION CLAIMS ACT

On July 9, 1956 Congress passed Public Law 673,[10] which further amended the Evacuation Claims Act of 1948. As noted before, the act had been amended in 1951 to authorize the attorney general of the United States to compromise and settle evacuation claims in amounts up to $2,500. Although a substantial number of claims had been settled and paid to the evacuees up to the statutory amount of $2,500, a large number of claims exceeding this amount still remained to be paid. These remaining claims involved amounts requiring appropriations by Congress.

To expedite the payment of almost all of the remaining claims, the Evacuation Claims Act was amended again in 1956 to authorize the attorney general to "compromise and settle and make an award in an amount not to exceed $100,000."

In addition, two other amendments were added. These involved the right of profit or nonprofit corporations, which had also sustained property losses due to the evacuation, to file their claims with the attorney general for compensation. These legal entities had been inadvertently overlooked in 1948 when the Evacuation Claims Act was under consideration. Under this act and the amendment in 1951, only a "person of Japanese ancestry" was eligible to file for losses. Now in 1956 various business organizations operated by persons of Japanese ancestry became eligible to file claims within the provisions of the Evacuation Claims Act. Churches, schools, and associations that had operated within the Japanese communities were allowed to file their claims for losses sustained when these nonprofit organizations were forced to dispose of or abandon their properties at the time of the evacuation.

Another group allowed to file claims for property losses included hundreds of persons of Japanese ancestry, mostly aliens, who had been apprehended by the FBI immediately after the outbreak of World War II and placed in special detention centers known as alien internment camps. These camps, as distinguished from concentration camps under the control of the War Relocation Authority, were known as the Alien Enemy Control Units of the United States Department of Justice. This special operation was headed by Edward J. Ennis, later a noted attorney in New York City.

These aliens had not been evacuated from their homes pursuant to Executive Order 9066 or under any of the exclusion orders promulgated by General DeWitt. After extensive investigations and hearings, almost all of the residents in the alien internment camps had been released to rejoin their families in the various concentration camps. Not having been evacuated under Executive Order 9066, they were ineligible to file for property losses under the Evacuation Claims Act.

The 1956 amendment to the act allowed claims "due to the exclusion of the families and relatives of such persons during their detention or internment. Any such person shall be deemed to have been excluded from such military areas and territories as of the date he would have been evacuated had he not been detained or interned." Under this amendment, such detainees were declared eligible to file within the original act.

The 1956 amendment accelerated the compromise and settlement of all the remaining claims except for one that had been filed by Jean and Ed Koda of Dos Palos, California. The Kodas had filed a claim in the amount of $2,497,500, the largest to be submitted by anyone evacuated in 1942. They claimed the loss of some 3,000 acres of farm property, a rice mill, a herd of hogs, machinery, inventory, and crops as well as management and legal expenses.

The Evacuation Claims Act had provided that the Court of Claims of the United States, situated in Washington, D.C., had jurisdiction to "determine any claim timely filed under this act," if the claim was more than $100,000.[11] On October 1, 1965 the Koda claim was settled. Chief Judge William Cowan of the court of claims approved the compromise settlement agreed to by the Attorney General's office and Jean and Ed Koda in the sum of $362,500.[12]

With the settlement of the Koda claim in 1965, the Evacuation Claims Program, sponsored by the JACL and authorized by law by the Congress in July 1948, came at long last to its termination.

ILLEGAL ALIENS ARE GRANTED PERMANENT RESIDENCY

After the passage of an amendment to Section 19(c) of the Immigration Act of 1917, aliens from Japan who had entered the United States legally as students, visitors, treaty traders, and teachers, but who had lost their status after World War II started, were able to apply for suspension of deportation and become permanent residents.

In addition, aliens from Japan who had entered the United States illegally before 1924 were allowed to become permanent residents if they were able to prove continuous residence in the country from before 1924 to the date of a hearing regarding their illegal status before officers of the Immigration Service. The basis for such an application by these illegal entrants was Section 249 of the Immigration and Nationality Act of 1952. This was known as a *registry proceeding*. Upon satisfactory evidence of continuous residence in the United States since before 1924, the Immigration Service would record that an applicant had been lawfully admitted for permanent residence in the United States as of the date of his original illegal entry. A registry proceeding also made such an alien eligible to apply for naturalization because he had resided at least five years in the United States.

However, the Immigration and Nationality Act of 1952 did not provide registry proceedings for aliens who had entered the United States illegally between 1924 and 1940, the period between the passage of the Japanese Exclusion Act of 1924 and the outbreak of World War II. Although many single aliens could apply for suspension of deportation if they produced evidence of "serious economic detriment" to themselves, other aliens who had entered the United States during this period were not able to do so and were subject to deportation.

In 1958 Congress amended the Immigration and Nationality Act to permit a registry proceeding if the illegal entry of the alien took place prior to June 28, 1940 instead of July 1, 1924.[13] This 1958 amendment was enacted primarily to prevent the deportation of aliens of Japanese ancestry who could not establish their date of entry prior to 1924.

Since all aliens of Japanese ancestry under deportation proceedings from 1946 to the date of the 1958 amendment had been in the United States as of 1940 and during World War II, their continuous residence was easily proved. The amendment proved eminently beneficial to a large number of Japanese aliens who were faced with the unhappy prospect of being returned to Japan because they could not prove that deportation would be of serious economic detriment to them.

LEGISLATION IN CALIFORNIA ASSISTS JAPANESE

Two bills passed in California are illustrative of efforts made to assist persons of Japanese ancestry, particularly Japanese aliens, and to accord them equal opportunities.

Many Japanese aliens had operated liquor stores, grocery stores, restaurants, and bars that required liquor licenses issued by the Alcoholic Beverage Control Board of California. Immediately after the outbreak of war on December 7, 1941, these licenses had been revoked for persons of Japanese ancestry regardless of whether the person was a United States citizen or an alien. As the Japanese returned to their homes, they were confronted by a state law that prohibited the issuance of liquor licenses to them.

On January 23, 1951 State Senator Gerald J. O'Gara introduced Senate Bill 1491, which added Section 7.1 to the Alcoholic Beverage Control Act of the State of California. It provided that any individual who held a license under this act immediately prior to December 7, 1941 and whose license was thereafter revoked "because of his enemy ancestry or because of internment or relocation of such person as a consequence of military necessity" could apply for a similar license upon the payment of the current fee.

Also in California, the Welfare and Institutions Code was amended in 1955 to permit Japanese aliens to apply for aid to the aged. For many years before the evacuation, the Japanese had prided themselves on the fact that they did not seek state or federal aid to assist them in their periods of economic distress, no matter how desperate their financial conditions. Organizations within the Japanese community, such as churches, prefectural societies, and Japanese associations, would contribute or loan money to tide individuals or families over times of economic difficulties. This strong sense of community self-help was so dominant a trait among the Japanese that it was considered a mark of shame for a Japanese to apply for governmental assistance for his individual support.

However, the evacuation had wiped out the bank accounts of many Japanese. Their properties had been abandoned or sold for only a few dollars of their actual value. Many of the Japanese churches, societies, and organizations had been discontinued or disbanded with no resources remaining in their coffers to care for their members.

In addition, many of the Japanese aliens, already reduced to a penniless status, could no longer obtain gainful employment because of their advancing age. Their children were living under crowded conditions and in most instances were married and attempting to raise their own families under hardship conditions. Although most of the destitute parents did live with their children wherever possible, some of these elderly Issei had no place to go. They lived in cheap, run-down rooming houses, eking out their daily existence under poverty-level conditions, dressed in shabby clothing, and subsisting on one or two inadequate meals a day. As a last resort, these aged Issei were compelled to ask for state or federal aid. The psychological impact of the "shame" connected with seeking government assistance was almost unbearable, but hunger and destitution were even worse.

In 1955 Assemblyman Edward Elliott, who represented a large number of these destitute Issei in the eastern section of Los Angeles, introduced a bill that made it possible for them to seek assistance from state funds. Section 2160.4 of the Welfare and Institutions Code removed the provision that aliens were not eligible for state aid and provided that "aid shall be granted to any person who had lived in the United States continuously for 25 years at time of making application."[14]

CONGRESS ASSISTS IN RETURN OF YEN DEPOSITS

Before the outbreak of World War II, several Japanese banks had opened branches in California. Chartered to conduct full banking services, they accepted deposits, loaned money for crops, automobiles, and homes, and financed the business operations of local merchants. These same banks also accepted American dollars from depositors to be converted into Japanese yen. At the time of the outbreak of World War II, the yen-dollar conversion rate was four yen to one dollar. Thus, twenty-five American dollars would reflect the equivalent of 100 yen on the international market.

Thousands of persons in the United States purchased yen certificates in order to take advantage of the conversion rate. These deposits amounted to several million dollars immediately after Pearl Harbor when the United States government "vested" such assets. They were held by the Office of Alien Property, a special unit of the United States Department of Justice under the attorney general.[15]

After the end of World War II, certain classes of depositors in these banks were permitted to file debt claims with the Office of Alien Property to recover their money. The yen deposit claim issues took over fifteen years, until 1972, to be resolved.

Thousands of claimants and the federal government clashed over three main problems. These issues were:

1. What was the status of the claimants who had failed to file before the prescribed statutory deadlines?

2. At what rate of exchange should the United States government return the bank deposits—at the prewar rate of four yen to one dollar or at the postwar rate of three hundred sixty yen to one dollar?

3. Were "internees" as distinguished from "evacuees" eligible to file for the recovery of their yen deposits?

Claimants numbering in the hundreds had failed to file their claims with the Office of Alien Property within a prescribed deadline. These claims were dismissed by the Office of Alien Property, even though the claimants' right to receive their money was not disputed. The initial deadline within which to file had been March 1, 1947. It was later extended by executive order to November 18, 1949.

The years between 1947 and 1949 were hectic ones for persons of Japanese ancestry. Most of these people had only recently left the concentration camps and were frantically seeking homes and employment. They were relocating in new and unfamiliar places throughout the United States. The Office of Alien Property had only their prewar addresses, which made it virtually impossible to keep in touch with them. The claimants themselves were not aware of the deadlines. Notices were officially published in the *Federal Register*, but who among them read it? Only by word of mouth were some claimants told of these deadlines.

To further aggravate the situation, the Office of Alien Property insisted that an original certificate of yen deposit be submitted with each claim. Many such documents had been lost or destroyed in the confusion of the evacuation and in the moves from camp to camp during the war.

In various areas of the United States, where large numbers of Japanese had resettled, committees to assist yen deposit claimants were formed. But locating the whereabouts of the claimants and assisting them in locating their yen certificates was a laborious task. In many instances, the deadline expired before the claims could be filed with the government. Hundreds of claims were dismissed by the Office of Alien Property because they missed the deadline. These claims had been filed for the return of yen deposits in the Yokohama Specie Bank, Ltd.,[16] the Sumitomo Bank, Ltd.,[17] and the Mitsui Bank, Ltd.[18]

The Federal Circuit Court of Appeals, in *Brownell* vs. *Morizo Nakashima*,[19] upheld the dismissal of those claims. In 1967 the Supreme Court of the United States reversed the judgment of the court of appeals. It held that the depositors had not understood the complicated procedures required to file their claims and thus were not barred from recovering their deposits even though the deadline had expired at the time of filing.

Another controversy raged between the claimants and the federal government after the Office of Alien Property had approved payment of deposits. The "eligible" claimants wanted their deposits returned at the prewar yen-dollar conversion rate of four yen to one dollar, the rate in effect when the bank assets were actually seized by the government after the outbreak of the war. However, the Government contended that the yen deposits should be repaid on the basis of the yen-dollar conversion rate at the postwar rate of three hundred sixty yen to one dollar.

In *Aratani* vs. *Kennedy*[20] the Federal Circuit Court of Appeals upheld the Government's contention that the deposits should be paid to the claimants "at the rate of exchange which prevailed when commercial intercourse first became lawful in post-war period and not at the rate prevailing on December 7, 1941, the last day that [Japanese] banks were open for business." (December 7, 1941 was a Sunday.)

The claimants appealed to the Supreme Court of the United States. In 1965, before the Court could decide the appeal, the Government accepted the depositors' position and agreed to pay their claims at the prewar conversion rate. However, the claims of alien internees or parolees had still to be resolved.

It was contended by the Government that Japanese internees were ineligible to file their claims because of the language contained in Section 34(a) of the Trading with the Enemy Act of 1946, as amended.[21] Claims would be paid by the government, upon approval of the Office of Alien Property only to citizens of the United States, or to those other natural persons who had been since the beginning of the war residents of the United States. Section 34(a)(2), however, went on to include those "who have not during the war been interned or paroled pursuant to the Alien Enemy Act."

Although all Japanese aliens were declared by the Presidential Proclamation of December 8, 1941 to be "alien enemies," persons who had
been removed to concentration camps were eligible to claim their yen
deposits. However, persons who had initially been apprehended by
the FBI immediately after the outbreak of World War II and interned
in camps operated by the Alien Enemy Control Unit of the Department
of Justice were not eligible to recover their yen claims.

The Department of Justice contended that an alien became an "alien
enemy" if the FBI considered him loyal to Japan in the first days after
Pearl Harbor and placed him in an internment camp. As a matter of
record, the Japanese aliens who were first apprehended were, for the
most part, language teachers, Buddhist priests, officers of Japanese
fraternal organizations, officers of cultural societies, or other leaders
who were respected by the Japanese community. During the time of
their internment, these persons had individual hearings bearing on
their loyalty and personal inclinations. Almost all of these internees
were ultimately released to rejoin their families in various concentration camps, freed outright, or freed under certain parole conditions.

The Office of Alien Property maintained that once a person had
been interned or paroled pursuant to the Alien Enemy Act, he was not
eligible to recover his yen deposits. After the Immigration and Nationality Act of 1952, these same internees and parolees had applied for
naturalization and had obtained their United States citizenship. In
spite of their newly acquired status, some 1,000 to 2,000 persons of
Japanese ancestry were unable to recover their yen deposits because
of the statutory provisions of Section 34(a)(2) of the Trading with
the Enemy Act.[22]

Although the controversy over the rate of the yen deposits was settled in 1965 and the right of claimants to recover their funds after the
deadline was affirmed in 1967, the issue of whether internees were eligible to file their claims still continued. Finally in 1971, a group of
persons called the Committee of Japanese American Yen Depositors
sought the assistance of the JACL. The league asked Representative
Spark Matsunaga to introduce a bill that would allow Japanese who
had been interned or paroled to file for recovery of their deposits.[23]

After the bill, known as H.R. 8215, was introduced by Representative Matsunaga in April 1971, the Justice Department delayed its
report on it for over a year, then finally stated that it would not object
to the proposed amendment. Once, this "no objection" report was
received, the bill quickly passed both the House of Representatives

and the Senate. Late Wednesday afternoon, October 4, 1972, President Richard Nixon signed H.R. 8215 into law.

The passage of this amendment to the Trading with the Enemy Act was the last major legislative act by the United States government that specifically benefited persons of Japanese ancestry after World War II. This praiseworthy bill, which benefited many persons in 1972, had come too late for hundreds of Issei who had died during the previous thirty-one years. These deposits had represented their entire life savings. Their heirs, however, enjoyed the benefits of the bill. It should be noted also that no interest was paid on the money while it was held by the United States government.

TITLE II OF THE INTERNAL SECURITY ACT IS REPEALED

In the waning days of September 1971, a historic meeting took place at Anchorage, Alaska. President Nixon was on an international tour of good will through the Orient. Emperor Hirohito was en route to visit Europe, the first time that a reigning ruler of Japan was to do so in the centuries-old history of that country. Their meeting symbolized close friendship between the United States and Japan, despite a war between the two countries some thirty years before.

For persons of Japanese ancestry in America, another event that took place at this time was also of great significance. President Nixon stopped in Portland, Oregon on his way to Anchorage. There, on September 25, 1971, he signed into law H.R. 234,[24] a bill that repealed the provisions of Title II of the Internal Security Act of 1950,[25] also called the Emergency Detention Act.

Title II was a part of the Internal Security Act, passed on September 23, 1950[26] at the height of the cold war with the Soviet Union and its threats of communistic encroachment. In justifying the provisions of the Emergency Detention Act, it was declared that "the precedents afforded by court decisions sustaining the validity of the Japanese relocation program in effect during World War II provide ample authority for the enactment of legislation to attain their objective."[27]

Title II provided that in the event of an invasion of the territory of the United States or its possessions, a declaration of war by Congress, or an insurrection within the United States in aid to a foreign enemy,

the President is authorized to make public proclamation of the existence of an "Internal Security Emergency."

. . . the President [is] . . . authorized to apprehend and by order detain . . . each person as to whom there is reasonable ground to believe that such person probably will engage in, probably will conspire with others to engage in, acts of espionage or of sabotage.

Persons apprehended or detained under this title shall be confined in such places of detention as may be prescribed by the Attorney General.

For those under suspicion, there was to be a preliminary hearing; if sufficient evidence was introduced against them, they were to be detained for an indefinite period of time for further proceedings through a board of detention review.

In his veto message regarding the Emergency Detention Act, President Truman stated:

The mere fact that it could be done shows clearly how the bill would open a Pandora's Box of opportunities for official condemnation of organizations and individuals for perfectly honest opinions. The basic error of these sections is that they move in the direction of suppressing opinion and belief—a long step towards totalitarianism.

The Emergency Detention Act of 1950, in spite of these warnings by President Truman, passed over his veto. The act provided facilities that bore not only a melancholy resemblance to the concentration camps for Japanese-Americans in the United States but also to those established for Jews by the Nazis during the Third Reich.

In 1952 the Justice Department designated six sites for concentration camps within the United States, to be administered by the United States Bureau of Prisons. These were

1. Allenwood, Pennsylvania, 4,200 acres.

2. Avon Park, Florida, part of the Florida prison system.

3. El Reno, Oklahoma, now pasture land.

4. Florence, Arizona, a federal prison.

5. Wickenburg, Arizona, a federal prison.

6. Tule Lake, California, formerly a concentration camp for persons of Japanese ancestry during World War II.

Funds were appropriated by Congress from 1952 to 1958 to prepare and administer these camps. In 1958 further appropriations stopped because it had been ascertained by the Justice Department that there was no need for these facilities. Few Americans even knew of the existence of Title II or of the fact that the government had prepared these camps for the wholesale detention of some of its citizens.

After President Lyndon B. Johnson succeeded President John F. Kennedy in 1963, the federal government quietly reactivated the concentration camp program. The Viet Nam War was "heating up" during President Johnson's administration. The Selective Service System was drafting thousands of eligible males; reserves were being called up for combat duty. Military supplies and equipment were being manufactured in massive quantities. Thousands of planes and helicopters were being shipped to the battle zones. The Seventh Fleet of the United States Navy was on alert in the South China Sea. Thailand and Cambodia were being shipped arms and other war materials. Okinawa, still under the control of the United States government, was used as a jumping-off place for American fighting forces bound for Viet Nam.

Voices of protest, particularly on college campuses throughout the United States, rose to crescendo heights from the mid-1960s on. Huge demonstrations, both peaceful and violent, by antiwar agitators began to tear the nation apart. Coupled with student demonstrations over the Viet Nam War were the cries of anger by minorities, particularly the blacks, who were increasingly frustrated by the slowness on the part of the government to implement provisions of the Civil Rights Act of 1964.

It was in this setting that the federal government began to consider enforcing the provisions of the Emergency Detention Act of 1950. On May 6, 1968 Chairman Edwin E. Willis of the House Committee on Un-American Activities suggested the use of Title II to imprison black militants, labeling them as "communists, and therefore insurrectionists in aid of a foreign enemy." The House committee released a report entitled "Guerilla Warfare Advocates in the United States." Chairman Willis declared that the "black militants have essentially declared war on the United States, and therefore they lose all constitutional rights and should be imprisoned in detention camps."

Government officials openly began to quote the 1950 act to proclaim that there was a crisis in the United States and that direct action to apprehend undesirable persons should be taken. Rumors became rampant throughout the black areas that the federal government was preparing the concentration camps for militant Negroes because of their vociferous protests of the conditions existing in ghettos and against which they were raising their fists as well as their voices.

In the turbulent period of the later 1960s, however, one small segment of the American public viewed the rising tide of hysteria with increasing alarm. To the Japanese-Americans the threat of imprisoning racial minorities and war protestors seemed strikingly similar to the atmosphere of panic that had caused their own mass removal and detention into concentration camps in 1942.

They remembered the legal authority of their mass evacuation as set down by the Supreme Court in *Korematsu* vs. *United States*.[28] But they also remembered the powerful dissenting opinion of Associate Justice Robert H. Jackson in the same case, who declared the mass evacuation to be unconstitutional and solemnly warned:

> Once a judicial opinion rationalizes such an order to show that it conforms to the Constitution, or rather rationalizes the Constitution to show that the Constitution sanctions such an order, the Court for all time has validated the principle of racial discrimination in criminal procedure and of transplanting American citizens. The principle then lies about like a loaded weapon ready for the hand of any authority that can bring forward a plausible claim of an urgent need. Every repetition imbeds that principle more deeply in our law and thinking and expands it to new purposes.

On August 23, 1968, at its biennial national convention held in San Jose, California, the JACL officially approved a resolution calling for the repeal of Title II. By 1968 the JACL had grown in strength and stature; it was now composed of over ninety chapters operating within almost every state where persons of Japanese ancestry were concentrated. Mike Masaoka, its Washington representative, was now the senior congressional representative for any civil rights organization, having served in his post continuously since 1946. His ability to persuade members of Congress to repeal discriminatory laws and to replace them with others reflecting the true spirit of American democracy was respected and honored. It was he who marshaled the necessary forces to support the repeal of Title II. His efforts were supported by two vigorous and dedicated members of the JACL, Ray Okamura and Paul Yamamoto, who were appointed cochairmen of an ad hoc antidetention committee.

The campaign in the beginning was confronted with the usual problems of apathy. However, as the committee expanded its activities throughout the United States, momentum in favor of the project increased. What was particularly alarming was the provision in Title II that stated that during periods of "internal security emergency" any person who probably would engage in, or probably would conspire with others to engage in, acts of espionage or sabotage could be incarcerated in detention camps.

Thus, any person could be summarily apprehended, detained, and incarcerated on the basis of rumors, gossip, lies, hearsay, or just being inadvertently present somewhere. The provision was frightening in its scope since it could be directed against any person, at any time, at any place, or under any circumstances, based solely upon the whim or will of a government official.

Soon, support for the repeal of Title II poured into the offices of the JACL. Newspapers and other media, public officials, and hundreds of organizations—civic, veterans, and religious—proclaimed their willingness to help.

On April 18, 1969 United States Senator Dan K. Inouye (D-Hawaii), a Nisei war hero, introduced S. 1872 to repeal Title II. The bill was cosponsored by Senator George Murphy (R-Calif.). They were soon joined by twenty-one other senators from sixteen states. In the 1971 session of Congress, the same bill, now known as H.R. 234, was overwhelmingly approved.

The threat of concentration camps in the United States, once the symbol of racial intolerance against the Japanese, was quietly laid to rest on September 25, 1971, only a few days before President Nixon met Emperor Hirohito at Anchorage. For persons of Japanese ancestry, the repeal of Title II was just as historic an event as the meeting between the heads of state in Alaska.[29]

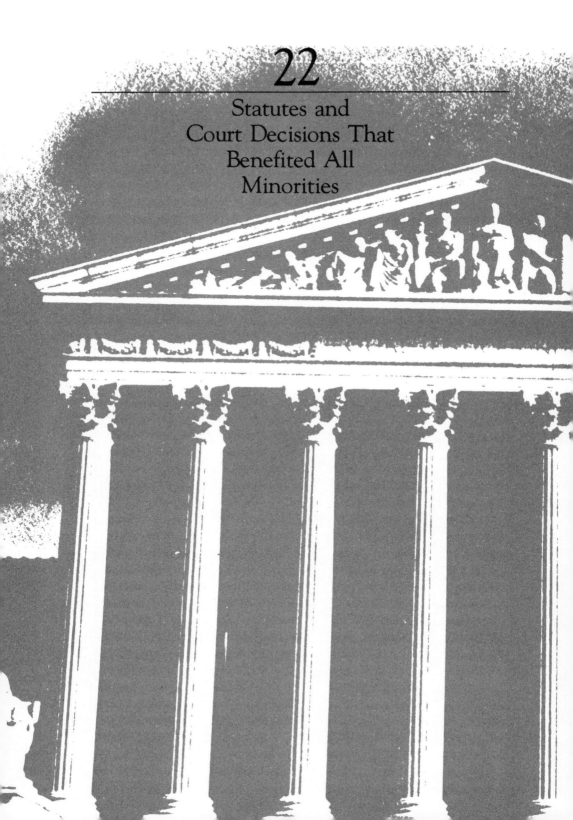

22
Statutes and Court Decisions That Benefited All Minorities

Iₙ ALMOST EVERY STATE of the United States there was at one time an antimiscegenation statute prohibiting marriage between those of the "white" race and persons of any other origin. California's first miscegenation statute was enacted in 1850.[1] This statute prohibited the marriage of whites and Negroes. Again, in 1880, the California Legislature considered, but did not pass, a bill to extend the prohibition of marriage of white persons with Mongolians. Such marriages were to be declared illegal and void.[2]

In 1941 the California Legislature considered two bills with respect to antimiscegenation. One bill sought to declare void, in the state of California, marriages of persons of different races who had been legally married in another state.[3] The other bill prohibited the issuance of a license for the marriage "of a white person with a Negro, Mulatto, Mongolian or member of the Malay race."[4] In 1945, during World War II, the California Legislature enacted Assembly Bill 321 prohibiting the marriage of "a white person with a Negro, Mulatto, Mongolian or member of the Malay race."[5] The bill was approved by Governor Earl Warren on May 31, 1946.

The obvious intent of all miscegenation statutes was to condemn certain races as "unfit" to marry with Caucasians regardless of the desires of the individuals concerned. The rationale for these antimiscegenation statutes was that persons wishing to marry in contravention of race barriers would produce progeny that would dilute "white racial purity."

ANTIMISCEGENATION STATUTES ARE STRUCK DOWN

In 1948 the antimiscegenation statute in California came under attack by Andrea Perez, a white resident of Los Angeles County, who sought to marry Sylvester Davis, a Negro. Both Perez and Davis were members of the Roman Catholic church. When the county clerk of Los Angeles County refused to issue them a marriage license, Miss Perez instituted a civil action to compel the county clerk to issue the license.[6]

Miss Perez contended that Section 69 of the California Civil Code was unconstitutional on the grounds that the statute prohibited the free exercise of her religion and denied to her and her fiancé the right to participate fully in the sacraments of that religion. She maintained that since the Roman Catholic church had no rule forbidding marriages between Negroes and Caucasians, they were entitled to receive the sacrament of matrimony.

Justice Roger Traynor of the California Supreme Court, later to become its chief justice, speaking for the majority of the court, held that Section 69 of the Civil Code was unconstitutional. "By restricting the individual's right to marry on the basis of race alone, . . . [the statute] violates the equal protection of the laws clause of the United States Constitution."

In the decision Justice Traynor particularly noted three landmark cases that involved persons of Japanese ancestry: *Hirabayashi* vs. *United States*,[7] *Oyama* vs. *California*,[8] and *Takahashi* vs. *Fish and Game Commission*.[9] In these three cases, which had become precedent decisions within the fabric of American constitutional law, the Supreme Court of the United States had stated that "distinctions between citizens solely because of ancestry are, by their very nature, odious to a free people whose institutions are founded upon the doctrine of equality. For that reason legislative classification or discrimination based on race alone has often been held to be a denial of equal protection."

In *Perez* vs. *Sharp* Justice Traynor held that there was "absent the compelling justification which would be needed to sustain discrimination of that nature . . . the fact that discrimination has been sanctioned by the State for many years does not supply such justification."

He brushed aside the contentions of County Clerk Sharp that Negroes, and by implication other persons mentioned in Section 60 of the Civil Code, were mentally inferior to Caucasians. Justice Traynor noted that many of the progeny of mixed marriages had made important contributions to the community. He further criticized the classification of races in the statute as "too vague and uncertain to constitute a valid regulation" since the number of races distinguished by systems of classification "varies from three or four to thirty-four."

The death blow to the antimiscegenation statute in California was the statement by Justice Traynor that

marriage . . . is something more than a civil contract subject to regulation by the State; it is a fundamental right of free man. . . .

The right to marry is the right of individuals, not of racial groups. . . . The equal protection clause of the United States Constitution does not refer to rights of the Negro race, the Caucasian race, or another race, but to the rights of individuals.

The concept of the right of individuals to marry was subsequently extended to the right of a husband and wife, even if not of the same blood or ancestry, to adopt a person of still another ancestry.

In 1962 a three-year-old blonde girl, born of an unwed mother of English descent and a Puerto Rican father, had previously been rejected by five other couples seeking to adopt children. Merl H. Baker, a Caucasian, had married Yoshiko Okuda in Japan in 1949 when he was stationed there in the army. Mrs. Baker was the daughter of a wealthy paper manufacturer in Japan. She was trained in the traditional Japanese dances and other arts. Mr. Baker was preparing for a new career in business machines.[10] Probate Judge Leonard S. Frost in Cleveland, Ohio ruled that little Jean could not be adopted by the Bakers because of the difference in the racial background between the adopting parents. Judge Frost was quoted as saying, "The good Lord created five races, and if He intended to have only one He would have done so. It was never intended that the races should be mixed."

On September 6, 1962 the Court of Appeals of Ohio reversed Judge Frost's decision and approved the right of a Caucasian and his Japanese wife to adopt Jean. The opinion written by Appellate Judge Lehr Fess, and concurred in by Judges Paul W. Brown and Raymond W. Younger, stated:

> We are constrained to hold upon the record presented that the best interests of the child will be promoted by granting the petition for adoption. We therefore conclude that the order denying adoption is unreasonable, unsupported by substantial evidence, and consequently contrary to law. . . .
>
> As we view it, the only alternative, if the [earlier] judgment is affirmed, is to have the child remain an illegitimate orphan to be reared in an institution. Orphanages are well and good, but they do not provide a real home with the attendant care, love, and affection incident to the relation of parent and child.

Many states prohibited cohabitation of spouses of mixed ancestry and provided criminal penalties even though such marriages were legal in the state where they were performed. In 1967 the Supreme Court of the United States declared unconstitutional a statute of the State of Virginia that prohibited cohabitation of persons of mixed ancestry, even if married.[12] The Honorable William Marutani, later to become a judge of the Court of Common Pleas in Philadelphia, appeared before the Supreme Court in this case as legal counsel for the JACL. This marked the first time that a Nisei had argued a case before this august tribunal.

RACE-RESTRICTIVE COVENANTS ARE RULED UNENFORCEABLE

Within the five hundred acres of rolling hills that constitute the beautiful campus of the University of California, Los Angeles, almost one acre of ground has been set aside by the university for use as the official residence of the chancellor. This property is situated on the southwest corner of Sunset Boulevard and Hilgard Avenue, across the street from the prestigious residential area of Bel Air, developed in the late 1920s and early 1930s by the late father of Congressman Alphonso Bell.

The deed to the chancellor's residence, duly recorded in the office of the County Recorder of Los Angeles County, contains a race-restrictive covenant, which states that "no part of said property or any portion thereof shall be . . . occupied by any person not of the Caucasian race, it being intended hereby to restrict the use of said property against the occupancy as owners or tenants of any portion of said property residence or other purpose by people of the Negro or Mongolian race, except as servants or employees."[13]

Throughout other parts of the United States from as early as 1911 to as recently as 1948, such restrictive covenants blanketed vast areas of residential subdivisions. Some covenants were even more blunt in precluding the use or occupancy of property by persons of other than the Caucasian race even as employees or servants. Most of these covenants were to be in effect for fifty years or longer, depending upon the whims and desires of the real-estate developers. This often forced non-Caucasians to live in deteriorating neighborhoods, which ultimately resulted in the areas becoming ghettos with appallingly crowded living conditions.

These race-restrictive covenants caused racial tensions, particularly among Negroes who could not move into the areas blanketed by these covenants during the period of time when the Caucasians were fleeing the inner cities, particularly after World War II. The race restrictions also affected all Orientals, who were included within the generic term "Mongolians" used in these covenants.

The mechanics for enforcing race restrictions were comparatively easy to apply up to the year 1948. In given tracts bound by the race-restrictive covenants, each of the owners purchased his home with knowledge of and consent to these restrictions. Since they were in the form of a written agreement, each of the homeowners was bound by these terms and conditions in concert with all other homeowners in the same tract. These covenants were mutually binding and were encumbrances on each parcel of property and affected the land and home in which the homeowner resided.

If any one of the landowners breached the covenant, that is, violated the terms or conditions of the covenant by selling to a person other than to one of the Caucasian race, the other property owners could institute a lawsuit in the state courts to have the covenant enforced. The state courts could then issue an injunction to prevent the non-Caucasian from entering his new home or to compel him to vacate the premises he had purchased. The refusal of the non-Caucasian to obey the injunction of the court would result in punitive action against him for violating a court order. He could have been jailed.

The courts offered no relief to the flood of cases involving non-Caucasians who attempted to purchase these properties, and there was no hope for legislative help. Realtors and real-estate boards, through their powerful lobbies, saw to it that any bills to eliminate the effect of these race-restrictive covenants were stopped.

There was little hope of congressional relief either. Prior to 1965 Congress had not passed a civil rights bill since 1875. Because of the seniority system, southern congressmen and senators were in control. Public sentiment was apathetic, indeed hostile, to any change in living conditions for racial minorities.

The federal government itself was the principal culprit in the encouragement of these covenants. The Federal Housing Administration required the imposition of race-restrictive covenants as a condition of extending mortgage insurance to home loans. City and county planning and zoning commissions manipulated rules and regulations to preserve and strengthen restrictions that kept the minorities in the ghettos.

Arguments by non-Caucasians in the courts that they were being denied equal protection of the law fell on deaf or unsympathetic ears. By 1948 supreme courts in nineteen states and the District of Columbia had upheld the legality of racial restrictions applied to real property.[14] Even the Supreme Court of the United States had circuitously but effectively upheld judicial enforcement of race-restrictive covenants as early as 1926 in *Corrigan* vs. *Buckley*.[15] For over two decades, the Supreme Court resolutely clung to the rule in the *Corrigan* decision by refusing all requests for review of subsequent court cases that challenged that decision.

Suddenly in 1947 the Supreme Court agreed to review two such cases, one from Missouri and the other from Michigan. Both of these cases contended that judicial enforcement of race-restrictive covenants violated basic constitutional guarantees contained in the federal Constitution.

The Missouri case, a landmark one known as *Shelley* vs. *Kraemer*, [16] involved J. D. Shelley and his wife Ethel Lee, both black, who purchased a home from a white person and moved into the house in St. Louis, Missouri on August 11, 1945. Their home was in a tract containing fifty-seven parcels. In 1911 its previous owner had signed an agreement under which its use and occupancy were prohibited to "people of the Negro or Mongolian race." If the covenant was violated, the agreement provided that the owner who permitted the violation was to forfeit his title to the property. Other tract owners, led by Louis Kraemer and his wife Fern, sued Mr. and Mrs. Shelley. The Missouri Supreme Court ordered the Shelleys out of their new home.

The Michigan case, *McGhee* vs. *Sipes*, [17] involved Orsel McGhee and his wife Minnie, who were also black and who had purchased a home in Detroit, Michigan from a white person. The McGhees moved into their new home on November 30, 1944. A committee of neighbors, headed by Mr. and Mrs. Benjamin Sipes, visited the McGhees in January 1945 and demanded that the McGhees vacate their home because their ownership and occupancy violated a 1934 agreement, signed by the previous owner, restricting its use and occupancy by "any person except those of the Caucasian race." The McGhees refused to move out, and Mr. Sipes filed suit. The Michigan Supreme Court ordered the McGhees out of their home within ninety days after the decree.

When the *Shelley* case was argued before the United States Supreme Court on January 15 and 16, 1948, for reasons not stated, Associate Justices Stanley Reed, Robert Jackson, and Wiley Rutledge took no part in the consideration or decision. On May 3, 1948 the enforcement of race-restrictive covenants by state courts was declared unconstitutional.

Chief Justice Frederick M. Vinson, speaking for the six-man court, declared,

> We hold that in granting judicial enforcement of the restrictive agreements in these cases, the States have denied petitioners the equal protection of the laws and that, therefore, the action of the state courts cannot stand.

In a footnote to this decision, Chief Justice Vinson remarked:

. . . restrictive agreements of the sort involved in these cases have been used to exclude other than Negroes from the ownership or occupancy of real property. We are informed that such agreements have been directed against Indians, Jews, Chinese, Japanese, Mexicans, Hawaiians, Puerto Ricans, and Filipinos, among others.[18]

Referring to the case of *Oyama* vs. *California*,[19] which had been decided by the Supreme Court only five months earlier (January 19, 1948), Chief Justice Vinson stated,

Only recently this Court had occasion to declare that a state law which denied equal enjoyment of property rights to a designated class of citizens of specified race and ancestry, was not a legitimate exercise of the state's police power but violated the guarantee of the equal protection of the laws.

The Supreme Court was careful to point out in *Shelley* vs. *Kraemer* that it did not declare race-restrictive covenants illegal or void per se. Neither did these race-restrictive covenants, standing alone, violate any rights guaranteed by the Fourteenth Amendment. If individuals wished to abide by these covenants on a voluntary basis, the Fourteenth Amendment did not extend to include private conduct "however discriminatory or wrongful." It was only when the individuals attempted to seek judicial enforcement in state courts of the restrictive terms of these covenants that state courts could no longer enforce these covenants under the *Shelley* decision. Other lawsuits to test the true dimensions of the *Shelley* case followed.

A lawsuit for breach of agreement, seeking damages against an owner of property who had previously signed a race-restrictive covenant, but who later sold the property to Negroes, was dismissed.[20] States could not entertain such damage suits since these suits were indirect attempts to enforce the covenants. Indirect enforcement as well as direct enforcement denied equal protection of law to owners of property.

Segregation in public housing on the basis of race was also held to be in violation of the equal protection clause of the Fourteenth Amendment.[21] Continued patterns of segregated public housing in other states became moot when President Kennedy, by executive order in 1962, proclaimed the end to all segregation in low-rent public-housing developments.

The Federal Housing Authority, historically the worst offender in the preservation of racially segregated subdivisions of homes, was ordered to deny federal insurance or mortgage money to home construction projects that tried to enforce race-restrictive covenants. The Veterans Administration, which insured federal funds for low-cost homes for eligible veterans, was ordered to adopt the same policy of nondiscrimination. In the same year President Kennedy ordered a national policy to be put in force, by executive order, that forbade all discrimination in sale or rental of federally assisted housing. State fair-housing statutes soon followed.

The courts finally came to recognize, after almost one hundred years, that the spirit of the 1866 Civil Rights Act should be followed and that non-Caucasians, particularly Negroes, were entitled to the same rights as all other Americans, including the right to purchase, own, and enjoy their own property.

EQUAL OPPORTUNITY MOVES ACROSS THE NATION

The years during World War II and afterwards witnessed a great internal migration of population in the United States. Millions of Americans left their homes to flock to the great war-related factories of the North, the East, and especially to those of the Far West. Negroes in the southern states left to seek new vistas, new job opportunities, and new homes. Other millions of Americans in the armed forces were shuttled from their homes to army, navy, and marine bases scattered throughout the country. Persons of all races, creeds, and colors were swept up into the maelstrom of the war effort, producing an intermingling of people from all walks of life never before experienced in America. The quiet, stable, stratified prewar society was shattered.

"Race problems" took on new dimensions and new realities. The urbanization of racial minorities was growing. Blacks, especially, became political factions that compelled their recognition, especially in the larger northern and far-western cities. Racial minorities who had served in the armed forces in the European and Pacific Theatres returned home with new concepts about their rightful places in the social order. Their insistence on equal constitutional rights and privileges became more demanding.

During this same period of time, the attitudes of many white Americans were also undergoing some profound changes, especially on racial issues. Studies by social scientists further helped to shatter the comfortable theories of white supremacy. The conservative, heretofore racially exclusive labor unions were forced to adapt themselves to the increasing number of Negroes and other racial minorities in their work force. Local, state, and national politicians, spurred on by an increasingly large number of minorities within their districts, openly bid for votes from these minorities in the interest of their political self-preservation.

As new judges were appointed to the bench in various state and federal courts, they brought with them fresh ideas and new attitudes toward racial discrimination and its deleterious impact upon the moral fiber of the nation.

The Federal Civil Rights Act of 1875 signed by President Ulysses S. Grant provided, in part, that "all persons within the jurisdiction of the United States shall be entitled to the full and equal accommodations, advantages, facilities and privileges of inns, theaters . . . and other places . . . of public accommodations." Fines and imprisonment were prescribed for violators.

On October 15, 1833 the Supreme Court of the United States, by an eight to one vote, held that the Fourteenth Amendment of the Constitution did not extend to the Civil Rights Act of 1875.[22] The Fourteenth Amendment stated that "no State shall . . . deny to any person within its jurisdiction the equal protection of the law." However, the Supreme Court held that Congress did not have constitutional authority to prohibit discrimination in public accommodations on the basis of race.

Nearly ninety years later, on July 2, 1964, Congress approved the Civil Rights Act of 1964.[23] This giant step forward in the field of civil rights provided equal opportunities for all persons in the United States, regardless of their race, religion, creed, or national origin.

The new act consolidated a series of executive orders. During his third term, President Franklin D. Roosevelt issued such an order establishing a fair employment practices committee. Other executive orders ended segregation in the armed forces, discrimination in government contracts, and the unequal financing of home mortgages. The act also incorporated provisions of the Civil Rights Act of 1957[24] and the Civil Rights Act of 1960.[25]

By the Act of 1964, the attorney general was empowered to enforce its various provisions. Federal district courts were specifically authorized to determine the facts relative to alleged violations of the act, and criminal penalties were provided for disobedience of any provision of the act. On December 14, 1964 two test cases arose involving the constitutionality of the Civil Rights Act of 1964: *Heart of Atlanta Motel Inc.* vs. *United States*,[26] and *Katzenbach* vs. *McClung*.[27]

The *Heart of Atlanta* case involved a large Georgia motel that carried extensive advertisements in national magazines. It solicited national conventions from organizations throughout the United States. More than three-fourths of its commercial income was derived from out-of-state guests. To meet the huge requirements of such an operation, food, supplies, drinks, and merchandise were bought from all parts of the nation. The motel sued the United States to prevent enforcement of the Civil Rights Act of 1964.

The *Katzenbach* case involved a family-owned restaurant in Birmingham, Alabama that purchased approximately $150,000 worth of food per year, $69,783 of which was for meat bought from a local supplier who had procured it from outside the state. Thus, a substantial portion of the food served in this restaurant, which specialized in barbecue meat, was obtained through interstate commerce. Nicholas deB. Katzenbach, as United States attorney general, sued Ollie McClung, the proprietor, to restrain him from discriminating against Negro customers.

The Supreme Court of the United States in both these cases held that Congress had constitutional authority to prohibit racial discrimination by innkeepers and that Negroes were entitled to the full and equal facilities of places of public accommodation. The decision was based on the power of the Congress to "regulate commerce . . . among the several states,"[28] and to "make all laws which shall be necessary and proper for carrying that section into effect."[29] The *Heart of Atlanta Motel Inc.* vs. *United States* and *Katzenbach* vs. *McClung* are landmark cases in affording "equal justice under law," the motto engraved above the entrance to the United States Supreme Court.

EQUALITY IN IMMIGRATION FOR ALL PERSONS

On a clear, crisp, autumn Sunday, October 3, 1965, at 3:25 P.M., a symbolic ceremony took place at the base of the Statue of Liberty on Liberty Island in New York Bay. President Johnson signed Public Law 89-236, which eliminated racism from the immigration laws that had been on the statute books for over eighty years.[30] It was appropriate that the signing took place at the foot of the Statue of Liberty, a monument that had symbolized for the past eighty years the hopes and dreams of over 45 million immigrants, most of whom were from European nations and who had entered the United States to begin new lives in the land of liberty and freedom. It might have been even more appropriate to have had the signing ceremonies at Angel Island in San Francisco Harbor, an entry point that had not welcomed Orientals into the United States for the previous eighty-three years.

Since the passage of the Chinese Exclusion Act of 1882, as a matter of national policy, the United States had practiced racial discrimination in a most flagrant manner. The immigration statutes during the next eighty-three years were directed primarily against Asiatics through such devices as the Asiatic Barred Zone in the Immigration Act of 1917, the National Origins Quota in the Japanese Exclusion Act of 1924, and the Asia-Pacific Triangle contained in the Immigration and Nationality Act of 1952.

The self-proclaimed stance of the United States government as the "bastion of democracy" was seen by other nations as a fraud because of the racially discriminatory features in its immigration statutes, which became increasingly embarrassing in international relations, particularly with Asiatic nations.

During the administration of President Kennedy, a study was commenced to consider changes in the basic quota provisions of the Immigration and Nationality Act of 1952. President Kennedy was personally in favor of abolishing the national origins quota system for the allocation of immigration visas because it was grounded on racial discrimination. He recommended instead a system of preferences that would extend priorities in the issuance of immigrant visas to (1) close relatives of United States citizens, (2) aliens lawfully admitted for permanent residence, (3) aliens who were members of the professions, arts, or sciences, (4) skilled or unskilled alien laborers who were needed in the United States, and (5) certain refugees. These recommendations were incorporated in S. 1932, which was submitted on July 23, 1963 to the Eighty-eighth Congress.

After President Kennedy's assassination, his successor, President Johnson, urged the Congress to enact these reforms. A prominent member of the United States Senate, Daniel K. Inouye (D-Hawaii), strongly supported President Johnson on the measures, declaring that "the action is long overdue." Senator Inouye had become the first Japanese-American to be elected to Congress after Hawaii was granted statehood.

Senator Inouye had earned a battlefield commission as a member of the famed 442nd Regimental Combat Team. In the fierce fighting nine days before the end of the war in Italy, he led an assault against a German position on Mount Nebbione and lost his right arm during the action. On his way home in 1945, Captain Inouye, his empty sleeve pinned to an army jacket covered with ribbons for heroic deeds in numerous campaigns, was denied a haircut in a San Francisco barbershop. The barber said, "We don't serve Japs here." The discriminatory provisions of the immigration statutes were very real and very painful to him, a man whose parents had gone from Japan to Hawaii many years before.

Another prominent member of the United States Senate, Hiram L. Fong (R-Hawaii), a Chinese-American who also knew well the pains of racial discrimination, cosponsored H.R. 2580 in the Eighty-ninth Congress. Senator Fong stated, "Revision of our Immigration laws is a logical extension of our efforts to achieve this ideal [of equality]. Last year we enacted the historic Civil Rights Act, which was designed to wipe out the last vestiges of racial discrimination against our own citizens. . . . We should also move to erase racial barriers against citizens of other lands in our immigration laws."[31]

Both H.R. 2580 and its companion bill S. 500 were the subject of extensive public hearings before the Subcommittee on Immigration and Naturalization. There were twenty-nine days of hearings, between February and August 1965. Testimony was received from fifty-six witnesses, including congressional sponsors of the proposed legislation, cabinet officers, government officials, and representatives of labor, religious, patriotic, and veterans organizations, as well as the public.

On March 25, 1965 the JACL submitted a voluminous brief of 111 pages in support of S. 500 and H.R. 2580. The JACL brief contained seventy-nine pages of scholarly and forceful arguments supporting the two bills, as well as an additional thirty-two pages of factual data. Written by Mike Masaoka, it is perhaps the most comprehensive report extant concerning our shameful history of discrimination against Orientals in the areas of immigration and naturalization.

The positions of both the proponents and opponents of change to the existing law were presented to the subcommittee in depth.[32] In the end, H.R. 2580 was signed into law by President Johnson as an amendment to the omnibus Immigration and Naturalization Act of 1952. Of particular interest to persons of Japanese ancestry and to persons of other Asiatic countries, the Asia-Pacific Triangle provisions of the 1952 act were eliminated.

Now, persons from all over the world, regardless of their race, were able to apply for permanent residence on a first come, first served basis.

Thus, after almost two hundred years, the United States returned to the noble ideals expressed in the Declaration of Independence:

We hold these Truths to be self-evident, that all Men are created equal, that they are endowed by their Creator with certain unalienable Rights, that among these are Life, Liberty, and the Pursuit of Happiness.

May it always be so.

NOTES

1

1. *Pacific Citizen*, Special Holiday Issue, December 20–27, 1968, Section C. *Los Angeles Times*, January 25, 1969.
2. 11 Stat 597, March 31, 1854.
3. *Hariasides* vs. *Shaughnessy*, 342 U.S. 580, March 10, 1952.
4. 1 Stat 103, March 26, 1790.
5. 1 Stat 414, January 29, 1795.
6. *In re Saito*, 62 F. R. 126 (C.C.D. Mass.), June 27, 1894.
7. 2 Stat 153, April 14, 1802. This act was considered in the case of *In re Saito*, 62 F. R. 126 (C.C.D. Mass.), June 27, 1894.
8. Thomas E. LaForgue, *China's First Hundred* (Pullman, Wash.: Pullman State College, 1942), pp. 20–22.
9. U.S. Department of Justice, Immigration and Naturalization Service, *Annual Report* (Washington, D.C.: Government Printing Office, 1966), pp. 58–59.
10. Cheng Tsu-Wu, *Chink* (New York: World Publishing Co., 1972), p. 109.
11. 16 Stat 739, July 28, 1868.
12. *Chy Lung* vs. *Freeman*, 92 U.S. 275, October term, 1875.
13. 22 Stat 826, November 17, 1880.
14. 22 Stat 58, May 6, 1882.
15. 14 Stat 27, April 9, 1866.
16. California Constitution, Article II, May 7, 1879.
17. Japanese Charter Oath of April 6, 1868.
18. 23 Stat 332, February 26, 1885.
19. Yamato Ichihashi, *Japanese in the United States* (New York: Arno Press, 1969), p. 229.
20. 22 Stat 214, August 3, 1882.
21. 26 Stat 1084, March 3, 1891.
22. Ichihashi, op. cit., pp. 74–75.
23. 26 Stat 1084, March 3, 1891.
24. *Ekiu Nishimura* vs. *U.S.*, 142 U.S. 651, January 18, 1892.
25. 29 Stat 848, November 22, 1894, treaty between U.S. and Japan known as the Treaty of Commerce and Navigation, proclaimed March 21, 1895. This treaty was discussed in *Yamataya* vs. *Fisher*, 189 U.S. 86, April 6, 1903.
26. 29 Stat 848, November 22, 1894. Under Article XVIII of the Treaty of Commerce and Navigation of 1895, the following treaties, conventions, arrangements, and other agreements were to cease to be binding:
   a. The Treaty of Peace and Amity, concluded March 31, 1854 (Commodore Matthew Perry).
   b. The Treaty of Amity and Commerce of July 29, 1858 (Townsend Harris).
   c. The Tariff Convention of June 25, 1866 (establishing tariff of duties between Japan and the United States, Great Britain, France, and the Netherlands).
   d. The Convention of July 25, 1878.
   e. "All other arrangements and agreements subsidiary thereto or existing between the high contracting parties."

27. Rafael Steinberg, *Japan* (New York: Macmillan, 1969), p. 73.

28. Roger Daniels, *The Politics of Prejudice* (New York: Atheneum, 1970), p. 20.

29. *Yamataya* vs. *Fisher*, 189 U.S. 86, April 6, 1903.

30. 25 Stat 566, October 19, 1888.

31. 142 U.S. 651, January 18, 1892.

32. Compare *In re Yamasaka*, 95 F. 652 (Wash., D.C.), July 20, 1899, and *U.S.* vs. *Yamasaka*, 100 F. 404 (C.A. 9) February 5, 1900, which discusses the right of an alien already residing in the United States to be accorded a full hearing by the federal courts under Section 13 of the Act of March 3, 1891 and the idea that no ministerial officer could arrest and deport an alien unless explicity empowered to do so.

33. Daniels, op. cit., p. 28.

2

1. Victor H. Metcalf, *Report of Secretary of Commerce and Labor to President Theodore Roosevelt.*
Herbert B. Johnson, *Discrimination Against the Japanese in California* (Berkeley, Calif.: Courier Publishing Co., 1907).

2. A. Whitney Griswold, *Far Eastern Policy of the United States* (New York: Harcourt Brace, 1962), p. 347.

3. Resolutions of the San Francisco Board of Education, October 11, 1906.

4. Yamato Ichihashi, *The Japanese in the United States* (New York: Arno Press, 1969), p. 103.

5. Raymond H. Esthus, *Theodore Roosevelt and Japan* (Seattle: University of Washington Press, 1966), p. 148.

6. Rafael Steinberg, *Japan* (New York: Macmillan, 1969), pp. 73–74.

7. Ichihashi, op. cit., p. 284.

8. The threat of war was rapidly becoming a matter for discussion and planning. In November 1906, within one month after the school board resolution of October 11, *Harper's Weekly*, a prestigious magazine with a nationwide circulation, wrote that "Japan is at this moment the strongest naval power in the Pacific, and she has entered moreover into an offensive and defensive alliance with Great Britain. . . . In a word, rich as we are, and poor as she is, we could not afford to go to war with Japan, for in the Philippines, in Hawaii, and on our Pacific Coast, we are vulnerable." In *The Pacific Rivals* (New York: Weatherhill; Tokyo: Asahi, 1972), a compilation of articles on the Japanese view of Japanese-American relations, it is noted on p. 61, "In 1907, American military strategists, having taken note of the military might that Japan had demonstrated in the war with Russia, formulated the so-called 'Orange Plan,' a top secret scenario envisioning a possible war with Japan. Although Japan was forced by her financial obligations to maintain good relations with the United States, she nevertheless drew up a defense strategy of her own, listing Russia, the United States, and France as hypothetical enemies, in that order. The central feature of this strategy was the launching of the eight-naval build-up program, to add eight battleships and eight cruisers to the fleet."

9. Esthus, op. cit., p. 133.

10. Resolutions of the San Francisco Board of Education, October 11, 1906.

11. Metcalf, op. cit.
Johnson, op. cit., p. 8.

12. Esthus, op. cit., p. 149.

13. Ibid., p. 143.

14. Ibid., p. 144.

15. *Plessy vs. Ferguson*, 163 U.S. 537, May 18, 1896.

16. Walton Bean, *Boss Ruef's San Francisco* (Berkeley: University of California Press, 1952), pp. 65–66.

17. Griswold, op. cit., p. 351.

18. Ichihashi, op. cit., on p. 284 he quotes *Treaty, Japan and the United States* (Palo Alto, Calif.: Stanford University Press, 1928), p. 18.

19. California Assembly Concurrent Resolution No. 9, January 18, 1907.
California Senate Joint Resolution No. 1, January 4, 1907.
California Assembly Concurrent Resolution No. 2, January 14, 1907
California Senate Joint Resolution No. 11, February 6, 1907.

20. 34 Stat 898, February 20, 1907.

21. Roger Daniels, *The Politics of Prejudice* (New York: Atheneum, 1970), p. 42. On July 8, 1907 Judge Dunne of the San Francisco Superior Court sentenced Schmitz to five years in the state penitentiary at San Quentin after Schmitz was found guilty. The court, the district attorney of the County of San Francisco, and the board of supervisors all permitted Mayor Schmitz to go to Washington, D.C. on this matter.

22. Esthus, op. cit., p. 158.

23. Griswold, op. cit., p. 353.

24. 34 Stat 898, February 20, 1907.

25. Congress did create a Joint Commission on Immigration consisting of three senators, three congressmen, and three other persons. It finished its investigation by 1911 and published its report, which was contained in forty-two volumes. This exhaustive study became the basis for the Immigration Act of February 5, 1917, 39 Stat 874.

26. Johnson, op. cit., pp. 83–84.

27. Ichihashi, op. cit., p. 244.

28. *Annual Report of the United States Commissioner-General of Immigration* (Washington, D.C.: Government Printing Office, 1908), pp. 221–222.

29. Roy Hidemichi Akagi, *Japan's Foreign Relations* (Tokyo: Hokuseido Press, 1936), p. 434.

30. 43 Stat 153, May 26, 1924.

31. Esthus, op. cit.
    a. Letter from Ambassador O'Brien to Foreign Minister Hayashi, dated January 25, 1908, with instructions from Secretary of State Root to diplomatic and consular offices of the United States.
    b. Letter from Foreign Minister Hayashi to Ambassador O'Brien, dated February 18, 1908, with accompanying memorandum.
    c. Letter from Ambassador O'Brien to Foreign Minister Hayashi, dated February 21, 1908.
    d. Letter from Foreign Minister Hayashi to Ambassador O'Brien, dated February 23, 1908, with accompanying memorandum.
    e. Letter from Ambassador O'Brien to Foreign Minister Hayashi, dated March 12, 1908.
    f. Letter from Foreign Minister Hayashi to Ambassador O'Brien, dated March 25, 1908, with public manifesto.

32. Akagi, op. cit., p. 434.

33. Ibid.
34. *Annual Report of the United States Commissioner-General of Immigration,* op. cit.
35. *Foreign Relations,* Vol. II (1921), p. 330.
36. Griswold, op. cit., p. 358.
37. Ibid., p. 351.
38. Ibid., p. 359.

3

1. *Geer* vs. *Connecticut,* 161 U.S. 519, March 2, 1896.
2. *Mager* vs. *Grima,* 49 U.S. 490, January 1850.
3. *McCready* vs. *Virginia,* 94 U.S. 391, October 1876.
4. *Hauenstein* vs. *Lynham,* 100 U.S. 483, October 1879.
5. Yamato Ichihashi, *Japanese in the United States* (New York: Arno Press, 1969), p. 250, footnote 13.
6. Franklin Hichborn, *Story of the Session of the California Legislature of 1909* (San Francisco: Press of the James H. Barry Co., 1909), p. 203.
7. California Legislature, S. B. 338, January 24, 1889.
   California Legislature, A. B. 374, January 28, 1889.
8. Ichihashi, op. cit., p. 262, footnote 5.
9. Ibid., p. 254. footnote 18.
10. Ibid., footnote 20.
11. California Legislature, S. B. 24, January 5, 1911.
    California Legislature, A. B. 30, January 6, 1911.
    California Legislature, A. B. 34, January 6, 1911.
    California Legislature, S. B. 1074, January 10, 1911.
12. Ichihashi, op. cit., p. 255.
13. Ibid., pp. 265–266.
14. Ch. 113 Cal. Stats, 1913.
15. Ichihashi, op. cit., p. 275.
16. Law cases affecting Japanese in the United States, compiled by the consulate general of Japan at San Francisco, California, 1925.
17. *Suwa* vs. *Johnson,* 54 C. A. 119, August 31, 1921.

4

1. 1 Stat 570, June 25, 1798.
2. 3 Stat 488, March 2, 1819.
   9 Stat 127, February 22, 1847.
   9 Stat 220, May 17, 1848.
   10 Stat 715, March 3, 1855.
3. 13 Stat 385, July 4, 1864.
   15 Stat 58, March 30, 1868.
4. Paul M. De Falla, "Lantern in the Western Sky," *The Historical Society of Southern California Quarterly,* Vol. XLII (June 1960), pp. 161–162.
5. 18 Stat 477, March 3, 1875.
6. 22 Stat 58, May 6, 1882.

7. 22 Stat 214, August 3, 1882.

8. 25 Stat 566, October 19, 1888.

9. 26 Stat 1084, March 3, 1891.

10. 33 Stat 1213, March 3, 1903.

11. 34 Stat 898, February 20, 1907.

12. 39 Stat 874, February 5, 1917.

13. 43 Stat 153, May 26, 1924.

14. *Kaoru Yamataya* vs. *Fisher,* 189 U.S. 86, April 6, 1903.

15. *U.S.* vs. *Nakashima,* 160 F.R. 842 (C.C.A. 9), February 17, 1908.
    U.S. vs. *Tsuji,* 199 F.R. 750 (C.C.A. 9), October 7, 1912.
    U.S. vs. *Nakao,* 17 F.R. 49 (C.C.A. 9), October 6, 1914.
    Kuwabara vs. *U.S.,* 260 F.R. 109 (C.C.A. 9), August 4, 1919.
    Kaneda vs. *U.S.,* 278 F.R. 694 (C.C.A. 9), February 13, 1922.

16. *Ex parte Keisuke Sata,* 215 F.R. 173 (D.C.N.D. Cal.), June 20, 1914.
    Ex parte Momo Tomimatsu, 232 F.R. 376 (D.C.N.D. Cal.), April 26, 1916.

17. *Ex parte Hosaye Sakaguchi,* 277 F.R. 913 (C.C.A. 9), January 9, 1922.

18. 26 Stat 1084, March 3, 1891.

19. *Harisiades* vs. *Shaughnessy,* 342 U.S. 580, March 10, 1952.

20. 83rd Congress, 1st session, 100 *Congressional Record,* Part 6, p. 8127.

21. Presidential Commission Report, p. 193.

22. *Bugajewitz* vs. *Adams,* 228 U.S. 585, May 12, 1913.
    Harisiades vs. *Shaughnessy,* 342 U.S. 580, March 10, 1952.

23. *Ng Fung Ho* vs. *White,* 259 U.S. 276, May 29, 1922.

24. *Klonis* vs. *Davis,* 13 F. 2d 630 (C.C.A. 2), July 13, 1926.

25. *Ex parte Hamaguchi,* 161 F. 184 (C.C.D. Ore.), April 6, 1908.
    Akira Ono vs. *U.S.,* 267 F.R. 359 (C.C.A. 9), September 7, 1920.

26. *Ex parte Kunijiro Toguchi,* 238 F. 632 (D.C.W.D. Wash. D.C.),
    December 29, 1916.

27. *Suzuki* vs. *Higgins,* 187 F. 603 (C.C.A. 9), May 23, 1911.
    Matsumura vs. *Higgins,* 187 F. 601 (C.C.A. 9), May 23, 1911.
    Ex parte Hidekuni Iwata, 219 F. 601 (D.C.S.D. Cal.), January 2, 1915.
    Toku Sakai vs. *U.S.,* 239 F. 492 (C.C.A. 9), February 5, 1917.
    U.S. vs. *Kimi Yamamoto,* 240 F. 390 (C.C.A. 9), February 5, 1917.
    Tama Miyake vs. *U.S.,* 257 F.R. 732 (C.C.A. 9), May 12, 1919.

28. *Mototaro Eguchi* vs. *U.S.,* 260 F.R. 144 (C.C.A. 9), August 4, 1919.

29. *Ex parte Gin Kato,* 270 F.R. 343 (D.C.W.D. Wash. D.C.), December 2, 1920.
    Nishimura vs. *Mansfield,* 277 F. 792 (C.C.A. 8), December 12, 1921.

30. *Ex parte Tsunetaro Machida,* 277 F.R. 239 (D.C.W.D. Wash. D.C.),
    September 16, 1921.
    Ex parte Yoshimasa Nomura, 297 F. 191 (C.C.A. 9), March 24, 1924.
    Rokuji Tambara vs. *Weedin,* 299 F.R. 299 (C.C.A. 9), June 2, 1924.

31. *U.S.* vs. *Miroku Komai,* 286 F.R. 450 (D.C.S.D. Cal. S.D.), February 8, 1923.

32. *Masanori Tanaka* vs. *Weedin,* 299 F. 216 (C.C.A. 9), June 2, 1924.

33. *Weedin* vs. *Sanzo Okada,* 2 F. 2d 321 (C.C.A. 9), November 24, 1924.

34. *Weedin* vs. *Tayokichi Yamada,* 4 F. 2d 455 (C.C.A. 9), March 23, 1925.

35. *Takeyo Koyama* vs. *Burnett,* 8 F. 2d 940 (C.C.A. 9), November 23, 1925.

36. 29 Stat 848, November 22, 1894.

37. 1 Stat 103, March 26, 1790.

38. 1 Stat 414, January 29, 1795.

39. *Elk* vs. *Wilkins*, 112 U.S. 94, November 3, 1884.

40. 16 Stat 254, July 14, 1780.

41. 54 Stat 1137, October 14, 1940.

42. 57 Stat 600, December 17, 1943.

43. 60 Stat 416, July 2, 1946.

44. 54 Stat 1140, October 14, 1940. The Nationality Act of 1940 relaxed the racial bar for certain Filipinos with military service in the United States armed forces during World War II.

45. 66 Stat 163, June 27, 1952.

46. *In re Saito*, 62 F. 126 (C.C.D. Mass.), June 27, 1894.

47. *In re Buntaro Kumagai*, 163 F.R. 922 (D.C.W.D. Wash. N.D.), September 3, 1908.

48. 12 Stat 594, July 17, 1862.

49. 31 Stat 1091, March 3, 1901.

50. *Bessho* vs. *U.S.*, 178 F. 245 (C.C.A. 4), February 1, 1910.

51. 28 Stat 123, July 26, 1894.

52. 6 Fed. Stat Anno. 2d Ed., p. 994, June 29, 1906.

53. *Hidemitsu Toyota* vs. *U.S.*, 268 U.S. 402, May 25, 1925.

54. 40 Stat 542, May 9, 1918.

55. *Ichizo Sato* vs. *Hall*, 191 Cal. 510, July 26, 1923.

56. 40 Stat 542, May 9, 1918.

57. 12 Stat 597, July 17, 1862.

58. 40 Stat 542, May 9, 1918.

59. *Yamashita* vs. *Hinkle*, 260 U.S. 199, November 13, 1922.

60. *Ozawa* vs. *U.S.*, 260 U.S. 178, November 13, 1922.

61. 34 Stat 596, June 29, 1906.

5

1-8. Roger Daniels, *The Politics of Prejudice* (New York: Atheneum, 1970), pp. 66–77. I am greatly indebted to this book for an excellent review of the anti-Japanese forces in California up to the Japanese Exclusion Act of 1924.

9. Yamato Ichihashi, *Japanese in the United States* (New York: Arno Press, 1969), p. 163.

10. California Board of Control, "California and the Oriental," 1920, p. 47.

11. Arizona Laws, 1917, p. 56.

12. Washington, Remington's Revised Statutes, Sec. 10581.

13. Oregon Laws, 1923, p. 145; Ore. Comp. Laws, 1940, Sec. 61.101 and 61.111. Idaho Laws, 1923, p. 160; Idaho Code, 1932, Sec. 23.101 and 23.112. Revised Statutes of Nebraska, 1943, Ch. 76, Sec. 401, 403, 405. 1.5 Texas Stats 166, 1921. Kansas Laws, 1925, p. 277; General Statutes of Kansas, 1935, Sec. 67.701–67.711; 1943 Supplement, Ch. 59, Sec. 511, 512; Chapter 67, Sec. 701.

Louisiana Constitution, 1921, Article XIX, Sec. 21.
Revised Codes of Montana, 1935, Sec. 6802.1–6802.4.
New Mexico Constitution, Article 2, Sec. 22.
Minnesota, Session Laws, 1945, Ch. 280.
Revised Statutes of Missouri, 1939, Sec. 15228–15230.

14. Cal. Stats, 1921, Initiative Act of 1920, LXXXIII.

15. Cal. Stats, 1913, Ch. 113, May 19, 1913.

16. Daniels, op. cit., p. 83. Twenty-two years later, in 1942, General John L.
    DeWitt, commanding general of the Western Defense Command,
    was to use the same words, "A Jap is a Jap," in urging the evacuation of
    over 110,000 persons of Japanese ancestry, citizens and aliens alike, from
    the Pacific Coast states and detaining them in ten concentration
    camps during World War II.

17. Ibid., p. 144. Besides these groups, Daniels mentions more than twenty-eight
    other established organizations that supported the platform of the
    Los Angeles Anti-Asiatic Association (part of the California Oriental
    Exclusion League); these organizations included the Los Angeles
    County Employees Association, the Parent-Teacher Association, and the
    Ebell Club.

18. Cal. Stats, 1921, Initiative Act of 1920, LXXXIII.

19. *Oyama* vs. *California,* 332 U.S. 633, January 19, 1948.

20. *Estate of Tetsubumi Yano,* 188 Cal. 645, May 1, 1922.

21. *In re Y. Akado,* 188 Cal. 739, May 16, 1922.

22. *In re K. Okahara,* 191 Cal. 353, June 28, 1923.

23. *Jones* vs. *Webb,* 195 Cal. 88, December 9, 1924.

24. *In re Nose,* 195 Cal. 91, December 9, 1924.

25. *Terrace* vs. *Thompson,* 263 U.S. 197, November 12, 1923.

26. *Porterfield* vs. *Webb,* 263 U.S. 225, November 12, 1923.

27. *Webb* vs. *O'Brien,* 263 U.S. 313, November 19, 1923.

28. *Frick* vs. *Webb,* 263 U.S. 326, November 19, 1923.

29. 45 Cal. Stats 1020, June 20, 1923.

30. California Legislature, A. B. 1319, introduced by Mrs. Woodbridge to
    add the new Section 1751(a) to the Code of Civil Procedure of California,
    enacted May 31, 1923.

31. As compared to 457,054 acres in 1920.

32. *15th Census of the United States,* Vol. IV (Washington, D.C.: Government
    Printing Office, 1930), p. 302.

33. *Fujii* vs. *California,* 38 Cal. 2d 718, April 17, 1952.
    Masaoka vs. *California,* 39 Cal. 2d 883, July 9, 1952.

6

1. Yamato Ichihashi, *Japanese in the United States* (New York: Arno Press,
   1969), p. 287.

2. Yukio Ozaki, "The Washington Conference," in Staff of the Asahi, *The
   Pacific Rivals* (New York: Weatherhill; Tokyo: Asahi, 1972), pp. 74–75.

3. Ibid., p. 76.

4. 42 Stat 540, May 19, 1921.

5. 67th Congress, 1st session, Document No. 55, *McClatchy* vs. *United States Japanese Immigration and Colonization* (Washington, D.C.: Government Printing Office, 1921).

6. Roger Daniels, *The Politics of Prejudice* (New York: Atheneum, 1970), p. 96.

7. Julia E. Johnsen, *Japanese Exclusion*, Vol. III, No. 4 (New York: H.W. Wilson Company, 1925), p. 64.

8. 68th Congress, 1st session, 1923, S. 2576.

9. Ichihashi, op. cit., p. 300.

10. Ibid., p. 305, referring to House Report No. 350, 68th Congress, 1st session, March 24, 1924, pp. 6–9.

11. Daniels, op. cit., p. 100, referring to U.S. Department of State, *Foreign Relations of the United States, 1924* (Washington, D.C.: Government Printing Office, 1939), p. 338.

12. Ichihashi, op. cit., p. 306, referring to Department of Foreign Affairs (Japan), *Document Relating to the Immigration Act of 1924* (Tokyo, 1924), p. 204.

13. 68th Congress, 1st session, Vol. 65, Part 6 (1924), p. 5810, entitled "Aliens Entitled to Enter the United States Under the Provision of an Agreement Relating Solely to Immigration."

14. Ichihashi, op. cit., p. 307.

15. 43 Stat 153, May 26, 1924.

16. Ichihashi, op. cit., p. 309.

17. Johnsen, op. cit., p. 64.

18. 66 Stat 163, June 27, 1952.

7

1. Roger Daniels, *The Politics of Prejudice* (New York: Atheneum, 1970), p. 105.

2. Harry L. Kitano, *Japanese-Americans: The Evolution of a Sub-Culture*, (Englewood Cliffs, N.J.: Prentice Hall, 1969), p. 162, table 13.

3. Ibid., p. 167, table 19.

4. Ibid.

5. Ibid.

6. Carey McWilliams, *Prejudice* (Boston: Little Brown and Co., 1944), p. 78.

7. Ibid., p. 87.

8. Ibid.

9. Ibid.

10. All references are to bills submitted in the California Legislature:
    S.B. 472, introduced by Senator Maloney, January 22, 1925.
    S.B. 112, introduced by Senator Hurley, January 8, 1929.
    A.B. 54, introduced by Assemblyman Quayley, January 12, 1931.
    A.B. 1368, introduced by Assemblyman Bliss, January 23, 1931.
    A.B. 83, introduced by Senator Maloney, April 22, 1931.
    A.B. 1061, introduced by Senator Seawell, January 26, 1935.
    A.B. 1926, introduced by Assemblyman Reaves, January 26, 1935.

11. Abraham Hoffman, *Unwanted Mexican-Americans in the Great Depression* (Tucson: University of Arizona Press, 1974), p. 39.

12. Ibid., p. 58.

13. Ibid., pp. 64, 124, and 125. It was not until the appointment of Frances Perkins as secretary of labor under President Franklin Roosevelt that the use of telegraphic warrants from the Immigration Service in Washington, D.C. was discontinued.

14. Alien Seamen:
    Ex parte T. Nagata, 11 F. 2d 178 (D.C.S.D. Calif. S.D.), February 19, 1926; compare *Nagle* vs. *Naoichi Misho*, 33 F. 2d 470 (C.C.A. 9), June 24, 1929.
    Ex parte Tatsuo Saiki and *Ex parte Hyoichi Ohashi*, 49 F. 2d 469 (D.C.W.D. Wash. N.D.), December 15, 1930.
    Matsutaka vs. *Carr*, 47 F. 2d 601 (C.C.A. 9), February 24, 1931.
    Ex parte Kojiro Sugimori, 58 F. 2d 782 (D.C.S.D. Calif. N.D.), May 6, 1932.
    Yonejiro Nakasugi vs. *Seager*, 73 F. 2d 37 (C.C.A. 9), October 8, 1934.

15. Prostitution:
    Kii Tanaka vs. *Weedin*, 15 F. 2d 844 (C.C.A. 9), December 20, 1926.
    Imazo Itow vs. *Nagle*, 24 F. 2d 526 (C.C.A. 9), February 27, 1928.
    Iku Kono Ishihama vs. *Carr*, 81 F. 2d 1012 (C.C.A. 9), February 19, 1936.
    Chiuye Inouye vs. *Carr*, 98 F. 2d 46 (C.C.A. 9), July 20, 1938.

16. The right to enter the United States:
    Shizuko Kumanomido vs. *Nagle*, 40 F. 2d 42 (C.C.A. 9), April 7, 1930.
    Ex parte Keizo Kamiyama, 44 F. 2d 503 (C.C.A. 9), November 3, 1930.
    Heizaburo Hirose vs. *Berkshire*, 73 F. 2d 86 (C.C.A. 9), October 22, 1934.

17. The right to reenter the United States:
    Kaichiro Sugimoto vs. *Nagle*, 38 F. 2d 207 (C.C.A. 9), February 17, 1930.
    Ex parte Tsugio Miyazono, 53 F. 2d 172 (C.C.A. 9), October 19, 1931.
    In re Katsujiro Akiyama, 58 F. 2d 363 (D.C.S.D. Calif. C.D.), April 12, 1932.
    Yasuji Fugita vs. *Nagle*, 58 F. 2d 184 (C.C.A. 9), May 4, 1932.

18. Communists:
    Kenmotsu vs. *Nagle*, 44 F. 2d 953 (C.C.A. 9), November 17, 1930.

19. Aliens likely to become a public charge:
    Ex parte Koji Saito, 18 F. 2d 116 (D.C.W.D. Wash. N.D.), March 23, 1927.
    Ex parte Himi Yasuda, 22 F. 2d 864 (D.C.N.D. Calif. S.D.), June 22, 1927.
    Hayashida vs. *Kakimoto*, 132 C.A. 743, June 23, 1933.

20. Deportation cases involving the five-year statute of limitations:
    Ex parte Yoshinobu Magami, 47 F. 2d 946 (D.C.S.D. Calif. C.D.), March 13, 1931.
    Takaji Mukai vs. *Burnett*, 62 F. 2d 355 (C.C.A. 9), December 19, 1932.

21. Crimes involving moral turpitude:
    Perjury—*Ex parte Keizo Shibata*, 30 F. 2d 942 (D.C.S.D. Calif. S.D.), February 27, 1929.
    Crime—*Nishimoto* vs. *Nagle*, 44 F. 2d 304 (C.C.A. 9), November 3, 1930.
    Fraudulent Passport—*Shimi Miho* vs. *U.S.*, 57 F. 2d 491 (C.C.A. 9), April 4, 1932.
    Smuggling aliens—*Yenkichi Ito* vs. *U.S.*, 64 F. 2d 73 (C.C.A. 9), March 27, 1933.

22. Fair hearings:
    Ematsu Kishimoto vs. *Carr*, 32 F. 2d 991 (C.C.A. 9), May 27, 1929.
    In re Sugano, 40 F. 2d 961 (D.C.S.D. Calif. S.D.), February 15, 1930.
    Ex parte Gunji Une, 41 F. 2d 239 (D.C.S.D. Calif. S.D.), May 29, 1931.
    Ex parte Shigenari Mayemura, 53 F. 2d 621 (C.C.A. 9), November 9, 1931.

Fair hearings: (continued)

Ex parte Seisuke Fukumoto, 53 F. 2d 618 (C.C.A. 9), November 9, 1931.

Tsutako Murakami vs. Burnett, 63 F. 2d 641 (C.C.A. 9), February 20, 1933.

Keitaro Karamoto vs. Burnett, 68 F. 2d 278 (C.C.A. 9), December 22, 1933.

23. Treaty traders:

Ex parte Naoe Minamiji, 36 F. 2d 422 (D.C.S.D. Calif. C.D.),
December 4, 1929.

Ex parte Haruye Suzuki, 36 F. 2d 424 (D.C.S.D. Calif. C.D.),
December 4, 1929.

Shizuko Kumanomido vs. Nagle, 40 F. 2d 42 (C.C.A. 9), April 7, 1930.

Kumaki Koga vs. Berkshire, 75 F. 2d 820 (C.C.A. 9), February 25, 1935.

Sugaya vs. Haff, 78 F. 2d 989 (C.C.A. 9), August 12, 1935.

Kaname Susuki vs. Harris, 29 F.S. 46 (D.C.E.D. Texas), August 1, 1939.

24. Aliens who remained longer than permitted:

Ex parte Masuda Tatsumi, 49 F. 2d 935 (D.C.N.D. Calif. S.D.),
May 8, 1931.

Masahiko Inouye vs. Carr, 89 F. 2d 447 (C.C.A. 9), April 12, 1937.

25. Loss of U.S. citizenship by marriage to an alien:

Toshiko Inaba vs. Nagle, 36 F. 2d 481 (C.C.A. 9), December 17, 1929.

26. Illegal entry:

Ex parte Masamichi Ikeda, 68 F. 2d 276 (C.C.A. 9), December 13, 1933.

Nakazo Matsuda vs. Burnett, 68 F. 2d 272 (C.C.A. 9), December 22, 1933.

Kunimori Ohara vs. Berkshire, 76 F. 2d 204 (C.C.A. 9), March 11, 1935.

Morikichi Suwa vs. Carr, 88 F. 2d 119 (C.C.A. 9), February 15, 1937.

Ohama vs. United States, 88 F. 2d 27 (C.C.A. 9), February 8, 1937.

Monji Uyemura vs. Carr, 99 F. 2d 729 (C.C.A. 9), October 18, 1938.

Yoshihara vs. Carmichael, 115 F. 2d 110 (C.C.A. 9), October 25, 1940.

Kazue Sumi vs. Carmichael, 118 F. 2d 110 (C.C.A. 9), October 25, 1940.

Misuye Kobayashi vs. Carmichael, 120 F. 2d 752 (C.C.A. 9), June 6, 1941.

27. *Ex parte T. Nagata*, 11 F. 2d 178 (D.C.S.D. Calif. S.D.), February 19, 1926.
The same results were reached in *Matsukata vs. Carr*, 47 F. 2d 601
(C.C.A. 9), February 24, 1931. However, opposite results were reached by
the federal district court in the State of Washington. Two Japanese
aliens were denied entry into the United States. The two aliens had
originally entered the United States illegally but later were on board an
American vessel that sailed into Canadian waters. The aliens never
left the vessel (*Ex parte Tatsuo Saiki* and *Ex parte Hyoichi Ohashi*, 49 F. 2d
469 [D.C.W.D. Wash. N.D.], December 15, 1930).

28. See footnote 15.

29. *Ex parte Keizo Kamiyama*, 44 F. 2d 503 (C.C.A. 9), November 3, 1930.

30. *Kaichiro Sugimoto vs. Nagle*, 38 F. 2d 942 (D.C.S.D. Calif. S.D.),
February 27, 1929.

31. *Ex parte Keizo Shibata*, 30 F. 2d 942 (D.C.S.D. Calif. S.D.), February 27, 1929.

32. *Nishimoto vs. Nagle*, 44 F. 2d 304 (C.C.A. 9), November 3, 1930.

33. *Shimi Miho vs. U.S.*, 57 F. 2d 491 (C.C.A. 9), April 4, 1932.

34. *Yenkichi Ito vs. U.S.*, 64 F. 2d 73 (C.C.A. 9), March 27, 1929.

35. *Ex parte Ematsu Kishimoto*, 32 F. 2d 991 (C.C.A. 9), March 27, 1929.

36. *In re Sugano*, 40 F. 2d 961 (D.C.S.D. Calif. S.D.), February 15, 1930.

37. *Shizuko Kumanomido vs. Nagle*, 40 F. 2d 42 (C.C.A. 9), April 7, 1930.

38. *Ex parte Naoe Minamiji*, 36 F. 2d 422 (D.C.S.D. Calif. C.D.), December 4, 1929.
39. *Ex parte Haruye Suzuki*, 36 F. 2d 424 (D.C.S.D. Calif. C.D.), December 4, 1929.
40. *In re Katsujiro Akiyama*, 58 F. 2d 363 (D.C.S.D. Calif. C.D.), April 12, 1932.
41. *Kumaki Koga* vs. *Berkshire*, 75 F. 2d 820 (C.C.A. 9), February 25, 1935.
42. *Asakura* vs. *Seattle*, 265 U.S. 332, May 26, 1924.
43. *State* vs. *Tagami*, 195 Cal. 522, February 27, 1924.
44. *Jordan* vs. *Tashiro*, 278 U.S. 123, November 19, 1928.
45. *Taro Shiba* vs. *James Yeiki Chikuda*, 214 Cal. 786, February 5, 1932.
46. *Gonzales* vs. *Ito*, 12 C.A. 2d 124, February 25, 1936.
47. *Thomas T. Sashihara* vs. *State Board of Pharmacy*, 7 C.A. 2d 563, June 13, 1935.
48. *State* vs. *Kosai*, 133 Wash. 422, March 16, 1925.
49. *State* vs. *Ishikawa*, 139 Wash. 484, July 8, 1926. See also *Mori Saiki* vs. *Luke Hammock*, 207 Cal. 90, April 19, 1929.
50. *Kiyoko Nishi* vs. *Downing*, 21 C.A. 2d 1, May 11, 1937.
51. *Jones* vs. *Webb*, 195 Cal. 88, December 9, 1924.
52. *In re Nose*, 195 Cal. 91, December 9, 1924. Same results in *Dudley* vs. *Lowell*, 201 Cal. 376, June 11, 1927. Note opposite results in *Takiguchi* vs. *State*, 47 Ariz. 302, March 16, 1936, *E. Takehara* vs. *State*, 55 P. 2d 806, March 16, 1936, and *Morimoto* vs. *State of Arizona* 55 P. 2d 806, March 16, 1936, in which it was decided that an agricultural employee possessed no interest in the land. The Supreme Court of Arizona held that the Arizona Alien Land Law of 1921 was not intended to prevent ineligible aliens from earning a living in a common occupation of the community.
53. *Cockrill* vs. *Calif.*, 268 U.S. 258, May 11, 1925; compare *Haruko Takeuchi* vs. *Schmuck*, 206 Cal. 782, April 1, 1929.
54. *People* vs. *Osaki*, 209 Cal. 169, March 26, 1930; see also *People* vs. *Morrison*, 125 C.A. 282, August 5, 1932.
55. *People* vs. *Nakamura*, 125 C.A. 268, August 5, 1932.
56. *State* vs. *Hirabayashi*, 133 Wash. 462, March 16, 1925.
57. *State* vs. *Natsuhara*, 136 Wash. 437, November 5, 1925. To the same effect, *State* vs. *Motomatsu*, 136 Wash. 637, July 16, 1926.
58. *State* vs. *Kusumi*, 136 Wash. 426, November 3, 1925.
59. California Legislature, A.B. 1270, introduced by Assemblyman Hornblower, March 30, 1925.
60. California Legislature, A.B. 1019, introduced by Assemblyman Hunt, January 20, 1937. Note, a similar bill (A.B. 1823) was introduced by Assemblyman Allen on January 25, 1941.
61. California Legislature, S.B. 749, introduced by Senator Law, January 22, 1937.
62. California Legislature, A.B. 1386, introduced by Assemblyman Williamson, April 24, 1939.
63. California Legislature, House Resolution No. 39, *Assembly Journal*, December 22, 1941.
64. California Legislature, A.B. 453, introduced by Assemblyman Jones, January 21, 1935.

65. California Legislature, A.B. 2798, introduced by Assemblyman Neisinger, April 13, 1939.
66. California Legislature, Senate Concurrent Resolution No. 16, March 12, 1925.
67. California Legislature, Senate Joint Resolution No. 6, February 27, 1929. California Legislature, Assembly Joint Resolution No. 11, May 1, 1929. California Legislature, Assembly Joint Resolution No. 21, May 8, 1929.
68. California Legislature, S.B. 231, January 22, 1935.
69. *Tokaji* vs. *Board of Equalization*, 20 C.A. 2d 612, April 30, 1937, involved a California law that prohibited the issuance of an on-sale distilled spirits license by the State Board of Equalization to any applicant who was not a citizen of the United States.
70. McWilliams, op. cit., p. 70.
71. Ibid., p. 72.

8

1. David Bergamini, *Japan's Imperial Conspiracy* (New York: William Morrow, 1971), p. 383.
2. Yamato Ichihashi, *Japanese in the United States* (New York: Arno Press, 1969), p. 365.
3. Bergamini, op. cit., p. 6.
4. Jon Livingston, Joe Moore, and Felicia Oldfather, eds., *Imperial Japan, 1800–1945* (New York: Random House, 1973), p. 349.
5. Ichihashi, op. cit., p. 369.
6. Ibid.
7. Livingston, Moore, Oldfather, op. cit.
8. Ibid., p. 350.
9. Bergamini, op. cit., p. 389.
10. Staff of the Asahi, *The Pacific Rivals* (New York: John Weatherhill; Tokyo: Asahi, 1972), p. 76.
11. John Toland, *The Rising Sun* (New York: Random House, 1970), pp. 6–8.
12. Bergamini, op. cit., p. 398.
13. Ibid., p. 486.
14. Ibid., p. 501.
15. Ibid., p. 636.
16. Richard N. Current, *Secretary of State Stimson* (New Brunswick, N.J.: Rutgers University Press, 1954), pp. 103–104.
17. Bergamini, op. cit., p. 396.
18. Ibid., p. 430.
19. Ibid., p. 480.
20. 48 Stat 1697, June 16, 1933.
21. Toland, op. cit., p. 50.
22. *Department of State Bulletin*, Vol. 1, No. 1, Publication 1349 (1939), p. 81.
23. 54 Stat 2743, September 30, 1940, Presidential Proclamation No. 2428.
24. 54 Stat 2770, December 20, 1940, Presidential Proclamation No. 2451.
25. Current, op. cit., p. 147–148.
26. Staff of the Asahi, op. cit., p. 89.
27. Mount Niitaka, on the island of Taiwan, is 13,599 feet high and was, at that time, the highest peak in the Japanese Empire (it exceeds the much

more famous Mount Fuji by 1,211 feet). "Climb Mt. Niitaka 1208" was the code message flashed by Grand Admiral Yamamoto to the special naval air squadron standing by to attack Pearl Harbor. The numerals 1208 meant December 8, which was the date in Japan at the time of the attack.

9

1. United States Department of the Interior, *People in Motion* (Washington, D.C.: Government Printing Office). The total number of persons in custody of the War Relocation Authority was 120,313.
2. Dillon S. Myer, *Uprooted Americans* (Tucson: University of Arizona Press, 1971), p. 32.
3. Center Regulations, Western Defense Command and Fourth Army, W.C.C.A., July 18, 1942, p. 3.
4. Only some of the books are listed below:
    a. Dillon S. Myer, *Uprooted Americans* (Tucson: University of Arizona Press, 1971).
    b. Roger Daniels, *Concentration Camps USA* (New York: Holt, Rinehart and Winston, 1972).
    c. Edward H. Spicer, et al., *Impounded People* (Tucson: University of Arizona Press, 1969).
    d. Allan R. Bosworth, *America's Concentration Camps* (New York: Norton, 1967).
    e. Daisuke Kitagawa, *Issei and Nisei: The Internment Years* (New York: Seabury Press, 1967).
    f. Paul Bailey, *Concentration Camp, U.S.A.* (New York: Tower Publications, 1972).
    g. Leonard Bloom and Ruth Reimer, *Removal and Return* (Berkeley: University of California Press, 1949).
    h. Maisie and Richard Conrad, *Executive Order 9066* (San Francisco: California Historical Society, 1972).
    i. Anne Reeploeg Fisher, *Exile of a Race* (Seattle: F. and T. Publishers, 1965).
    j. Audrie Girdner and Anne Loftis, *The Great Betrayal* (New York: Macmillan, 1969).
    k. Morton Grodzin, *Americans Betrayed* (Chicago: University of Chicago Press, 1949).
5. John Toland, *The Rising Sun* (New York: Random House, 1970), flyleaf map at the front of the book.
6. Myer, op. cit., p. 15.
    Bosworth, op. cit., p. 54; Bosworth reports that the newspaper was the *San Luis Obispo Independent*, December 12, 1941.
7. Myer, op. cit., p. 16.
8. Ibid., p. 15.
9. Grodzin, op. cit., pp. 253–254.
10. Myer, op. cit., p. 18.
11. Ibid.
12. Ibid., p. 21.
13. Bosworth, op. cit., p. 86. Twelve years later, on September 2, 1954, Mayor Bowron admitted his mistake when he appeared before a congressional committee that was looking into property claims resulting from the evacuation: "I was Mayor during all of the war years . . . and I know of the hysteria, the wild rumors, the reports, that pervaded the atmosphere and worried a great many of us in responsible positions.

We were quite disorganized. There were many rumors floating around, as a
result of which, this order of evacuation was made. . . . I rather hold
myself somewhat responsible, with others. . . . I realized that
great injustices were done. . . . I thought it was the right thing to do at
the time; in the light of after events, I think it was wrong, now. . . .
I have been impressed with the fortitude of the Japanese people, the way
they took it, and then how they came back and re-established
themselves in this community."

14. Ibid., p. 66. The Tolan committee had been created by House Resolution 113
"to inquire further into the interstate migration of citizens . . .
caused by the national defense program."

15. Ibid., p. 79.

16. *Time,* March 5, 1965, p. 41.

17. Bosworth, op. cit., p. 62.

18. Daniels, op. cit., p. 36.

19. Ibid., p. 37.

20. Stetson Conn, *Japanese Evacuation from the West Coast* (Washington, D.C.:
Government Printing Office, 1964), pp. 116–118.

21. Department of the Army, Office of the Chief of Military History, *Command
Decisions* (Washington, D.C.: Government Printing Office, 1960), p. 125.

22. Ibid., p. 126.

23. Ibid.

24. Daniels, op. cit., p. 39, footnote 16.

25. Ibid., p. 40.

26. Department of the Army, op. cit., p. 128.

27. Presidential proclamation, December 7, 1941.
Presidential proclamation, December 8, 1941.

28. Department of the Army, op. cit., p. 132.

29. Ibid.

30. Ibid., p. 133.

31. Ibid., pp. 134–135.

32. Ibid., pp. 141–142.

33. Ibid., pp. 142–143.

34. Daniels, op. cit., pp. 69–72.

35. Department of the Army, op. cit., pp. 145–146.

36. U.S. Code, Congressional Service, 77th Congress, 2nd Session, 1942, p. 157,
Executive Order 9066, February 19, 1942. This order was rescinded
by Presidential Proclamation No. 2714 on February 19, 1976 by President
Gerald R. Ford.

37. Daniels, op. cit., p. 71.

38. Department of the Army, op. cit., p. 149.

39. 55 Stat 1647, Presidential Proclamation No. 2487, May 21, 1941.

40. 55 Stat 1696, Presidential Proclamation No. 2523, November 14, 1941.

41. 55 Stat 1701, Presidential Proclamation No. 2525, December 7, 1941.

42. 55 Stat 1705, Presidential Proclamation No. 2526 (Germany),
December 8, 1941.
55 Stat 1707, Presidential Proclamation No. 2527 (Italy),
December 8, 1941.

43. 56 Stat 173, March 21, 1942.

44. War Department, Public Proclamation No. 3, March 24, 1942.

45. Note civilian exclusion orders dated May 10, 1942, which excluded persons
    of Japanese ancestry from King County, Washington (No. 57),
    Pierce County, Washington (No. 58), Orange and San Diego Counties,
    California (No. 59), and Orange County, California (Nos. 60 and 61).

46. Memorandum from General DeWitt to the secretary of war dated February 14,
    1942. This memorandum became available January 19, 1944 and
    was published as an appendix to Chapter III of General DeWitt's final report
    on the Japanese evacuation from the West Coast.

47. John L. Dewitt, "Final Report: Japanese Evacuation from the West Coast"
    (Washington, D.C.: Government Printing Office, 1943).

48. Each of these accusations and other allegations were masterfully refuted
    in the amicus curiae brief filed with the Supreme Court of the United States
    by the JACL in October 1944 in the landmark case of *Korematsu
    vs. U.S.*, 323 U.S. 214, December 18, 1944.

49. U.S. Code, Congressional Service, 77th Congress, 2nd session, 1942,
    p. 267, Executive Order 9102, March 18, 1942, "Establishing the War
    Relocation Authority in the Executive Office of the President and Defining
    its Functions and Duties."

10

1. Saburo Kido, "Living with JACL," *Pacific Citizen*, January 20, 1961.
   Part I is a series of articles written in 1961 and 1962 for the *Pacific Citizen*,
   the official weekly publication of the JACL. This series covers
   Kido's recollections of the JACL between 1930 and 1942.

2. 42 Stat 1021, September 22, 1922.

3. 49 Stat 1917, June 25, 1936.

4. 49 Stat 397, June 24, 1935.

5. U.S. Constitution, 14th Amendment, Sec. 1.

6. 34 Stat 1228, March 2, 1907.

7. Saburo Kido, "Living with JACL," *Pacific Citizen*, January 12, 1962.

8. Karl R. Bendetsen, "An Obligation Discharged," address to personnel of
   Wartime Civilian Control Administration at the Commonwealth
   Club, San Francisco, November 3, 1942.

9. Dillon S. Myer, *Uprooted Americans* (Tucson: University of Arizona Press,
   1971), p. 245.

10. Ibid., p. 246.

11. Ibid.

12. Ibid., p. 247.

13. Ibid., p. 248.

14. Ibid., p. 249.

15. Ibid., p. 313, Appendix E. President Roosevelt's letter to the secretary of war
    approving the proposed formation of the Japanese-American combat
    team, February 1, 1943.

16. Ibid., p. 253.

17. Allan R. Bosworth, *America's Concentration Camps* (New York: Norton,
    1967), p. 164.

18. Ibid., p. 165.

19. Myer, op. cit., p. 326, Appendix H.

20. Bosworth, op. cit., p. 15, referring to figures released by the adjutant general, Department of the Army.

21. Orville D. Shirey, *Americans: The Story of the 442nd Combat Team* (Washington, D.C.: Infantry Journal Press, 1946).

22. Bosworth, op. cit., photograph facing p. 161.

11

1. *Ex parte Milligin,* 71 U.S. 2, December term, 1866.

2. *Ex parte Quirin,* 317 U.S. 1, July 31, 1942.

3. *Regan vs. King,* 49 F.S. 222 (D.C.N.D. Calif. S.D.), July 2, 1942.

4. *U.S. vs. Wong Kim Ark,* 169 U.S. 649, March 28, 1898.

5. *Morrison vs. California,* 291 U.S. 82, January 8, 1934.

6. *Perkins vs. Elg,* 307 U.S. 325, May 29, 1939.

7. *Ex parte Kumezo Kawato,* 317 U.S. 69, November 9, 1942.

8. 7 Federal Register 2543, March 24, 1942.

9. *U.S. vs. Yasui,* 48 F.S. 40 (D.C.N. Ore.), November 16, 1942.

10. *Hirabayashi vs. U.S.,* 320 U.S. 81, June 21, 1943.

11. *Yasui vs. U.S.,* 320 U.S. 115, June 21, 1943.

12. *Korematsu vs. U.S.,* 323 U.S. 214, December 18, 1944; see dissenting opinion of Associate Justice Frank Murphy.

13. *Korematsu vs. U.S.,* 323 U.S. 214, December 18, 1944. The brief submitted by the Japanese American Citizens League, "The Case for the Nisei" as amicus curie for Korematsu, contains one of the most concise but also one of the most enlightening refutations of the accusations against the Japanese regarding the factors that resulted in the evacuation order.

14. ACLU, "The Korematsu Case" (amicus curie brief), *Pacific Citizen,* Special Holiday Issue, December 22–29, 1967, Section A, p. 3.

15. Allan Bosworth, *America's Concentration Camps* (New York: Norton, 1967), p. 98.

16. 64 Stat 987, September 23, 1950. Title II, also known as the Emergency Detention Act, of the Internal Security Act of 1950 provides that in time of emergency the attorney general or his representative is authorized to issue "a warrant for the apprehension of each person as to whom there is a reasonable ground to believe that such person probably will engage in, or probably will conspire with others to engage in, acts of espionage or sabotage" (Sec. 401[a]). A member of the staff of the Senate Internal Security Committee in support of Section 104(a) cited *Korematsu vs. U.S.* as authority for the bill. Title II provided for further evacuation of persons, not only on the basis of race or color but also on the far broader and more dangerous ground of thought itself. Title II was repealed in 1970 through the efforts of the Japanese American Citizens League, which saw the danger to all Americans because of its own experiences during World War II.

17. *Ex parte Mitsuye Endo,* 323 U.S. 283, December 18, 1944.

18. Dillon S. Myer, *Uprooted Americans* (Tucson: University of Arizona Press, 1971), p. 67.

12

1. Dillon S. Myer, *Uprooted Americans* (Tucson: University of Arizona Press, 1971), pp. 322–328, Appendix H.
2. Allan R. Bosworth, *America's Concentration Camps* (New York: Norton, 1967), p. 234.
3. California Alien Land Law, May 1927.
4. California Alien Land Law, February 1935.
5. California Alien Land Law, 1937.
6. 1943 Session of the California Legislature:

January 7	Assembly Joint Resolution No. 34	Thurman
January 8	S.B. 18	Engle
January 10	A.B. 23	Lowrey, Hoyden, Lowry
January 10	A.B. 17	Hastain, Dilworth, Kraft, Stream, Watson, Niehouse, Fourt, Waters, Weybret, Erwin, Bashore.
January 11	A.B. 374	Erwin, Erwin, Fourt, Price, Leonard, Stream, Miller, Robertson, Bashore.
January 26	A.B. 921	Erwin, Fourt, Armstrong, Stream, Watson, Erwin.
March 17	S.B. 140	Engle, Luckey, Cunningham, Quinn, McBride, Ward, Dorsey, Tenney, Burns, Deuel, Dillinger, Powers, Salsman, Collier, Slater, McCormack.
March 20	A.B. 493	Call
May 5	A.B. 31	Thurman

7. Carey McWilliams, *Prejudice* (Boston: Little Brown, 1944), p. 65.
8. 1945 Session of the California Legislature:

January 15	S.B. 139	Donnelly, Hatfield, Quinn, Slater, Dorsey
January 23	S.B. 414	Donnelly, Dorsey, Quinn, Hatfield, Slater
January 23	S.B. 415	Donnelly, Quinn, Hatfield, Dorsey, Slater, Crittenden, Weybret, Judah
January 26	S.B. 877	Fletcher
January 27	A.B. 1682	Kraft, Field, Lawrey, Erwin, Hollibaugh, Clarke, Stephenson, Stream, Thorp, Watson, and Mrs. Niehouse.
May 7	S.B. 1293	Burns
May 18	Senate Constitutional Amendment	Tenney, Fletcher, Burns, Salsman, Cunningham,

1945 Session of the California Legislature: (continued)

		Seawell, Hulse, Sutton, Weybret, Crittenden, Brown, Dilworth, Deuel, Mayo, Dillinger, Powers, Keating, Mixter, Biggar, McBride.
May 24	A.B. 2130	Lowrey

9. Cal. Stats, 1945, Ch. 1136, Sec. 2.

10. Audre Girdner, and Anne Loftis, *The Great Betrayal* (New York: Macmillan, 1969), p. 429.

11. *Oyama vs. California*, 332 U.S. 633, January 19, 1948. Brief for petitioners (Oyama) filed with the Supreme Court of the United States, October term, 1947, p. 63, Appendix B.

12. Bill Hosokawa, *Nisei: The Quiet Americans* (New York: William Morrow, 1969), pp. 447–448.

13. *Pacific Citizen*, February 2, 1946.

14. *Estate of Yano*, 118 Cal. 645, May 1, 1922.

15. *People vs. Oyama*, 29 Cal. 2nd 164, October 31, 1946.

16. *Oyama vs. California*, 332 U.S. 633, January 19, 1948.

17. U.S. Department of the Interior, *People in Motion* (Washington, D.C.: Government Printing Office), pp. 41–42.

18. *Mott vs. Cline*, 200 Cal. 434, February 17, 1927.

19. *Webb vs. O'Brien*, 279 F.R.117 (D.C.N.D. Calif. 2d Div.), December 20, 1921.

20. *In re Y. Akado*, 188 Cal. 739, May 16, 1922.

21. *Terrace vs. Thompson*, 263 U.S. 225, November 12, 1923.

22. *Porterfield vs. Webb*, 263 U.S. 225, November 12, 1923.

23. *Morrison vs. California*, 291 U.S. 82, January 8, 1934.

24. *Cockrill vs. California*, 268 U.S. 258, May 11, 1925.

25. 56 Stat 182, March 27, 1942. 8 U.S.C.A., Sec. 42 provides, "All citizens of the United States shall have the same right, in every state and territory, as is enjoyed by white citizens thereof, to inherit, purchase, lease, sell, hold and convey real and personal property."

26. *Oyama vs. California*, 332 U.S. 633, January 19, 1948. Brief for respondent (State of California) filed in the Supreme Court of the United States, October term, 1947, p. 24.

27. *Oyama vs. California*, 332 U.S. 633, January 19, 1948. Brief for respondent (State of California) filed in the Supreme Court of the United States, October term, 1947, p. 24, citing the *Estate of Yano*, 188 Cal. 645, May 1, 1922, and *People vs. Fujita*, 215 Cal. 166, March 1, 1932.

28. California Probate Code, Sec. 1407; *Estate of Yano*, 188 Cal. 645, May 1, 1922.

29. *De Greayer vs. Superior Court*, 117 Cal. 640, August 21, 1897.

30. 59 Stat 1046, June 26, 1945; United Nations Charter, Articles 55(c) and 56.

31. *Terrace vs. Thompson*, 263 U.S. 225, November 12, 1923.
Porterfield vs. Webb, 263 U.S. 313, November 12, 1923.
Webb vs. O'Brien, 263 U.S. 313, November 19, 1923.
Frick vs. Webb, 263 U.S. 326, November 19, 1923.

32. *Terrace* vs. *Thompson*, 263 U.S. 197, November 12, 1923.
    Porterfield vs. *Webb*, 263 U.S. 225, November 12, 1923.
    Webb vs. *O'Brien*, 263 U.S. 313, November 19, 1923.
    Frick vs. *Webb*, 263 U.S. 326, November 19, 1923.
33. U.S. Department of the Interior, op. cit., pp. 64–65.
34. California Legislature, A.B. 951, January 18, 1949.
35. *Palermo* vs. *Stockton Theatres, Inc.*, 32 Cal. 2d 53, June 15, 1948.
36. *U.S. Department of State Bulletin*, Vol. 1, No. 1, Publication 1349
    (1940), p. 81.
37. *Kenji Namba* vs. *McCourt*, 185 Ore. 579, March 29, 1949.
38. Oregon Alien Land Law, 1945, Ch. 436.
39. Oregon Laws, 1923, p. 145.
40. *Sei Fujii* vs. *State of California*, 38 Cal. 2d 718, April 17, 1952.
41. *Haruye Masaoka* vs. *State of California*, 39 Cal. 2d 883, July 9, 1952.
42. *Porterfield* vs. *Webb*, 263 U.S. 225, November 12, 1923.
43. Bosworth, op. cit., p. 57.
44. *Haruye Masaoka et al.* vs. *State of California*. Memorandum of opinion,
    Thurmond J. Clarke, Los Angeles County Superior Court, No. 3306,
    March 16, 1950.
45. *Haruye Masaoka* vs. *State of California*, 39 Cal. 2d 883, July 9, 1952.
46. *Los Angeles Examiner*, October 18, 1956.

13

1. Eiji Tanabe, "The History of Japanese Commercial Fishing," *Pacific Citizen*,
   March 27, 1948, pp. 2–5.
2. Paul Bailey, *Concentration Camp, U.S.A.* (New York: Tower Publications,
   1972), p. 31.
3. Tanabe, op. cit., pp. 15–20.
4. State of California 1909, Ch. 197, approved March 13, 1909.
5. United States citizens only; all references are to the California Legislature:

January 25, 1935	S.B. 444	Edwards
January 22, 1937	A.B. 2653	Boyle
May 16, 1937	A.B. 336	Yorty, Tenney, Waters, Poulson
January 16, 1939	S.B. 278	Metzger
January 25, 1939	A.B. 2415	Millington
April 20, 1939	A.B. 1883	Heisinger
January 7, 1941	A.B. 32	Thomas
January 8, 1941	A.B. 57	Tenney, Waters, Poulson, Doyle
January 22, 1941	A.B. 965	Voigt
January 25, 1941	A.B. 2350	Tenney, Waters, Field, Millington, Allen, Cooke, Poole, Poulson
January 19, 1943	S.B. 286	Tenney

6. United States citizens and aliens eligible for citizenship; both references are to the California Legislature:

January 8, 1943	S.B. 19	Engle
January 7, 1943	A.B. 46	Lowrey, Gannon

7. United States citizens and aliens who have declared their intention to become United States citizens; both references are to the California Legislature:

January 15, 1919	A.B. 135	Mitchell
April 9, 1943	A.B. 407	Erwin, Bashore, McCollister, Fourt, Price, Hollibaugh, Call, Weybret, Middough

8. Prohibits aliens not eligible for citizenship in the state of California or the United States; all references are to the California Legislature:

January 17, 1921	A.B. 346	Mitchell
January 31, 1923	A.B. 826	Dawson
January 21, 1925	A.B. 415	Cleveland
January 18, 1929	A.B. 1026	Williams
January 6, 1933	A.B. 425	Hunt
January 18, 1935	A.B. 307	Hunt

Cal. Stats 1945, Chapter 181, Section 990, September 15, 1945.

9. Persons who have continuously resided within the state of California or the United States for a period of one year immediately prior to the time application is made for a license; all references are to the California Legislature:
Cal. Stats, 1933, Ch. 696, amending Ch. 5, Article 1, Sec. 990.

January 21, 1933	S.B. 157	Snyder
January 24, 1935	A.B. 718	Reaves
January 18, 1937	A.B. 801	Reaves
January 7, 1941	A.B. 31	Thomas

10. Alien Japanese prohibited from commercial fishing licenses; both references are to the California Legislature:
Cal. Stats, 1943, Ch. 1100, p. 394, August 4, 1943.

May 25, 1945	A.B. 700	Watson

11. Howard Goldstein surveyed the commercial fishing licenses issued by the Fish and Game Commission of California. The survey was reported in the *Pacific Citizen*, January 17, 1948.

12. Cal. Stats, 1933, p. 479, April 11, 1933.

13. 9 Cal. App. 2d 300, September 27, 1935.

14. Cal. Stats, 1943, Ch. 1100, August 4, 1943, which amended Cal. Stats, 1933, p. 394.

15. *Takahashi* vs. *Fish and Game Commission*, 334 U.S. 410, June 7, 1948. Note Justice Murphy's concurring opinion.

16. Cal. Stats, 1945, Ch. 181, Section 990, September 15, 1945.

18. *Takahashi* vs. *Fish and Game Commission*, L.A. Superior Court No. 19835, 1947.

17. *Takahashi* vs. *Fish and Game Commission*, 30 Cal. 2d 719, October 17, 1947.

19. *Takahashi* vs. *Fish and Game Commission*, 334 U.S. 410, June 7, 1948.

14

1. Dillon S. Myer, *Uprooted Americans* (Tucson: University of Arizona Press, 1971), Chronology XXIX.
2. Ibid., p. 185.
3. Ibid., Chronology XXIX.
4. Ibid., Chronology XXVIII.
5. Ibid., Chronology XXVI.
6. Ibid., Chronology XXIX.
7. Ibid.
8. Ibid.
9. Ibid., Chronology XXX.
10. Ibid.
11. Ibid.
12. Bill Hosokawa, *Nisei: The Quiet Americans* (New York: William Morrow, 1969), p. 440.
13. Ibid., p. 442.
14. 62 Stat 1231, July 2, 1948.
15. Hosokawa, op. cit., p. 445.
16. Although the federal records show 23,689, the breakdown shows 22,903, or a discrepancy of 786. The discrepancy may possibly be explained by different members of the family filing for the same property losses at different times, which were later consolidated into one claim.
17. Hosokawa, op. cit., p. 446.
18. 65 Stat 192, August 17, 1951. Amended Section 4(a) and Section 7 of 62 Stat 1231, July 2, 1948.
19. Japanese-American evacuation claims hearings before Subcommittee No. 5 of the Committee on the Judiciary, House of Representatives, San Francisco, August 30–31, 1954, pp. 95–96.
20. Audrie Girdner and Anne Loftis, *The Great Betrayal* (New York: Macmillan, 1969), pp. 436–437.
21. Roger Daniels, *Concentration Camps USA* (New York: Holt, Rinehart and Winston, 1972), p. 169.

15

1. Roger Daniels, *Concentration Camps USA* (New York: Holt, Rinehart and Winston, 1972), p. 112.
2. Ibid.
   Dillon S. Myer, *Uprooted Americans* (Tucson: University of Arizona Press, 1971), p. 72.
3. Daniels, op. cit., p. 113.
   Myer, op. cit.
4. Myer, op. cit., p. 76.
5. Daniels, op. cit.
6. Ibid.
7. Ibid., p. 107.

8. Myer, op. cit., p. 73.

9. Daniels, op. cit., p. 113.

10. Myer, op. cit., p. 76.

11. Daniels, op. cit., p. 115.

12. Ibid., p. 114.

13. Bill Hosokawa, *Nisei: The Quiet Americans* (New York: William Morrow, 1969), p. 365.

14. Ibid.

15. Myer, op. cit., p. 326, Appendix H.

16. Daniels, op. cit., p. 114.

17. 54 Stat 885, September 16, 1940.

18. *Masaaki Kuwabara et al., vs. United States,* 56 F.S. 716 (D.C.N.D. Calif. N.D.), July 22, 1944.

19. *United States vs. Shigeru Fujii et al.,* 55 F.S. 928 (D.C.D. Wyoming), June 26, 1944.

20. Daniels, op. cit., p. 120.

21. Ibid., p. 121.

22. Ibid., p. 123.

23. Ibid., p. 125.

24. Ibid., p. 126.

25. Ibid.

26. *United States vs. Shigeru Fujii et al.,* 55 F.S. 928 (D.C.D. Wyoming), June 26, 1944.

27. *Shigeru Fujii et al., vs. United States,* 148 F 2d 298 (C.C.A. 10), March 12, 1945.

28. *Tamesa vs. United States,* 325 U.S. 868 (writ of certiorari denied May 28, 1945). This case was originally known as *Shigeru Fujii et al., vs. United States,* 148 F 2d 298 (C.C.A. 10), March 12, 1945.

29. *Shigeru Fujii et al., vs. United States,* 148 F 2d 298 (C.C.A. 10), March 12, 1945.

30. *Kiyoshi Okamoto et al., vs. United States,* 152 F 2d 905 (C.C.A. 10), December 26, 1945.

31. *Kiyoshi Okamoto et al., vs. United States,* 152 F 2d 905 (C.C.A. 10), December 26, 1945.

32. *Keegan vs. United States,* 325 U.S. 478, June 11, 1945.

33. Daniels, op. cit., p. 128.

34. 66 Stat 1441, December 23, 1947. Names of Nisei noted in the presidential pardon by Proclamation No. 2762. Breakdown is number of draft violators by various concentration camps of the WRA:

District Court	Convictions
Arizona	109 (99 convicted same date)
Arkansas (Eastern)	3
California (Northern)	2
Colorado	30
Idaho (Northern)	33
Idaho (Southern)	1
Kansas (Eastern)	1
Montana	1
Utah	5

66 Stat 1441, December 23, 1947. (continued)

Washington (Eastern)	1
Wyoming	81 (63 convicted same date)
Total	267

35. 66 Stat 1441, December 23, 1947, Presidential Proclamation No. 2762.
36. Daniels, op. cit., p. 129.

16

1. Carey McWilliams, *Prejudice* (Boston: Little Brown, 1944), p. 171.
2. Ibid.
3. Allan R. Bosworth, *America's Concentration Camps* (New York: Norton, 1967), p. 171.
4. Ibid., p. 177.
5. Ibid., p. 179.
6. Ibid., p. 189.
7. Ibid., p. 191.
8. Ibid., p. 190.
9. Dillon S. Myer, *Uprooted Americans* (Tucson: University of Arizona Press, 1971), p. 80.
10. California Legislature, 55th session, 3rd extra session, Senate Joint Resolution No. 9, Ch. 36, February 4, 1944.
11. U.S. Congress, House Resolution 3012, Congressman Leroy Johnson, 1944.
12. Bosworth, op. cit., p. 198.
13. Myer, op. cit., p. 101.
14. Ibid., p. 104.
15. 8 U.S.C.A. Section 801(i), July 1, 1944.
16. *Pacific Citizen*, July 8, 1944.
    Myer, op. cit., p. 90.
17. Bosworth, op. cit., p. 200.
18. Ibid., p. 204.
19. Myer, op. cit., p. 90.
20. Bosworth, op. cit., p. 233;
    Myer, op. cit., p. 226.
21. *Yuichi Inouye et al.*, vs. *Clark*, 73 F.S. 1000 (D.C.S.D. Calif. C.D.), September 5, 1947.
22. *Acheson* vs. *Murakami*, 176 F 2d 953 (C.C.A. 9), August 26, 1949.
23. *Tadayasu Abo* vs. *Clark*, 76 F.S. 664 (D.C.N.D. Calif. S.D.), June 30, 1947.
24. 50 U.S.C.A. Sec. 21–23, 1798.
25. *Tadayasu Abo* vs. *Clark*, 77 F.S. 806 (D.C.N.D. Calif. S.D.), April 29, 1948.
26. *Tadayasu Abo* vs. *McGrath*, 186 F 2d 766 (C.C.A. 9), January 17, 1951.
27. Myer, op. cit., p. 225.

17

1. 8 U.S.C.A. Sec. 801(a) through (j).
2. 8 U.S.C.A. Sec. 802.
3. *Meiji Fujisawa* vs. *Acheson*, 85 F.S. 674 (D.C.S.D. Calif. S.D.), August 23, 1949.

4. *William S. Ishikawa* vs. *Acheson*, 8 F.S. 1 (D.C.C.C. Hawaii), August 12, 1949.
5. *Noboru Kato* vs. *Acheson*, 94 F.S. 415 (D.C.S.D. Calif. C.D.),
   November 14, 1950.
6. *Ozasa* vs. *Acheson*, 94 F.S. 436 (D.C.S.D. Calif. C.D.), November 14, 1950.
7. *Mitsugi Nishikawa* vs. *Dulles*, 356 U.S. 129, March 31, 1958.
8. *Etsuko Arikawa* vs. *Acheson*, 83 F.S. 483 (D.C.S.D. Calif. C.D.),
   April 4, 1949.
   Miyoko Tsunashima vs. *Acheson*, 83 F.S. 483 (D.C.S.D. Calif. C.D.),
   April 4, 1949.
   Hatsuye Ouye vs. *Acheson*, 91 F.S. 129 (D.C.D. Hawaii), May 12, 1950.
   Yamamoto vs. *Acheson*, 93 F.S. 346 (D.C.D. Ariz.), June 23, 1950.
   Kuniyuki vs. *Acheson*, 94 F.S. 358, (D.C.W.D. Wash. N.D.),
   August 24, 1950.
   Haruko Furuno vs. *Acheson*, 94 F.S. 381 (D.C.S.D. Calif. C.D.),
   November 14, 1950.
   Haruko Kai vs. *Acheson*, 94 F.S. 383 (D.C.S.D. Calif. C.D.),
   November 14, 1950.
   Harumi Seki vs. *Acheson* and *Yada* vs. *Acheson*, 94 F.S. 438 (D.C.S.D.
   Calif. C.D.), November 22, 1950.
   Fumi Rokui vs. *Acheson*, 94 F.S. 439 (D.C.S.D. Calif. C.D.),
   November 22, 1950.
   Fujiko Furusho vs. *Acheson*, 94 F.S. 1021, (D.C.D. Hawaii),
   January 23, 1951.
   Akio Kuwabara vs. *Acheson*, 96 F.S. 38 (D.C.S.D. Calif. C.D.),
   March 5, 1951.
   Hichino Uyeno vs. *Acheson*, 96 F.S. 310 (D.C.W.D. Wash. N.D.),
   March 23, 1951.
   Kikukuro Okumura vs. *Acheson*, 99 F.S. 587, (D.C.D. Hawaii),
   September 12, 1951.
   Teruo Naito vs. *Acheson*, 106 F.S. 770 (D.C.S.D. Calif. C.D.),
   July 24, 1952.
   Minoru Furuno vs. *Acheson*, 106 F.S. 775 (D.C.S.D. Calif. C.D.),
   July 24, 1952.
   Fusae Yamamoto vs. *Dulles*, 16 F.R.D. 195 (D.C.D. Hawaii),
   September 21, 1954.
9. *Etsuko Arikawa* vs. *Acheson*, 83 F.S. 483 (D.C.S.D. Calif. C.D.),
   April 4, 1949.
   Miyoko Tsunashima vs. *Acheson*, 83 F.S. 483 (D.C.S.D. Calif. C.D.),
   April 4, 1949.
   Yamamoto vs. *Acheson*, 93 F.S. 346 (D.C.D. Ariz.), June 23, 1950.
   Haruko Kai vs. *Acheson*, 94 F.S. 383 (D.C.S.D. Calif. C.D.),
   November 14, 1950.
   Fumi Rokui vs. *Acheson*, 94 F.S. 439 (D.C.S.D. Calif. C.D.),
   November 22, 1950.
   Fujiko Furusho vs. *Acheson*, 94 F.S. 1021 (D.C.D. Hawaii),
   January 23, 1951.
10. *Kikukuro Okamura* vs. *Acheson*, 99 F.S. 587 (D.C.D. Hawaii),
    September 12, 1951.
    Hisao Murata vs. *Acheson*, 99 F.S. 591 (D.C.D. Hawaii),
    September 12, 1951.
11. U.S. Constitution, 14th Amendment, Sec. 1.
12. U.S. Constitution, Article I, Sec. 8.

13. *Nishikawa* vs. *Dulles*, 356 U.S. 129, March 31, 1958.
14. *Teruo Naito* vs. *Acheson*, 106 F.S. 770 (D.C.S.D. Calif. C.D.), July 24, 1952.
15. *Baumgartner* vs. *U.S.*, 322 U.S. 665, June 12, 1944.
16. *Schneiderman* vs. *U.S.*, 320 U.S. 118, June 21, 1943.
17. 62 Stat 807, June 25, 1948.
18. U.S. Constitution, 14th Amendment, Article 1.
19. Nationality Law of Japan, Article 1 and Article 20, Sec. 3, Ordinance No. 26, November 17, 1924.
20. *U.S.* vs. *Tomoya Kawakita*, 96 F.S. 824 (U.S.D.C.S.D. Cal. C.D.), November 1, 1950.
21. *Tomoya Kawakita* vs. *U.S.*, 343 U.S. 717, June 2, 1952. Justice Felix Frankfurter, not having heard the argument because of illness, and Justice Tom Clark, having been attorney general of the United States during the prosecution of Kawakita, took no part in the consideration or decision of the case. Chief Justice Fred M. Vinson, Justice Hugo L. Black, and Justice Harold H. Burton dissented.
22. William A. Reuben, *The Legend of Tokyo Rose* (San Francisco: William A. Reuben), p. 2.
23. *Iva Ikuko Toguri D'Aquino* vs. *U.S.*, 192 F 2d 338 (U.S.C.A. 9), October 1, 1951.
24. *Iva Ikuko Toguri D'Aquino* vs. *U.S.*, 343 U.S. 935, April 28, 1952, petition for writ of certiorari denied; 343 U.S. 958, May 29, 1952, petition for rehearing denied.
25. 66 Stat 267, June 27, 1952.
26. Japanese American Citizens League, *Iva Toguri (D'Aquino): Victim of a Legend*, (San Francisco: National Committee for Iva Toguri, 1975), p. 29.

18

1. John Toland, *The Rising Sun* (New York: Random House, 1970), p. 838.
2. Edwin O. Reischauer, *Japan: Past and Present* (New York: Charles E. Tuttle Co., 1971), p. 240.
3. Staff of the Asahi, *The Pacific Rivals* (New York: Weatherhill; Tokyo: Asahi, 1971), p. 109.
4. Willard Price, *The Japanese Miracle and Peril* (New York: Hayden Book Co., 1971), p. 240.
5. 57 Stat 600, December 17, 1943.
6. 60 Stat 416, July 2, 1946.
7. 60 Stat 339, June 29, 1946.
8. 63 Stat 56, April 21, 1949.
9. 64 Stat 464, August 19, 1950.

19

1. 39 Stat 874, February 5, 1917.
2. 43 Stat 153, May 26, 1924.
3. 62 Stat 1206, July 1, 1948.

20

1. 66 Stat 163, June 27, 1952. For a full discussion of this law, see Frank L. Auerbach, *Immigration Laws of the United States* (New York: Bobbs-Merrill, 1955), pp. 17–19.
2. 80th Congress, 1st session, Senate Resolution 137.
3. 81st Congress, 2nd session, Senate Report 1515.
4. 82nd Congress, 2nd session, House of Representatives, House Document 520.
5. Japanese American Citizens League, "To Eliminate Racial Discrimination in Immigration," a brief in support of administration's immigration bill S. 500 and H.R. 2580, 1965, p. 32.
6. 43 Stat 153, May 26, 1924.
7. 1 Stat 153, March 26, 1790.
8. Japanese American Citizens League, op. cit., pp. 8 ff.
9. Ibid.
10. Bill Hosokawa, *Nisei: The Quiet Americans* (New York: William Morrow, 1969), p. 455.

21

1. 66 Stat 634, July 15, 1952.
2. 54 Stat 1137, October 14, 1940.
3. *Acheson vs. Okimura*, 342 U.S. 899, January 2, 1952.
4. *Nishikawa vs. Dulles*, 356 U.S. 129, March 31, 1958.
5. *Dulles vs. Katamoto*, 256 F 2d 545 (C.A. 9), June 6, 1958.
   Kiyama vs. Dulles, 268 F 2d 110 (C.A. 9), April 27, 1959.
   Yukio Yamamoto vs. Dulles, 268 F 2d 111 (C.A. 9), April 27, 1959.
   Kozuki vs. Dulles, 268 F 2d 207 (C.A. 9), May 19, 1959.
6. 63 Stat 191, August 16, 1951. Public Law 114, H.R. 400, passed August 16, 1951, had previously provided an expeditious method of restoring citizenship to United States citizens of Italian descent who had voted in the elections in Italy in 1946 and 1949.
7. 68 Stat 495, July 20, 1954.
8. 32 Stat 389, June 17, 1902.
9. 70 Stat 131, May 10, 1956.
10. 70 Stat 513, July 9, 1956.
11. 50 U.S.C.A., Appendix 1984, Section 4(b).
12. Mike Masaoka, "Last Evacuation Claim," *Pacific Citizen*, October 22, 1965, p. 2.
13. 72 Stat 546, August 8, 1958.
14. California Legislature, Assembly Bill No. 941, introduced by Assemblyman Edward Elliott, January 19, 1955.
15. 7 Federal Register 8665, Sumitomo Bank, Ltd., October 23, 1942, Vesting Order No. 162.
   7 Federal Register 8813, Yokohama Specie Bank, Ltd., October 29, 1942, Vesting Order No. 170.
   8 Federal Register 2456, Mitsui Bank, Ltd., February 25, 1943, Vesting Order No. 912.

16. Office of Alien Property, U.S. Department of Justice, *In the matter of Tokio Okamoto,* Claim no. 53,620.

17. Office of Alien Property, U.S. Department of Justice, *In the matter of Katsu Arai,* Claim No. 53,621.

18. Office of Alien Property, U.S. Department of Justice, *In the matter of Hatsumi Ishii,* Claim No. 53,720.

19. *Brownell* vs. *Nakashima,* 243 F 2d 787 (C.A. 9), June 7, 1957.

20. *Aratani* vs. *Kennedy,* 317 F 2d 161, (C.A. District of Columbia), March 28, 1963.

21. 50 U.S.C.A. Appendix Section 34.

22. 50 U.S.C.A. Appendix Section 34.

23. Both the Sumitomo Bank and the Mitsui Bank had already liquidated their assets to pay other claimants and were therefore not included in H.R. 8215.

24. 85 Stat 347, September 25, 1971.

25. 64 Stat 987, September 23, 1950.

26. 64 Stat 987, September 23, 1950.

27. U.S. Code, Congressional Service, 81st Congress, 1950, p. 3917.

28. *Korematsu* vs. *United States,* 323 U.S. 214, December 18, 1944.

29. 85 Stat 347, September 25, 1971.

22

1. Cal. Stats 1850, Ch. 140, p. 424.

2. California Legislature, A. B. 536, introduced by Assemblyman Young, March 16, 1880.

3. California Legislature, S. B. 804, introduced by Senator Jesperson, January 24, 1941.

4. California Legislature, A. B. 48, introduced by Assemblyman Crowley, May 2, 1941.

5. California Legislature, A. B. 321, introduced by Assemblymen Miller, Johnson, and Sherwin, March 7, 1945.

6. *Perez* vs. *Sharp,* 32 Cal. 2d 711, October 1, 1948.

7. *Hirabayashi* vs. *United States,* 320 U.S. 81, June 21, 1943.

8. *Oyama* vs. *California,* 332 U.S. 633, January 19, 1948.

9. *Takahashi* vs. *Fish and Game Commission,* 334 U.S. 410, June 7, 1948.

10. *Cleveland Plain Dealer,* September 6, 1962.

11. State of Ohio, Court of Appeals, Cuyahoga County, Eighth District, No. 26040.

12. *Loving* vs. *Virginia,* 388 U.S. 1, June 12, 1967.

13. James R. Martin, "The University of California (in Los Angeles)" (a resume of the selection and acquisition of the Westwood site, Los Angeles, California, 1925), p. 232.

14. Loren Miller, *The Petitioners* (Cleveland: Meridian Books, 1966), p. 322.

15. *Corrigan* vs. *Buckley,* 271 U.S. 323, May 24, 1926.

16. *Shelley* vs. *Kraemer,* 334 U.S. 1, May 3, 1926.

17. *McGhee* vs. *Sipes,* 334 U.S. 1, May 3, 1948.

18. *Shelley* vs. *Kraemer,* 334 U.S. 1, May 3, 1948, p. 21, footnote 26.

19. *Oyama* vs. *California,* 332 U.S. 633, January 19, 1948.

20. *Barrows* vs. *Johnson,* 346 U.S. 249, June 15, 1953.

21. *Banks* vs. *Housing Authority,* 120 C.A. 2d 1, August 26, 1953.

22. *Civil Rights Cases,* 109 U.S. 3, October 15, 1883.

23. 78 Stat 241, July 2, 1964.

24. 71 Stat 634, September 9, 1957.

25. 74 Stat 86, May 6, 1960.

26. *Heart of Atlanta Motel Inc.* vs. *United States,* 379 U.S. 241, December 14, 1964.

27. *Katzenbach* vs. *McClung,* 379 U.S. 294, December 14, 1964.

28. U.S. Constitution, Article I, Sec. 8, Clause 3.

29. U.S. Constitution, Article I, Sec. 8, Clause 18.

30. 79 Stat 911, October 3, 1965.

31. *Pacific Citizen,* January 22, 1965.

32. 89th Congress, 1st session, Report No. 748 of the Committee of the Judiciary to accompany H.R. 2580, Calendar No. 733, September 15, 1965, p. 12.

INDEX

PHOTO ACKNOWLEDGEMENTS

2: California Historical Society; 18: courtesy of Dr. Kazuye Togasaki; 38: Visual Communications Center, Los Angeles; 52: Frank F. Chuman; 72: United Press International; 90, 104: Visual Communications Center; 126: United Press International; 142: Japanese American Citizens League; 164: United Press International; 182: Visual Communications Center; 198: courtesy of the California State Archives; 224: courtesy of Toyo Miyatake; 234: Visual Communications Center; 246: courtesy of the Japanese Section, Reference Department, The Library of Congress; 262: courtesy of Toyo Miyatake; 278, 296: United Press International; 302: courtesy of the Western Region, Immigration and Naturalization Service; 308: courtesy of the *Pacific Citizen;* 314: United Press International; 332: Frank F. Chuman.

Insert Photos
A, B: United Press International; C, D, E, F: Visual Communications Center; G: courtesy of Dr. Kazuye Togasaki; H: courtesy of the *Pacific Citizen;* I, J: Visual Communications Center; K: United Press International; L: Visual Communications Center; M: United Press International; N, O, P: courtesy of the *Pacific Citizen;* Q: United Press International; R: courtesy of the *Pacific Citizen;* S: United Press International.

Copy Editor : Nancy Sjoberg
Designer : John Odam
Production : Jane Bremner
Compositor : Chapman's Phototypesetting
Fullerton, California
Typeface : Goudy Old Style
Paper : 60-pound Dontique Antique
Color Separation : Color Graphics Inc.
San Diego, California
Photo Insert Printer : Atlas Lithograph
San Diego, California
Printer : R. R. Donnelley & Sons Company
Crawsfordsville, Indiana